23,—

MW01273741

Nakae Ushikichi in China

HARVARD EAST ASIAN MONOGRAPHS
139

Nakae Ushikichi and his dog Huang (Peking, circa 1937)

NAKAE USHIKICHI IN CHINA
The Mourning of Spirit

JOSHUA A. FOGEL

Published by COUNCIL ON EAST ASIAN STUDIES, HARVARD UNIVERSITY, and distributed by HARVARD UNIVERSITY PRESS, Cambridge (Massachusetts) and London   1989

The Council on East Asian Studies at Harvard University publishes a monograph series and, through the John King Fairbank Center for East Asian Research and the Edwin O. Reischauer Institute of Japanese Studies, administers research projects deisgned to further scholarly understanding of China, Japan, Korea, Vietnam, Inner Asia, and adjacent areas.

Publication of this volume has been assisted by a grant from the Shell Companies Foundation.

Index by Katherine Frost Bruner

Printed in the United States of America

Library of Congress Cataloging in Publication Data

Fogel, Joshua A., 1950–
    Nakae Ushikichi in China : the mourning of spirit / Joshua A. Fogel.
        p. cm. – (Harvard East Asian monographs : 139)
        Bibliography: p.
        Includes index.
        ISBN 0-674-59842-3
        1. Nakae, Ushikichi, 1889–1942. 2. Sinologists–Japan–Biography.
    3. Sinologists–China–Biography. 4. China–Study and teaching.
    I. Title. II. Series.
    DS734.9.N34F64 1989
    951.04'092–dc20
    [B]   89-7101
                                             CIP

Contents

Illustrations

Acknowledgments

No one helped me more in the research that went into this book than Mr. Sakatani Yoshinao, then of Tōkyū Hotels International, now of Kanagawa University. Despite an inordinately busy schedule, Mr. Sakatani was more than generous with his time. He read with great care my translation of Nakae Ushikichi's wartime diary, which constitutes the Appendix, and offered numerous corrections and suggestions. He provided me with several books and with a photocopy of Nakae's reading notes on Hegel's *Phenomenology of Spirit*. The latter has never been seen before, let alone studied, by any scholar. All other debts incurred, intellectual or otherwise, in the course of this study pale by comparison.

Nonetheless, I would like to thank the library staff of the Jinbun kagaku kenkyūjo (Research Institute for Humanistic Sciences) at Kyoto University, where Nakae's personal library is now housed, who tolerated my examining twenty to thirty volumes at a time, day in and day out. Will the dust ever come off all of our hands? Kida Tomoo and Yasuko Watt helped me decipher several of Nakae's handwritten marginalia. I also received a grant from the National Endowment for the Humanities to pursue the research and writing of this book.

My wife, Susan Margolis, was as always fairly patient with the vicissitudes of life with an East Asian historian, whose moods hinge on the basis of such serious matters as the availability of library books and the legibility of handwritten letters.

Joshua A. Fogel
New York City

Preface

This study into the life and work of Nakae Ushikichi (1889–1942), like my earlier work on Naitō Konan (1866–1934), proceeds on the fruitful assumption that the modern histories of China and Japan are inextricably intertwined.[1] As important as this view is to a proper understanding of modern Chinese and modern Japanese history generally, it is essential in assessing pivotal figures in the cultural dimension of Sino-Japanese relations, such as Naitō, Nakae, and countless others. Accordingly, this is not a study in either Chinese history *or* Japanese history, but in both.

Except in rare cases, Western historians of modern China and Japan have focused on one country and have been content to reduce the history of the other to a set of clichés. They have, moreover, been unduly influenced by native scholars: Chinese historians have tended to see modern Japan primarily in relation to the development and execution of imperialism on the mainland; Japanese historians have tended to find modern China abhorrently disorderly and mismanaged, one rebellion after another, one meaningless regime after another. No one would deny that these perceptions are central to the main story of modern Japan and China, but the main story is not the whole story. Nor in any case, should historians ever be content with caricatures.

In addition to the personal inclinations of those attracted either to China or to Japan, academic divisions have also militated against examining the two histories together. In most East Asian universities, Chinese and Japanese history are taught in separate departments. In the West, where both languages have to be learned, there is usually little dialogue of a serious scholarly nature between historians of the two countries even if they do teach in the same department. Nonetheless, we get nowhere in our understanding of either country's modern history by ignoring or caricaturing the other.

Over three decades ago, Marius Jansen began to blaze a trail in the study of the cultural and political dimensions of Sino-Japanese history with his book *The Japanese and Sun Yat-sen*.[2] The implications of this extremely important work proved too difficult for many scholars in the West as well as East Asia to accept. Sun Yat-sen was deeply influenced by Japanese notions of Pan-Asianism, some of whose advocates later propounded the cause of Japanese imperialism. This was tantamount to blasphemy of the "national father." But it was also true.

In recent years, the work of Akira Iriye, Noriko Kamachi, and others have begun to address the many untouched or badly handled issues at the core of Sino-Japanese relations.[3] We have only begun. In the People's Republic of China, and to a lesser degree in Taiwan as well, virtually no historical research into the cultural dimension of Sino-Japanese relations existed until recently. To the extent that it has emerged in recent years, particularly in China, it has done so in the writing of a kind of historical autobiography. Certain Japanese scholars, such as Sanetō Keishū and Takeuchi Minoru, have been attentive to these issues for some time. Nonetheless, postwar guilt for Japanese imperialism and the war brought by the Japanese military all over Asia has made serious research into any Sino-Japanese area of the prewar period except imperialism difficult to pursue. That situation is now changing, at last.

China and Japan have influenced each other historically and culturally for over 1500 years. Even with the intrusion of the West in the modern period, no country influenced either China or Japan more than each did the other. As they draw closer together in trade and diplomacy and as old animosities ease with the passage of time, the atmosphere for examining their shared histories may improve within these countries themselves. In the West, the problems are, first, a tendency to allow intellectual fads to dictate the questions asked and the methods used in historical discourse, and, second, the assumption that recognizing the need to work from a comparative perspective is the same thing as attempting or achieving it. Greater attention to this dimension in modern East

Asian history will enhance our understanding of the history of both countries. Failure to do so at this point in the development of our own research on East Asia will keep Western views limited and provincial. It is high time we picked up where Marius Jansen began in the early 1950s.

Nakae Ushikichi in China

Introduction

In many ways Nakae Ushikichi (1889–1942) is the anomaly of his generation. He was a man endowed with opportunities for a successful career in Japan, and he spurned them all. Although he grew up in the last decades of the Meiji era (1868–1912) and came of age in the vibrant Taishō era (1912–1926), he chose to leave Japan altogether. Becoming a private scholar in China, he might have had his innovative Sinological essays published and gained a deserved reputation from them; but he rejected all offers of publication. He abandoned life in Japan itself and rejected the world of scholarship, preferring the existence of a semi-eremetic expatriate among the common people.

What causes a man to take such steps? How was he able to see in Taishō liberalism the roots of Shōwa ultranationalism? What was his great fascination with China, a country slipping further and further into political, social, and economic decay? These are among the questions this study seeks to answer. Even more central will be an examination of a Japanese expatriate, living in China for nearly three decades, and watching with a unique sense of distance and extraordinary insight the emergence of the Chinese revolution, the Japanese invasion, and the conflagrations of World War II all develop before his eyes. All the time, he retained his surgically critical perspective on developments in Japan and an unfailing opposition to them all. Throughout his self-imposed exile he was also trying to make logical, philosophical sense of where the world was going and what the future would bring.

Nakae was little known in his own day primarily because he shunned the public spotlight and refused (with one exception) to have his essays published. After his death in 1942 and with the conclusion of the Pacific War in 1945, his works and his letters appeared in Japanese bookstores and interest in him burgeoned. One of Japan's foremost critics, Hashikawa Bunzō, made the case most enthusiastically: "The keystone of his greatness was an unbounded faith in and love for humanity combined with an historical vision so broad that he almost seemed to be the world spirit incarnate."[1]

It is no wonder that after World War II the Japanese intellectual community should search for links between the prewar era and the growth of the Japanese military machine in Asia; nor is it any wonder that Japanese should look for lost chances, avenues not taken, seminal figures who understood all along, and approaches untried from the prewar period, to uncover roots of the democracy they sought to build in the postwar years. Nakae provided just such an example of a man who had managed to live a life without ever compromising his values. For him that had meant that if he had to leave his native country, to predict and even welcome the defeat of his homeland in World War II, then so be it. This sense of priorities and values impressed the famous critic Hasegawa Nyozekan (1875–1969) and prompted him to say that when he himself was in a quandary, he often "would think: 'What would Nakae Ushikichi have done had he been in this situation?'"[2]

The issue raised by Hashikawa that will become the central problem of this study is how Nakae combined the defining aspects of his life as an expatriate, Sinologist, philosopher, and political critic with this "unbounded faith in and love for humanity." One generally expects to find the kernel of an adult's life in the influence exerted upon him in youth. A commitment to any of these roles in life or anything else during Nakae's youth and college years seemed far beyond the realm of possibilities. His father, Nakae Chōmin (1847–1901), was one of the most famous men of the Meiji period and modern Japanese history generally. What characterized Ushikichi's relationship with his father, the celebrated defender of individual liberties and translator of Rousseau? What lasting influence did Chōmin exert on the young Ushikichi before his death in 1901?

When Ushikichi, orphaned at age twelve, graduated from the Faculty of Law of Tokyo University in 1914, a successful career was assured him, if he had chosen for it to be. But, for some reason, he forsook the orthodox career pattern altogether and went off to China to work as a secretary far in the recesses of the Yuan Shih-k'ai government. After floundering for several years, he underwent a personal crisis around 1919, and the Nakae Ushikichi as he would later be known began to emerge. Considerable attention will be devoted to what caused this remarkable change of direction in his life and the concomitant decision to continue living in China, a highly uncommon practice in the intellectually exciting Taishō period in Japan, a politically chaotic time in Republican China.

After a number of years of self-directed study of classical Chinese texts, Nakae tried his hand at scholarship and produced a 200-page essay on the history of ancient Chinese political thought that is remarkable for a host of reasons. Not the least among them are the essay's breadth of vision, comparative perspective, and close attention to the logic of analysis. In this and his other Sinological essays Nakae invested considerable energy to developing his own system of thought as an approach to the Chinese classical tradition. He borrowed from German philosophy, particularly German idealism, but he borrowed selectively. What he used and how he used it will be the main themes of this part of the study, as will the lasting import, if any, of these essays.

Although most of his writing dealt with the history and manipulation of Chinese thought, the only essay he published in a scholarly journal concerned an entirely different topic. This was the time-honored problem of "feudalism" in Chinese society, ultimately as fascinating and as tedious an issue as exists in Chinese social history. While much of the analysis in this essay may now be dated, one theoretical construct, involving the nature of Chinese rural society and the question of *kyōdōtai* (local community), proved influential enough in Japanese Sinological circles to spawn several generations of debate. This debate continues today, although no longer connected directly to Nakae.

Why did Nakae feel compelled to engross himself in the kind of detailed and often picayune Sinological research he did? Why would a man deeply concerned with the destruction of war around him devote many long hours to solving the mysteries of the *Shang-shu* (or *Shu-ching*, Book of history or Book of documents)? What unique perspective on the Chinese classics, particularly the *Shang-shu*, did Nakae bring to his scholarship, and is it tied to broader concerns? The late scholar of Chinese literature, Takeuchi Yoshimi (1910–1977), although fully cognizant of the importance of Nakae's scholarship, commented that he found himself more drawn to Nakae Ushikichi as a person than as a scholar, but that the two issues are not easily separated, nor should they necessarily be.[3]

Whereas Nakae Chōmin was drawn to French political thought and adored French culture, Ushikichi was attracted to German philosophy (though not German culture). He especially took inspiration from the great thinkers in the German idealist tradition, Kant and Hegel, and from certain of Karl Marx's works as well. But his admiration remained critical throughout his life, for he found elements in their works with which he could not agree. How did Nakae understand and use these and other thinkers (such as Max Weber), and how did his reading of their works influence his Sinological theories? What influence did the German idealist tradition exercise on Nakae's own philosophical ideas?

Although he wrote no works of philosophy, we can extract from his writings—his essays, letters, recorded conversations, and reading notes—something closely approximating a philosophy of life or a philosophy of history. At this point Nakae's efforts to develop and simultaneously live a philosophy based on the ultimate belief in the future of humanity will be examined. From this perspective we can try to understand the reasons for his anti-war views, for his harsh criticism of Japan's military invasion of the Asian mainland, and for his pursuing the life of an expatriate in China. Unfortunately the whole picture does not coalesce in a perfectly neat way. There are large gaps, frustrations, and unpolished edges in Nakae's *Weltanschauung*. But, one element that never flagged was his uncommonly strong sense of the ultimate sanctity of human life.

It is this conception of the value of human life that postwar Japanese critics find so admirable in him and, indeed, a more enlightened view would be difficult to imagine. That he maintained this view despite all the adversities of the 1930s; that unlike many left-leaning Japanese, he refused to compromise with the right-wing authorities in Japan; and that he lived his belief in humanity by not seeking to rise above the average man have all rendered him a kind of beacon of light shining across a dark divide that separates the prewar from the postwar Japan. The playwright Kinoshita Junji, in remarking how attracted he felt to Nakae, noted that Ushikichi's life was truly the stuff of drama.[4]

As we shall see, Ushikichi differed in many ways from Chōmin. He lived the quiet life of a recluse; his father was one of the most famous social and political activists of the entire Meiji period. He wrote little; his father wrote in quantity. From his father, however, he inherited this core belief in the human being, although he couched it in different terms and traditions of thought. For Chōmin this view involved the guarantee of individual liberties to all, and even meant the disavowal of the theistic element that was part of the French intellectual tradition he popularized in Japan. Both men, though, regarded human life as precious. On his deathbed, Chōmin is reported to have told his faithful disciple Kōtoku Shūsui: "Of course, I was for the [French] Revolution. But, all the same, if they made me sit and watch King Louis XVI mount the steps to the guillotine, I'd have had no choice but to run over, knock down the executioner, and help the king to escape."[5] Ushikichi shared with his father this belief that protecting a human life, regardless of whose it was, transcended all else.

Part One
Nakae Ushikichi's Early Life

Nakae Ushikichi with his father Chōmin, circa *1901*

ONE

The Years in Japan

Meiji Japan produced many colorful and brilliant figures, many of whom led lives fraught with frustration and melodrama. For the first time in several centuries of Japanese history, overseas travel and study became permissible, and this change came just at a time when scientific developments made travel accessible and study desirable. But yearning for knowledge about the outside world and efforts to change Japan, either to meet the challenge of the West or to make Japan a more modern country, frequently ran up against obstacles. The life of Nakae Chōmin (1847–1901) describes just such a conflict and introduces the unusual intellectual atmosphere in which his son Ushikichi spent his first impressionable years.

NAKAE CHŌMIN AND MEIJI INTELLECTUAL LIFE

Chōmin was born in the last years of the Tokugawa bakufu into a low-ranking samurai household in Kōchi, seat of the domain of Tosa. Tosa was famous in its day not for being a great or powerful domain but as the home of the men, such as Sakamoto Ryōma (1835–1867), who facilitated the compromise between the great domains of Satsuma and Chōshū to bring about the Meiji Restoration. How well Chōmin ever knew his father, Motosuke, remains a matter of conjecture inasmuch as the latter spent long periods away from home at work in the Edo office of the lord of Tosa. He died when his son was only fourteen years old.[1]

Before then, though, he had launched his son on the standard educational path befitting a member of the elite, albeit an impoverished segment of that class. As a result, Chōmin studied the Chinese classics, retaining particular fondness for the Taoist masterpiece *Chuang-tzu* and the progenitor of East Asian historiography, the *Shih-chi* (Memoirs of the grand historian) of Ssu-ma Ch'ien (135?–93 B.C.E.). For Japanese well-trained in Chinese learning or Kangaku, the *Shih-chi* was a special favorite as much for the form and manner in which it described ancient Chinese history as for Ssu-ma Ch'ien's elegant style as a writer of prose.[2] Chōmin combined an avid interest in Kangaku and Kanbun (Japanese writings in Chinese) with all the proper attributes of a serious student, studying many long and hard hours. It apparently paid off, for he is still remembered as one of the finest writers of Kanbun in his time.

Chōmin also showed signs from his youth of knowing that the future boded ill for samurai society. This foresight fitted nicely with his own predilection for a kind of radical egalitarianism and strong belief in individual liberties. While still in Tosa he began studying Dutch and English, perhaps with an eye to future advancement. He continued his studies at the Chidōkan in Edo and from 1865 in Nagasaki. There he began to learn French, and thereafter the whole course of his Western studies moved in a Gallic direction. Two years later (1867) he enrolled in the most prestigious institution for training in the French language, the Tatsuridō in Edo. Shortly after he was expelled from this school for misconduct (assiduous participation in the life of the local brothels and bars), the government selected him as interpreter for Léon Roches, the special French emissary in Japan. He was twenty years old at the time, in possession of the rare Japanese ability to speak and read French. It was in this set of circumstances that Nakae Chōmin witnessed the events of the Meiji Restoration of 1867–1868.

Shortly thereafter he moved to Edo (now renamed Tokyo), where he assumed a post teaching French at the Daigaku nankō, a forerunner of Tokyo University. The association proved short-lived, as Chōmin, having somehow gained the attention of Meiji statesman Ōkubo Toshimichi (1830–1878), obtained his help and became one of fifty students accompanying the Iwakura Mission to America and Europe in late

1871. He then stayed on in France for three years as a student sponsored by the Ministry of Justice.

Arriving in the capital shortly after the fall of the Paris Commune, Chōmin immediately defied his government's injunction to study French law and immersed himself in the study of French philosophy, history, literature, and culture. Perhaps as a way to improve his French and absorb French culture firsthand, he threw himself as well into the good life of French café society. He found willing compatriots in his fellow Japanese students then in Paris, in particular Prince Saionji Kinmochi (1849–1940). From these years his inner tendency toward egalitarianism found expression in a wholesale commitment to the Western principles embodying it. At times he would even criticize the West for failure to live up to these noble ideals. At some point before he returned to Japan in January 1875, Chōmin began a translation of Rousseau's *Du contrat social*, which would subsequently earn him the nickname "the Rousseau of East Asia."[3]

Back in Japan, Chōmin assumed a post teaching French at the Tokyo Foreign Languages School. When he demanded that classical Chinese education become part of the school curriculum, inasmuch as Japan's cultural heritage was so deeply indebted to China (no educated European, after all, lacked a comparable knowledge of Latin and Greek), the Ministry of Education turned him down flat. In protest he resigned; thus, a conservative government had refused a radical's call for the injection of classical Chinese into the modern education of students.[4] This curious mixture of classical, traditional culture with new values and impulses of Western derivation characterize Chōmin's thought and behavior generally. In this his son closely resembled him.

In the meantime, drafts of his translation of Rousseau's *Du contrat social* began to circulate in 1877. This document proved extraordinarily impressive to the leaders of the young movement for popular rights that had been organized in orderly opposition to the Japanese government. When they formed the Jiyūtō in early 1881, Chōmin made his entrance into politics; and it was the French explanation of natural rights (gleaned undoubtedly from his translation) that the movement adopted. From February 1882 his bimonthly journal *Seiri sōdan* serialized a fully annotated edition of his translation, and from then on his name became forever linked with Rousseau's.

The mixture of new and old elements in his thought are interestingly reflected in this translation. From his annotations it becomes ever so clear that Chōmin wanted to stress the idea that all political power resides with the people. This principle, made in the strongest and most uncompromising fashion, rejects any sharing of power between a hereditary sovereign and subjects, even a constitutional monarchy.[5] The essence of a republic made any compromise with the ultimate sanctity of the imperial institution in matters political impossible for Chōmin, and it made the stance of the Jiyūtō in the Meiji period rather more radical than might appear at first glance.

If he was intent on a course of action that rested on a belief in the sanctity of the popular will and that would be dependent on popular support alone, why then did he translate Rousseau into elegant classical Chinese? No one has adequately answered this question yet. One of the more satisfying answers may closely approximate Chōmin's motivation: In his mind, Rousseau's *Du contrat social* constituted the most important text for his fellows to read, at least within the bounds of explicating the principles of republicanism; as such, it deserved the kind of treatment insuring its immortality, translation into the true language of the East Asian intelligentsia and the larger East Asian community. Perhaps also in the back of his mind lay the possibility that a translation into Chinese might someday serve some purpose in Chinese and Korean reform.[6]

Several years later, in 1887, Chōmin wrote his most popular piece of the day, *Sansuijin keirin mondō* (Three inebriates discuss politics). In this book three drunken men, each representing a distinct and current point of view, argue about the future and nature of politics. It has been commented on and analyzed at great length by Japanese scholars, and translated into English twice.[7] Suffice it to say here that, through one of his characters, Chōmin articulated a position fully in accord with his earlier views on republicanism and individual liberties. From this time forward he exclusively used the style "Chōmin," a name which accentuated his attempt to identify with the masses of the people.

However impressed the leaders of the Jiyūtō may have been with

Chōmin's writings and translations, these written works proved insufficient to keep the party together. Factionalism and the government's harassment broke it apart in 1884. That year formed a turning point of sorts for Nakae Chōmin, now thirty-seven years old, as he participated in a number of schemes apparently aimed at spreading the liberal republican message to other countries in East Asia.

CHINA AND JAPAN FOR NAKAE CHŌMIN

Chōmin's long friendship with Tōyama Mitsuru (1855–1944), forerunner of right-wing ultranationalism in twentieth-century Japan, also began in 1884 when several members of the pro-Japanese party of reformers in Korea took refuge in Japan after a failed coup. Both he and Tōyama participated in the plan to found a foreign language school, the Zenrinkan, in Pusan; but their efforts were soon frustrated by the Osaka Incident. At the same time, Hiraoka Kōtarō (1851–1906) of Tōyama's organization, the Gen'yōsha, left for China to train activists and adventurers for future political and social action in China; and to this end he founded the Tōyō gakkan in Shanghai. Among the seven "comrades" who joined in its creation we find the name of Nakae Chōmin.[8]

What was Chōmin doing in China? And what possible reason could a man of his personal and philosophical inclinations have to maintain a friendship with the likes of Tōyama Mitsuru? With the collapse of the Jiyūtō in 1884, Chōmin set off on a trip to China with fellow "liberal" Sugita Tei'ichi (1851–1920). They hoped to spread the republican message there, with the ultimate aim of increasing their prestige back home by presenting proof of Chinese converts to their cause. The Chinese, however, failed to show much interest.

The reactions of Sugita and Chōmin to this Chinese venture demonstrate clearly how divergent Japanese ideals confronted Chinese realities and how China was often only of subsidiary importance in the minds of Japanese thinkers. Sugita returned to Japan utterly despondent over China's present state and future and convinced that Japan had a choice between immediately plunging in to seize some piece of the China pie, or else becoming part of the "main course" soon to be devoured by the Western imperialists.[9] Chōmin, in contrast, returned with renewed inter-

est in East Asian unity and Sino-Japanese cooperation; and this theme
of the shared Sino-Japanese cultural bonds comes out in his *Sansuijin keirin mondō* written several years later. He was not in principle opposed
to adventurism in China, but he did oppose both extremism at home
and the use of military expansionism as Japanese policy overseas. In
principle, he thought the best way for increasing national strength lay
not in militarism but in domestic reforms.[10]

Although Chōmin and Tōyama reacted differently to what they saw,
their interests had a basic similarity: Ultimately neither was much concerned with what was happening in China except insofar as events there
might influence politics back home for the better. Both were centrally
concerned with how to make Japan a better place, and both sought
reforms to that end. Where Tōyama and his followers called for a Japanese invasion or annexation in East Asia, Chōmin sought solidarity. But
their ends are less important for our understanding the differences
between them than are the means they advocated; for in the final analysis they represent two sides of the predominant Japanese system of
thought—nationalism. For Tōyama national security and national
strength were attainable through militarism and increased state power.
For Chōmin the way to keep Japan from becoming a second Romania,
as he put it in his last work *Ichinen yūhan* (One Year and a Half), was
through further insuring individual and popular rights at home.[11]

In March of 1887 Chōmin's first child, a girl, was born (d. 1971). Out
of a proclivity for simple names, he named her Chibi (a homonym for
"Shorty" or "Cutie")—much to her later consternation.[12] In December
he was forced to take his family and leave Tokyo because of the newly
enacted Peace Preservation Law. Two years later the ban on his travel to
the capital was lifted with the promulgation of the Meiji Constitution.
Leaving Mrs. Nakae, who was pregnant again, in Osaka until the birth
of their son in August, Chōmin took Chibi and returned at once to the
center of political action.

The Meiji Constitution disappointed Chōmin by relegating only
ambiguous powers to the Diet. He decided to run for office from Osaka
and was easily elected because of his popularity. The political haggling
and deals behind the scenes so disgusted him, though, that within a year
he resigned his post and swore off all politics until he could regain

financial security. He also quit his long and sustained habit of drinking and decided to go into business. This venture proved to be a complete failure; and by 1897 he was back in the political arena with a newly formed party, the Kokumintō. His last years found him in a losing battle against the rising tide of extreme nationalism in Japan.

In sum, what sort of man was Nakae Chōmin and what legacy did he bequeath his son? Professor Kuwabara Takeo, dean of Nakae Chōmin studies, sees him as someone who deeply felt himself to be a loner in the world, a man of inordinate talents and capabilities but with so few successes and so few devoted followers that he must have imagined himself cutting his own pathway. Another scholar, Katō Shūichi, sees him as a marginal man in Japanese society, a man with an insider's knowledge of the society and an outsider's intellectual distance from it. This combination provided him with tremendous insight but with little immediate influence, particularly in Japan's group-oriented and homogeneous society; his combination of power, weakness, and perception was similar to that of court women in Heian times. It was a fitting testament to his personal integrity that, at the time of his death, his funeral arrangements reflected the essential simplicity of one ordinary man who had been devoted to individual independence.[13] He had his body devoted to medical research (a rare practice in his day); and no religious service was to be held at the funeral because he considered Western beliefs in divinity and the immutability of the soul (apriorisms in the minds of the Europeans he most admired) to be irrational and unscientific.[14] By all accounts he died a sad and decidedly poor man.

CHŌMIN'S LAST YEARS AND NAKAE USHIKICHI

Little information survives concerning Chōmin's relationship with his son. We know the father was forty-two years old and living in Tokyo at the time of Ushikichi's birth, 14 August 1889, in Sonezaki, Osaka. Like his sister, Ushikichi was given a simple name, composed of the words for "cow" (*ushi*), since he was born in the year of the cow, and for "good luck" (*kichi*). After his mother arrived with him in Tokyo, the family settled down in the former Koishikawa ward (now part of Bunkyō ward). A little over a year later, Chōmin purchased a home in nearby Take-

shima; it was fairly large with a garden, a pond, trees, and even a small
vegetable patch. In February of 1892 Chōmin left his family to take a
position on the staff of the *Hokumon shinpō* (Northern news) in far-off
Otaru, Hokkaidō. He quit that job and turned in August to his own business ventures in the Sapporo timber industry; but when those went
bankrupt, he returned to Tokyo at the end of the year.[15]

The only real information we have about Ushikichi's youth—and it
is slight—comes from an interview with his sister in 1964 and her
memoir of 1965. Chibi recalled never having seen her brother studying
when he was a youngster because he was always playing. The two of
them had a black cat named Neguro, concerning whom a set of rules
had either been established from above or agreed upon between them.
In the morning when they awoke in their separate beds, each would
raise the blanket and try to get Neguro to crawl under, but neither was
allowed to grab the cat. Neguro learned from experience that Ushikichi
knew little of holding cats, would fumble with him, and often inadver-
tently inflict pain. Despite these strict guidelines, Ushikichi regularly
jumped up and grabbed the unsuspecting feline for himself. If he was
home, Chōmin would break in and scold his son; Chibi would become
angry with her younger brother; and only the mother would defend
him.[16]

Despite the fact that brother and sister never got along very well (in
fact, they fought a great deal), she painted a happy picture of home life
in the years before her father's death. Ushikichi had an endless array of
things with which to play and fruit to pick from the family's trees.
Chōmin taught his children the names of all the trees and flowers from
a botany text he had purchased years before in France, and Ushikichi
retained an interest in plant life throughout his life. "People have said
that Nakae Chōmin was a strange man," wrote his daughter many years
later, "but at home he was a wonderful father."[17]

In 1893 Ushikichi entered the Yamada Kindergarten where he met
Ishimoto Kenji, a man who would become a life-long friend. As a
young boy, Ushikichi was thin and quite small because of a weak
stomach. He needed a carefully balanced diet, and at the time the
Nakae family budget had no trouble accommodating his needs. There
were times, however, when the family did not have enough to eat. Chibi

did not remember wanting for food; but the older Kōtoku Shūsui (1871–1911), who had lived with the Nakaes earlier and rejoined them in April 1893, filled in this detail, a form of "noble poverty" (*seihin*) as Chōmin imagined it. Like the great majority of Japanese mothers to this day, Iyoko doted on her son, always letting him do as he wished. Chibi recalled not being accorded such special treatment herself. Ushikichi was an incessant chatterer, and his father chastised him for it.[18]

In 1895 Ushikichi moved on to the elementary school attached to the normal school for girls in the Takehaya area (still in Koishikawa ward). His record there was remarkable only for being undistinguished; he was apparently easily excitable (as Chōmin had been as a youth) and preferred outdoor play above all else. Chōmin took an active hand in his son's education several years later, when the boy reached age ten, and had him begin studying Kanbun and Kangaku.[19] It seems, however, that the young Ushikichi looked upon study as a burdensome waste of time.

One reason for the scarcity of information about Ushikichi's early years and his relationship with Chōmin in the father's last years is that Ushikichi all but refused to talk about his youth. He reportedly once summed up his father's contribution to Japanese history by saying Chōmin "was merely one enlightened scholar" of his day.[20] One of the few descriptions he ever gave of his youth was in a letter (dated 5 August 1936) to his friend Katō Koretaka (1910–1972). Upon seeing a local variety of wild peach in Peking, he wrote:

> My father used to explain to us about the wonderful taste of the wild peach, for even when he was suffering from his incurable illness and lay on his sickbed, he retained an abiding affection for the wild peach of his home town. He made a note of this in a work from that time [*Ichinen yūhan*], just after lauding the tastiness of the Tosa bonito. . . .
>
> I never had a chance to go with my father to Tosa and partake of the wild peach; but a fair time after his death, I recalled in my childish mind just how delicious the wild peach is, precisely as my father had put it.
>
> As I'm now approaching the age at which my father died, my own desire to pursue this childish affection of my father's for wild peaches. . . . has gotten the best of me.
>
> Although this [local Chinese] wild peach has a sturdy tree trunk and beautiful leaves, not once have I been able to find the essential fruit that my father so adored.[21]

Ushikichi's reasons for remaining so taciturn about his family life and particularly about his father are difficult to surmise. In addition to whatever problems may have arisen from being the son of a famous man, I think in part the explanation has to do with the shock, perhaps trauma, of Chōmin's sudden illness and death when Ushikichi was only twelve years of age. Many years later, in a letter to his good friend Suzue Gen'ichi (1895–1946), Ushikichi was trying to describe how the various qualities of joy change as one matures. Something compelled him at this point to remember his father's last year of life, how Chōmin's sense of humor improved "at a time when his life was in its eleventh hour, hanging on the verge of extinction, and while suffering he would listen to the sounds of insects and gaze at the moonlight visiting him in bed through the window at night."[22]

In March 1901 when Chōmin paid his doctor a visit, complaining of throat pain, he was not overly surprised at the diagnosis of cancer of the larynx. Given eighteen months to live, he made his wife and doctor keep the severity of his illness a secret from everyone, including his two children.

> After news of my tracheotomy became known in Osaka and Tokyo, I received a daily stream of letters asking about my recovery. I had my wife reply that my progress was excellent. Many people, unaware of the meaning of a tracheotomy in cases of cancer, automatically assumed that the operation had successfully cured my disease and sent letters of congratulations. The "year and a half" was known only to my wife and myself. Even my two children sent postcards and letters from Tokyo saying, "dearest Father, in due course you will recover." As a father I adopted a stoic philosophy; I had to protect my secrecy. Ah, but human beings are such fools.[23]

He then set about, in constant pain the entire time, dictating to his devoted disciple Kōtoku Shūsui his final work, a memoir of sorts and a summation of his philosophy and outlook on life. From April 1901 on, Ushikichi hustled off each morning to Waseda Middle School, unaware of the gravity of his father's illness. Despite the doctor's prognosis, Chōmin lived only nine months till his death on 13 December 1901 at home in Tokyo.

In addition to whatever one might easily imagine as a twelve-year-old's response to his father's sudden death, the only eyewitness account we have is Chibi's memoir. Although less than entirely sympathetic, she claimed a vivid memory of Ushikichi at the time of their father's death: "My brother

Ushikichi was nearby at the time and watched [apparently without emotion] in amazement at Mr. Kōtoku's terribly sad state of mind. Looking over at Ushikichi, I thought to myself: What kind of a son is this anyway?"[24] One wonders what she (only fourteen years old herself) expected of her little brother at that moment. When the father of a friend of his died in 1941, Ushikichi wrote to his friend Katō Koretaka of his own persistent sense of distress and sadness.

> As you know, the Chinese have the expression: "When the trees seek to be calm, the wind will not die down; when the child seeks to be filial, the parent is not there." In the past when I have read these phrases, maybe several hundred times, I have had scarcely any feeling at all. But now through the passing . . . [of this friend's father] the reality of the [Chinese] expression has been driven home to me.[25]

I think there can be little doubt he later grieved in his own quiet way for having failed to be as good a son as he came to wish he had been. The difficulty, of course, was that he became a full person only after his father's death and was never able to communicate this feeling. Late in life, Ushikichi reputedly hung an example of his father's calligraphy on the wall of his bedroom and would ironically say to visitors, ostensibly about the calligraphy but clearly with broader implications: "My, how the son does not measure up to the father."[26]

Short of engaging in amateur psychohistory, we cannot describe the nature and enduring import of the relationship between father and son. From our external and temporally distant perspective, though, I think we can surmise that it must have had a lasting effect on Ushikichi if only because he always remained so reticent about it. It may also be worth noting certain similarities in their personalities and circumstances. Although the boy Ushikichi showed none of his father's prodigious penchant for learning, he did already resemble his father in his youthful rambunctiousness and an early proclivity for misconduct. What is more, Chōmin, too, had lost his father at an early age and had been raised primarily by his mother. In the case of Ushikichi, this early loss had more than psychological consequences: Hard times were now in store for the Nakae family.

USHIKICHI'S YOUTH IN LATE MEIJI TOKYO

Several months after Chōmin's death, Mrs. Nakae was forced to sell their home in Takeshima-chō. With help from one of Chōmin's former students, Itō Daihachi (1858–1927), who was now a Jiyūtō representative in the Diet, the Nakae family was able to move to a house in Kōjimachi. Chōmin's old friends and disciples were instrumental in keeping the Nakaes afloat. Tōyama Mitsuru, who continued for some time to aid them financially, arranged through the famous woman educator Shimoda Utako (1854–1936) to rent several of the rooms in Mrs. Nakae's home to overseas Chinese students in Tokyo. She let the first room to Chang Tsung-hsiang (1877–194?), an overseas Chinese student in the Faculty of Law, Tokyo University; and the next year Chang's friend, Ts'ao Ju-lin (1876–1966), who was then studying at Chūō University, took a room in the Nakae home and stayed for two years. Both men retained a lifelong affection for the Nakaes, particularly for Ushikichi. Ts'ao's memoirs are full of his positive impressions of the reform efforts underway in Meiji Japan. Interestingly enough, however, neither he nor Chang showed any interest in the circles of radical and revolutionary Chinese students then in Tokyo.[27]

In 1903 Mrs. Nakae sold her house in Kōjimachi and moved to a rented place nearby in Motozono-chō, which was where Ts'ao roomed with them. Difficult times pursued her, though; and without the help of four men in particular, her situation might have seriously worsened. Monetary aid came directly from Dr. Asakawa Norihiko (1865–1907), a microbiologist of note and one of Chōmin's maternal cousins; Kurihara Ryōichi (1855–1911), a Chōmin disciple and member of the diet; and Kaneko Motozaburō, a Hokkaidō businessman who owned a mine jointly with Tōyama Mitsuru. And all the while Kōtoku Shūsui labored long hours to prepare Chōmin's manuscripts for publication in order to bring in royalties.

Despite whatever money Mrs. Nakae received from these sources, as well as from several of Kōtoku's friends and classmates, it was not enough to provide for her two teenagers. She chose to move again, this time outside the municipality of Tokyo to the village of Nippori, Shimotoshima County, Tokyo Prefecture. Chibi graduated in 1904 from

Takehaya Girls Middle School; and in December of 1905 she married Takeuchi Toraji, third son of the popular rights activist Takeuchi Tsuna and half-brother of Japan's future prime minister Yoshida Shigeru (1878–1967).[28]

Ushikichi graduated from Waseda Middle School in March 1906 and began preparing for the entrance examinations into Japan's elite senior high school of this era, Dai'ichi kōtō gakkō or First Senior High School. He sat for the exams in July, failed them, and was forced to settle for the Seventh Senior High School in Kagoshima the next summer. Again he posted no impressive record in school, aside from a marked ability at foreign languages. His activities and course work from these years through graduation from college several years later remain obscure, but we know that he became an avid reader of literature. He read Russian and French fiction in English and German translations, as well as German literature in the original. He also apparently was a great fan of the works of such contemporary Japanese authors as Natsume Sōseki (1867–1916), Kunikida Doppo (1871–1908), and a number of popular *haiku* poets. However, these activities and a particular predilection for taking long walks about Kagoshima and elsewhere in Kyūshū betrayed no scholarly urge on his part.

In the meantime, Kōtoku returned from a trip to the United States in 1906, with a gift of a rare fountain pen for the seventeen-year-old Ushikichi. Somewhat later he suggested in a letter to Mrs. Nakae that she sell the rights to a new edition of her husband's works and thereby garner enough income to secure her family's future income. Kōtoku moved out of the Nakae household around 1908, on the surface so as not to continue being a bother, but probably in fact so as not to involve the Nakae family in his own political activities. In December 1910 he was arrested by the authorities, together with his wife and others, allegedly for plotting the assassination of the Meiji Emperor. Although to anarchists and others around the world his case became a *cause célèbre*, he, his wife, and several comrades were executed the following month.[29] Ushikichi had grown up with Kōtoku always around the house and was known to have been fond of him. His response to the arrest and execution of Kōtoku remains unknown, but it must have come as a great shock to him as well as to his mother.

In July of 1910 he entered the political science department of the Faculty of Law at Tokyo University. Despite his entirely unremarkable scholastic record, matriculation from his elite high school enabled his entrance into the single most prestigious university faculty in all of Japan. There he met Sakatani Ki'ichi (1889–1957) and Sasaki Tadashi, with whom he later became close friends in China. Two other notable members of his class were Nanbara Shigeru (1889–1974), a liberal, Christian political scientist who later taught at his alma mater, spoke out against Japanese militarism during World War II, and became president of Tokyo University after the war; and Morito Tatsuo (b. 1888), whose arrest and imprisonment in 1920 for publishing an article sympathetic to Kropotkin's social thought became known as the Morito Incident. Nagayo Yoshirō (1889–1961), a novelist and playwright of a liberal, humanist bent in the face of Japan's growing involvement in World War II, was also studying at Tokyo University; but because he was in the Faculty of Letters, Ushikichi hardly knew him at the time.[30]

During his first year in college, Ushikichi rented a room in a university building in the Hongō section of Tokyo. Whenever his money ran out, he made pilgrimages to his mother in Nippori for more. According to a record of several years later, Mrs. Nakae was allocating roughly a fifth of her monthly budget of fifty yen to her son. The favored son, however, is not necessarily the dedicated scholar; and again, Ushikichi fell short of a model student's behavior. Never overly concerned about such things as his appearance or studies, he used to come to class in his wooden sandals, sporting a hunting cap, and station himself at the very back of the classroom.

Although he was apparently influenced to some small extent by Professor Onozuka Kiheiji (1870–1944) and took a minor interest in diplomatic history, what he absorbed from the lectures is difficult to say. He devoted the bulk of those waking hours in which he was sober to pursuing his earlier passion—literary works in foreign languages. His stock response to his mother's query about where he had ranked in his class was, "*biri*" (the tail end, the very last one). Finding Nakae Ushikichi during his college years usually required a trip to one of Tokyo's many music halls, theaters, vaudeville-type shows, or bars. He still enjoyed taking walks and reading English and German novels, but nothing intellectual or legal sparked much interest in him.

In March 1914 he went off to Yugashima to study for his graduation exams; and when he returned home shortly thereafter, he found his mother gravely ill. She died on 17 April, even more suddenly than his father had. Although he managed to graduate that July, he took his mother's death hard. As much as he may have taken her (and her monetary support) for granted, her death left him bereft. When he was later living in Peking, every year on the anniversary of her death he walked to Peking's central park to see the peonies, his mother's favorite flowers.[31] His "War Diary" (see Appendix 1) provides further evidence that every April 17 he took special note of his mother's passing.

Graduation from the Faculty of Law of Tokyo University could have assured Ushikichi a career in government. But, if the structure of life in law school was too constricting for Ushikichi, a bureaucrat's job hardly offered an appropriate alternative. Although his youth had had its share of traumatic events and the threat of financial disaster had always hovered about the threshold, still Ushikichi was raised as the son of a privileged family. Whenever he squandered his money or did poorly in school, he seems to have found a doting mother and friends of his father willing to contribute to keep him going. We have no evidence that he ever worked, considered leaving school to take a job and help support the family, or even seriously planned for his own future. While one can sympathize with his reluctance to enter the world of the white-collar bureaucrat, one can only come to the conclusion that his entire life to this point, age twenty-five in 1914, was that of a very spoiled young man.

If we did not know that he would become one of Japan's most original Sinologists and thinkers of the Taishō and Shōwa eras, Nakae Ushikichi's story would be mundane, indeed boring, in the extreme. But his life was about to take a radical turn over the next several years, prompted by a number of events to be described in the next chapter. Around September 1914 he received an offer from Itō Daihachi, now a vice-president of the South Manchurian Railway Company (SMR), to join the firm; and he proceeded to their main office in Dairen. Although he soon abandoned this tack, the course was set to bring him to China.

TWO

A Life Transformed: The 1910s

Not the least significant element of modern political history is contained in the constant growth of individual personality accompanied by the limitation of the State.[1]

Georg Jellinek, 1892

FIRST TRIP TO CHINA AND THE JAPANESE COMMUNITY IN PEKING

When Nakae grew bored with working for the South Manchurian Railway Company, once again his benefactors came to his rescue and found something else for him. Around October 1914, his mother's former boarder, Ts'ao Ju-lin, managed to land him an offer. Ts'ao summoned Nakae to Peking with a one-year contract to work as secretary to Ariga Nagao (1860–1921). Ariga was a professor of international law at Waseda University and had been a friend of Ushikichi's father, although their political views diverged sharply. Apparently, years before, Mrs. Nakae out of concern for her wayward son's future had prevailed on the ever grateful Ts'ao to intercede on behalf of Ushikichi if necessary. Nakae received the handsome monthly salary of one hundred *yuan* for responsibilities neither especially demanding nor explicit. One suspects that he held this sinecure, which might otherwise not have existed, because of his mother's earlier appeal. We know, however, that Nakae spent a great deal of his time in China that year leading what he himself would later refer to as the life of a "profligate villain" (*hōtō burai*).[2]

In 1914 Ariga accepted an invitation to serve as an advisor to the government of Yuan Shih-k'ai (1859–1916), which had taken power several years earlier in the young Republic of China. Yuan's advisor Ts'ao Ju-lin, who had been a student in Tokyo a decade earlier, may have engineered the invitation to Nakae by using his own political clout. Along with Yuan's other foreign advisors, Frank J. Goodnow (1859–1939) and George Ernest Morrison (1862–1920), Ariga had been hired in the capacity of a legal scholar to help draft a constitution for Yuan's regime. Ariga doubted that China was adequately prepared for a "liberal democracy," and he encouraged Yuan to seek a balance between a monarchy and a republic. He feared the wide extension of the franchise for several reasons: It insured rule by the poor; it blindly followed a Western model of government; and it ignored China's glorious political traditions. In general he advised "conservative centralization," highly restricted suffrage, and permission for the convening of a national assembly only if the political situation demanded it. As Ernest Young has argued: "It might not be unfair to say that Ariga's main influence on Yuan Shih-k'ai was to reinforce his scepticism about the value of vigorous representative institutions."[3]

No sooner had Ariga (and Nakae) come to Japan than in January of 1915 the Japanese government laid its infamous Twenty-One Demands before the Yuan regime. Although Yuan was cleverly able to leak news of these secret demands to the press and claim no choice but to reject them, an ultimatum by Japan forced his acceptance of all but the last of them, the heinous fifth group, which virtually ceded to Japan powers of military and police intervention into Chinese affairs. Ariga may have been no radical democrat, but he was outraged by the excessive expansionist zeal of Foreign Minister Katō Kōmei (1869–1926). Taking Yuan's side in the negotiations, he informed Japan's elder statesmen (the *genrō*) of Katō's actions and the gravity of the demands foisted upon the Chinese. Katō was vigorously chastised by the *genrō* for his insensitivity, just as Ariga was criticized by Japanese ultranationalists for insufficient expansionist desires. The actual signing of the demands, on 25 May 1915, devolved upon Chinese Foreign Minister Lu Cheng-hsiang, although responsibility for Chinese policy actually lay with Yuan and Ts'ao Ju-lin, then the Vice-Minister of Foreign Affairs.[4]

Ts'ao, who had already played a part in Nakae Ushikichi's life and was to play a larger one, was a central figure in Peking politics into the 1920s. Having studied law at Chūō University from 1899 to 1905, he had returned to China and held a number of governmental posts in the last years of the Ch'ing dynasty. After the 1911 Revolution, he was associated first with Yuan Shih-k'ai and then, after Yuan's abortive attempt to reinstitute the monarchy (which he had, in fact, supported), with Yuan's successor as Prime Minister, Tuan Ch'i-jui (1865–1936), whose government he joined in 1916 as Minister of Communications. It was Ts'ao who instigated the "war loans" plan that called for China to declare war on Germany and apply for loans from Japan, ostensibly to fight on the Allied side in World War I but primarily to strengthen Tuan's troops and enable him to reunify warlord-ridden China. President Li Yuan-hung (1864–1928) rejected the idea; but Ts'ao continued negotiating privately with the Japanese; and eventually a deal was made with Nishihara Kamezō (1872–1954), the emissary of Japanese Premier Terauchi Masatake (1852–1919). Tuan declared war on Germany in August 1917; and by September, seven installments of what came to be called the Nishihara Loans, totalling 145 million yen, had been paid. In return, large concessions were offered the Japanese in railways, banking, mining, and other industries.[5] During all this, Ts'ao made no secret of his affinity for Japan; but to many Chinese, his role in the negotiations over the Twenty-One Demands and particularly in the Nishihara Loans looked more like treacherous collusion than mere admiration and sympathy. To the public, he had become the most identifiable pro-Japanese official in the government, and it was an image that served him poorly in the coming years.

Nakae probably had little idea of what he was sailing into in 1914. He surely played no role of any importance in the events just described, although he served the Chinese government from mid 1914 through 1915. Ts'ao and the Chinese ambassador to Tokyo, Chang Tsung-hsiang, both of whom he had known now for a decade, introduced him to many of their associates in these years. Ts'ao, for instance, introduced him to Army Colonel Banzai Rihachirō (1870–1950), who was officially a military advisor to the Yuan government but was also for many years an intelligence operative for the Japanese government and instrumental in arranging the Nishihara loans.[6] In mid 1915 when Nakae's old college friend Sasaki Tadashi became the editor-in-chief of the Japanese-run, Chinese-language newspaper *Shun-t'ien shih-pao* (Capital news), Nakae's introduction enabled Sasaki to live at Colonel Banzai's residence. Nakae himself had been living in Ariga's residence since his arrival in China, although he made no secret of his frequent sorties to a Japanese restaurant, the Chōshuntei, in Peking.

When his contract expired in 1915, Nakae requested an extension; but Ariga having turned him down, he had no choice but to return to Japan. Back in Tokyo and looking for work, he made it clear to his sister that he planned to set up house with one Matsui Satoko, a geisha at the Chōshuntei Restaurant in Peking. Satoko came originally from Shiga prefecture where her father ran a candy store, but difficult times had later forced her to become a geisha in Osaka. Nakae's sister, aware of her own roots and now married into the illustrious Takeuchi family, was horrified and opposed the marriage wholeheartedly. Disheartened, Nakae philandered the rest of 1915 in Tokyo before returning to Peking at the end of the year. For the next seventeen he did not leave China once.[7]

Among the many other figures Nakae came to know through Ts'ao in the mid 1910s were Lu Tsung-yü (1875–1941), also a Waseda graduate; and Ting Shih-yuan (b. 1879), member of the militaristic Anfu Club and, in the mid 1910s, head administrator of the Peking-Suiyüan and Peking-Hankow Railways. Nakae also made the acquaintance of Fujiwara Masafumi (b. 1879), a graduate of Tokyo University whom Nishihara Kamezō appointed as an advisor to the Bank of Communications. In 1918 he met Professor Uesugi Shinkichi (1878–1929) of Tokyo University, a celebrated, conservative expert on constitutional law, whom he may have heard during a famous debate on the Japanese Constitution held at the Faculty of Law while he was a student there. Like Fujiwara, Uesugi had come to Peking at the behest of the Japanese Finance Ministry and Ts'ao Ju-lin. It is highly unlikely that Nakae would have met such illustrious men had it not been for his contact with Ts'ao, and he was soon to return the favor handsomely.

Some time shortly after his return to China, at the end of 1915 or the beginning of 1916, Nakae became more closely acquainted with Colonel Banzai, an advisor to the Tuan regime after the death of Yuan Shih-k'ai. Knowing Nakae's ability to read foreign languages rapidly, the Colonel asked him to peruse the foreign press in China and to prepare summaries of the news and editorial arguments with respect primarily to foreign affairs. Nakae thus began reading such newspapers as the *China Press, North China Daily News, Peking Gazette,* and *Peking-Tientsin Times* on a daily basis. Although the task was not especially rewarding to Nakae, except as a means of survival for about two years, Banzai was highly enthusiastic about the results because of the information thus made available to him. Banzai's residence itself had become a center for the handling and transmission of intelligence, and it was to serve as a training ground for young Japanese military men in China. Through Banzai and his predecessor in China, Aoki Norizumi (1859–1924), who stayed on in a different capacity after Banzai's arrival, Nakae came to know Doihara Kenji (1883–1948), who later became a General in the Japanese Army active in North China; Captain Tada Hayao (1882–1948), with whom Nakae forged an acquaintanceship sufficiently close for him to offer critical advice over the years; and Captain Okamura Yasuji (1884–1966), later convicted and imprisoned as a major war criminal.[8]

One must not hastily conclude that, because he knew these men and in fact worked for Banzai in a private capacity for a time, he shared their views on politics or anything else. We do not know what Nakae was thinking at the time; but twenty years later in a 1938 letter to Lieutenant Colonel Imada Shintarō of the Japanese Army General Staff, he had the following to say:

> I have no objection to the fact that he's a "great China hand" (*dai Shinatsū*), and he's probably remarkably adept in matters concerning contacts with the Chinese people . . . Although I was fed in this man's home for over a month at one point, it is my belief that, contrary to the loud claims of the vulgar world about his character, he combines an immense mixture of both good and bad, and I'm unable to distinguish quality in the man. He fully lacks the aesthetic sentiment, the purity, as well as the morality of a great man. Although not miserly in offering nourishment to those who enter his home, he lacks the plain honesty to improve himself.

Nakae concluded his letter by noting that, in the final analysis, Banzai was not terribly bright.[9] As we shall see, Nakae would over the years cultivate acquaintances from every political corner and every walk of life; and he was unusually frank in his opinions with them.

That development in his character, however, was still several years away. Despite all the activity in Chinese and world politics, to say nothing of the troubling developments in Sino-Japanese relations, at this time Nakae demonstrated little or no interest in any of it. We indeed have evidence only that he continued his philandering with gusto. His friend Sasaki Tadashi had heard of his ability to prepare news summaries and had Nakae write some political commentaries for *Shun-t'ien shih-pao*. After he moved out of Ariga's official residence, Nakae lived for a time with Colonel Banzai; but in 1918 he and Matsui Satoko finally decided to live together in spite of familial efforts to discourage them. Although they later separated and she returned to Japan, she was, according to Nakae, a devoted, intelligent, and capable wife.[10]

In an essay on Meiji-Taishō Japanese feelings and sense of distance with respect to China, Professor Takeuchi Minoru argues that "generally from the Taishō period on . . . life in Peking for Japanese was an idyllic honeymoon for those stricken by an 'infatuation for Peking (*Pekin koi*).'"[11] As the Taishō period progressed, the Japanese population of Peking, and elsewhere in China (and Manchuria), increased dramatically, as this "sense of distance" Takeuchi describes dwindled to an unprecedented point in Sino-Japanese intercultural relations. As it did, Nakae, who became one of the infatuated, came to know more people. But the increased number of personal contacts had the effect of making him increasingly covet his privacy. Where Peking had once been a refuge from life in Japan for Nakae, as many Japanese moved there, it began to lose the qualities Nakae had found most appealing.

In the mid 1910s, there were only about 500 Japanese living in Peking, though aside from Sasaki, Fujiwara, and few others, Nakae had scarcely any contact with them. Of this group many were businessmen employed in the Peking branch of their Japanese firms; reporters and editors for the Japanese press (some worked for newspapers based in China, others as correspondents for Japanese papers); educators; officials of the Japanese government working in the embassy; and advisors in everything from military affairs to educational matters to agronomy. Nakae found it difficult to become accustomed to Japanese society in Peking, in part surely because he shared little besides a university degree with most of them.[12] Like many overseas communities, the Japanese in Peking tended to re-create many of their own institutions in China in a manner more convention-bound and stratified than even back in Japan, and this was precisely what Nakae had abandoned rather than accommodate himself to the standard career route set before him. Through Satoko he became friendly with one Okamoto Torao (b. 1894), proprietor of a dyed goods store in Peking, and his elder sister Kikuko (b. 1891) whom everyone called *anego* (roughly the equivalent of "Big Sis"). They all remained friends for many years.

Although Nakae may have felt the increased Japanese presence in Peking, the physical distance from Japan itself was still great enough to make coping with his sister's objections to his setting up housekeeping with Matsui Satoko considerably easier. Across the North China Sea, he could simply ignore them. It also allowed him to make friends without regard to class or political viewpoint. Aside from hinting at a certain spiritual restlessness, however, his domestic arrangements and the other indications of Nakae's increasing disaffection with conventional society do little to hint at the suddenness with which his life would change or the startlingly individualistic shape it would take.

NAKAE BECOMES A SCHOLAR: THE INFLUENCE OF GEORG JELLINEK

Around 1918, perhaps early 1919, Nakae hired a Chinese teacher with whom he began to study conversational Chinese as well as to brush up on his classical. He also obtained some instruction in English, German, and French composition and conversation from members of the Western community in Peking. German was his particular favorite; and he is said to have read German books every day from this point on, although with no special aim or program.

Among the German-language books available to him, perhaps found in Ariga's office or home, was Georg Jellinek's oft-reprinted *Allgemeine Staatslehre* (A general theory of the state) of 1900. Although no longer widely read, in his day and at the time Nakae read his work, Jellinek (1851–1911), who was close friends with Max Weber (1864–1920) and Ernst Troeltsch (1865–1923), was a major force in the theory and sociology of the modern state. *Allgemeine Staatslehre* was, in fact, immensely popular at Tokyo University when Nakae was there, and some have speculated that rediscovering it in Peking shook him out of his intellectual doldrums.[13]

Jellinek and especially *Allgemeine Staatslehre* had found an avid disciple in one of Nakae's teachers, Tokyo University Law Professor Minobe Tatsukichi (1873–1948). Minobe shared Jellinek's methodological concerns, admired the politically liberal bent of his view of the state and its constitution, and considered him a true internationalist because of the French and Anglo-American influences in his thought. Johann Kaspar Bluntschli (1808–1881) was, as several scholars have noted, the other most popular and widely read political scientist in mid- and late-Meiji Japan; but "[t]he intellectual universality and tolerance of Jellinek seem to have carried the greater and more enduring influence in Japan," writes one of Minobe's biographers.[14]

Constitutional studies became immensely popular even before Tokyo University opened its doors in 1877. The Meiji Restoration had raised such fundamental issues as: What body (the people, the Emperor, a Diet) held ultimate national sovereignty? What was the nature of the modern state? And what role did a constitution play in elaborating the functions and powers of the constituent elements of state authority? In 1872, Katō Hiroyuki (1836–1916) published a translation of Bluntschli's *Allgemeines Staatsrecht* (General state law), and he later pushed German studies at Tokyo University both as teacher and as president there. In contrast to Katō's decidedly anti-parliamentary views, however, liberal constitutional thought also flourished at Tokyo University under the influence of German theorists and the leadership of "the Jellinek of Japan," Minobe.[15]

Allgemeine Staatslehre was a mammoth synthesis of Jellinek's entire intellectual oeuvre, and systematically explicated his jurisprudential ideas. Central among the latter was the theory of "auto-limitation," by which the state restricted itself in imposing its will on its subjects. This notion was essential to the popular concept of *Rechtsstaat* (*hōchikoku*, in Japanese): the state in which the rule of law reigns and the individual is legally protected against arbitrary intrusion.[16] Jellinek argued that the modern state always retained highest sovereignty, and that meant it held supreme power. But the modern state also limited its control or restricted itself through the promulgation of a constitution and laws.

Thus, while only the state could impose "binding commands," at the same time those would always be tempered by the restrictions of the law. And the law, in the final analysis, derived from social relations and other factors completely external to the legislative operations of the state.

Jellinek's opponents questioned, obviously, whether the state would in fact limit itself through law; or, whether, if the state retained highest authority, it *could* actually limit itself. His response was that his concept of "auto-limitation" not only applied to the law, but was central to all modern ethical thought and was opposed to rule by arbitrary force in any context. As one expert in this field summarized Jellinek's ideas in this vein:

> The ultimate foundation of law, Jellinek held to be its rationality and its objectification of the ethical consciousness of the community and of the existing balance of power in the community. That international law was less stable and secure than the public law within each State, he attributed not to a lack of coercive authority over the States, but to the fact that the common consciousness of the community to which it applied was at a considerably lower stage of development than that existing within the borders of the individual States.[17]

The law reflects the ethical and cultural values of the societal community that produces it, and the rights of the individual, as a constituent member of that society, were to be protected in law. Auto-limitation insured that the state would be legally restricted in all of is dealings with the citizenry that formed it. Thus, auto-limitation created the relationship between the state and the individual subject in legal terms, rendering it no longer merely that of ruler over ruled. The basic principle was that the central government was "confined within the limits of the law, that it may not demand anything of the individual or command him in anything except that to which it is expressly authorized by legal prescription."[18]

Allgemeine Staatslehre, in good Kantian form, recognized the dichotomous relationship between the "is" (*sein*) and the "ought" (*sollen*), between the societal and the jurisprudential. Beyond this methodological dualism, however, lay the belief that the law took form and gained validity insofar as it was based on the society it governed. Although he attempted the monumental task of discussing both the sociology of the state and juristic philosophy in an effort to bridge the gap between them, Jellinek's Neo-Kantian background seems to have made that an elusive goal.[19] Ultimately, his main contribution to the German theory of the modern constitutional state was this stress on the safeguards for the rights of the individual before the sovereignty of the state.

In 1910, the year in which Nakae entered the Law Faculty of Tokyo University, Uesugi Shinkichi became professor of law there. Owing to his extreme right-wing views, he soon clashed sharply with his colleague Minobe Tatsukichi; and from 1912 on, a bitter feud developed between them. Ironically, Uesugi had actually studied under Jellinek in Heidelberg and felt sufficiently close to him to dedicate his *Teikoku kenpō* (The imperial constitution) both to Jellinek and to his other mentor, the extremely conservative Hozumi Yatsuka (1860–1912). Uesugi charged that Minobe, in his liberal interpretation of the constitution and the Japanese state, had misconstrued *kokutai* (national polity) by equating it with *seitai* (*Staatsform*, or the form of state). Nothing, in Uesugi's view, could limit the sovereignty of the Japanese emperor, and this illimitability was the hallmark of Japan's unchangeable and unique *kokutai*. A new *seitai* may have taken shape in 1889 as a result of the promulgation of the Meiji Constitution, but it was merely a new structure through which the emperor ruled.

Minobe responded in good Jellinekian form by arguing that the state was a corporate body that united the monarch with his people in pursuance of a common goal. The monarch acted in the capacity of sovereign on behalf of the entire populace, much as one would find in the other monarchies of the late nineteenth century. In other words, Japan was not unique in this regard, as Uesugi strenuously claimed. This acute disagreement over juristic ideas was closely linked to sharp political differences between the two men.[20] It threw into sharp relief the two principal interpretations of Japanese sovereignty and the state under the Meiji Constitution.

In the first decade of the twentieth century, Minobe translated, summarized, and introduced many of Jellinek's writings, including his short volume on *The Declaration of the Rights of Man and Citizens* and large excerpts from *Allgemeine Staatslehre*. These appeared in publications available to students at the time, and they were undoubtedly widely read by students in the Faculty of Law of Minobe's own university. As he further digested the many ideas in these works and their applicability in Japan, Minobe's attraction to Jellinek's interpretation of the issues only grew stronger. His *Nihon kenpō* (The Japanese constitution, 1921, reprinted several times) "is virtually an *Allgemeine Staatslehre*," according to Frank Miller, replete with whole passsages drawn from Jellinek's masterwork with the essential social-juristic dichotomy structurally intact. In addition, Ienaga Saburō has shown how Minobe later came to disagree, albeit only slightly, with the great power attributed to the government by Jellinek.[21]

Minobe developed and published his early work on and by Jellinek in the few years immediately preceding Nakae's entry into Tokyo University; and the Minobe-Uesugi debate erupted precisely while Nakae was there. Jellinek's ideas were, thus, widely known in the original and in Japanese translation by 1910, principally owing to Minobe's efforts. If sides were being taken, Nakae's background would have inclined him toward Minobe, and from there perhaps to Jellinek himself. Even if he had not read Jellinek's work in school, Nakae certainly knew his name and probably the bent of his argument.

Although somewhat dated now, Jellinek's ideas remain curiously interesting even in hindsight and were indeed more liberally inclined than those of Ariga or Uesugi, both of whom served as advisors on constitutional law to the Peking government in power. Jellinek's emphasis on the state's restricting its own sphere of activity and so enabling the individual greater areas of freedom, his idea that law had to reflect its societal basis, and his overall position of support for the progress hailed by the French and American Revolutions may have struck respondent chords in Nakae Ushikichi. Nakae Chōmin had spent the better part of his life fighting for the guarantee of individual liberties that Jellinek argued were the essence of the modern constitutional state.

Something besides the substance of Jellinek's major work interested Ushikichi: his style of reasoned argument and the complexity of his analysis. Some of us are of a cast of mind receptive to German idealist philosophy, and some can even lay claim to understanding it. Nakae apparently was among that select group, and Jellinek's Neo-Kantianism seems to have awakened in him hitherto dormant inclinations. We can only surmise this from Nakae's subsequent immersion in the writings of Kant, Hegel, and Marx, as well as numerous lesser figures in German philosophy, psychology, and sociology. *Allgemeine Staatslehre* was a wide-ranging magisterial work of brilliant scholarly organization; and as we shall soon see, Nakae's first essay on Chinese political thought, written several years later, reflects an enormous conceptual debt to Jellinek and probably as well to Minobe.

It was both Jellinek's juristic philosophy and his style of reasoned analysis that molded Nakae's future patterns of thought. This influence, though, proved more formative than lasting. Whereas Minobe, by contrast, continually returned to Jellinek's ideas, even after World War II, Nakae moved back into eighteenth- and nineteenth-century German thought, as well as laterally into nineteenth- and twentieth-century European social science, for intellectual sustenance after he completed his first work. Nakae rarely mentioned Jellinek after the mid 1920s; and in the four hundred pages of his letters that have been reprinted (mostly from the mid 1930s until his death), there is not a single reference to Jellinek. What Jellinek and his work had done for Nakae was provide access into the world of German idealism and social science. From January 1919 Nakae began to fill the first of his forty-two extant notebooks with reading notes, and he continued in this purposeful and scholarly manner until his death.

THE MAY FOURTH INCIDENT: ANOTHER AWAKENING

While Nakae was reading Georg Jellinek, World War I came to an end and the Powers met in Versailles to decide Germany's fate. There, to the shock and dismay of the Chinese, the European powers allowed a geopolitical recognition of Japan's growing might to override the principle of self-determination; and Japan retained sovereignty over the Shantung peninsula. The incident that resulted has been so glorified in modern Chinese historiography, Communist and Republican alike, that it is difficult to present an even-handed version of the events nearly three-quarters of a century later.

When the news of the decision in Europe reached China at the beginning of May 1919, the already active student movement grew violent. The stories of what actually occurred on 4 May 1919 vary, but we can piece together the essentials. In the afternoon, a group of demonstrators, between 3,000 and 5,000 in number, sought to make their feelings known to the ministers of the European governments resident in Peking. Finding the American, British, French, and Italian ministers indisposed, they began marching in the direction of Ts'ao Ju-lin's home on Chao-chia-lou Street, still in an orderly procession.[22]

The names of Ts'ao Ju-lin, Chang Tsung-hsiang, and Lu Tsung-yü were all associated with pro-Japanese sentiments by reason of their roles in the negotiations concerning the Twenty-One Demands and the Nishihara Loans. In the mushrooming press of that time, the students had been daily vilifying them for their alleged dealings with the Japanese, with vituperative outbursts like "The names of Ts'ao Ju-lin, Lu Tsung-yu, and Chang Tsung-hsiang will stink for a thousand years."[23] The residents of a perceived traitor made a natural destination for the demonstrators frustrated by the Western ministers. The none too sympathetic *North-China Herald* published several accounts of the demonstration, one of which blamed certain "repressive measures taken by the Police" for the violent turn that the demonstration soon took. Another report in the same newspaper noted that

> the change which came over this procession of apparently innocent schoolboys was astounding, and it was most disconcerting to the 50 police who had assembled at the Cabinet Minister's [Ts'ao's] gate. The 3,000 bunched up in the narrow street . . . and went through police, gates and all in a fine indifferent frenzy and set about making a ruin of Ts'ao Ju-lin's residence in the most systematic manner.[24]

What drove the students from peacefully demonstrating to the use of brute force may simply have to do with the psychology of the mob. Why the trouble broke out specifically on Chao-chia-lou Street is another question. Ts'ao was an understandable object of their anger, but the burning of his house to the ground has become so emblazoned and glorified in the collective memory of the Chinese that few have yet examined other reasons for the demonstration's having ended in front of his residence. Factional fighting among the cliques in Peking may have played a considerable role here.

The leader of the Research Clique, Lin Ch'ang-min (1876–1925), despite having been educated at Waseda University and maintaining friendships with individual Japanese, had long warned against governmental dealings with Japan. A longtime fighter for parliamentary government, he had written newspaper articles vigorously opposing the policies of Ts'ao Ju-lin and the New Communications Clique. Although his writings never advocated violence, some members of the foreign press maintained years later that Lin's polemics had stirred up the demonstrators; and this was a view easily accepted by Ts'ao and others who had feuded with him.[25]

In point of fact, however severe Lin's attack on the negotiations with the Japanese and on the pro-Japanese group in the Tuan regime, Lin never openly advocated violence. According to one long-time Japanese resident in China, Lin spoke Japanese with the fluency of a native and cultivated many Japanese friends. His opposition to the activities of Ts'ao Ju-lin and his group was motivated by a strenuous disagreement over policy, not any deep-seated enmity for Japanese. He simply feared the consequences of the Nishihara Loans greatly and worked painstakingly to raise public consciousness against them, authoring an "open letter" to the Japanese people entitled "Ching-kao Jih-pen jen shu" (A letter of warning to the Japanese people) in the early 1920s.[26]

Nonetheless, during the afternoon of 4 May 1919, the demonstrators descended on Ts'ao's home. Nakae was spending that afternoon at the home of his friend Sasaki Tadashi along Huang-shou-i Lane nearby. He could see that the police were expecting a large crowd to assemble at the home of Lu Tsung-yü. In the early evening, Nakae got wind of the storm brewing at Ts'ao's home and rushed over to see whether he could help. Chang Tsung-hsiang and Lu Tsung-yü (one account places Ting Shih-yuan and not Lu at the scene) were with Ts'ao at the time. Ts'ao found a hiding place to avoid danger, but Chang was severely beaten.[27]

In wholly untypical fashion, Nakae jumped into the fray, helped Ts'ao to escape, and carried Chang to safety just as Ts'ao's mansion began burning. Nakae then allegedly screamed at the students in his accented, broken Chinese: "This is my friend; if you want someone to assault, beat me up!" According to one eyewitness account, by Po Ch'i-ch'ang, the demonstrators complied and whacked him with metal rods and sticks.[28] Another Chinese account mentions "a Japanese who right at the critical moment braved death to plunge into the crowd and save Chang's life." Nakae then carried Chang to the Dōjin Hospital where both men were treated for the injuries they had sustained. Although the *North-China Herald* ran an obituary for Chang several days later, he lived for another twenty or more years, thanks to Nakae.[29]

What impelled Nakae to jump into the melee at the risk of his own life is difficult to say, for he would never speak of it. His action has sometimes been interpreted in light of his father's remark that he would have been unable to witness the execution of King Louis XVI without helping him to escape. But aside from the obvious difference between stating a hypothesis about oneself and actually taking a seriously dangerous action, there is a real difference between rescuing a person one thinks of primarily as a political despot and rescuing a friend. The May Fourth Incident has been studied with so overwhelmingly a pro-student a bias that Ts'ao and Chang have routinely been cast as political villains and the students' right to burn the house of one and attempt the murder of both routinely accepted. It is doubtful, however, that Nakae thought of the situation in that way. What he saw was an attack on human life and more particularly on the life of a friend and benefactor. It seems to me more likely that he responded on impulse with the courage of friendship than that he reckoned with any political principle. But if a political comment is useful in interpreting his action, it is not Chōmin's on the doomed Bourbon so much as one of Ushikichi's own remarks, as reported by Nakamura Shintarō: "Even if I betray the state, I cannot betray a friend."[30]

THE NEW NAKAE USHIKICHI

Needless to say, the events of 4 May 1919 brought Nakae and Ts'ao closer together as friends. Either that year or early in 1920, Nakae moved at Ts'ao's invitation into a house owned by Ts'ao along Eastern Kuan-yin-ssu Lane. The grounds had a lovely garden with numerous trees. Nakae lived there rent-free for the next twenty years. Also, around this time Nakae had his wife appear in his stead at the commemorative ceremony for his mother at a temple in Tokyo. He had apparently won his sister's approval to have Satoko's name entered in the Nakae family register. This event seems to have warmed the rather chilly relations that had prevailed between him and his sister for some time.[31]

The experiences of May 1919, his newfound interest in scholarship and German thought, and his personal familial security dating from this time all combined to produce an entirely renewed Nakae Ushiki-chi. They made him realize that life and personal freedom are meaningless without direction. He decided to remake totally the pattern and substance of his daily life. The many persons who came to know him over the next two decades met this new Nakae Ushikichi and were deeply impressed, often unaware of his earlier incarnation.

Nakae's personal reformation meant first of all complete abstention from alcohol and prostitutes. He also began to impose on himself a rigid daily regimen. He would usually rise before dawn, 4:00 A.M. according to most accounts, and begin the day by reading the foreign-language newspapers in English, German, and later French; the Chinese paper *Ta-kung-pao*; and (grudgingly) the Japanese daily *Asahi shinbun*. After several hours of newspapers, breakfast, and viewing his yard, he would return to his study, lock the door, and spend the remaining hours before lunch reading texts. In the 1920s these texts were mostly classical Chinese originals or works in English, German, and French. From the mid 1930s on, philosophical works in European languages predominated, but he did continue reading Chinese texts till the end of his life. Each day he apportioned himself a set amount of reading to accomplish before the day's work could come to a close, often reading materials three times before moving on to a new segment.

Although he ate lunch promptly at noon, he often read during the meal. His penchant for taking invigoratingly long walks, which predated this change of character, became part of his afternoon schedule, usually around 3:30 P.M.; and he was ordinarily accompanied by his faithful and beloved German shepherd Huang. Guests that arrived at this time of day either joined him walking or waited back at Ts'ao's house. In the early 1920s Nakae might pay a visit to the Japanese Club

of Peking, although he discontinued this practice later. There he met
Ōnishi Itsuki (1887–1947) of the *Asahi shinbun* and Tachibana Shiraki
(1881–1945) then of the *Kei-Shin nichinichi shinbun* (Peking-Tientsin
daily news). Tachibana had already won notoriety in the Japanese press
with his acerbic editorials for the *Shun-t'ien shih-pao*. Like Nakae, he
spent nearly thirty years in China; but their careers evolved in different
directions, as we shall soon see.

Nakae usually returned home from his walk after 5:00 P.M., washed,
recorded the day's temperature at that time, the names of that day's visitors, whether or not he had spoken any Japanese during the day, and
the letters written and received. In an interview many years later, his ser-
vant told Katō Koretaka that Nakae then spent about three minutes in
silent prayer. Then he returned to work, often by looking up the many
unfamiliar expressions he had encountered during the day in European-
language works. After dinner at 7:00 P.M., his reading continued but the
content varied widely over the years, anything from the *Tzu-chih t'ung-
chien* (A comprehensive mirror for aid in government) by Ssu-ma
Kuang (1019–1089) to Prosper Merimée's *Carmen* to the *Chuang-tzu*. In
his later years, Nakae read from the Bible before retiring. It was one of
the few works he allowed himself the luxury of reading in translation,
and it moved him deeply. He usually went to sleep between 9:00 and
10:00 P.M.[32]

Maintaining this rigid schedule became an obsession of sorts for
Nakae, perhaps because he better than anyone knew how easy it was to
fall back into a dissolute life. Until his dying day, when he was bedrid-
den and feverish, he tried to keep to a regimen. He viewed it as his primary contact with the real world, as can be seen in the diary he kept of
his last weeks in the hospital.[33]

Because of this strict schedule and his general indifference to the activities of the Japanese community in China, many of the Japanese in Peking considered Nakae a bit of an eccentric. Among his early Japanese
friends in Peking were Hashikawa Tokio (1894–1983), a reporter for the
Shun-t'ien shih-pao and later director of the Cultural Affairs Department
of the Japanese Ministry of Foreign Affairs in Peking; Ishibashi Ushio
(b. 1892), a worker at the Japanese Consulate and private scholar of
Peking's history and geography; Dr. Kosuge Isamu, Chief of Staff at

Dōjin Hospital in Peking, who later went into private practice; Shimizu Yasuzō (b. 1891), a Christian businessman who ran the Ch'ung-chen School for impoverished Chinese girls; and Tsujino Sakujirō (1876– 1940) an expert in telecommunications who was invited to China from the Japanese Communications Ministry at the time of the Russo- Japanese War to install telephone equipment in major cities along the Yangtze River and who remained an advisor to the Peking Telephone Bureau as well as one of Nakae's closest friends.[34]

By 1922–1923 Nakae's life had so changed that what preceded it resembled the life of an altogether different person. By the early 1920s he had completed his first major work of Sinology, become acquainted with numerous members of the staff of the South Manchurian Railway Company (in particular, Itō Takeo [1895–1985]), met a number of the outstanding Sinologists of the day, and harbored in his home several of Japan's best known Communist leaders. In 1923 he also met a Japanese friend of Itō's who was probably the only Japanese to have open as well as secret contacts with the central figures in the Chinese Communist Party organization and was, moreover, probably the only Japanese to join the Chinese Communist Party without simultaneous membership in the Japan Communist Party. This was Suzue Gen'ichi, and he was to become Nakae's closest friend.

SUZUE GEN'ICHI: A LIFE DEDICATED TO THE CHINESE REVOLUTION

In some ways the life of Suzue, who was born near ancient Izumo in what is now Shimane prefecture, parallels that of Nakae. He, too, was the son of a member of the first Diet; and he, too, lost his father when he was a schoolboy. The death of the elder Suzue, at a time when a num- ber of local enterprises he had established had gone bankrupt, plunged the family into desperate poverty; but in the case of the young Gen'ichi, there were no old family friends and benefactors to ensure his educa- tion. While Nakae Ushikichi was studying law at Tokyo University, Suzue in his teens was working in the law offices of Tasaka Sadao in the Nihonbashi section of Tokyo. After completing military service in 1917, he pulled a rickshaw for a doctor in the Yūrakuchō section of the city and delivered newspapers. In September 1917 he enrolled in a special course in the department of politics and economics of Meiji University, a course designed for people who had not graduated from middle school; but having ignored the examinations and required fees, he was expelled the next year.

In the summer of 1918 he participated in the famous rice riots in Japan but escaped the police investigation that followed.[35] Nevertheless, he seems to have decided it was wise to take Tasaka's suggestion and move to Peking. In March 1919 he arrived carrying a letter of introduction from Tasaka to Fujiwara Kamae (1878–195?), editor-in-chief of *Shin Shina* (New China), the first (and at that time the only) Japanese-language newspaper published in China. Like Nakae, therefore, he arrived in the city that was to become his home and the country that was to become his passion more or less by accident and certainly without any inkling of the impact that this fortuitous solution to an immediate problem would have on the rest of his life. But, again as in the case of Nakae, it took a while for the pattern to take hold.

Suzue wrote for *Shin Shina* and occasionally contributed pieces to *Hōchikoku* (the organ of Tasaka's legal offices back in Tokyo) and to *Taishō nichinichi shinbun* (Taishō daily news). He was in China at the time of the May Fourth Movement and may have witnessed the incident that gave the movement its name. Certainly he would have witnessed other demonstrations; but in 1919 he showed no particular concern for the activities of nationalistic Chinese, and he considered the issue of sovereignty over Shangtung "a trifling affair" at the time. In fact, the notion that China could look upon Japan as some sort of enemy was still unthinkable to him. From 1920 when he wrote his first essays in Peking for Fujiwara and *Shin Shina*, he adopted the peculiar pen name "Indo no karasu" (Indian crow), as well as simply the Chinese surname "Wang."[36]

Suzue was not immediately committed to the idea and practice of a Chinese revolution; but in 1921, when Nakae was becoming absorbed by ancient China, he began to immerse himself in the life of the common people in the China of their own day. Probably under the influence of Fujiwara and others, he began in earnest to master the Chinese language, to wear old Chinese clothes daily, and to attend Chinese theater. It was from this time that he adopted another pen name which he often used in public and in his writings, "Wang Tzu-yen." That same year, when the Peking branch of the International News Service was opened under bureau chief Furuno Inosuke (1891–1966), Suzue was hired. Like Suzue, Furuno was a man of no academic background whatsoever, a completely self-made figure; and he served as a great inspiration to Suzue.[37]

Suzue ultimately made his contribution in life by publicizing the plight of the working masses in China through numerous journalistic and some scholarly publications. In contrast to Nakae he published widely and often. In further contrast he became an activist; he participated in the Chinese revolution during most of his twenty-seven years in China. In 1922, while Nakae undertook revisions on the essay on ancient Chinese political thought that will be examined in the next chapter, Suzue began work on a systematic study of the Chinese labor movement and through his research came into daily contact with Peking working men and women by interviewing them as well as radical organizers. From this time on, he also became acquainted with more and more activist students who had been at the center of the May Fourth Movement at Peking University.[38]

During the fall of 1922 Suzue met Itō Takeo of the Research Department of the South Manchurian Railway Company in Peking. Itō himself had arrived in Peking only in the fall of 1921, but in the fall of 1923 he was made editor of the SMR journal *Pekin Mantetsu geppō*. He wanted to be able to introduce to Japan a "scientific" explanation of contemporary Chinese society, that is, one based on the theme of the "development of capitalism in China." From that time forward he worked closely with Suzue, who was now writing extensively on Chinese laborers. With his contacts in activist circles, Suzue was able to provide Itō with many documents, and they shared a great deal of material and many experiences over the next twenty-five years.[39]

Suzue's contacts with the Chinese revolutionary movement grew deeper with the passage of time, and eventually he even served in certain official capacities. Interestingly, he had virtually no contacts with Japanese radical circles; he was devoted to China. In May of 1925, on the eve of the May Thirtieth Incident, in talks with striking workers in Tsingtao, he came to know Su Chao-cheng (1885–1929), the leader of the strike. On many occasions he interpreted for visiting Japanese Communists in international or bilateral meetings in China. His most famous activity was his participation in the abortive Wuhan government of the "left" Kuomintang for three months (April through July) in 1927, following Chiang Kai-shek's coup of 1927 and the purge of Communists. In Wuhan he apparently served under Su Chao-cheng, head of the Labor Bureau, and at the All-Pacific Workers Conference in May he addressed the assembled delegates in Chinese.[40] His interest in contemporary events and Marxism in particular would later exert a marked influence on Nakae.

In 1923, when they met for the first time—in the billiard parlor of the Japanese Club of Peking—the full development of Suzue's activism lay ahead but the direction had already been set. Nakae's course, too, had been set; but at the time, especially to anyone with revolutionary sympathies, Nakae Ushikichi with his ties to Ts'ao Ju-lin, his association with Colonel Banzai, and his friendship with members of the Anfu Club was unlikely to appear to be primarily a scholar with a deep devotion to individual liberties and the development of the human spirit. They had probably known each other somewhat earlier, because Nakae had already met Itō and a number of his associates. Suzue's involvement in the left-wing Chinese movement was already sufficiently well known for him to have been given the nickname "Mr. Principle." When Nakae asked Suzue whether he had purposefully ignored him on the grounds of principle, Suzue said "No." Thereafter the self-made journalistic activist and the self-taught critical Sinologist embarked on a friendship that lasted the rest of Nakae's life.[41]

Part Two
Penetrating the World of Ancient China

THREE

Politics and Thought

Everywhere under Heaven
Is no land that is not the king's.
To the borders of all these lands
None but is the king's slave.[1]

In 1922 Nakae completed a draft of his first Sinological essay, "Shina kodai seiji shisō shi" (A history of ancient Chinese political thought). He dedicated it (in its final form) to Ts'ao Ju-lin and Chang Tsung-hsiang as acknowledgment of their support, particularly to Ts'ao for giving him money with no strings attached. Since he had never studied Sinology or the Chinese classics at any recognized institution of higher learning and since he was shy about his intellectual prowess, before passing this essay around widely, he showed the draft to his friend, the eminent and fascinating China scholar Ojima Sukema (1881–1966).

Eight years older than Nakae and like him a native of Tosa, Ojima had graduated from the Faculty of Law of Kyoto Imperial University, spent time in China, and then returned to Kyoto to study for a degree from the Faculty of Letters, which at that time was Japan's foremost center for historical and cultural research on China. He was the only scholar among Nakae's close friends. Not only a scholar but a Sinologist, he read Nakae's manuscript and was so impressed with it that he urged him to have it published. Over the years he also introduced Nakae to other notable Japanese Sinologists like Kuraishi Takeshirō (1897–1975), a scholar of Chinese literature and bibliographic science;

Yoshikawa Kōjirō (1904–1980), Japan's foremost scholar of Chinese literature, particularly T'ang poetry; Kimura Eiichi (1906–1985), a scholar of ancient Chinese thought; and Ono Katsutoshi (b. 1905), a scholar of Chinese and Japanese art history. In the early 1920s, he also came to know Okazaki Fumio (1888–1950), a pioneering scholar of medieval Chinese history; Aoki Masaru (1887–1964), a scholar of Chinese literature, especially drama; and two more old-fashioned Kangaku scholars, Imazeki Tenpō (1884–1970) and Matsuzaki Tsuruo (1867–1949).[2]

By the mid 1920s Nakae had acquired a circle of friends and acquaintances with whom he could discuss the most intricate of Sinological questions. It is interesting and a little puzzling that he apparently approached no Chinese scholars to talk about the matter to which he was devoting all his energies at this time. Classical Chinese scholarship was unfashionable in China (although it had not disappeared) at a time when the New Culture Movement dominated intellectual life, particularly in Peking. Perhaps the men who engaged in the kind of research on which Nakae was now concentrating were not the sorts he wanted to have as friends; or perhaps he was embarrassed by his lack of education in traditional Chinese subjects, his imperfect Chinese, or the fact that he was writing in Japanese. Whatever his reasons, he remained rigidly eremetic in his work habits, only showing his essays to a few others after he had finished drafts.

If anything can be said to characterize all of Nakae's Sinological essays, collected after the war under the title *Chūgoku kodai seiji shisō* (Ancient Chinese political thought), it would be his groping search for a method by which the scholarly mind of the present could understand the universe of classical Chinese scholarship and ancient Chinese thought. Nakae's lack of a formal education in Sinology, although he had indeed learned the Chinese classics and Kanbun like any young man of his class and generation, may have been a blessing in disguise. It forced him to keep as wide a perspective as possible and allowed him none of the biases or partisan characteristics of the rival schools of Sinology in Japan. This quality of breadth, in which all the disciplines, particularly comparative history and philosophy, might contribute to a clearer picture of reality and in which the wider the body of evidence the better, are among Nakae's lasting contributions to the study of ancient Chinese thought.

The only attention Nakae's first essay has ever received was in a few short, though glowing, reviews in Japan when his writings were published after the war. The essay as it was published (under the title "Chūgoku kodai seiji shisō shi") represents a reedited version, completed probably in the spring of 1925. We know this from Nakae's citations to works published as late as 1924, and from the marginal annotations (dated as late as early 1925) in his personal copies of these works. Nakae had three hundred copies of the essay privately printed in July 1925.

When the critic Takeuchi Yoshimi (1910–1977) wrote a short review of Nakae's book in 1950, he noted that the most striking quality running through the entire volume was a "fierce spirit for organization (*taikei*)." The Japanese scholarly world, particularly in the China field, had lacked this systematic approach, according to Takeuchi; and Nakae had transcended the limitations of the academy, toward which he was wholeheartedly antipathetic.[3] In order, though, to understand the past in a systematic way requires either borrowing a model or models into which one can place data and make sense of it, or creating a model of one's own. Drawing on disciplines from philosophy to psychology, Nakae examined a good number of systematic approaches to various aspects of his project and ultimately formed his own system, albeit with heavy debts to others.

Nakae devoted the entire first quarter of his essay on ancient Chinese political thought to the quest for a method. He was prepared to assume absolutely nothing, to question everything, and to define every term he used conceptually. Consistency and organization were clearly essential to the project as he envisioned it. Indeed, he was so rigorous in his "scientific method" that the work reads much more like the work of a systematic philosopher than of a historian.

The essay begins by questioning itself. What is "politics" and where can you locate it? When do you find it in history? By the same token, what constitutes "thought" (*shisō*)? Is the state a necessary intermediary in the formulation of thought? Why do we speak of "political thought" (*seiji shisō*) and not "political science" (*seijigaku*) or "theories of politics" (*seiji gakusetsu*)? What is meant by "ancient"? Is it prior to the evolution of historical time, or is it the earliest period after pre-history? What constituted "China" in "antiquity," and how can one identify it from the texts that survive? These are the kinds of questions Nakae asks and begins to try to answer in the first few pages of his work.

Methodology then occupies a central place both here and throughout Nakae's writings. How, he asks many times, are we to approach a "text" presumably written two thousand years ago? It may be partially destroyed, either naturally over time or consciously by men; or, it may be a forgery altogether. Even if it is provably authentic, how are we, two millennia removed, capable of entering the minds and the society of the men who composed these works? Scholars often take for granted that being as rigorous or as scientific as possible in weighing evidence enables the investigator to get at the essence of the investigated. Inasmuch as Nakae takes nothing for granted, he has to devote considerable attention to this problem.[4]

Another of Nakae's strengths was his penchant for comparisons from other cultures and systems of thought. Citing the work of Lewis Morgan (1818–1881), Nakae demonstrates that an ancient body of thought, even in its own day, can give rise to radically different interpretations among its followers. The example given by Nakae is that of Socrates. We have no way of knowing now what Socrates thought except through the works of Plato and Xenophon. Which of these two widely divergent disciples are we to trust? Here we are forced to look for corroborative evidence from other fields, such as the archeological work of Heinrich Schliemann (1822–1890) that tended to support Plato.[5] The point, however, is that secondhand information, even that claiming direct access to the original source, can be deceiving unless it is put under equally close scrutiny.

Many of the works of antiquity, particularly the pre-Socratics in the West and the pre-Ch'in philosophers in China, are left to us now in fragments. We can thank Renaissance thinkers in the West and particularly Ch'ing-period exegetical scholars in China for reconstructing ancient texts. But, even with the welcome help of these great scholars, we still must confront the texts. The words are Chinese, a language that remains in use today; but words change in meaning as historical conditions change, sometimes fundamentally. Thus, reconstitution of the original meaning of the characters in these texts becomes an inordinately difficult, though entirely indispensable, task. Quoting at length from the work of Gustav Le Bon (1841–1931), Nakae argues that only by attempting to approach the atmosphere of the time in which a text was written can that world begin to become clear to us; only then can we begin to understand ancient texts. Nakae defines this as the first necessary precondition for historical knowledge in the history of political thought.

He goes on to define a second precondition: As sources of our understanding of ancient political thought, these ancient texts must be seen without any intervening restrictions. They may indeed have been moral or religious in nature at the time of their composition, but in Nakae's system they must remain "objects of free criticism."[6]

This query leads to yet another quandary. How are we now to come to terms with ancient morality when we examine the writings of antiquity? Morality, he argues, is a conscious phenomenon in the collective life of human beings and human society. It is not, though, something hard and fixed; therefore contemporary man cannot assume an easy conformity between ancient beliefs and his own conceptions of morality. Because of the general East Asian reverence for antiquity, the ancient texts were rarely, if ever, treated with the kind of "free criticism" Nakae proposes, even in the Ch'ing era. A scholar might have proven a given edition of an ancient text to be spurious but that never invalidated the essential sanctity of the "real" text. A similar phenomenon can be identified in the West, where the Bible was treated as an inspired historical account of antiquity until approximately 150 years ago. Ernest Renan's (1823–1892) famous biography of Jesus caused a great stir in the religious world. His depiction of Jesus as a "martyr for free thought"[7] stressed the secularity of Jesus' martyrdom, to the great consternation of many clergymen.

As sources of information about ancient political thought, all the texts of antiquity have potentially equal value for the contemporary scholar, and they must be treated equally. Equally, but not statically, for the ancient texts we now have in our possession were not dropped into the modern scholar's lap, nor were they the work of a single hand. Critical assessment requires a hard look at the changing meanings of the characters in the texts as a reflection of changing conceptions over time in antiquity.

Nakae offers a fascinating example of this phenomenon by examining the ancient conceptions of what we now would refer to as the "state." As long as the idea of a state exists, a people may produce "political thought" even though they are not inhabitants of their own political entity that could be identified as a state. However, the fullest form of what he calls a "continuous legal society" is a society in which a state does exist. The state may take different forms in different societies and at different times in the same society because of the social groupings that are central to its composition: lineages, families, races, and the like.

Nakae's analysis of the state in ancient China focuses primarily on the meaning of the characters *i* and *kuo*. He demonstrates that in ancient times an *i* (a town or "nucleated settlement," according to K. C. Chang[8]) was not territorial in the sense that it was definable in the first instance by an attachment to the land on which it was settled, as described by Wilhelm Wundt (1832–1920), Nakae's comparative example here, although land was important nonetheless. At the center lived the head of the local ruling lineage, and in the region around the *i* farmers lived and worked the land. The concept of *i* implied a notion of bounded regionality, and it was tied to a conception of political life. Even reputedly in the times of Yao and Shun, he argues, following the research of the great Ch'ing scholar Tuan Yü-ts'ai (1735–1815), the classical feudal levels of society implied a parceling of lands within boundaries. Nakae agrees with Wu Ta-ch'eng (1835–1902) that the character *kuo* originally implied a specified area with a border that was protected militarily. Thus, as in ancient Greece and Rome, *kuo* denoted a city-state, not a sense of regionality as in the case of *i*. He agrees with the modern scholar Lo Chen-yü (1866–1940) that by contrast the character *i* as it appeared in ancient inscriptions meant a "place where people lived." With these and many further examples, Nakae comes to the conclusion that in its original formulation, a conception of "state" (as the unit for meaningful political activity) in China implied the site where people congregated, not an area given by a king to a feudal lord as part of a feudal system.[9]

Through early Chou times, in this analysis, the basic political unit or "state" was the *i*, a lineage-based residential area or *Geschlechterstaat* (*shuzoku teki kokka*); it dominated a land area, but habitation by a ruling lineage and those who served them rather than geography defined it. The change toward understanding the land itself as the characteristic that defined the basic polity—the change to understanding the state as a *Territorialerstaat* (*zokuchi teki kokka*)—occurred, Nakae argues, only with the Ch'in unification of 221 B.C.E. Before the Ch'in dynasty, four points characterized the relationship within a given region between members of the local ruling bloodline and residents outside that line. Politically, they were the rulers and the ruled. Economically, the efforts of all served primarily to meet the material desires of the ruling house; those not party to the inner life of that ruling house worked for it and lived only on its surpluses. Religiously, they were linked by an important ceremonial or ritual bond. And regionally, they were linked in a common defense of lives and property against any incursion by the rest of the world.

Thus, in Nakae's view, each *i* constituted a miniature state ruled by a single lineage (*tsu*) or bloodline, with as yet no complex, interregional, nationwide network of *i*. Only individual links between individual *i* existed. There was, however, a "national confederation of *i*" that cohered through ritual (see below), and often the reason given in ancient texts for conquest was closely tied to ritual matters. One problem that Nakae recognizes for identifying even the larger confederation of *i* with a conception of "state" is the lack of an independent and firm ruling authority, the root of a sovereign community. The various *i* lacked an aggregate, unified existence as a recognizable, independent entity apart from the confederation through ritual; by the same token together they had no independent legal authority. Ultimately, Nakae is led to the conclusion that, although the Hsia-Shang organization of *i* did possess certain of the salient characteristics of a state, it cannot strictly speaking be called one.[10]

Nakae's central concern here with the "state" and "state life" reflects

the great influence of his readings in German political science, which
was fixated on the *Staat*. *Staatslehre* (state theory), *Staatsrechtlehre*
(science of state law), and *Staatswissenschaft* (political science) dominated late-nineteenth-century German political thought, of which Jellinek was a part, and exerted an overwhelming influence not only on
Nakae but on the entire Japanese academy. And, this stress on the state,
whether directly attributable to Jellinek or to a larger intellectual *Zeit-*
geist, remained with Nakae through his life and work.

Kaizuka Shigeki (1904–1987), the dean of contemporary Japanese
studies of ancient China, agreed with Nakae's thesis that the Chou state
became primarily land-oriented or territorial only as the main lineage's
bloodline ceased to be its essence.[11] As the Chou period unfolded, the
concept of territory developed as part of the emergence of a defined feudal system. By the Warring States era, as the power of the house of Chou
declined, the Chou Emperor retained only nominal and ceremonial
powers. The state had come to be conceived territorially; but the feudal
lords who theoretically held subkingdoms from the Emperor had, in
fact, become contending "sovereigns" of distinct territories. At the same
time, inequalities in regional economic power were growing. Gradually
the assumption that all land was publicly owned by the Emperor had to
yield to the emergence of private ownership. As the population continued to grow and the more powerful of the warring states strengthened
themselves further, the old land apportionment system could no longer
provide a legal basis for the state. In this way, Nakae describes the dissolution of the "public" property system of the Chou, often nostalgically
dubbed the *ching-t'ien* (well-field) system by Chinese scholars.[12] Thus,
the notion of the "state" changed markedly over the period we broadly
refer to as "ancient."

Nakae offers two final methodological tools for approaching ancient
Chinese texts. One is the use of comparison or analogy. The texts are
explained by making comparisons among them, as the Ch'ing textual
scholars did so remarkably well, or by comparing them to the ancient
works of other peoples. Analogy to other cultures, however, can lead,
Nakae warns, to all but moronic conclusions (Lao-tzu as an anarchist,
or Mo-tzu as a socialist) if it is not strictly and carefully applied. Nakae
was more than a little wary of the wild comparisons being made by cer-

tain Chinese scholars of the day between, for example, Chinese thinkers of the late Chou and contemporary European theorists of natural law. The two sides of a comparison can and should be similar, but they are decidedly not the same thing: superficially, ancient Chinese philosophers and modern European legal thinkers may share numerous qualities, but an "unbridgeable gulf" still separates them. This is the point at which the historical level a society has reached must enter the comparative equation, for it is missing in the kind of comparison Nakae criticizes.[13]

Nakae's other suggested approach to ancient texts is to examine them in a unified manner. In other words, in addition to the continuity and change that one must look for in the ancient texts, he appeals for a systematic approach to the entire body of literature as a whole. Nakae wants the unity, the overall life of the era under examination, to receive scrutiny. Thus, no discipline that purports to study Chinese social life, the living Chinese community of the past, can ignore the fact that human consciousness of a sort distinctive to each era pervades all the texts of that time. In consequence, the scholar has to establish what that fundamental conception was in each age and examine how it underwent change with the passage of historical time.[14]

This immensely complicated task assumes the reality of a *Zeitgeist* — that is, of a set of common beliefs and assumptions underlying the outlook of people at a given time, though not necessarily recognized by them as such, so fundamental to thought is it. Although Nakae had not yet begun the serious study of Kant and Hegel that would occupy much of his thought during the 1930s, he had already read some Kant and encountered German Idealist historiography through Jellinek. During the period between 1922 and 1925, when he was revising this essay, he was also reading the social theorists Ludwig Gumplowicz (1838-1909), Karl Bücher (1847-1930), and Franz Oppenheimer (1868-1943); and his marginal notations in books by them indicate that he was particularly influenced by their theories of the stages through which societies develop. It is just possible, moreover, that his experience in China as an alien disposed him to perceive a need to understand a culture as a whole in order to understand it at all. In any case, his conception of the historian's task reveals that he was attempting to write something larger than a history of ancient political writings and expressed thought. He was instead trying to capture the history of what was thought politically, the conceptual foundations of the political realm, in ancient China. Thus, unlike virtually any other book on Chinese thought, Nakae's work did not examine each of the ancient political thinkers and their writings, but was concerned with coming to general conclusions in an unusually systematic way about the conception of politics underlying antiquity itself. Working out all the methodological intricacies of this analysis at length may appear tedious in retrospect: To Nakae, however, as he embarked on an exploration of ancient Chinese writings, a methodological introduction seemed a necessary first step; and indeed, the work he did here served him in his subsequent Sinological essays.

Nakae was not the first student of historiography to be concerned with how the mind of the present investigator penetrates the intellectual world of the past; but more than most historians he was unwilling to proceed in practice as though historical truth could emerge from a close reading of texts, fitted to modern assumptions through a cut-and-paste reordering. It is all too easy to set aside, as primarily a philosophical matter, the basic problem of how one achieves an understanding of the intellectual, spiritual foundations of the minds that created these documents. Can we simply assume that our categories neatly fit theirs? Nakae thought not and wanted to work alert at all times to this methodological problem, although perhaps he did not foresee how difficult and even debilitating such an attempt must inevitably be (just as the rest of us too often overlook the extent to which ignoring the problem must inevitably vitiate our results).

Jellinek may have provided Nakae with some methodological guidance or at least some awareness of a problem. In *Allgemeine Staatslehre*, and with further developments in a 1906 work entitled *Verfassungsänderung und Verfassungswandlung*, he examined the nature and origins of constitutional change; and he argued that while constitutions often change, change is not a result of revolution or the enactment of new laws but a response to new trends. Thus, change in a state's constitution, its basic law which by definition reflected its social constituency, was for Jellinek tied to historical change. Changes in law ultimately derived from other historical changes.[15]

Wilhelm Dilthey (1833–1911), the German philosopher and historian who died in the same year as Jellinek, pioneered the study of historical change. Concerned with delineating that sphere distinctive to the methodology of the historian, Dilthey (like many historicists) rejected the use of methods from the natural sciences. Instead, he set out to build a "generalized science of human cultural behavior" on the basis of data from a huge variety of sources. For Dilthey, history dealt with the concrete and the individual, while the natural sciences were concerned with coming to abstract generalizations. Where the natural scientist looked to laws determining a sequence of events, the historian began with an analysis of causation and looked to psychological and other motivations behind human activity.

Dilthey presupposed that "the whole of reality is one vast historical process." The historian could understand that process through examination of its objectifications (books, paintings, documents, inscriptions, and the like) as cultural symbols and by studying them one came to understand what they represented in a given age or historical actor. Here was the difficulty that Nakae Ushikichi confronted: How can we be sure we understand the symbols as they were meant and understood in the past? Dilthey responded that the mind of the contemporary investigator can penetrate the minds of distant historical subjects because our minds and theirs operate according to the same "categories," as described principally by Immanuel Kant (1724–1804). The categories of the mind transcend the universal historical process. Thus, Dilthey posited both a universality and a necessity to the functioning of men's minds throughout history. We possess the capacity to understand men of the past because they thought in the same universal and transtemporal categories as we now do. Knowledge, in his conception, was itself an internal, subjective process (not external and objective as in the natural sciences) and changed with time and the viewpoint of the observing historian. But, *historical* knowledge enabled the observer to overcome this sort of relativism.[16] Dilthey thus believed that he had created a science for comprehending history because he could show:

(1) that the process of history was the process of the development of ideas out of a life-situation and the progression of action from those ideas, (2) that ideas arose in history within certain necessary and universal types of world-views, and (3) that the investigator's mind could understand those ideas because his mind functioned in similar patterns.[17]

These were the kinds of intellectual concerns with which Nakae was struggling in the early 1920s, when he was just beginning to read the great German philosophers and historians.

After his lengthy methodological discussion, Nakae began his examination of the furthest reaches of Chinese antiquity with a question as natural as it difficult to answer: Who were the Hsia people of ancient times? To this day there is no hard evidence concerning a Hsia "dynasty," save as legendary material, but its absence does not lead Nakae to reject the many legends about them out of hand. The very name *Hsia* seems to imply a sense of cultural superiority with respect to alien ethnic groups. He argues that their migration to the area we now call China as opposed to their having been native to that region does not imply, as some have suggested, a lower cultural level than that of the native populace. Although Nakae is partial to the migration idea, he feels the evidence is much too weak for such a conclusion. He does sharply disagree with the theory of Chang Ping-lin (1869–1936), the brilliant scholar and anti-Manchu revolutionary of the 1911 period, that *Hsia* was a racial name deriving from the old name of a local waterway. What then, Nakae rebuts, were the residents of the area near this waterway known as before the arrival of the people later called Hsia? In fairness to Chang, this response hardly refutes his theory, although no one has yet come up with a firm answer; and Chang was predisposed to Chinese superiority in issues of race.

Nakae's main point is to focus on the fact that a clear distinction between a state's territory and a racial or ethnic name can arise only after the development of social life. He notes that although the *Shuowen chieh-tzu*, an early dictionary of ancient Chinese characters, claimed that *Hsia* implied the people of China, the term *Chung-kuo* (the central kingdom or kingdoms, namely China) really referred only to the area under the control of the Chou ruler. Tribal structure (Nakae uses the German expression *Stammesverfassung*) precedes state structure (*Staatsverfassung*), but the state's name always postdates the name of the ethnic or racial group. Similarly, the alien peoples living along ancient

China's borders were given specific names (*i, ti, jung,* and *man*) by the Chinese which carried different connotations at different times. Nakae's point, though, is that as soon as such peoples and their alien customs were identified and distinguished from those of the Hsia, an ethnic or racial consciousness had developed.[18]

From as early as the Hsia (pre-Shang) era, Nakae argues, one can speak of China as agricultural. He completely rejects the suggestion put forth by Liang Ch'i-ch'ao (1873–1929) that the Chinese became farmers only in the Spring and Autumn period (770–476 B.C.E.), because the firmness of the Hsia attachment to the soil, Nakae claims, was essential to their cultural development and to the growth of political thought. Liang based his views on the developmental scheme of Friedrich List (1789–1846) in which all societies are said to move from hunting and gathering, to livestock-raising, to agriculture, and finally to commerce and industry. Nakae wants to debunk such theories denying the agricultural foundations of Chinese historical antiquity. Even the ancient Chinese attitude of superiority over alien peoples, for example, was ultimately based on the fact that China had agriculture and they (the others) reputedly did not. King Yü, the alleged founder of the Hsia according to extant texts, was revered, Nakae argues, because he controlled the floods, the whole purpose of which was to facilitate use of the land for growing crops. The fact that the Shang moved its capital often had nothing to do necessarily, as some have argued, with its people's being a group of hunters; and he points to extant inscriptional material as evidence to the contrary. In fact, the Chou was extremely proud of its agricultural past, popularly remembered in its legends, which, in effect, bespoke an ethnic consciousness on the part of the Chou for the agricultural legacy bequeathed it by the Hsia.[19]

Nakae, like the Germans he was reading, believed that what people thought about, wrote about, and recorded in their physical artifacts was as much the result of the fabric of their society as of their conscious choices; but the modern scholar who could discern the loom on which that fabric was woven could also correctly understand the meaning of a society's cultural and political manifestations. It is, therefore, important to him in this essay to establish that ancient China was in fact an agricultural society; for he believes that roots in agriculture explain the formation of Chinese thought concerning not only such phenomena as the seasons but more importantly the nature of the cosmos and structures of order. He sees beliefs in man's fixed relationship to the land and in the supremacy of nature over human effort as fundamental to ancient Chinese perceptions and responses to the world. In other words, sedentary agriculture determined more than economic practices; it also determined the basic social organization and underlying political assumptions. For this reason, Nakae concludes that "the fact that the Hsia were farmers must be a key to the study of ancient Chinese political thought."[20]

The Hsia-Shang "state," insofar as it existed, was of the *i* variety described above, with a concomitant lineage structure. Even when the Chou began to institute a system of "feudal" lords, King Wu selected men from his own lineage. The significant difference, according to Nakae, was that the Chou house placed itself at the center of the realm to give orders to its vassals all around, whereas the Hsia-Shang ruling lineage gathered wherever the main *i* was to be found, which was not always at the center of the realm. The location of the main *i* in the Hsia and Shang eras, moreover, often changed. The scale of the *i* was probably small, certainly in comparison to the fortified capitals of later eras. They were usually located on a hill, for purposes of community defense, making use of the natural topography in an age when knowledge of public works was still rudimentary; in this they resembled other ancient city-states, such as Rome and Troy. Furthermore, the *Shang-shu* (Book of history, or Book of documents) claimed that the small size of the capital *i* facilitated frequent changes in its site, but the text did not clearly explain why the moves were made. The answer remains shrouded in mystery, for obvious explanations, such as civil war, foreign invasion, and natural disaster, do not characterize developments in Shang history. Nakae suggests a religious element in these repeated decisions to move, and we shall examine this dimension of ancient Chinese life soon.

Economic life in ancient China, according to Nakae's ordering of things, centered on the *i* where the ruler resided. He characterizes the economy of that time as a *dokuritsu shitsuka keizai* (private household economy), a term he derived from Karl Bücher's idea of *geschlosse Haus-*

wirtschaft. The "household" on which the entire economy of the *i* was based was the ruler's. Nonetheless, he notes that to support the classes of people (peasants, artisans, and merchants) outside that "household," the ruler allowed perforce a measure of exchange and some markets. Although the *Chou-li* (Rites of Chou) described provisions for all manner of exchange at the time, Nakae insists that this depiction concerned only the family economy of the ruler, which was ultimately self-sufficient. As a whole it was a non-exchange economy, and the common people were severely restricted in their movements which purposefully inhibited trade.

Nakae lays considerable stress on the complete lack of independence and freedom of the members of the non-elite families of ancient China, given the structure of the economy. Their low status and assigned work were fixed from birth, he claims; and they functioned as cogs, pure and simple, in the ruler's economy. In no case were they independent producers, and even the merchants of ancient China were primarily responsible for securing luxury items for the ruler and his family. Nor did the urban centers give rise to an exchange or market economy with a thriving merchant class. On the contrary, unlike medieval European cities which developed from an economically and politically independent "market," the Chinese *shih* or "market" that can be seen in the oldest extant texts resembled European markets only superficially. The merchant in the *shih* had no specific power or rights in ancient China, unlike the *Bürger* with his *Burgrecht* or *Marktrecht*, which decreased subservience to one's lord and the Crown. The *Marktherr* of European markets had the power to set market taxes and mint his own money; although similar functionaries existed in China, Nakae notes, they never gained the kind of power of the *Marktherr*. Whereas European markets emerged with the dissolution of the independent household economy, in China the *shih* stood at the pinnacle of that economy and were controlled by it; in fact, *shih* were ridiculed by the powerful of ancient China as the arena in which petty men ran around seeking profit. Thus, one rarely would find a ruler there, and the *shih* were never located in the *i*.[21]

Nakae argued that ancient China effectively had two classes: those with power, whose household provided the centerpiece for the economy, and those without power, who had nothing. The latter produced all the food, clothing, dwellings, and the like to satisfy the needs of the former within each *i* region. In the Chou era, state affairs were principally concerned with fulfilling the material needs of the king's family. The institution of the *ta-tsai*, mentioned in the *Chou-li* as the man who "assisted the king in ruling the enfeoffed states," resembled the *Meier* (steward or majordomo) of an estate in Europe. In early medieval France, Nakae notes in comparison, a similar functionary became an exceedingly powerful hereditary office.

Nakae firmly disagrees with the theory that ancient China was a matriarchal society, the view advanced for all ancient societies by Friedrich Engels (1820–1895) in his *Der Ursprung der Familie, des Privateigentums und des Staats* (The origin of the family, private property, and the state) of 1884, and a view beginning to gain adherents among young Chinese Marxists in Nakae's day.[22] Among those lacking power, he argues, women were no more exalted or subservient than men. They had all but a monopoly of work in certain handicrafts, such as weaving: The character *nü* (female) suggests to Nakae a woman kneeling as she wove. Again following the explanation found in the *Shuo-wen chieh-tzu*, he sees in the character *fu* (woman, wife) a woman working with a broom. The nature of these tasks specifically associated with women, however, is certainly no basis for assuming a matriarchy. On the basis of work by Tuan Yü-ts'ai and Wu Ta-ch'eng among others, moreover, he argues that in distant antiquity the character *hsing* (made up of the elements for "female" and "birth") meant "sex" or "to give birth," and that only later did it gain its modern meaning of "surname." An early association of lineage with the female, therefore, cannot be argued on etymological grounds.

Although recognizing in ancient China domination by a ruling family and strict regulation of the society centered on the *i*, Nakae stops short of calling it a caste society. He does, however, clearly point out the absence of any freedom (political or economic) and the strict, inherited social status of the powerless. He likens their situation to the fate of aliens captured by African or Indian conquerors in military engagements and put to work back home for the ruler.[23]

Thus, in the Shang (and presumably the Hsia as well) there were those with power and everyone else without so much as a hint of it.

One found one's place in this bifurcated situation on the basis of blood ties. There were a few exceptions of resistance by the powerless (and the record may simply be incomplete in that regard), but Nakae argues that class struggle cannot be identified in ancient China. The same can be said for resistance to laboring in an economy that served only the ruler. The people, Nakae concludes in an increasingly depressing portrayal, were the object of rule; they were of use to the rulers, like livestock.

Following the work of Ludwig Gumplowicz, he argues that states take form through the use of might, often when a powerful foreign race (or ethnic group) conquers a weak, entrenched one. In peasant societies, Nakae notes in agreement with Franz Oppenheimer, because peasants are not usually well trained militarily and cannot simply run off the land, they are unable to sustain any long-term resistance and are most often forced by circumstances to accept subservience to their conquerors.[24]

Because there was no independent life for the powerless outside their service to the rulers of the "state," political control pervaded every area of social and economic life in ancient China. As elsewhere, law reflected social priorities; and in ancient China the law codified the control of those with power over those without it. Citing the work of Henry Sumner Maine (1822–1888), for comparisons, Nakae adds that Chinese law is like other ancient legal systems in being concerned largely with what would now be called criminal law. Then suddenly Nakae Ushikichi is unable to sit back with detachment in his scholar's armchair and continue offering a detailed picture of the sad life endured by the powerless of ancient China who suffered the severe punishments of the law's sanctions. He bursts out, "I've been explaining these [legal matters in the] classical texts item by item, dispassionately, but the life of the common people at that time, the class without any power, was wretched indeed!"[25] This sentence, inserted without warning, has the effect of grabbing the reader by the lapels and insisting it be remembered that those subject to the laws under discussion had once been living, feeling human beings who were treated mercilessly and whose miserable existence was defined by the values of their society solely in terms of their function in meeting the needs of a ruler.

RELIGION AND POWER IN ANCIENT CHINA

The ruler and his proxies held all the cards—military, economic, political—in ancient Chinese society. One is still left with a lingering sense of bewilderment: Why did the lower classes tolerate this situation? To be sure, they had little choice in the matter when an invading army enslaved them; but is the use of brute force or its potential use sufficient to explain why the ruling elite of antiquity was able to enjoy such incomparable power unchecked? Nakae suggests part of the solution to this puzzling issue when he cites Oppenheimer on the failure of peasants in ancient societies to form cohesive bonds. One of the most interesting arguments in his entire work supplies another element in this explanation, the role of religion in ancient China and its conception of kingship.

Nakae sees the basis of religious belief in ancient China to be the idea that life on earth must be enjoyed; a fear of the awesome power of nature he sees as secondary. More than most ancient peoples, the Chinese tended to place mankind at the center of the cosmos and to form contractual kinds of bonds with the gods. In the Shang, *shen* or spirits were seen as responsible for natural phenomena and resident in nature (such as in rivers); the Chinese response to the presence of these *shen* was to try to avoid harm and accrue benefits. *T'ien*, or heaven, was the highest expression of nature's power as well as the object of ancestor worship for the ruler or Son of Heaven. However, the way in which Chou rulers used this neat, unified spiritual conception to unify the realm leads Nakae to doubt that the Hsia and Shang rulers had enjoyed the same recognition of absolute power. He typifies the earlier Sons of Heaven primarily as heads of allied religious communities, and it is in this capacity that he cites their ultimate authority.

Many ancient peoples personified elements of their systems of worship, but not so the Chinese. Ancient China's religion seems not to have centered on natural phenomena but on themselves and to have sought rational explanations of the world. Nakae argues that the Chinese were relentlessly this-worldly (*gensei teki*) even in their religious concerns and practices with the result that religious expression tended to take political forms. Here also lies the reason that ancient Chinese religion never developed a priesthood: It was too bound to the development of the political realm. The idea of a clergy's mediating between the spiritual and the human worlds existed in most ancient societies, but not in China. There were Shang officials who carried out divinations, but they seem not to have possessed any political authority. Since in essence the Chinese conception of the spirits was grounded in this world, where the gods watch over human affairs, anyone in this world could have contact with them and needed no priestly intermediary. In this, he concludes, ancient China was thoroughly unlike Egypt and Mesopotamia.

Nakae attributes another reason for the failure of an independent church to develop in ancient China to the entrenched position of the family head or paterfamilias, who exercised virtually absolute political and ceremonial authority over the family or kin group. The failure to produce a priestly class led to an unusually free atmosphere in ancient China for the generation of a wide variety of theories and ideas; for, unlike other parts of the globe, China lacked religious repression. This, of course, all changed under the Ch'in and Han dynasties, when the avenues of intellectual freedom began to be blocked.[26]

Whatever military or political powers the Son of Heaven could claim (and they changed in relation to his actual power), his power as the leader of religious rituals to heaven was absolute. The larger "national" federation of allied *i* of the Shang was first and foremost, according to Nakae, a ritual or religious community. The king did not rest atop this structure because he was a priest, so that one cannot conclude that the root of kingly power in China was religious; rather, his authority as head priest derived from his being the king. He further allocated, in bureaucratic fashion, assistant positions in the performance of ritual to his subordinates, the heads of various *i*. In turn, his inferiors within the ruling elite paid him tribute in items that gave pleasure, such as luxury goods, and not in the necessities of life as a demonstration, as with rituals, that he was the boss. Nakae goes so far as to claim that the king exercised his entire authority as if it ultimately derived from his position in charge of ritual.[27]

Rulership in China at this time was entirely a function of blood. Political position derived from a one-to-one mapping of kin relations within the ruling *tsu* or lineage. Military organization itself was based precisely on kin groups, and Nakae asserts on the basis of inscriptional and oracle bone material that the Chinese character *tsu* originally contained a military component. Following the controversial work of Lewis Morgan, Nakae concludes that Hsia-Shang society was basically at the *gens* stage. With the Chou, he notes changes in political life away from the Shang "tribal" era into a state covering the realm.[28]

POLITICAL THOUGHT

Having labored over methodology, having described in as great detail as possible at the time the nature and functioning of state and society in ancient China, and having portrayed the role of ancient ritual and religion, Nakae finally turns in the last quarter of his lengthy essay to his original theme, political thought. Nakae implicitly assumes that without the preceding 150 pages of tightly argued text, any discussion of "political thought" would be unfounded. Prior to the late Chou, he claims, political thought was not concerned with the individual. The *tsu*-based state in Shang times militated against any individual's actions having social significance. In an era when tradition and custom possessed unconditional authority, one would not expect to see theories claiming that the importance of life lay in individual freedom or in the value of the individual. Nakae similarly argues that a critical attitude toward religious theories of the origins of the cosmos is essential to the emergence of philosophical theory concerned with the individual, and spiritual or religious belief itself is, of course, not critical in this sense. The *Analects* of Confucius, for example, is not oriented toward the individual but to the larger ethnic group.

For the roots of political thought as a cultural phenomenon in the Hsia and Shang eras, one has to look primarily at the classic known as the *Shang-shu*, with its many textual problems. Life at that time centered on the *i* and its surrounding territory, what might be called a *tsu* state or, in the words of Wilhelm Wundt, a *Geschlechterstaat*. The *tsu* was the essential ingredient of all social organization, perhaps best expressed in the famous phrase from the *Tso-chuan*: "If he be not of my *tsu*, then he must have a different mind (*hsin*)." The leaders of the *tsu* were able to rule over the majority through their claim, not based on some intellectual argument but on an absolute order of belief, to direct descent from and contact with the gods by virtue of their bloodline.

Nakae ultimately argues that political thought (or, rather, how politics was thought of) in this period was theocratic in nature. He adopts Georg Jellinek's classification to characterize the ancient Chinese state in this way, because the origin of state power and the discretion of its usage all belong to the supernatural. In *Allgemeine Staatslehre*, Jellinek posited two kinds of theocracy: one in which the ruler serves as the representative of divine authority; and another in which the will of God restricts the ruler, usually through other agencies. The former of these is absolute, the latter limited. The power of the king in ancient Chinese theocracy fails to fit either of these paradigms precisely. In China the king ruled as the Son of Heaven and as the representative of the will of heaven (*t'ien-i*), like a ruler in the former of Jellinek's categories. Nevertheless, the conception of *t'ien-ming*, or the mandate of heaven, imposed potential limitations on the ruler—yet not through any clear agency as in Jellinek's definition, but apparently with some sway over the imperial institution through a process of "self-regulation" (*jiko seigen*). This last term is Jellinek's, ordinarily rendered "auto-limitation."

Until Ch'in Shih Huang-ti, the king's power could not rest solely on his military might; and he surely could not rely on the masses of alienated people, unless he took on a religious persona in making offerings to heaven or the gods. China's first Emperor eliminated the fundamental religious elements of kingly power and made brute force the sole arbiter. By taking the name Huang-ti (Emperor) for himself, he swept away the entire heavenly basis to kingship and established naked power in its stead. China was never the same thereafter.[29]

So, ancient China was a kind of *i* state in form, *tsu*-based in organizational reality, and theocratic at the root of its power. Basing himself on oracle bone evidence, Nakae argues that "heaven" through the early Chou was a deity that gave orders (*ming*) to the head of a specific *i*, and this formed the basis for the succession of kingly power. Thus, *t'ien-ming* is to be taken literally for this period, not metaphorically. The idea that any individual could become the king on the basis of personal character or charisma alone, at a time when *tsu* groups were the basic units of social life, is impossible, he argues. It was the religious dimension of kingship that enabled the ruler to hold on to his mandate.

What about the idea, though, that popular will or the mind of the people played a determining role in the retention of heaven's mandate? First of all, Nakae reiterates, the "people" (*min*) of ancient China were the "ruled class," those without power. The "will of the ruled class" as a player in the changing of heaven's mandate demonstrates a remarkable strain of democratic thought in ancient China that never was able to effect the creation of democratic institutions. The essential problem is that this "will" always lacked the power of organized resistance and an independent consciousness with respect to the holders of power. The "will of the people" never developed into a Chinese conception of popular sovereignty. Even as late as the Warring States period (475–221 B.C.E.), when many theories of politics emerged in China, only one theory of the state—monarchy—was to be found. This point reflects the essence of the Minobe-Uesugi debate: Chinese thought had evolved many theories of the political form of government (*seitai*) but only one conception of the essence of the Chinese polity (*kokutai*).

Chinese thought consistently approved of the "change of the mandate" (*ko-ming*) both historically and theoretically. This change reflected a change in heaven's orders, so that a new man should subsequently carry out the ceremonies to heaven. Had Chinese thought lacked this concept of *ko-ming*, brute force would have been the sole determinant of rulership. Still, *ko-ming* was the business only of the highest echelons of the elite, the common people having no influence in this arena; and it signified structurally a change only within the leadership class. The object of seizing the mandate was to gain access to the religious powers held by the ruler. Essential to Nakae's point is that *ko-ming* in ancient China bore no resemblance to its modern meaning as "revolution."[30]

NAKAE AND HIS SOURCES (I)

At the time Nakae set out to study ancient China, modern scholarship on the subject was only just beginning. The Shang oracle bones were discovered at the turn of the century, but scholarly collections of these and other inscriptional material did not appear until the middle of the 1910s. As a result, whereas contemporary scholars around the world can now turn to two generations of solid research, Nakae had to do most of the groundwork for himself. He used the first major works in this field by Lo Chen-yü and Wang Kuo-wei (1877–1927), and a handful of early specialized studies in various languages. Most of his conclusions, though, were drawn from his own critical examination of the extant sources, such as the *Shang-shu*, and from the work of Ch'ing textual scholars.

The paucity of scholarship in this young field and his own penchant for comparative analysis led Nakae to draw on the work of a large number of European historians and social scientists of the late nineteenth and early twentieth centuries. Most of the names of the scholars whose work he used are no longer well known except as figures themselves in the intellectual history of Western social science, but in their day they were widely read and debated. A look at their writings, to which Nakae so often had recourse, can help to understand his general approach to ancient China. From Ernest Renan, for example, we have seen how Nakae learned an approach to figures from antiquity who have been buried under centuries of obfuscation. Renan's efforts to uncover what Jesus of Nazareth was like as a man provided Nakae with a case study for penetrating the minds and the times of two thousand years ago.[31]

In distinctive ways, three scholars on whom Nakae relied for important ideas—Gumplowicz, Bücher, and Oppenheimer—adopted theories of societal development in which universal laws claimed applicability. In Gumplowicz's schema, mankind is pictured first in small, natural, ethnic or blood-kin groups held together by consanguinity. Then, through a process of conflict, subjugation, and assimilation, states inevitably were formed; and social evolution proceeded therefrom in stages in which the organization for control in state and society would always be reflected in the law.

In Bücher's more clearly defined system of societal stages, mankind is said to have moved from the closed household economy, to the town economy of the Middle Ages, and finally to the national economy (*Volkswirtschaft*) of modern times. This three-tiered process was accompanied by progressive growth in the importance of exchange: At first goods went directly from producers to consumers without exchange, and, in fact, exchange was regarded with hostility; eventually some craftsmen working directly for consumers or selling in local markets received payment in exchange for goods and services; and finally exchange became widespread in modern times.

Oppenheimer believed sociology to be a general science of collective human life and that it established laws about change. One of his better known ideas concerned the conquest and subjugation by nomadic herdsmen and others of tribal society as the end of prehistory and the dawn of civilization. What followed was the gradual development of states from their primitive through their modern constitutional forms.[32]

In addition to a general belief in a universal social evolution through states, Nakae borrowed from Gumplowicz's ideas of the centrality of blood ties in ancient society, the origin of states in conquest, and the importance of law as a reflection of class control. From Bücher, he borrowed ideas about the nature of the ancient Chinese economy. Oppenheimer's thesis on the formation of states clearly influenced him as well. Lesser figures whom Nakae used, such as Lewis Morgan and Julius Lippert (1839–1909), also adopted evolutionary, developmental schemes in their anthropological research, as did Wilhelm Wundt, the tireless scholar of psychology and science, whose ten-volume *Völkerpsychologie* (Ethnic psychology; 1900–1909) was intended to describe the natural history of mankind through stages.[33]

One of the reasons that theories of social evolution based on universally applicable stages of development were so prevalent in the nineteenth century lay in the explanatory capacity of such notions for people of many different political bents. A conservative, even reactionary, thinker might be attracted to a state theory because it proved just how far contemporary society (that is, Western society), the pinnacle of civilization, had come from its primitive, tribal past when men behaved liked heathens; and those people living in stone age "societies" as late as the nineteenth century could be simultaneously pitied and studied. Liberals, as well as radicals like Karl Marx (1818–1883), might find in a theory of developmental stages an explanation for why some people lived in the advanced West and others not so fortunate were held back in a primeval past; it offered those tribes living in the stone age "societies" and Asians victimized by the West the promise of a future in which they, too, would develop to the level of the contemporary West and beyond.

The two great historical works on Western antiquity to which Nakae returned time and again are no longer widely read as they once were: *Römische Geschichte* by Theodor Mommsen (1817–1903) and *Griechische Geschichte* by Karl Julius Beloch (1854–1929). From both men Nakae learned, among other things, that understanding ancient political thought required investigation of every kind of available material, no matter how foreign to politics it might seem on the surface.[34] The work of many other now-forgotten authors influenced Nakae, including Rudolph Stammler (1856–1938) on law and society and Denis Numa Fustel de Coulanges (1830–1889) on the ancient city.[35]

Virtually all of these secondary works can be found in Nakae's library collection with his annotations in them and a date in his own hand indicating when he began (and sometimes when he completed) reading them. If these dates are accurate, Nakae read all of the comparative and social science material just discussed between April 1921 and February 1925. In other words, he read the vast majority of it after he had completed the first draft of the essay he gave to Ojima Sukema in 1922 and worked it into the revised edition of July 1925. Counting just the books in which he noted the date at which he began to read, during the period from early 1921 to early 1925 he read in addition sixty-five other tomes in the same vein, all presumably to get a firmer and more balanced perspective on antiquity.

Nakae's numerous marginal notes concern comparisons with aspects of East Asian history, refer him back to some other work, or render a judgment on the quality of the ideas being expounded. For instance, in Nakae's copy of *Die Geschlechtsgenossenschaft der Urzeit und die Entstehung der Ehe* (Tribal society in primitive times and the origin of marriage) by Albert Hermann Post (1839–1935), there are many notes comparing statements by Post to propositions about endogamy in China or the well-field system and the like. Or, in his copy of *Die Geschichte der neueren Philosophie* (The history of modern philosophy) by Wilhelm Windelband (1848–1915), he notes next to the author's treatment of a particular point about Kant that this "is comparable to [the place of] Confucius in [Chinese] classical scholarship."[36]

In the three years between the first draft of his essay on the history of ancient Chinese political thought and its printing in mid 1925, as he consumed the ancient Chinese texts and countless Western works, Nakae continued to live the rigorously ascetic, virtually eremetic existence he planned for himself in 1919. Through the mid 1920s, he was becoming ever more engrossed in the Chinese classics and Chinese scholarship on them. Although he had 300 copies of his first essay printed in 1925 for distribution to friends and others who might have been interested, over 200 of them were found after his death among the papers in his library.[37] No sooner had he completed that essay, than he began to see the holes in its arguments and to feel ever more incompetent as a scholar of antiquity. The basic methodological issues still plagued him; and it seemed that the closer he came to the sources, the further they receded from his understanding.

"*SHŌSHO GAIRON*": *A CORRELATIVE STUDY OF THE* SHANG-SHU

This dilemma of gaining a true understanding of the texts available from antiquity was especially severe in the case of the source he considered most crucial. Nakae had noted at one point in his first essay that the *Shang-shu* was the single most important extant work for the study of ancient Chinese political thought. Therefore, a systematic knowledge of it and the traditions of scholarly commentary on it over the subsequent 2000 years became essential to his gaining further access to the world of ancient China. Nakae wrestled with the *Shang-shu* for the next decade, coming back to it in 1931, early 1934, and finally in 1935. All the time he was working toward a methodology that would break through the endless layers of mystery surrounding the text and, hence, the world it described.

While he was working on revisions of his first essay and reading Western-language books to that end, he found time to write a long essay on the *Shang-shu*. Nakae not only never distributed this piece; he never even had it printed. After the war it was discovered in manuscript among his papers and books deposited in the library of the Research Institute for Humanistic Sciences at Kyoto University. Professor Kimura Eiichi edited it for publication in 1948 in the university's Sinological journal *Shinagaku*.[38] Today, it reads like the kind of rigorous exercise Nakae would have inflicted on himself to make sure he was staying on top of the confusing mass of arguments about virtually every aspect of the text. One of the sharpest differences between this essay, "Shōsho gairon" (An outline of the *Shang-shu*), and his longer first piece of work was the complete lack of any citations to Western philosophical, historical, or social science writings in this essay. Aside from one brief comparison with Western traditions of philology, Nakae devoted this study of the *Shang-shu* entirely to Sinological issues.

The essay centers on the main problems confronting the scholar of the *Shang-shu*. For example, Nakae asks, why has the *Shang-shu* been considered different from other ancient Chinese texts? He offers a series of detailed answers, among them the lack of sufficient materials to corroborate its contents; the confusion of having both a New Text (or New Script) and Old Text (or Old Script) edition of the book, because the original was proscribed and destroyed during the Ch'in book-burning; and the complex relationship between these two editions of the text. By laying out these problems and the means by which subsequent scholars and schools of thought have handled them, Nakae sets the stage for an investigation that he deemed necessary to further work into the much deeper complexities of the *Shang-shu*.

What does the title of this text mean and where did it come from? Nakae suggests three possibilities, noting that the evidence cannot as yet sustain any of them. He leans toward the position that the "shang" of *Shang-shu* is homophonous with the Chinese character meaning "above" or "supreme." The implication is "antiquity," and hence this text is the "book" or "documents" (*shu*) of the ancient sage kings. Such a view fits well with our understanding of the Chinese reverence for antiquity. Other scholars such as Cheng Hsüan (127–200) and Wang Ming-sheng (1722–1798), argued at widely disparate times that the work was originally known only as the *Shu* and that Confucius revered (*shang*) it and renamed it accordingly. Not only is there no way to corroborate such a notion, Nakae points out, but if Confucius did just this, why did he not do the same for the other classics? Others, such as K'ung An-kuo (second century B.C.E.) and K'ung Yin-ta (574–648), claimed that it was named by Fu Sheng (c. 200 B.C.E.), who allegedly secreted the book in a wall of his house to save it from destruction and brought it (the New Text edition) to light during the reign of Emperor Wen (r. 179–156 B.C.E.)

of the Han dynasty. Again, Nakae concludes that the evidence is too weak to draw such a conclusion.[39]

One of the major problems for those working on the *Shang-shu* is that it was on several occasions destroyed (partially or wholly) or lost, and hence it is never entirely clear what text a given commentator had before him. Generally, scholars have followed the theory that the *ur*-text had one hundred chapters, but even this cannot be proven. One of the most difficult issues in this connection, and one to which Nakae would return in the mid 1930s, was the number of chapters (*p'ien*) in Fu Sheng's edition of the text. The number is either twenty-eight or twenty-nine, but there were variations even among the proponents of each number. Should one count the *hsü*, the purported "introduction" to the *Shang-shu*, or is it an interpolation from much later? What did Ssu-ma Ch'ien mean when he gave the number as twenty-nine in his *Shih-chi*? Did certain chapter titles in fact cover what we now consider two chapters? Such questions plagued Chinese scholars for over two millennia.[40]

The question to most readers of Nakae's essay today is why it mattered so much to him. Certainly it is important to know whether Fu Sheng had twenty-eight or twenty-nine chapters in his edition of the *Shang-shu*, but need one devote years of study to it? Nakae was more persuaded by the theory of twenty-nine for a number of reasons too complicated to warrant the explanatory space necessary; but the essay gives few clues to what larger issue seemed to him to hinge on the correct answer—only an occasional clause here and there goes beyond technicalities. This may have been because this essay was not intended for other's use. Nakae clearly felt that the *Shang-shu* was a political work or a volume concerned with the practices of government, centering on the words and deeds of ancient rulers and officials. And, he regarded it as the key work for understanding ancient Chinese political thought. He also seems to have felt that the *Shang-shu*, with all its complexities and all the arguments surrounding it, was sufficiently important as a guide to antiquity to warrant years of attention.

It was not just the text of the *Shang-shu* that attracted him to these issues. For example, he claims to accept the argument put forth by Yen Jo-chü (1636–1704) that the Old Text version of the *Shang-shu* was spurious. Interestingly, though, he does not dwell on this problem, nor does

he cease analyzing the Old Text edition at this point. Nakae was fasci-
nated, often to the point of great praise or equivalent anger, with the
development of traditions of thought over the years about the *Shang-
shu.* How were the editions of the text transmitted and changed? How
did Chinese scholars substantiate their suppositions about points in the
text? And, how did Chinese philology develop? It thus became histori-
ographically important to him to know not whether the *Shang-shu* had
twenty-eight or twenty-nine chapters when Fu Sheng presented it to the
throne, but which scholars over the years believed which numbers, how
they arrived at their findings, and what philological tools they had developed to come to their conclusions.

The Even though the Old Text *Shang-shu* proved to be unauthentic,
Nakae had great respect for the scholars who taught and supported it,
certainly much more that he had for the New Text scholars. He considered the New Text theory that Liu Hsin (53?–23 B.C.E.) had forged large
sections of the Old Text *Shang-shu* to be all but moronic. He admired
the less rigid, more open, and more individual style of the Old Text phi-
lologists who, he felt, were more interested in finding out what the text
really meant than in suppressing and destroying their "enemies" in the
New Text school. In fact he likened the Old Text school in scholarly
atmosphere to the Italian school in the Renaissance who used linguistic
methods to get at the essential meaning of Plato and Aristotle, long mis-
understood by Arabic and Church scholars.

The Old Text edition of the *Shang-shu* thrived in the intellectual
world of the Eastern Han (as the New Text version had in the Western
Han), and with it a sound basis for classical philology was laid. The educational system of the Han dynasty, the *shih-fa* or *chia-fa* system, was
such that each of the ancient texts had specific teachers and schools
through which traditions of interpretation were passed down. Among
the foremost scholar-teachers of the Old Text *Shang-shu* who were the
founders of Han philology, Nakae reserved special praise for Tu Lin (d.
47 B.C.E.), Chia K'uei (30–101), and a long list of others. Unfortunately,
much of Old Text scholarship from the Eastern Han was destroyed in
the warfare of the early third century, but scholars, such as Wang Su
(195–256) in the Wei dynasty (220–265), worked hard at reviving it.[41]

Although he devoted many long hours to uncovering the textual intri-

cacies of the *Shang-shu*, Nakae ultimately was just as interested in the
scholarly traditions of transmission and various treatments of the text as
he was in solving the puzzles. In subsequent years he developed a
method for organizing lineages of chapters within the text of the *Shang-
shu*, and, in so doing, he relied on the technical expertise of these traditions. This unpresumptuous essay of 1924 allowed him to lay out the
work he planned to carry out over the next decade on both the *Shang-
shu* and the *Kung-yang chuan* (Kung-yang commentary).

Things, though, did not go entirely as planned; for the distresses of
the outside world began to menace Nakae's carefully guarded detachment. In Europe Nazism and Fascism were rising; and what was more
difficult to ignore, in Asia the Japanese Army had invaded Manchuria
and was putting pressure on North China. How could Nakae continue
calmly to live in a borrowed house in Peking, studying Chinese antiquities? While staying under Nakae's roof, the Japanese Communist
Katayama Sen (1859–1933) chided his host by remarking, "I can't imagine how you can really be interested in this ancient stuff."[42] The comment may have lacked tact, but it hardly lacked point at a time when
the world seemed to be falling apart. Nakae wrestled with its implications for a long time and came to a resolution only years later.

FOUR

A Critique of Classicism

In 1927 Nakae and his wife Satoko decided to separate. She left for Japan with Suzue Gen'ichi in the fall, and eventually settled there the following year. The divorce, finalized in 1931, was harmonious, if painful, and Nakae continued to send her money each month until his death. He spent the next fifteen years living alone, his existence one step closer to that of a hermit.[1]

Between July 1925 when Nakae printed his revised version of "Shina kodai seiji shisō shi" and July 1930, he wrote nothing. Those who knew him well insist that by early 1926 he was dissatisfied even with the revised essay and that he had decided to reassess his whole approach to ancient China. He was not faced with any pressure to publish (nor any apparent desire to do so). In any case, he had no intention of hurrying to conclusions about the bases of a systematic approach to understanding antiquity. Around 1926 Suzue Gen'ichi, who had spent the last few years in close contact with the Chinese labor movement, undoubtedly influenced Nakae to begin shifting his reading toward a focus on more left-wing materials, like Marx's *Das Kapital*, which Nakae began for the first time that year.[1]

From the marginal notes in his books, we know that Nakae had begun reading works by socialists and other leftist thinkers as early as 1920 or 1921. At that time they were just part of his larger reading schedule. In the early 1920's he developed an interest in the work of Immanuel Kant, and in January 1924 began to plough through *Kritik der*

reinen Vernuft (The critique of pure reason). Nakae's copies of Kant's
books are now so fully marked up with pencil and ink that it is all but
impossible to read his marginal notations. He reread this *Critique* several times over the years and, apparently, each time added more notes. In
addition to *Das Kapital*, which he also read at least three times, Nakae
read others of Marx's works between 1925 and 1930, as well as writings
by Vladimir Ilyitch Lenin (1870–1924), Rosa Luxemburg (1870–1919),
and Nikolai Bukharin (1888–1938). He also began reading works by
two of the founders of contemporary sociology, Max Weber (1864–1920)
and Émile Durkheim (1858–1917).[2]

Despite this prodigious program in Western scholarship and philosophy, the years from 1924 to 1930 belonged to the works of the Chinese. We know this from the wealth of data he brought to the essays he
published from 1930. He never made a marginal note in any of his thousands of volumes of Chinese writings, as if these texts were in some odd
way sacrosanct (or else the paper was too thin to be marked up). How
then was his newly found interest in late-nineteenth- and early-twentieth-
century European philosophy and social activism to be reconciled with
his continuing proclivity for the distant Chinese past and the mysteries
of its texts? Nakae began to resolve this problem in his scholarly work
through a critique of classical authority in the history of Chinese scholarship on the *Shang-shu*. This was in effect a critique of authority itself.

As with his work on ancient Chinese thought, when Nakae set out
again to work on the *Shang-shu*, he basically had the texts of antiquity
and traditional scholarship by Chinese on the subject. There was little
secondary work to build on, though a number of important collections
of oracle bone materials had been prepared by Liu E (1857–1909), Lo
Chen-yü, Wang Kuo-wei, Hayashi Taisuke (1854–1922), and several
other Chinese scholars.[3] Lo and Wang had contributed important
works, and between 1925 and 1930 Tung Tso-pin (1895–1963) entered
the field and began publishing.

Among early Japanese scholars of China in the Shang period, Nakae
cited the work of two men. Hayashi Taisuke, who had been trained
along traditional lines, came under fire in the late Meiji period for his
"old-fashioned" Kangaku approach to the Chinese classics; but he pioneered Japanese studies of Shang China and the oracle bones. Similarly,

the even less well known Tazaki Masayoshi (1880–1976) wrote a number of essays on the *Shang-shu* that Nakae thought were brilliant (and Nakae rarely cited the work of any Japanese scholar). Tazaki was among the first to use the text as a way to understand politics, society, and the economy of Shang China.[4]

A METHODOLOGY FOR APPROACHING THE SHANG-SHU

By August 1931 Nakae had returned to his favorite text and he then had one hundred copies of a moderately long essay printed for distribution to friends. It was entitled "Shōsho Hankō hen ni tsuite" (On the P'an Keng chapter of the *Shang-shu*), and was dedicated to Prince Saionji.

P'an Keng (r. late fourteenth century B.C.E.) was the seventeenth, eighteenth, or nineteenth king of the Shang dynasty, depending on whom one consults.[5] Inasmuch as no oracle bone material has yet been discovered to corroborate the entire story, the actual facts remain cloudy. In the *Shang-shu* chapter bearing his name, P'an Keng makes three speeches exhorting the "people" to move the capital with him to a new site at Yin (An-Yang). The authenticity of this chapter, its three constituent parts, and the date of its composition have long troubled scholars, in part because, as K. C. Chang notes: "*P'an keng* is considered one of the most important texts pertaining to the Shang, because it is believed to contain many genuinely Shang elements and because, made up of words that are both pleading and threatening, it reveals some of the essence of the governing art of the Shang dynasty."[6] No consensus, however, has yet been reached about the veracity or dating of the text; and the debate has continued through recent years.[7]

Despite widespread disagreement by scholars of ancient China on virtually every aspect of the "P'an Keng" chapter, there is also a widespread belief in its importance. The Sung philosopher Chu Hsi (1130–1200) noted in his *Chu-tzu yü-lei* (Recorded conversations of Master Chu) that the *Shang-shu* consisted of two kinds of chapters, "those extremely easy to understand" and "those extremely difficult to understand." He placed "P'an Keng" in the latter group because, he suggested, it was probably written in an ancient local dialect or a complicated spoken style of the time.[8] Nonetheless, significant strides had been made by Chinese scholars over the years toward penetrating the linguistic opacity of the text. Nakae was especially inclined to praise the work of classicists of the Ch'ing period.

Scouring all the available texts of the pre-Ch'in period, as well as efforts by later scholars to reconstruct those texts, for citations from the "P'an Keng," Nakae finds scant mention of it. Yet, by the time Lü Pu-wei (d. 235 B.C.E.) compiled his *Lü-shih ch'un-ch'iu* at the end of the Chou, the expression "P'an Keng chih cheng" (the government of P'an Keng) had apparently passed into current usage. In the Han dynasty, P'an Keng represented the political model of a king who dispensed with luxury and honored frugality, as well as a prime example of moving the capital. The importance of this chapter within the *Shang-shu* rose, Nakae argues, because its stress on peace and adherence to political authorities proved pleasing to the New Text scholars of the Western Han, virtually all of whom served as scholar-officials and were thus beholden to the powers that be. Here was the emergence and solidification of "classical scholarship" (*keigaku*) about which Nakae would later write at length.[9]

Nakae's major contribution to studies of this chapter of the *Shang-shu* was to take the three parts of the "P'an Keng" apart and examine them separately. If whole chapters or books of the *Shang-shu* could be spurious or later interpolations, then why not parts of chapters? If entire chapters could be shown to possess systems of thought, character usage, and written styles out of kilter with what we know of the period in which they are alleged to have been written, perhaps sections of chapters were mechanically (or intentionally) patched together by adding later material to earlier.

Traditionally, scholars regarded the speeches which constitute the first two sections of "P'an Keng" as having been delivered before the capital was moved: the first being the king's admonition to his court officials who opposed the move, the second a speech to the populace. The speech given in the third section then occurred after the move to Yin. Because classical scholars generally failed to understand the relationship in Shang times between the ruler and the general populace, Nakae claims, they mistakenly distinguished the first two sections in this way. He argues that the "populace" (*chung*) was in no way excluded from the first admonition, nor were court officials ignored in the second. In fact, based on this analysis and his other work on the *Shang-shu*, Nakae identified as one of the characteristics of ancient Chinese society the point that an admonition of the ruler to his kinsmen-officials first took the form of an admonition to the "people."

The first two sections essentially describe the same set of circumstances impelling, in the king's view, a move to Yin; but the third part, while covering the same content, is fundamentally different in style. When Chu Hsi complained about how difficult the whole chapter was, he overlooked this distinction. Close examination of the third section reveals a simpler, more refined prose with an economy of style, unlike the coarser two sections preceding it. A comparison of the third section phrase for phrase with the previous parts of "P'an Keng" reveals a remarkable parallel in the events described.

King P'an Keng of the last part is no longer, as he was in the first two parts, a king in a lineage-based society; but he has been transformed into an ideal Son of Heaven of post-Shang vintage. What we have here, Nakae argues, is not two aspects of the same P'an Keng but descriptions of him from two different eras and two different conceptions of society and polity. In effect, it was the intent of the author of the third section to translate, perhaps "modernize," the essence of the earlier sections into a more elegant, simpler prose of his own day. And, this third section is considerably shorter. In addition, the conceptions of morality, the self-reflective mind, the replacement of reverence for ancestors with a kind of religious dread, and a variety of other subjective factors demonstrate that different ideas are at work within the "P'an Keng" chapter of the *Shang-shu*.[10]

One significant contribution of Nakae's essay is thus based on a structural analysis of the ancient text; another reflects his reading in leftist thought. By referring for the first time to the work of Karl Marx, he now elaborates the picture of politics and society that he painted in that first piece. Nakae introduces the whole machinery of "production relations" as the underpinning for ancient society. Earlier, when seeking the essence of the bond between ruler and ruled, he had found it in the source of the ruler's political authority; now he finds it in the economic effect of power. Whereas before he had stressed the king's position as head of the dominant lineage, he now focuses on the entire ruling lineage as an owning class, with subject lineages as producers. The general populace, the direct producers, were "the ruled" because they were subjugated lineages put to work for the ruler in agriculture. In other words, farming lineages were ipso facto "ruled" lineages, the exploited class.[11] To engage in agricultural labor was a sign of subjugation.

To make this argument iron clad, Nakae had to eliminate any suggestion that the king in "P'an Keng" actually was appealing to the people to move the capital. Some scholars have argued that the *chung* who appear in this chapter of the *Shang-shu* were "free farmers," perhaps lowly members of the ruler's lineage; Professor Ho Ping-ti has even claimed that there was social mobility for *chung* and that they could rise on the basis of merit.[12] Nakae may have been wrong, but he would have found such arguments appalling. This was a society, he believed, in which one owed one's identity to the lineage into which one had been born. The very conceptions of individuality, individual merit, and the like were entirely alien to that world. While stopping short of dubbing the "ruled" slaves, Nakae took pains to demonstrate the utter lack of control they possessed over their own lives.

Summarizing the interrelations between society, religion, and now the economy, Nakae argues:

> The basis of the lineage state took its form from the direct relationship between the ruling lineage, possessors of the conditions of production upon which their lineage bonds as ruler were founded, and the ruled lineages who were agricultural lineages, the direct producers. Furthermore, the same lineage grouping that comprised the ruling class possessed a religious consciousness as such which formed the fulcrum of their societal consciousness at that time. Hence, they comprised a ceremonial grouping that became the motive force to all social activity.[13]

The king represented this ceremonial group; and his link with the general populace was indirect, because they were by definition from other lineages and thus outside the ceremonial group. As ruling bonds based on lineage died out, the ruler's link to the populace and control over them became more direct. The passage containing the ruler's appeal to the "people" in the P'an Keng chapter must be metaphoric if it is genuine; or else it, like the third section, must be an interpolation containing Chou conceptions of sovereignty. In this last part of "P'an Keng," one no longer sees the ruling lineage's religious consciousness at the core of social life, controlling all social phenomena; but a shift has occurred toward political and moral ideas that break down the barriers to the social existence of the individual which had been set up by lineage society. It represents a wholly new societal spirit.[14]

Looking back many years later at the debate over whether the "P'an Keng" chapter was originally one or three sections, Kaizuka Shigeki expressed the highest regard for Nakae's insight and his talent as a social-economic historian; but he could not agree with the Marxist overtones of this essay. He also offered high praise for Nakae's opening the discussion of ancient Chinese society to comparative perspectives with other ancient societies, although again he had trouble with some of Nakae's conclusions.[15]

Ultimately, the strength of this essay both in the context of Nakae's own personal intellectual development and as a scholarly contribution to posterity lies less in the conclusions than in the methodology. As we have seen, the Marxist overlay was obvious, indeed obtrusive. Nakae was searching for an encompassing method that would help make sense of the historical materials. He relied, albeit critically, on classical traditions of textual scholarship concerning the Chinese sources; and he was beginning to develop his own methods for reading texts and analyzing their formation. But, when he turned to make social and economic historical sense out of ancient China, he looked to Western philosophy, history, and social science. Like many of his day he was extraordinarily impressed by his first reading of Marx, and it shows in this essay written shortly after he had finished *Das Kapital* for the first time.

Several years later, at the home of a friend, he was leafing through a book by a young, anti-traditional Chinese scholar:

> I was astonished to read [in this book] that, because the "Pan Keng" chapter expressed a belief in ghosts, it was a forgery . . . I find such an idiotic point of view unbearably disheartening. When I confront such completely wrong-headed arguments, my first feeling is that these iconoclasts [lit., *shinjin* or new men] of China are nothing but rocks from head to foot. This may reflect my own foolishness; but inasmuch as contemporary Chinese society has completely lost its foundations, it should not seem strange that in the academic world, as elsewhere, brilliant men are impossible to find.[16]

The "iconoclastic" view to which Nakae referred here seems to be the argument popular in the 1920s and 1930s, and in certain quarters even today, that religion as generally understood in the West was absent from China; therefore, anything of a religious nature in an old text betrayed the text's spuriousness. More generally Nakae was bemoaning the low level of contemporary Chinese scholarship on China's own history. The lack of seriousness he pointed to revealed its primarily political critique of the burden of Chinese tradition, not a focussed, structured effort to understand ancient history.

Nakae returned to the *Shang-shu* for his two last works of Sinology in early 1934 and 1935. Only one hundred copies of the first of these, "Sho nijūkyū hen ni kansuru shiken ni tsuite (1)" (My views on the twenty-nine chapters of the *Shang-shu*, part 1), were printed. The second piece, a continuation of the first, was never completed and appeared only when Nakae's collected articles were published after World War II. As a whole Nakae attempts to draw from the methodology he developed for dissecting the "P'an Keng" chapter and bring it to bear on the entire *Shang-shu*. At the same time he tries to pare away the layers of *keigaku* (classical) interpretation that had become central to the accepted understanding of the text. The *Shang-shu* was both the most often studied *keigaku* text and the one debated the longest.

For Nakae, the main problem with *keigaku* as scholarship was that despite the tremendous technical advances it had made, especially in the Ch'ing dynasty, it never achieved full independence from its object of study—the Chinese classics and commentaries. The very fact that we have a unified *Shang-shu* (we actually have two) and that it has become a classic are the result of the rise of the *keigaku* movement in the Han dynasty. Thus, the *keigaku* hold on the *Shang-shu* as we know it has always been particularly firm. Questions of how *keigaku* fashioned certain chapters within the *Shang-shu* or, for example, how Yao and Shun of the *Shang-shu* became model Chinese sage-emperors lay outside the realm of *keigaku* inquiry. The central problem for the contemporary scholar of the *Shang-shu*, Nakae argues, is how to distinguish *keigaku* "historical facts" from general historical facts. *Keigaku* fact is based on traditions and legends, not objective experience; the *keigaku* universe lies outside the experiential realm, a purely conceptual world of ideas. Nakae's important distinction here between these two kinds of facts will become clearer in the context of his analysis of the *Shang-shu*.[17]

In his essay on the "P'an Keng" chapter, Nakae had argued that, contrary to the claims of *keigaku* scholars, its first two parts were not sequential but instead duplicative, while the third section, by contrast, was a restatement from a later era when *keigaku* influence was strong and a different set of assumptions pertained. By examining the ideological content of different chapters, Nakae now argues, one can see that throughout the *Shang-shu* certain chapters served as prototypes for the composition of others. If the entire *Shang-shu* could be rearranged for analytical purposes to group chapters by the prototype on which they are based, then the reasons for the *keigaku* ordering of the chapters as we now have them would become clear and no longer accepted as objective fact.

Nakae offers as an example a comparison of the "To fang" (Numerous states) and "To shih" (Numerous officers) chapters of the text. He argues that both chapters address the same group of people. Following the work of Tuan Yü-ts'ai, Ch'ien Ta-hsin (1728–1804), and Wang Su, he does not translate *fang* as region (as Legge did) but shows that in ancient Chinese it was a homophone for *pang* and that both terms, as well as the character *kuo*, were probably used interchangeably. The *ssu-kuo* (literally, "four states") mentioned at the outset in "To fang" in fact did not refer to four specific states but to states in all four directions.[18] In both chapters, the announcements went out to the "officers and people of Yin."

By a painstakingly detailed comparison of the two chapters, phrase by phrase, Nakae confidently argues that much of "To shih" simply summarized passages in "To fang." *Keigaku* scholars over the years stressed the differences between them in order to provide a basis for the continued belief that they represented completely independent chapters. Nakae notes the inconsistencies in a perfect match, but he stresses the overwhelming similarities. These differences, he hypothesizes, were introduced after the completion of the "To shih" chapter when the legend of the Duke of Chou, central to the group of chapters to which it belongs, had become accepted with the authority of historical fact. Material was then inserted into the text in an infelicitous manner. He further surmises that the author of the "To shih" had no intention of writing in a style different from the "To fang," but aimed at composing an independent chapter based on "To fang." In style "To fang" is more "descriptive," while "To shih" is more "explanatory."

Thus, "To fang" appears to have been composed without reference to "To shih," while the latter was written on the basis of "To fang." "To fang" in general follows the basic ideological theme outlined in the "K'ang kao" (Announcement to [the Prince of] K'ang) chapter: *ming-te shen-fa* or "illustrate virtue and be careful in the use of punishments." However, the changes introduced into "To shih" brought it into closer accord with the principle of a changing heavenly mandate.[19] "To shih" described the same set of facts, in a slightly different fashion; but to see them as two entirely independent entities, Nakae argues, is *keigaku* fiction.

The method that Nakae developed here is to examine the chapters of the *Shang-shu* for ideologically similar themes and thereby establish filiations of chapters by systems of thought. He grouped these filiations around the chapters in which those systems are most clearly expressed. In the chapters of the "K'ang kao" group, the ideological underpinning is *ming-te shen-fa*. The "K'ang kao" chapter itself expresses this theme most succinctly. "To fang" belongs to the "K'ang kao" system of chapters, which has as its principal element the concept of *ming-te shen-fa*. This idea appears widely in the text, even in chapters not, strictly speaking, within the system for which it is the defining element. It is impossible to date with precision the order in which chapters of the "K'ang kao" system were written; for, as Nakae notes, certain of the chapters of this system probably predate the "K'ang kao" chapter itself. The reason Nakae labeled it the "K'ang kao" system is simply that in this particular chapter one finds the clearest and most intellectually original form of the central principle. In all, Nakae identifies five filiations of chapters, nine independent chapters with their own distinctive elements, and several miscellaneous chapters without any unique ideas. Ten chapters from the *Shang-shu* fall into the "K'ang kao" system.

The "K'ang kao" chapter itself is pure *ming-te shen-fa* from beginning to end. Its author explained with perfect clarity that King Wen "was able to illustrate his virtue and be careful in the use of punishments," and thus heaven enabled him to defeat the Shang and receive the mandate. Young Feng, the putative addressee of this announcement (*kao*), is counseled to learn from the wise rulers of the Shang, to help the people by spreading his goodness, and to make sure that punishments fit not the magnitude of the crimes committed but the intentions of the criminals. The point of this last element was to distinguish purposeful and accidental crimes, for the act of punishment is part and parcel of the ruler's guidance of the people. For members of the ruling elite who commit crimes, particularly the "detestable" crimes of being "unfilial" or "unbrotherly," the announcement counsels even greater severity than for commoners. Because the elite serves as the backbone of society, the fictive parents to the wayward and childlike people, no mercy can be shown them: "Let you quickly, according to what is recognized right, put them to death."

The text of this chapter offers eight observations on relationships among heaven, the recipient of the mandate (that is, the ruler), and the little people (the ruled), all of which in some way manifest aspects of *ming-te shen-fa*: Not everyone received the mandate, for King Wen was special. The people's feelings provide the ultimate proof that heaven is changing the recipient of its mandate. Calming the people's emotions is the object of government. Only a king can calm the people's minds. Heaven is forever watching over the king to ascertain whether he is carrying out the responsibilities entrusted to him by heaven. The content of these responsibilities lies in *ming-te shen-fa*. The complete attainment of *ming-te shen-fa* lies in the perfection of the king's moral nature. And, unless this kingly morality is achieved, there can be no government for instructing the people.[20]

The "K'ang kao" chapter is pregnant with ideas that bore fruit in late-Chou thought. It is quoted by numerous thinkers of the period; and its ideas about the relationship among heaven, the ruler, and the people have become identified with Chou China itself. Nakae next compares each of the other nine *Shang-shu* chapters in this filiation to the prototype just described. For example, "Chiu kao" (Announcement about drunkenness) appears close to "K'ang kao" in thrust. The reason for this, Nakae argues, is not because both are works in which announcements are made to K'ang Shu (young Feng), but because "Chiu kao" was written as an extension of the thought embodied in the "K'ang kao" chapter. Where they differ in literary style tells us differences between the authors, but, as Nakae demonstrates, there is no doubt about the fact that the author of "Chiu kao" based his text on "K'ang kao."

This new charge to Feng adds to the principle of illustrating virtue and being careful about punishments, according to Nakae, a new "somewhat unnatural and hyperbolic" injunction to be attentive to excessive drinking. The order of instructions to Feng follows "K'ang kao" almost exactly, and the addition of a warning about the evils of drink, Nakae argues, was abruptly inserted by the author. In fact, one can even see that the author, despite his attempted fidelity to the spirit and the content of "K'ang kao," did a poor job of explaining the relationship between the idea of being careful in meting out punishments and the thought of the former wise men. As early as the *Han-fei-tzu*, the Legalist text of the late Warring States period, the link between "K'ang kao" and "Chiu kao" was recognized, but the nature of the link was never uncovered.[21]

Utilizing the same basic format, Nakae goes on to compare each of the chapters he placed in the "K'ang kao" system with the prototype ("K'ang kao" itself) in an effort to show how the system took form. For example, Nakae attributes the abruptness of the "Tzu ts'ai" (Timber of the tzu tree) chapter and the resultant brevity (and difficulty) of its text to its author's efforts not to write a wholly independent chapter but a continuation of some earlier piece, an extension through examples of "K'ang kao."[22] Moving next to an examination of the "Wu i" (Against luxurious ease) chapter, Nakae notes: "Moving from 'Tzu ts'ai' to 'Wu i' makes one feel as if one is getting out of heavily patched, thickly padded cotton clothing and changing into brand new, lightweight clothes." He regarded it as the most freely flowing, elegant chapter of the entire *Shang-shu*, a beautiful, musical, rhythmical text. He argues that whereas "To Fang" and other chapters mimic "K'ang kao," "Wu i" possesses an integrity of style. Although he finds that this stylistic integrity gives "Wu i" a satisfying wholeness and self-sufficiency, he reiterates that the content is rooted in principles set forth in "K'ang kao": Its appeal to the sovereign to be wary of excessive luxury, for instance, flows directly from the the dictum that when the sovereign's morality approaches completeness, prosperity will follow. By establishing an opposition between those who carry the onus of rulership and those petty men with all their faults who must be ruled, the author of the text offers a warning to rulers to beware of greed and overindulgence.[23]

One of the most interesting chapters in this system is "Lü hsing" ([Marquis of] Lü on punishment) which contains elements nowhere else found in this filiation. Written in an extremely clear, unspecialized vocabulary, it is centrally concerned with illustrating virtue and being careful in punishment, but not as a simple extension of the "K'ang kao" chapter. Although we cannot establish an absolute order in which the chapters of the *Shang-shu* were written, we can say with certainty that *ming-te shen-fa* represented the standard ideological fare of the ruling class in China at the time of the text's composition, and that the "K'ang kao" chapter did not create the ideology. "Lü hsing" posits a single origin of all evil in the world: Ch'ih Yu, who "according to the teachings of ancient times . . . was the first to produce disorder—which spread among the quiet, orderly people until all became robbers and murderers." Ch'ih Yu appears in the text only as the initial instigator of disquiet; he is never mentioned again. By the same token, the misuse of punishments that led to the intrusion of heaven to set the world right is laid at the feet of the Miao people who "did not use the power of goodness but [only] the restraint of punishments. They made the five punishments into engines of oppression, calling them the laws." Again, the influence of evil leads to the people becoming evil until heaven intervenes and visits retribution upon the world. The Miao are not meant to typify Chinese views of alien racial or ethnic groups, but simple to serve as an allegory of what can happen to the Chou people if they fail to learn from the past.

Although both Ch'ih Yu and the Miao are mentioned nowhere else in the "K'ang kao" system, the passages concerning them in "Lü hsing" fit well with the "K'ang kao" system of thought. They provide a magnification of the whole conceptual system surrounding the need for care in the use of punishments. Thus, the author introduced the origin of evil in the character of Ch'ih Yu and the notion of heavenly retribution for crimes with the Miao people. The idea that evil has spread to one's own society from an alien group was common, Nakae argues, in ancient and pre-civilized polities. "The Nazis nowadays," he notes, "are no exception." Societies with a sense of cultural superiority are often threatened by alien societies. The result is often, as can be seen in embryonic form in "Lü hsing," the development of ethnic (or racial) self-conceptions. What the author of the "Lü hsing" did was to separate *ming-te* from *shen-fa* and emphasize the inner workings of the latter. Rather than examine the relationship between the two elements of this basic principle in the "K'ang kao" system, the author primarily stressed the portion dealing with how to combat crime, which undoubtedly means that at the time of its composition ideas on how to fight crime were being discussed widely.[24]

In sum, Nakae's methodology was to examine the chapters of the *Shang-shu* internally and see in what direction they inclined intellectually or ideologically. Then, he lined them up by systems of thought, putting to the side chapters that either had their own distinctive ideas or had no ideas at all, and planned to assign a conceptual underpinning of each filiation usually through that system's most typical chapter (after which the system was named). In the "K'ang kao" system, *ming-te shen-fa* provided its ten filiated chapters with a basic ideology to which each of them sought adherence. Exceptions and extensions of the general ideas of a given system usually tell us how a chapter was composed, perhaps when it took form, and maybe something of who wrote it. Nakae attributed, for example, the choppiness of abrupt disjunctures one finds in certain chapters to the inabilities of the authors to bring their work into alignment with "K'ang kao."

Nakae may be faulted for overly schematizing the structure of the *Shang-shu*, but the methodology he developed for penetrating its structure of the text was novel in Sinological studies and enabled him to perceive the *Shang-shu* in radically new ways. His study, however, could not be considered a finished product until all the systems identified within the *Shang-shu* had been analyzed in the way he dealt with the "K'ang kao" chapters, and Nakae never completed that task. He was sidetracked by other concerns, intellectual and otherwise. He did leave a much shorter study of the chapters in the "Lo kao" (Announcement concerning Lo) system, but he never published this essay or even had it printed. He planned for it to stand as the second part of his study of the organization of the chapters of the *Shang-shu*, as his title indicates: "Sho nijūkyū hen ni kansuru shikan ni tsuite (2): Rakkō keitō Shohen o ronzu" (My views on the twenty-nine chapters of the *Shang-shu*, part 2: An analysis of the "Lo kao" system of chapters in the *Shang-shu*).

The essay on the "Lo kao" system was apparently written some time in 1935. The principal theme of this system of chapters is the establishment of the capital at Lo by the Duke of Chou and the ethical implications of that action. Again Nakae takes as his task the stripping away of *keigaku* "truth" from what can be objectively determined. *Keigaku* scholars long argued that Lo was founded at the geographical center of the Chou empire, a concrete manifestation of the ethical-political ideal of moral uprightness and balance in ruling the realm. "Great peace" (*t'ai-p'ing*) in the *keigaku* view of history became the realization of ideal government, mythically centered in the legend of the Duke of Chou. *T'ai-p'ing* became the highest concept in Chinese political thought, the standard by which an emperor's achievements were measured. *Keigaku* scholars in advocating the ascendancy of this concept over the people attained positions of political authority, for the maintenance of peace always meant the pacification of popular uprisings. "Great peace" merely papered over an oppressive political order with a veneer of popular satisfaction. Nakae was as critical of many Chinese classicists for their scholarship as for the main political thrust of their work.

Although chapters outside the "Lo kao" system mention the legend of the Duke of Chou, for the chapters of the "Lo kao" filiation it is the crucial element. In the tale of the founding of the Lo capital, the Duke of Chou had not yet risen to distinctively heroic proportions, as he would in *Mencius*. Unlike this early portrayal of him as a denouncer of barbarians and pioneer settler in the land of the Chinese people, *keigaku* later pictured him as a creator of rituals and the founder of the way of Chou, the *keigaku* ideal state. He would become the central figure in *keigaku* historiography, its legend par excellence.

Nakae specifies that by *keigaku* legend he refers to a story about a person whom *keigaku* has recreated as a personification based on *keigaku* ideals and moral principles, and hence as an object deserving veneration.

This is the sense in which Wilhelm Wundt used the term *Legende*; it refers to a secular belief belonging to the ethical-political realm. The *keigaku* hero lacks sanguinary, martial qualities; for he represents the perfection of the civil peacemaker, the creator of *t'ai-p'ing*, a paragon of this-worldly political acumen. Thus, the *keigaku* spirit is embodied in this serious intellectual approach to the figures it "sanctified." In other chapters outside the "Lo kao" system, one finds the Duke of Chou eulogizing peace as a goal for the future; but in "Lo kao" in particular, peace is something unshakable and present.[25]

In contrast to systematic comparisons of chapters to an archetype in his essay on the "K'ang kao" system, in this second essay Nakae devotes more attention to the "Lo kao" system's central idea, the founding of the capital at Lo by the Duke of Chou. He also analyzes in detail how that legend was refracted through the other ancient classics. Unlike the *keigaku* portrayal of the Duke, the *Shih-ching* (Book of poetry) glorifies him for military conquests. Nakae argues that this conception of the hero more closely approximates that of other ancient societies than does the *keigaku* ideal. The *Shih-ching* presents a historical figure who becomes an object of veneration and legend different both from real, demonstrable historical actors and from legendary figures within *keigaku* contours, who came later when *keigaku* scholars reconstructed Chinese antiquity after their own values. Thus, Nakae concludes, "the Duke of Chou of the *Shih-ching* is no *keigaku* legendary type, but a legendary hero born to the ancient Chinese people from the natural process of their own ethnic life." *Mencius* and *Hsün-tzu* portray the Duke of Chou in a similar light to the *Shih-ching*. Confucius of the *Analects* speaks with the utmost reverence of the Duke of Chou, but he never once mentions the founding of the capital at Lo.[26]

Nakae has now described two models through which ancient Chinese heroes became exalted figures. Both render the central character beyond normal human proportions, the one attributing to him extraordinary military skills, the other making him the repository of the highest civil and cultural standards and royal guardian of peace. In short, the *keigaku* movement of the Han dynasty completely reversed the legendary qualities of the Duke of Chou, because what was considered essential to a hero had completely changed. In the stable times of the Han empire, in which *keigaku* scholars served as officials, there was no room for glorifying military prowess. Nakae does not mention it, but a similar phenomenon can be seen in the changing portrayals of Western heroes. Both the stern Deity of the Old Testament as well as Jesus Christ have been invoked for military and pacific movements alike.

One can sense in reading through Nakae's essays on the *Shang-shu* and on ancient Chinese thought generally that he was growing ever more exasperated by the twists introduced by *keigaku*. When he first began to discuss the *keigaku* movement, it was as a phenomenon in Chinese intellectual (and social) history as interesting in its own way as the texts it interpreted. By the conclusion of this last piece he would write on ancient China, Nakae still retains his scholarly approach but the emphasis has turned to the perversions of *keigaku*. After describing (with some irritation) how many of the chapter titles of the *Shang-shu* were invented by *keigaku* scholars of the Han dynasty, Nakae stops and wonders: "Why don't we plunge the same dagger into the body of the *Shang-shu* in the modern script" that Yen Jo-chü thrust into the Old Text version back in the eighteenth century?[27]

Scholars of the *Shang-shu* usually reserve a special place in twentieth century studies of the text for a path breaking essay by Naitō Konan (1866–1934), one of the principal founders of the Kyoto school of Japanese Sinology. In an essay published in 1921 (which Nakae may have seen), Naitō began the process of liberating the *Shang-shu* from the hands of *keigaku*, placing it in the arena of critical scholarship. He basically approached the text as a historian wondering how it took its present form. By critically examining its chapters, both in comparison to what allegedly later texts quote from them and from their use of language, he argued that one can reconstruct the development of Confucian thought. The changes in Confucian thought led scholars to insert numerous spurious elements into the text of the *Shang-shu*, and one can trace the history of Confucianism through them. This "intellectual prostitution" brought the text further and further from its original form. In the Han dynasty, as Confucianism became an ideology sanctioned by the state, the differences between various contending versions of the *Shang-shu* disappeared. "The fact that such [extensive] changes were made," Naitō concluded, "has to be the first consideration in studying the *Shang-shu*."[28]

Naitō was looking at the text externally as a whole, while Nakae was examining it internally. Nonetheless, both recognized that nothing historically significant could be said about the *Shang-shu* until the questions of how and why it took its present form were addressed. Naitō saw the history of Confucian thought written across the changes that the text had undergone, especially in the Han dynasty. Nakae did just what Naitō had suggested and devised a methodology to understand how chapters were composed in line with certain prototypes and basic lines of thought.

NAKAE'S APPROACH TO THE KUNG-YANG TEXTUAL TRADITION

Several years before he wrote these two pieces on the chapters of the *Shang-shu*, Nakae had written and printed (in one hundred copies) an essay on the *Kung-yang chuan* or *Kung-yang Commentary*, one of the three major commentaries on the ancient classic *Ch'un-ch'iu* (The spring and autumn annals), and the schools of thought that developed around it in the Han dynasty. In this long essay of June 1932, entitled "Kuyōden oyobi Kuyōgaku ni tsuite" (The *Kung-yang Commentary* and the *Kung-yang* school), Nakae first developed his ideas about how the *keigaku* movement influenced subsequent interpretations of texts and the institutionalization of Confucianism in the Han dynasty. It is undoubtedly the most complete of his later Sinological essays: It fits together as a unified whole, and he did not plan any further treatment of the subject.

This essay, written shortly after he printed his piece on the "P'an Keng" chapter of the *Shang-shu*, was heavily influenced by Nakae's newfound interest in Marxism. It includes a good number of passages that attempt, with only partial success, to carry the conclusions reached in the intellectual realm one step back to antecedent social, economic, or political causes. Those aspects of this essay will be addressed in the next chapter when we look at Nakae's understanding of the nature of Chinese society and the applicability of the label "feudalism" to describe it. Our main concerns here are the intellectual dimensions of the emergence and growth of classicism (*keigaku*) in the Han dynasty, the role of the *Kung-yang Commentary* in that process, and the development of distinctive *Kung-yang* schools of thought and what they did to the original text. In his essay cited above, Naitō Konan noted that the *Kung-yang Commentary* had been even more twisted by *keigaku* scholars in the Han to serve their own purposes than the *Shang-shu*. Nakae knew this and recognized as a result the central role that the *Kung-yang Commentary* must have played in the rise to prominence of *keigaku* itself.

Mencius once compared the compilation of the *Ch'un-ch'iu* by Confucius to the taming of the flood waters by Yü, reputed founder of the Hsia dynasty, and the pacification of the barbarians by the Duke of Chou. Given the great importance attached to this text by Chinese scholars right into the twentieth century, this is probably no exaggeration. Confucius was traditionally said to have written the *Ch'un-ch'iu*, a chronicle of his native state of Lu, and after his death Chinese interpreters of his work ferociously debated its meaning. A handful of commentaries on the *Ch'un-ch'iu* survived in the late Chou, of which three were most famous: *Kung-yang*, *Ku-liang*, and *Tso-chuan*. The former two represented the interpretations of the New Text school, the *Tso-chuan* that of the Old Text school.

In the Western Han dynasty, Confucian scholars made their peace with the state. Classical scholarship forged a bond with the imperial institution for mutual benefit, smoothly and rationally. The Han educational system (*shih-fa*) was based on specialization in a single classic or set of classics. In the process of the rise of *keigaku* to prominence in the world of thought, the *Ch'un-ch'iu* text managed to rise above the others in the scholarly debates of the time. Nakae suggests several possible reasons for how that occurred.

All *keigaku* scholars believed that Confucius had written the *Ch'un-ch'iu*. Already in the early Western Han there were many scholars who did not regard the text primarily as a chronology of historical events but as the fundament of knowledge itself. This was no mere record of historical facts spanning 242 years, in their eyes, but a record of how men should govern, in which Confucius had expressed himself through mundane historical facts.

Even more crucial to the rise of *Ch'un-ch'iu* studies in the Han era was the perception at the time that the text had been written with the Han (China's first, long-lasting, unified empire) in mind. The Han dynasty made the *Ch'un-ch'iu* its own. Ideas that scholars in the *keigaku* movement believed were in the text they tried to implement in Han society, and the bond between the Han state and *keigaku* gained added meaning by this approach to the *Ch'un-ch'iu* text. It not only strengthened the rise of *keigaku*, but it spelled the demise of the other non-Confucian schools of the late Chou (Mo-tzu, the Taoists, and others), usually referred as the *chu-tzu* (non-canonical schools). The scholars of the *Ch'un-ch'iu* and other Confucian scholars in the early *keigaku* movement not only successfully suppressed the *chu-tzu*, according to Nakae, but they borrowed and assimilated ideas original to the *chu-tzu*; and, they were able to affect reader's perceptions of the pre-Confucian texts (such as the *Shih-ching*, *Shang-shu*, and *I-ching* or *Book of Changes*) along the lines of their own substantial interpretations of them. As early as the early Eastern Han, Wang Ch'ung (27–90?) had perceptively noted that: "The Five Classics were established by the scholars of the Han dynasty."[29]

Only after the heyday of the New Text interpretations of the *Ch'un-ch'iu* did the *Tso-chuan* gain prominence. In other words, only after the Confucian *keigaku* movement had significantly vanquished study of the *chu-tzu* and had attained a position of ascendancy did the *Tso-chuan* emerge as a document to be studied seriously. Unlike the *Kung-yang* or *Ku-liang* commentaries, the *Tso-chuan* of the Old Text school in the Eastern Han treated the *Ch'un-ch'iu* as a historical record and could, Nakae argues, itself function as a historical account. Like Thucydides' history, the *Tso-chuan* reflects a conscious attempt to depict historical events faithfully at the time of conflict between the feudal lords and with special focus on the rivalry between the states of Lu and Ch'u. The New Text interpretations aimed at transmitting not the events but the "great idea" (*ta-i*) behind them. No major school of thought developed around *Ku-liang* but Nakae points out that the *Kung-yang Commentary* was important to a succession of intellectuals, even though the climate of thought underwent changes. He believed it was written as a Confucian philosophy of history based on the *Ch'un-ch'iu*, but in the Western Han was read by *keigaku* scholars as embodying their own interpretation of those annals. By the Eastern Han, Ho Hsiu (129–182) had created a *Kung-yang* school of thought as one branch of *keigaku*, completely different from his Western Han predecessors. This is the framework

Nakae uses for describing the process involved in the development of the *Kung-yang*: from a commentary on the *Ch'un-ch'iu*; to prominence as an established school of thought as seen in the work of Tung Chung-shu (ca. 179–ca. 104 B.C.E.), its representative in the Western Han; to a wholly new school of thought as seen in the writings of Ho Hsiu, its representative in the Eastern Han. By tracing the phenomenon in this way, one can also observe what elements became part of the *Kung-yang* school that cannot be found in the commentary itself. No other commentary on a classic in the Chinese cultural tradition became a text worthy of commentaries itself to the extent that the *Kung-yang Commentary* did. Able to spawn commentaries and interpretations of itself, the *Kung-yang Commentary* in the process transmogrified into a school of thought.

Nakae's first period is defined by the infancy and youth of the *Kung-yang Commentary*, when it still was regarded only as an interpretation of the *Ch'un-ch'iu*. At that point it was seen as providing not an explanation for the historical events depicted in Confucius' work but a philosophy of history based on the text of the sage. The text of the *Kung-yang Commentary* never denied the objective existence of the facts in the *Ch'un-ch'iu*, but used them as objects of analysis for a philosophical investigation. One of the elements Nakae sees as a possible cause for the appearance of a philosophy of history at this point in Chinese history is a confrontation between qualitatively different societies, as described below. In an extremely interesting comparison, Nakae argues that the first philosophy of history in the West, comparable to the *Kung-yang Commentary* in China, was Augustine's *De Civitate Dei*. Facing a clash with what he considered a fundamentally antagonistic system, Augustine wrote to attack heterodoxy, the social order of the Romans.[30]

As was the case with other ancient texts, the *Kung-yang*, the world's first philosophy of history in Nakae's view, was originally transmitted orally. It is in this sense of "transmission" or "tradition" that the character *chuan*, now usually translated as "commentary," should be understood. The text of the *Kung-yang* took its present written form, Nakae argues, in the early Western Han, before the full ascendency of *keigaku*. As proof, Nakae notes that Western Han *keigaku* emphasized the cosmological theories of *yin-yang* and the five elements in their explanations of phenomena natural or otherwise, and these notions are absent from the *Kung-yang Commentary*. These and other conceptions—such as a sophisticated theory of portents—are in fact not mentioned in the *Kung-yang Commentary*, but Tung Chung-shu, Ho Hsiu, and others working to develop schools of thought later effectively created these as points to be addressed in *Kung-yang* studies.

In Nakae's view, the *Kung-yang Commentary* embodied an interpretation of the *Ch'un-ch'iu* that saw in the annals' spare entries not a record of historical facts but the expression of ideas by means of those facts. It was the ideas that were of interest to those who composed and transmitted the *Kung-yang* text. He pointed out, for instance, that value judgments about the acquisition of hegemony appear throughout the *Kung-yang* text, but for elaboration of the *Ch'un-ch'iu's* entries that recorded fights for hegemony between two rulers, the *Tso-chuan*, with its narrative emphasis, was a better source than the *Kung-yang Commentary* which does not include them at all. This selective (or indifferent) treatment of historical facts in the *Kung-yang Commentary* suggests to Nakae that its compilers were less concerned with the events themselves than with the meaning events adumbrated. In Nakae's language, the *Kung-yang Commentary* was not history but the philosophy of history. Nakae likens this approach to Hegel's description of the idealist philosophy of history, in which the contemplative subject looks upon history as a means of creating a transcendent historical view without a crude reliance on factual experience. The same can be said of the *Kung-yang Commentary* in which historical facts are used as a medium or vessel for the Idea being communicated. The facts exist to give clarity to the "great idea," without which they are meaningless.

This posture assumed in the *Kung-yang Commentary*, Nakae warns, should not be seen as an expression of arrogance with respect to historical facts. On the contrary, the *Kung-yang Commentary* assumed a reverent attitude toward the facts recounted in the *Ch'un-ch'iu*. It could never, for instance, find errors in the text of the *Ch'un-ch'iu*, as the *Tso-chuan* claimed to have done. It contradicted the entire *Kung-yang* conception of the sanctity of Confucius' work to suppose even a mistaken or missing character, and the commentary went to pains to explain points where the problem is easily resolved by correcting a mistake in the transmission.[31]

In the *Kung-yang*, Nakae argues, the *Ch'un-ch'iu* is viewed as a call to raise the spirit of the "way of the king" (*wang-tao*) to fight off the alien "way of the barbarians" (*ti-tao*). The "way of the Chou" which had embodied this "way of the king" had tumbled into decline, taking society with it. The victory of the "way of the barbarians" symbolized the overturning of the proper social order, the demise of culture, and a gross impediment to the development of human life. Confucius understood this dilemma, in the perception of the *Kung-yang Commentary*, and was motivated to write the *Ch'un-ch'iu* to awaken the dormant "way of the king" and fend off tell-tale signs of creeping barbarism in Chinese society.

The *Kung-yang Commentary* made this distinction clearly between the Chinese and the aliens, between *hua* and *i* (2). Nakae notes, though, drawing on the work of Émile Durkheim, that it was not necessarily a moral distinction; rather, it seems to have been more on the order of a religious differentiation between the holy and the profane or impure. Although these two social orders were diametrically opposed, the *Kung-yang Commentary* recognized the possibility of passage from the unsacred to the sacred realm through a process of total transformation. The *Tso-chuan* took a stance of never the twain shall meet. For the *Tso-chuan*, an alien race or ethnicity meant, quite simply, a group of another order of species implying that those who were not Chinese were perforce barbarians.

The reason the *Kung-yang Commentary* counseled attack on the "way of the barbarian" was that the latter embodied a cultural antagonism (Nakae appropriated the term *Kulturfeindschaft* from the anthropological literature he was reading in German) to Chinese society and its "way of the king." It did not aim at repelling any particular alien society, but looked rather for the flourishing of the "way of the king" and the concomitant advances in civilized (Chinese) culture and society. Thus, the *hua-i* distinction was fundamentally one of culture. Although Nakae recognizes the possibility of movement from uncivilized to civilized within the general principles of the *Kung-yang Commentary*, he stops far short of arguing that a perfectly harmonious society with the complete abolition of the *hua-i* difference was the logical extension of ideals advocated in the text. This was the position of the *Kung-yang* school of the late Ch'ing dynasty, notably that of P'i Hsi-jui (1850–1908) and K'ang Yu-wei (1858–1927). The point here is that, as in the earlier cases of the *Kung-yang* schools of Tung Chung-shu and Ho Hsiu, not until some extraneous and entirely new element (in the case of the Ch'ing, Western thought linked to certain ideas from the "Li-yun" chapter of the *Li-chi*) was introduced into the system of this incarnation of the *Kung-yang* school could it read those new elements back into the original text and take on its new form.[32] One of the more interesting and telling aspects of the *Kung-yang Commentary* is its treatment of the "way of the king" in relations to the house of Chou. The Chou, symbol of the "way of the king," is held in the highest esteem throughout; but nowhere in the commentary is there any expectation that the house will be revived nor any hope placed on a new center for the "way of the king." *Kung-yang* schools in the Han dynasty did not look to re-create the Chou either, but they did aim for the creation of a new representative of the "way of the king." Thus, where the *Kung-yang Commentary* was thoroughly vague about the possibility of a new "way of the king," later *Kung-yang* scholars read in the "subtle words and great idea" of the text the need for a new one. This proved to be an important step toward their establishing legitimization of the Han dynasty in the text.

In earlier essays Nakae located the most basic of the Shang ruler's powers over his people in his control of ritual and religion. He was the ruler because he was master of all ceremonies, and he led the rituals because he was the head of the dominant lineage group. When the state emerged in importance as an entity unto itself, Nakae argues, a process of politicization affected the ceremonial grouping and began to dissolve the lineage organization of the Shang "state." While the Chou envisioned a state essentially similar to that of the Shang, the Chou ruling house boasted a more rationalized lineage organization and division of territory. In the Chou the Emperor remained head of a religious alliance within the state, while the feudal lords were simultaneously his assistants and counterparts within their states. In the early Chou, the feudal states were small and a power balance was easily maintained. As the dynasty proceeded and internal conflicts between contending feudal lords developed, the Chou house was unable to keep the balance as before; and gradually the ceremonial group around the ruler took on a greater political role, becoming concerned with military campaigns and the like.

Together with the politicization of the ceremonial group came the independence of politics from ceremony, for government was now no longer merely an accessory to ritual as it had been in Shang and early Chou theocracy. This development had a destructive effect on the old lineage organization, for local aristocrats were no longer willing to follow their sovereign's wishes where these collided with local power interests. In this manner, the ruler's power within the lineage organization as well as his authority that had derived from his position in the ritual community conflicted with the needs of the new state, and politics won. The intent of the *Kung-yang Commentary* seemed to point toward preservation of early Chou feudalism, but its conceptions of power and authority found fertile soil only within a state organization based on this more politicized structure contrary to the lineage basis of earlier times.

Another unresolved contradiction within the *Kung-yang Commentary* was its stress on land. Following his first lead in the world of Western social science, Georg Jellinek, Nakae argues that this emphasis is not the product of a lineage-based society but of the society that follows its demise. Only when the principle of personal jurisdiction declines does the significance of the land as inseparable from state life first arise. Similarly, the *Kung-yang Commentary* seems to stress the importance of the territory of the state more than the sovereign. While it links the ruler to the "gods of the soil and grains" (*she-chi*) and their fates for better or worse, the state's territory seems to possess a permanence above and beyond the sovereign. This represents a view altogether different from what we saw in the Nakae's understanding of ancient Chinese society. These apparent contradictions may reveal gaps in the *Kung-yang Commentary* as a full philosophy of history, but, Nakae argues, they also reflect conflicts within Chinese society at the time the text was set down.[33]

We now know from the work of scholars such as Nakae and George Kennedy that, contrary to the interpretation offered by the *Kung-yang Commentary*, the *Ch'un-ch'iu* made no special use of characters to indicate sanction and censure in a consistent manner and possessed no ethical unity.[34] The text began a process first to beatify Confucius as its reputed author, then to necessitate the finding of secret importance within the *Ch'un-ch'iu*, and finally to erect whole philosophies on that basis. By the Ch'ing dynasty, even the sanctification of Confucius was insufficient, and K'ang Yu-wei moved on to deification.

In the second period described by Nakae, *Kung-yang* scholarship appears as an ideology of a young Han society. This change required an effort to perceive a wholly new form and content in the *Kung-yang Commentary*, to arrive at an interpretation in which all of its seeming contradictions were resolved. More important, though, was the pivotal role played by *Kung-yang* studies and Tung Chung-shu, in particular, in the rise of *keigaku* in the Western Han. The *Kung-yang* school also facilitated the famous compromise of many Confucian scholars with the Legalist state by legitimizing that state with the authority of Confucius himself. The ideology that *keigaku* created, in Nakae's view, reached fruition only by the end of the Han, after which it had the generative capacity to serve subsequent centralized ruling houses. Although created for the Han, it was seized upon by later Chinese and "barbarian" rulers alike. In the Western Han, *keigaku* was still in its short-lived youth, still in its creative stage, whereas in the Eastern Han it aimed more ambitiously at a massive systematizing of many different strains of thought.

The fundamental distinctions Nakae draws between the *Kung-yang Commentary* of period one and the *Kung-yang* school of period two are all based on the conscious effort of the latter and Tung Chung-shu to establish a unified standard for learning within the context of life under the Han. *Keigaku* in the Western Han was vibrant, full of theories (portents, five elements, and the like) profoundly concerned with understanding life and natural phenomena in the world. *Kung-yang* studies in this second period introduced a wide panoply of new ideas into interpretations of the *Kung-yang Commentary*, among them the notions that Confucius was an "uncrowned king" (*su-wang*), that history might be periodized in "three eras" (*san-shih*), and that the *Ch'un-ch'iu* was a text that essentially taught the reform of institutions. What brought about this transition from period one to period two? Both the times and the social environment change, but in addition *Kung-yang* scholars began actively to combine their new conceptions of the universe with their scholarship. They accomplished this by reading into the *Ch'un-ch'iu* and the *Kung-yang Commentary* a theory of "revolution" or "change of mandate" (*ko-ming*) applicable really to Han society. This new reading gave the *Kung-yang Commentary* new meaning.

This highly synthetic notion of *ko-ming* claimed that, although the Ch'in had succeeded the Chou, its sovereigns had been unmandated. Therefore, to the Han fell the true mandate. Essential to this new view of things was that the *Ch'un-ch'iu* be outfitted with a full-fledged theory of *ko-ming*, which was of course absent until Western Han scholars provided it. The primary motivation for expounding the *ko-ming* idea in this way was to make the *Kung-yang Commentary* purely a Han commodity, a document that spoke from antiquity, with the authority of Confucius, directly to Han society. Given their instrumentalist approach to this text, clearly intellectuals of the *Kung-yang* school played an important role in the rise of *keigaku*, the legitimizing ideology of the new Han state.

Compared to the interpretative schemes of period one, those of Tung Chung-shu and his disciples expanded the scope of the *Kung-yang Commentary* immensely. In addition to dealing with questions of human nature, ethics, morality, and the reverence for the civil over the military, as well as reading the idea of the "rectification of names" into *Kung-yang* studies, the most conspicuous element of Tung's school was a view that the sovereign should nurture the people. Tung wrote on economic policy in an effort to impede further land annexations by the great clans of the Han, to restrict the extent of landownership allowed, to reclaim marsh and hill lands, to end the salt monopoly, and to limit sharply the number of persons forced into servitude. In Tung's view of the "way of the king," the "king" (*wang-che*) followed the will of heaven and brought moral instruction to the wayward people.[35]

An interesting example of how Tung expanded on the *Kung-yang Commentary* (and how Ho Hsiu and K'ang Yu-wei expanded on him) involved the notion of the "three eras" of history. At three points in the *Ch'un-ch'iu*—the death of Kung-tzu i-shih, the meeting of Duke Huan with several aristocrats, and the sighting of a *lin* (some sort of unicorn) during a hunt—the *Kung-yang Commentary* interrupts to pose a question and answer each time "different words are used for events seen, events heard, and events heard from others."[36] Somehow, Tung drew a parallel, although still a completely unclear one, with a conception of "disorder," "rising peace," and "great peace." Basically, all that Tung stated was that the idea of a coming "great peace" can be found in the *Ch'un-ch'iu*. It fell to Ho Hsiu, in Nakae's third period, to link the ideas of "great peace" and *ko-ming* in reading the *Ch'un-ch'iu*. In Ho's view "great peace" became a prediction exclusive to Han society. As Nakae puts it: "Tung Chung-shu's *Kung-yang* school bore the task of creating Han society, but the adulation of its perfection . . . belonged to Ho Hsiu."

The *Kung-yang* school of the Eastern Han, as typified by Ho Hsiu, had formally become one established part of a *keigaku* ascendant and complete. In content Ho combined the notion that the *Ch'un-ch'iu* had been written specifically for Han society with his view of the "three eras." Ho believed that Han society was indestructible. He also believed in the veracity of the popular works in the Han dynasty, written in imitation of the classics, that made predictions about the future (*wei-shu*) and used them as demonstrations of the Han's perfection of Confucianism: Confucius had envisioned some great structure as his objective in the *Ch'un-ch'iu*, according to Ho, and Han society encompassed it. Confucius had also predicted a society of "great peace," argued Ho, moving even further from the text, and so he wrote the *Ch'un-ch'iu* with the Han in mind. The notion of "great peace" is no longer vaguely associated with the text, because for Ho Hsiu the *Ch'un-ch'iu* was a book about "great peace" which Han society embodied.[37]

The revival of the *Kung-yang* school in the late Ch'ing was, significantly, a revival of Ho Hsiu's ideas more than those of Tung Chungshu's. K'ang Yu-wei's notion of the "three eras" now included some ideas impossible in Ho's day—Buddhist, Western—and the reinterpretation of other ancient works. The result was the mapping of the "three eras" onto Chinese history and the teleological invocation of a utopian future. The world of the late Ch'ing had changed much from Ho's day; and in the spirit of *Kung-yang* internationalism, K'ang graciously applied his periodization to the nations of the West as well.

The *Kung-yang* school had clearly come a long way from the *Ch'un-ch'iu* or even the *Kung-yang Commentary* itself. Although he has little to say about the late Ch'ing incarnation of *Kung-yang* studies, Nakae provided a scheme for the development of the *Kung-yang Commentary* from a philosophy of history, to an ideology for the new Han society, to a prophetic text singing the praises of Han peace. Few scholars have yet taken account of Nakae's contribution to the study of this issue; but the few who have, such as Niida Noboru (1904–1966),[38] have been deeply impressed. As with his major work on the organization of chapters in the *Shang-shu*, Nakae's study of the *Kung-yang* tradition may appear overly schematic, but in neither case has anyone done the appropriate work necessary to disprove his conclusions. That would be an immense task.

NAKAE AND HIS SOURCES (II)

More recent studies of the *Shang-shu* and the *Kung-yang Commentary* indicate that Nakae missed few, if any, Chinese sources or commentaries in organizing his analysis. Yet, in an otherwise definitive examination of the construction of the *Shang-shu*, Matsumoto Masaaki ignored or simply failed to mention Nakae's four essays on the subject. His work on the *Kung-yang Commentary* remains even less well known.[39] Few knew of his work before 1950 when the collection of his essays was first published, but since then those who have looked at these Sinological pieces have usually gone no further than to express awe at Nakae's painstaking work. With the possible exception of his essay on the "P'an Keng" chapter of the *Shang-shu*, little systematic effort has as yet been made by the specialists to incorporate Nakae's work on ancient China into scholarly debates.

In addition to its exhaustive detail from Chinese sources, another difficulty with Nakae's work for contemporary Japanese (to say nothing of contemporary Chinese) scholarship on ancient China is his insistence on bringing Western traditions of philosophy, history, and social science into his analytic framework. Not that scholars now ignore comparative perspectives, but by the early 1930s Nakae was no longer merely making comparisons. He was drawing directly on schools of European, particularly German, thought to elucidate his argument. Through the 1920s he read widely in a variety of fields and disciplines;

from the early 1930s he began to concentrate his reading in German idealism—Kant, Hegel, and Marx, in particular—and the Neo-Kantians of the early twentieth century as well. This predilection will find few followers in the world of contemporary studies of ancient China. Many Marxists may be upset by his special fondness for Kant or Hegel, and non-Marxists, such as Kaizuka Shigeki, find the "Marxist" nature of some of his conclusions difficult to accept.

As noted earlier, Nakae began reading Kant's *Kritik der reinen Vernunft* in January 1924, and in 1932 he read Kant's *Kritik der praktischen Vernunft* (Critique of practical reason). Over the next two years he perused both works a second time. The earliest work of Hegel's that Nakae cites is *Vorlesungen über die Philosophie der Weltgeschichte* (Lectures on the philosophy of history). Only later, after he had ceased doing Sinological research, did he read other works by Hegel. The other major thinkers he consulted in constructing the intellectual framework for these later Sinological essays all bore the Kantian imprint: Wilhelm Windelband, Wilhelm Dilthey, Heinrich Rickert (1863–1936), and, to a lesser extent, Georg Simmel (1858–1918).[40]

These men were all prolific German writers who, although they had taken issue with Kant, were nonetheless indebted to him for the philosophic structures on which they built their own work. All had also worked extensively in the field of the philosophy of history. We have seen Dilthey's concern with finding a methodology with the appropriate philosophical underpinning for historical inquiry. Nakae began reading Windelband, the earliest of all the neo-Kantians. The first to write a history of philosophy around issues rather than thinkers, Windelband was, like Nakae, concerned with methodological issues; whereas Nakae was more concerned with a rigorous method that would allow the contemporary scholar to understand the ancient past, Windelband sought to establish philosophy as its own discipline unencumbered by association with or reliance on other natural or human sciences. Nakae agreed with Windelband's thesis that the disciplines were separable only by virtue of their approaches, not the objects of their analysis. Natural (*nomothetic*) science seeks general laws, while historical (*idiographic*) science focuses on specific events.[41]

Rickert, whose work Nakae found least satisfying, disagreed both with Dilthey's subjective approach to the comprehension of historical reality and with Windelband's division of the natural and historical sciences. Insofar as it is possible to glean Nakae's view of this difference of opinion, his marginalia would indicate a preference for the views of Dilthey and Windelband. Simmel's view that the historian can never know the past because historical "facts" no longer exist and cannot be observed would find no support from Nakae.[42]

At the time Nakae began work on ancient Chinese thought, this debate over the philosophy of history was raging in scholarly circles in Europe. By one contemporaneous account, more scholars were involved in the study of the philosophy of history than in history itself.[43] This was the atmosphere in which Nakae puzzled through problems of Chinese philosophy. In his essay on the *Kung-yang Commentary*, Nakae was especially interested in the neo-Kantians not for their purely philosophical thought but for their views on the philosophy of history. Because he was arguing that the *Kung-yang Commentary* represented China's (and the world's) first work in the philosophy of history, it was essential to him to place his argument in the larger context of debate on the subject. He did not accept their views uncritically, as derisive notes in the margins of his copy of Rickert's *Die Probleme der Geschichtsphilosophie* (Problems in the philosophy of history) testify.[44]

At this point in his life, Nakae was not yet interested in establishing a philosophical stance of his own. He was no longer simply reading voluminously without design, and his philosophical preferences were becoming clearer. But his essays on the *Shang-shu* and the *Kung-yang Commentary* aimed specifically at devising methodologies to penetrate the *keigaku* world in which they had been formed, not at contributing to the philosophy of history. His work on the *Kung-yang Commentary*, though, did indirectly offer this text and the traditions of thought that followed it as an object worthy of analysis in the European debates on the philosophy of history and the history of textual traditions. No one has yet proceeded with the line of analysis Nakae initiated for the *Kung-yang Commentary*.

The events of the 1930s in Japan as well as in Western Europe were making it more difficult for Nakae to remain cloistered in Ts'ao Ju-lin's home. Despite his actions on 4 May 1919, Nakae was not a man of action. But he was deeply concerned by the rise of Fascism, Nazism, and militarism; and he found it increasingly troubling for his work to be so distant from the actualities of life in his day. We have seen how he allowed himself an occasional comparative or allegorical comment about his own time in his writing on antiquity. The larger philosophical question of how he could justify to himself and to his friends his continued work on the distant Chinese past, while the Japanese military was beginning to implement its plans to conquer Asia, was the most difficult to solve. His one written statement that directly confronts this subject appears in the introduction to his first essay on the organization of the *Shang-shu*; it is the subject of Chapter Six.

The essay in which Nakae brought past and present most closely together was his work on "feudalism" in China, to be discussed in the next chapter. Although not his strongest essay as Sinology, it was by far his most influential and the only one he allowed to be published. Examining it closely allows us also to understand somewhat better how Nakae was coping with the major issue of a scholar of antiquity concerned with a contemporary world going up in flames before his very eyes.

FIVE

The Nature of the Chinese Polity

China is quite peculiarly oriental.
G. W. F. HEGEL[1]

During Nakae's dry period from 1925 through mid 1930, his reading in Western works was directed mostly toward Western social science, philosophy, and Marxism. Under the influence of his friend Suzue Gen'ichi, he also began reading *International Press Correspondence* (organ of the Comintern) in English and *Rundschau* (a progressive daily) in German on a regular basis. One memoirist claims that Katayama Sen gave Nakae a complete set of Lenin's writings in the late 1920s, a point impossible to corroborate, though we do know he began reading works by Lenin, Engels, Kautsky, and a host of lesser Marxist figures. A set of Lenin's selected writings in German translation can now be found among Nakae's books, although there is not a note or any other mark on any of its pages.[2]

Given this direction to his reading and interests, it was indeed odd that Nakae's first essay after five years made no use whatsoever of Marxist thought. When he completed this piece in July 1930, he had only thirty copies printed, the shortest run he would ever issue. Either he realized that the three hundred he had ordered for his first essay was excessive, or, more likely, he was not planning to show this new piece to many people. It was, as a matter of fact, on a very narrow topic, the location of two fiefdoms of the late Chou. Its title, "Ei Ō no Shōyū to Chō

Gi no Shōo to ni tsuite" (Shang Yang's Shang-i and Chang I's Shang-yu) is bare; but no title is bare enough to prepare the reader for a text that so exhaustively reviews so many sources to solve so self-contained and limited a problem as this one does. His introduction to it reads now like an apology:

> To my honored friend, Mr. Ts'ao Ju-lin: It has been a long while since I have written anything. although the issue [I deal with here] is extremely trivial, I present it to you in the personal belief that it represents one small accomplishment. I think I would like next to write on the problem of why a feudal system like those in Europe and Japan never arose in China.[3]

Indeed, the last sentence points beyond the question at hand, as though some indication were needed that the author was capable of thinking about the larger issues he knew were absent from the present discussion. Despite the essay's limitations, however, to the student of Nakae's own intellectual development it at least offers concrete evidence that although his reading was taking him into ideological realms and theoretical historiographical systems, his own research methods continued to be characterized by thorough, empirical siftings through as much evidence on a point as he could gather.

The specific task of locating the two fiefdoms of Shang-i and Shang-yu necessitated reading through numerous texts, geographies, and gazetteers, and sorting out all the different place names and theories about them. In the end Nakae offers his own theory about where one might now look to find these ancient sites. The essay has none of the exciting suggestions offered in his first piece, nor any comparative perspective. It reads like a textual exercise on late Chou place names. It may be of interest to scholars of ancient China, but it has little wider interest.[4] One of the first people to whom Nakae showed this piece was his friend Itō Takeo of the South Manchurian Railway Company (SMR). As Itō remembered it: "It wasn't what I expected at all, and it seemed to me like a waste of time. I was ashamed of myself later, but I told Nakae [at the time] that I thought it was pedantic."[5]

Itō Takeo, although extraordinarily knowledgeable about contemporary China, knew little about earlier periods. Nakae may have been overly modest in deprecating this piece as "trivial," but it clearly covered a tiny corner in the universe of available antiquarian Sinology. One question never posed concerning this essay is why Nakae selected a topic in the Warring States period after having spent so much time and effort on the Shang and early Chou. Part of the answer, one must assume, has to do with the fact that heads of states in the Chou tried to found their capitals on the sites of known earlier capitals. Even when they did not, they used the names of earlier capitals, such as Shang-i and Shang-yu, in an effort to legitimize their actions. Thus, this work follows directly from his research on ancient Chinese cities.

Like his first work on ancient Chinese thought and his later writings, this essay stands out for its methodological rigor. No presumably informative text is left untouched, and nothing is accepted at face value. Here is the real importance of this essay. It was a strenuous effort to prove to himself (and perhaps to others) that he could do this sort of textual exercise. Nakae was forever conscious of the fact that he had never received formal Sinological training; and even though he had little good to say of the Japanese academy, he felt defensive about this lacuna in his background. Nakae reached his larger critique of the *keigaku* tradition only later. In this essay, he was still honing his own scholarly skills, sharpening his abilities to address more profound issues, at which time his Sinological talents in using a wide variety of Chinese sources, primary and secondary, would be taken for granted.

DID CHINA EVER HAVE FEUDALISM?

Nakae's next piece concerned the much larger question of why feudalism had not developed in China, a question that exercised the minds of many of the thinkers of his day. In December 1930 he had one hundred copies of an essay entitled "Shina no hōken seido ni tsuite" (On the feudal system in China) printed for distribution to friends and acquaintances. He asked Itō to publish this piece; and after reading it, Itō agreed to run it in the SMR scholarly journal *Mantetsu Shina gesshi* early the next year. This essay proved to be Nakae's most influential work on the Japanese world of China studies in the two generations after it first appeared. But, why did he all of a sudden want one of his essays published? And, why did he choose this particular piece, and no others before or after it, to appear in print?

In the late 1920s and early 1930s, Chinese intellectuals were vigorously debating the correct periodization of Chinese history. The controversy spawned large numbers of books and articles, and countless periodization schemes. Virtually all of the participants in what became known as the "debate on the history of society" accepted general Marxist notions of historical stages, and they mapped them as they saw fit onto three or four millennia of Chinese history. Most of the contributors were less specifically concerned with describing Chinese history accurately than they were with devising a scheme that properly explained the nature of the coming Chinese revolution: If China was currently a "feudal" society, then the country needed a bourgeois-democratic revolution; but if China could already be characterized as capitalist, then a socialist revolution was called for. A few participants in the debate (few, but some) argued that China was stuck, or had at some time been stuck, in the Asiatic mode of production; that analysis usually demanded an external impetus, such as foreign imperialism, to push China back onto the unilinear path to feudalism or capitalism.[6]

Because of the teleological nature of the debate, the conclusions of the debaters about earlier periods of Chinese history, however interesting they may be to the intellectual historian of twentieth century China, contain little of interest now to the historian of pre-modern China. Nakae was living in China during the entire controversy, and in Peking, one of the centers of it. He presumably was reading the material produced by the debate, although he never addressed himself to it directly. He usually confined his opinions about the contemporary Chinese scholarship with which he disagreed to his footnotes. And, there, hidden in the midst of this essay, one finds the following note concerning comparisons of Chinese and Western historical development, a central premise of the entire debate.

> Together with the spread of Western learning recently, the trend has grown among Chinese to make such meaningless comparisons. I haven't the least objection to applying Western methods and perspectives in Chinese studies, but it necessitates an attitude of exactitude and strictness. I simply cannot

fathom how these young Chinese, who should have a complete mastery of textual critical methods, so advanced in the Ch'ing dynasty, can make such infantile errors.[7]

In an untypical gesture, somewhat more directly addressed at the Chinese debate on periodization, Nakae "rejects altogether the so-called
Marxism popular recently among Chinese youth" and other theories
that are "basically crass materialism."[8] Elsewhere he says, again in a footnote, that: "It may be possible to overestimate the capacities of any one
individual, but the antithesis of this view can lead to an attitude which
completely ignores [the individual]. This notion that if something concerns emperors or aristocrats in the past that it cannot be of any importance, a historical view to be found among young Chinese [nowadays],
is deplorable."[9]

In his introduction to this essay on feudalism in Chinese history,
Nakae explains also that he planned to write this piece to work through
some of the doubts that he had had both about his own earlier work
and about the treatment that the issue of feudalism was receiving at the
hands of other scholars. He also mentions the comment made by "one
of my most trusted friends" (whom we now know to be Itō Takeo) that
his previous article on late-Chou place names was pedantry. Because he
was unwilling to concede the point, his reference to Itō's comment is
defensive; but this essay on feudalism was clearly meant to overcome
anyone's feeling that he was an ivory-tower pedant. Nakae seems to have
been upset by the "unexpected" remark, though one wonders what he
did expect from Itō, who was openly sympathetic to the radical workers' and students' movements in China, on the eve of the Japanese invasion. The comment did, though, make him rethink his ideas about the
character of peasant life in China's past.[10]

Nakae constructs his analysis around a counter-factual question:
Why had China *not* developed a feudal system like that of Europe or
Japan? The immediate dangers of plunging into the prefabricated net of
binding suppositions of a Marxist or other developmental scheme were
not lost on Nakae, but neither does he successfully avoid them. As soon
as one poses the question in the way Nakae does, one assumes that a society moves through stages of development, usually in a linear path,
toward some "modern" or "capitalist" (or both) point in time. Nakae

accepted the Marxist notion that the modern state represents the necessary product of the capitalist economy and that it emerges in a struggle
with its predecessor, feudalism. Not only Marx, but other late-
nineteenth century economists, historians, and sociologists (such as
Max Weber and Franz Oppenheimer) also recognized the transition
from feudal to capitalist society; and all had noted the apparent similarity between Japanese and European feudalism.

Nakae makes it clear from the outset that he does not believe China
ever developed anything remotely resembling European or Japanese feudalism with any staying power. Chinese society, he asserts, was "Asiatic"
from the beginning, by which he means that it was characterized by a
central authority that monopolized control of crucial public works like
irrigation systems and by the absence of private landownership among
the general population, which was distributed in villages rather than
cities. He is quick to distance himself from the prevailing Marxist argument concerning the "Asiatic mode of production," because those few
economists and historians who made the claim for China's being "Asiatic" in the Marxist sense usually forced it out of the few scattered
remarks on China and India by Marx and Engels on the subject. The
principal Soviet theorist of Asiatic society, some of whose work Nakae
read in German translation and some in Japanese translation, was Liudvig I. Mad'iar (the Russian name of the Hungarian-born Lajos Magyar,
1891–1940). "It's only natural," Nakae notes, "that Mad'iar who is a
Marxist esteems Marx's explanations as much as he possibly can, but
since I am not a Marxist, I need not assume such an attitude."[11] Be that
as it may, Nakae's views on "Asiatic" society in China strongly resemble
Marx's. Nakae's disdain for Marxists reflected a personal distaste for
unblinking fidelity to the master's theories, not for Marx's ideas
themselves.

Two topics actually underlie Nakae's argument, although it ostensibly deals only with the problem of why feudalism did not develop.
Closely connected to the stated question is the problem of explaining
the nature of China's "Asiatic" society and how it had prevented feudalism from developing as it had elsewhere. Both of these issues were more
widely fashionable in the late 1920s and 1930s than they are now, not
because we now have the answers but because the focus of our inquiries

has shifted. Many Chinese, Soviet, and Japanese (although considerably fewer than in the past) still struggle with these issues in their scholarly journals. Nakae's main contribution to the long debate on the nature of "Asiatic" society was to bring a non-Marxist perspective to bear on the sources. He used a wide variety of Chinese materials as well as European social science (including Marxist) writings in an effort to elucidate the problem.

In a statement that would now be considered either bold or completely misguided, Nakae claims that no independent, intermediary authority or power was ever recognized in principle between the Chinese people and their emperor. This framework fit well with his earlier depiction of Shang and Western Chou society: a ruler with complete control over his subjects in an *i* based on one ruling lineage. In that society, a person belonged either to the ruler's lineage or to the great mass of "the ruled." The ancient conception of a "state" was not territorial but described that residential area, which often changed, in which the ruler's lineage held sway. The economy of the *i* served the ruler and his family only; and it lacked so much as the hint of an exchange economy.[12]

In restating key points from his essay on ancient Chinese political thought, Nakae observes that the Chou had conquered the alien Shang and recreated what he had earlier referred to as the *Geschlechterstaat* (lineage-based state). From the Spring and Autumn and Warring States periods, however, the lineage-based state (the Chou "feudal" or *feng-chien* system) began to decline and the "territorial" state began to emerge in its place. The contention for power among small, locally based states brought the "land" conception of a state into currency, and gradually the theocratic foundation of the ruler's authority gave way to brute force as final arbiter. China was still divided, however, and would have to await the Ch'in era before a major transformation could occur.[13]

Although the Ch'in traditionally received the least sympathetic treatment of any dynasty in China's long history, it nonetheless played the most important role in the development of the Chinese state and society, according to Nakae. Shih Huang-ti established for China the only state form it would ever know, and the Asiatic economy on which it was founded repelled the dispersive trend of the late Chou back toward unity and away from something more closely resembling feudalism elsewhere. This "great state form" (*dai kokka tai*)—namely, the omnipotent state characteristic of a society dominated by the Asiatic mode of production—allowed for no meaningful opposition to the power of the throne. Similarly, in the Ch'in and the Western Han which followed it, a kind of enfeoffment was effected by the center but of meritorious individuals who had served the royal house, not of imperial relatives.

Chou "feudalism" had been lineage-based, while the Ch'in and Western Han states were absolute monarchies in which power resided with the imperial institution. While both systems aimed at supporting the imperial house, the Chou enjoyed a smoother integration between state and society because politics always reflected the Chou's structure of central power. In the Ch'in, Han, and subsequent dynasties, the fact that the emperor was head of the imperial lineage was irrelevant to political life because sovereign authority was based solely on power. Agriculture provided the basis for both societies, but the change brought about by the Ch'in greatly altered the position of the peasantry vis-à-vis the state. Whereas in the Shang and Western Chou peasant status resulted from belonging to a conquered or alien (non-aristocratic) lineage, from the Han on this was no longer at issue. The peasantry from that time forward constituted a ruled class plain and simple.

Liu Pang's (r. 206–194 B.C.E.) system of enfeoffment allowed his "feudal" lords certain legal, tax assessing, and military powers; but again, Nakae insists, China never developed a system of landholding and governance that invested real power in the feudal lords who were vassals to the king. This was true, Nakae argued, because the central government retained control of public works throughout the kingdom; the "great state" conception of the nation under the ruler did not allow for the development of regional centers of power where feudal lords could rule independently, rendering only nominal allegiance to the king. Instead, it was the extension of authority to lords by the king that was only nominal, and the lords were unable to wrest control of their territories from the central authority. When seven feudatories rebelled during the reign of Han Ching-ti (r. 156–149 B.C.E.), their lords were defeated and the powers of feudal lords generally were crushed. Strong policies against the accumulation of power by vassals accompanied the accession of Han

Wu-ti (r. 140–86 B.C.E.). Following reforms enacted by Ching-ti, Wu-ti moved further toward the centralization of power by dividing the "feudal" states into smaller units. In the end, the "feudal" lords were deprived of power. In sum, Nakae points out that the failure of the Han effort to invest the new imperial system with the spirit of Chou feudalism was due to the impossibility of coexistence between the "great state form" and its absolute autocracy together with territorial powers. China remained "Asiatic."[14]

The Eastern Han also attempted to implement a vague system of enfeoffment that allowed for a certain independent power on the part of the feudal lords; but having learned the lessons of previous eras, its "feudal" lords required imperial sanction for official appointment to local government. In this way the center kept a close watch on the "feudal" lords, and the latter were powerless with respect to the throne.

When the Eastern Han broke up in the early third century, the only basis for power in the Three Kingdoms (220–265) was real power itself; for legitimizing arguments and claims to be the true claimant to the throne provided nothing to buttress the position of a pretender. This would have been the time for a feudal aristocracy to develop in China as it did in Europe and Japan, an aristocracy with a measure of regional control that insured its becoming more than an imperial pawn. In this period of nearly four centuries of disunion, internecine warfare, continual foreign invasions, and repeated regicides, one might expect from the experience of other parts of the world to see the ascendancy of a feudal system with a regionally powerful military aristocracy. That a system easily identifiable as feudalism did not emerge is one of the great enigmas of Chinese history, and explanations have been debated by generations of scholars.[15] As Nakae notes, the Wei dynasty (220–265), founded by Ts'ao Ts'ao (155–220) and his son Ts'ao P'i (186–226), enfeoffed descendants of the Ts'ao family as feudal lords, but these lords lived in dread of the power of the Wei throne. When Ts'ao Chih (192–232), third son of Ts'ao Ts'ao, requested that they all return to the Wei capital and become court aristocrats, no unified opposition to the center was voiced.

The Western Chin (265–316) briefly reunified China; and, Nakae argues, having learned from the experience of the Han and Wei dynasties of the problems that could arise among royal princes, it avoided them by not enfeoffing members of the imperial house. Instead the highest military men were installed locally with responsibility directly to the center. This system institutionalized the presence of an imperial agent at the local level and served as a reminder that central power could be mobilized in bad times or when an alien invaded. Thus it was intended, says Nakae, to calm the people's mind. It might also have insured the generation of a military aristocracy over which the central government often had difficulty keeping control.

Feudal lords in the Western Chin had the right to appoint subordinate officials, although the center retained the right of appointment for all important posts. Nakae ultimately has to argue that they were not really feudal lords in anything but name, for in fact they were officials of the central government. The land belonged to the local Chin lord insofar as rent and tax collection were concerned, but he had no independent power over it as a territorial lord. As a result, vassalage was not highly prized whereas a position at the central court was. Removal from the center became a punishment visited on lords who lost out in struggles with the court. Although "feudal lords" in name, they more closely resembled their predecessors in the Western Han after the reforms of Wu-ti and in the Eastern Han. To the extent that subsequent states during the period of division had something resembling a "feudal" system, it followed this model.[16]

In the T'ang (618–907) system of regional commanderies Nakae finds the best evidence for feudalism in China. "Even school children," he notes, "know that the predominance of the regional commanderies was a cause of the fall of the T'ang dynasty, but how was it that they became so powerful as to last through the Five Dynasties period [907–960] as fully independent states in opposition, and then within a century Sung T'ai-tsu [founder of the Sung dynasty, r. 960–976] reverted to the old pattern of the 'great state form'? The reason is that China was an Asiatic society, and no other state form could be implemented."[17] Originally the regional commanderies had been founded as defensive outposts to protect against potential barbarian invaders. Eventually the generals who controlled them became extremely powerful, all but independent of the central government. T'ang efforts to destroy their might proved Pyrrhic at best, completely ineffective at worst.

Using the most famous examples of An Lu-shan (d. 757) and Shih Ssu-ming (d. 761), Nakae demonstrates that although the military commissioners who controlled the regional commanderies had private armies, the territory under their control, the predominantly non-Han populations living there, and the tax monies that came with local control, they did not attempt to create sovereign states. When the T'ang finally collapsed, the states of the Five Dynasties period retained the appearance of T'ang regional commanderies. In fact, he notes that the founders of the Latter Liang (907–923) and Latter T'ang (923–936) both had served as military commissioners in the T'ang. Following the work of Ou-yang Hsiu (1007–1072), Nakae argues that this era of continual warfare had all the ingredients for the formation of an independent military class. States were based on their military capacities, and yet no such military aristocracy as one sees in Japan and the West emerged. The reason, he argues, had to do with the fact that, because of the Asiatic despotic nature of Chinese society, soldiers served their officers like slaves, but when separated from the troops they became bandits; they were never able to generate a consciousness of themselves as a group. Eventually the Sung (960–1127) reunified China under the only state form conceivable, that of the all-powerful state. Later, the Ming (1368–1644) effected a feudal system in name, but like that of the Eastern Han its feudal lords had no significant power and no independent territorial control.[18]

Conquest dynasties—Khitans (907–1125), Jurchens (1115–1234), Mongols (1271–1368), and Manchus (1644–1911)—present a different kind of problem for Nakae's analysis. From the fall of the T'ang, China lived under the perpetual threat or actuality of foreign invasion and domination. These nomadic and semi-sedentary peoples of the North and West brought a system of control to bear on the Chinese similar on the surface, Nakae notes, to the dominant lineage-based system of the Shang and Chou. Unlike the Shang and Chou, though, the Mongols, for example, were completely ignorant of the advantages offered by an agrarian society. The famous case of the advice given to Chinggis Khan (1167?–1227) by his advisor Yeh-lü Ch'u-ts'ai (1190–1244) *not* to depopulate North China and turn it into grazing lands for the Mongol herds speaks to this underdeveloped economic sensibility. The same backwardness can be seen in the Mongols' initial understanding of the Chinese political system and its culture, although by the time they conquered China in 1271, the Mongols had advanced far beyond the Khitans and Jurchens at a comparable juncture on account of cultural contact in the Western regions of their empire.

A second trait of conquest dynasties was the military absolutism they used to control the domestic population. The conquerors differed from the Chinese in language, ethnicity, customs, and ways of life. They regarded the realm as their family property, and they instituted a form of despotism to control it. Nakae quickly differentiates the kind of despotism seen under the Khitan, Jurchen, and Mongol regimes from that of the Chinese themselves. The conquerors combined absolutism with the coercive force of a militaristic state. These herdsmen and hunters exercised an uninhibited tyrannical reign over the sedentary agrarian population. They understood far better than the Chinese the need for extreme autocratic military discipline, and as a result their troops were always better trained than those of any agricultural people. However, this distinction bore the seeds of destruction for military autocracy in China. The Chinese were thoroughly wedded to the land and were capable of absorbing considerable abuse from their conquerors, but in the end they marshaled resistance and the foreign invaders were always expelled.

A third characteristic of conquest dynasties cited by Nakae concerned the growth of a privileged class around the ruling lineage or clan. The Khitan and Mongol regimes kept everything for themselves, while the Jurchens and Manchus developed systems of ethnic privilege, particularly in their native military structure, with their ruling ethnic group on top. The Mongols went so far as to prohibit ownership of weapons by Han Chinese. As a conquering group, they possessed what Franz Oppenheimer referred to as the mentality of a *Junker*, the privileged landowning class. But even the distinctive military organizations of the Jurchens and Manchus never developed into an ascendant military class like those of Europe and Japan. These "primitive conquest states" effectively exerted no influence on the state form of the conquered. "In the immense majority of cases," Nakae quotes from Engels's *Anti-Dühring*, "where conquest is [effectively] permanent [as in the Ch'ing dynasty], the more barbarian conqueror had to adapt himself to the higher 'economic situation' as it emerges from the conquest; he is assimilated by the vanquished and in most cases he has even to adopt their language."[19]

In sum, Nakae argues that although China had on several occasions developed in the direction of a feudal system, it never fully reached that point. Every time China had been on the verge of feudalism, it had been held back by internal social and political forces which it apparently was unable to overcome. It remained an "Asiatic" society.

Nakae's conception of "Asiatic" society breaks down into four characterics. First, public works were the responsibility of the central government alone, and local initiatives in this direction had to be channeled through the center. Second, aside from a handful of large cities, China in its entirety was divided into many thousands of "village bodies" (*sonraku dantai*), each of which formed its own universe with its own fully independent structure. Third, the most basic requirement for agriculture, irrigation, was the responsibility at various levels of the "village body," the local administrative unit, or the central government. And, finally, no system of free landownership existed, because the state was the sole owner of the land.

Nakae was not so naïve as to think that these four conditions were absolutes in China's case. He knew, for instance, that Chinese cities had long developed commercial relations and that urban dwellers had used commercial (or usury) capital in coercive relations with village peasants. The point was that the basis of China's economic structure remained, *mutatis mutandis*, one of "village bodies" grounded in their local autonomous structures. These numerous cells knew no intermediary power between themselves and the emperor (who ultimately owned all of their land), and they had little lateral contact with other cells like themselves.[20]

Thus, in Nakae's view, China's economic structure had persistently remained at precisely the same level since Ch'in Shih Huang-ti assumed the throne in 221 B.C.E. It was "Asiatic" with the "great state form" imposed on top. The former insured that local society would never organize to contest the center for local authority; the latter insured the center the full complement of autocracy it required. And, no intermediary of consequence—no vassal system as in Europe or daimyō system as in Japan—emerged in the great vacuum between the two. In place of the standard of feudalism that "no land lacks for a lord," the Chinese state might be characterized as all land under heaven belonged to the monarch. In *Allgemeine Staatslehre* Georg Jellinek argued that "the feudal system creates independent power in land. Its background, together with the substance of state power, gradually disappear from historical memory." This development, Nakae concludes, never occurred in Chinese history: "The first step in the process of moving toward a modern state, conflict between the king and the aristocrats, cannot so much as be sensed in a dream in China."[21]

China's classical scholarship (*keigaku*) developed its distinctive character because it had been nurtured in its growth by "Asiatic" society and the economic base accompanying it. *Keigaku*, as he describes it in his essay on the *Kung-yang Commentary*, provided the "great state form" with an ideology in the Han dynasty because it tied its fate to the rise and fall of the Han. The very concept of a supreme "Son of Heaven" was in large part the creation of *keigaku*. Long after the Han dynasty had collapsed, the "great state form," Asiatic society, the imperial system, and *keigaku* lived on. The reason that *keigaku*, ostensibly created for Han society, was able to survive the demise of the Han lay in the simple fact that *keigaku* as it emerged full force in the Eastern Han was even more fully equipped for "Asiatic" society in general. It continued to reign through the rise and fall of dynastic houses, even in the culturally less developed regimes of foreign conquerors. Of course, new elements, from Buddhism and elsewhere, entered the larger *keigaku* system; but it always retained its essential "Asiatic" core, at least until the time of the Opium War.[22]

THE THEORY OF "ASIATIC" SOCIETY:
NAKAE'S CONTRIBUTIONS AND INFLUENCE

The concept of "Asiatic" society has a long history in Western political thought. Until modern times, it usually was a designation for alien societies in the East (the Orient) where despotism reigned and history stood still; and it was never the result of scholarly inquiry or even extensive travel and observation. With the rare exception of those who used it as a foil to attack absolutism or papism (as in the cases of Montesquieu [1689–1755] and Rousseau [1712–1778]), terms such as "Oriental" or "Asiatic" society became terms of derogation.

In the late eighteenth and nineteenth century, these earlier portrayals of Eastern society as having attained perfect stability and stasis became the foundation for historicizing it into the distant past of world historical progress. As progress became the quintessential element of modernity, the Orient was found woefully lacking; and the overarching might of Oriental despotism was cited as the cause for this. Such ideas as that China had no history, remained unchanged for centuries, knew nothing of private property and individual liberty, and the like were common among such varied thinkers of the time as Johann Gottfried von Herder (1744–1803), Georg Wilhelm Friedrich Hegel (1770–1831), Karl Marx (1818–1883), Adam Smith (1723–1790), James Mill (1773–1836) and his son John Stuart Mill (1806–1873).[23]

Marx argued here and there in his writings that the all-powerful state in Asia monopolized economic initiative, inhibited class competition, and thus caused stagnation.[24] After Marx's death, Engels labored, largely without success, to integrate his ideas into their larger theoretical system. Shortly after the founding of the Soviet Union, a debate that spilled over into China and Japan developed over what was now dubbed the "Asiatic mode of production."[25] In theory, it was concerned primarily with elucidating a theory of Asiatic society consistent with what Marx and Engels had written on the subject; in fact, it was more concerned with fitting the theory to the actions to be taken in the Chinese revolution of the late 1920s.

The foremost supporter of the idea that Marx and Engels had advocated a distinctive mode of production that characterized Asian society was Liudvig Ignat'evich Mad'iar, whose views most closely resembled Nakae's own. Born in Hungary and arrested for his activities in the 1919 revolution there, Mad'iar was released in a prisoner exchange with the Soviet Union. In Russia he worked for both TASS and *Pravda*, before accepting a position with the diplomatic service in China from 1926 through 1927. He returned to Moscow to become chief of the Oriental Department of the International Agrarian Institute (1928–1929) and later deputy chief of the Oriental Secretariat of the Executive Committee of the Comintern (1929–1934). In 1934 he fell victim to the great purges.

During his stay in China, Mad'iar collected the materials for his most influential work, *Ekonomika sel'skogo khozaiastva v Kitae* (China's rural economy), published in 1928 and soon translated into Chinese several times. Mad'iar argued that the Asiatic mode of production had characterized Chinese society until the beginning of the twentieth century, at which time feudal and bourgeois notions of private property began to color China's overall economy. Nonetheless, Asiatic remnants (important to the direction of the Chinese revolution) remained in place. This volume represented the most developed exposition of the Asiatic mode of production then available in the Marxist world.[26]

Like other "Aziatchiki" (Mikhail D. Kokin [1906–1939], S. A. Dalin, G. Papaian, and A. I. Lomakin), as the supporters of an Asiatic mode became known by their opponents, Mad'iar accepted the geographical specificity of Marx's original Asiatic mode. As a result, he rejected a single universal, unilinear, developmental path along which *all* societies travel. In subsequent writings prior to 1931, such as his *Ocherki po ekonomike Kitaia* (Studies on the Chinese Economy, 1930), and his lengthy introduction to *"Tszin'-Tian": Agrarnyi stroi drevnogo Kitaia* (*Ching-t'ien*: The agrarian structure of ancient China, 1930) by Kokin and Papaian, Mad'iar continued to develop his theory of the Asiatic mode production in China. In the last of these works, he argued that four characteristics of Oriental society could be drawn from the work of Marx and Engels: the absence of private landownership; the necessity of artificial irrigation and a massive public works structure; the rural commune; and despotism as the form of the state.[27]

Nakae entered the discussion of Asiatic society as the debate in the

Soviet Union was winding down and just as it was growing more heated in China and Japan. His work was nonetheless distinctive in several ways. First, although not to his own mind a Marxist, he accepted the standards for Asiatic society as elaborated by the foremost Aziatchik, Liudvig Mad'iar. Although Mad'iar had, under pressure in the Kremlin, revised his original book to exclude the prominent place he had given the Asiatic mode, Nakae once told his friend Katō Koretaka that he was "satisfied with Mad'iar's [original] explanations." Niida Noboru noted in a review essay after the war that Nakae's essay "virtually nailed down Mad'iar's theories on Asiatic society," though Niida himself was far from being in full agreement.[28] Second, Nakae never used the Japanese expression then and now current for the Asiatic mode of production, *Ajia teki seisan yōshiki*, or the Chinese term *Ya-hsi-ya sheng-ch'an fang-shih*. Instead, he spoke of *Ajia teki shakai* (Asiatic society) and occasionally of *Ajia teki keizai shakai* (Asiatic economy and society). His reluctance to use the accepted term for the Asiatic mode of production probably derived from a desire not to be seen as a participant in a debate of Marxist insiders, many of whose writings he found considerably wanting. Nonetheless, his initial motivation for addressing the issue of feudalism in China derived from what he perceived as the sloppy way many Chinese and Japanese Marxists used such terms.

The Aziatchiki in the Soviet Union were ultimately crushed because their views ran counter to the regime's desired direction in the Chinese revolution. While an "Asiatic" designation could arguably have made China ready to fight the socialist revolution, Stalin was only prepared for China to fight for bourgeois democracy. The most striking quality of Nakae's contribution was his ability to use numerous Chinese sources in support of his argument for Asiatic society, without having his vision obstructed by a primary concern for the future of the Chinese revolution. No one before or since, including Karl A. Wittfogel (b. 1891), who has seriously entertained the Asiatic mode of production as an adequate description of China at any time in its history, has been so well based in the original Chinese materials.

In basically accepting Mad'iar's arguments about Chinese society, Nakae may actually have been closer to Marx's own position than many "Marxists" who attacked Mad'iar. Nakae's notion of the "great state form" with one ruler and no intermediate authority between him and the people was identical to Mad'iar's conception of the despotic state. His notion that large-scale public works were the responsibility of the central government and the related idea that China lacked a developed sense of free landownership both closely resembled Mad'iar's ideas. His understanding of the conditions necessary for a feudal system far exceeded that of Mad'iar or any of the Aziatichiki, probably because they were usually more concerned with finding China's proper road to revolution. Nevertheless, he and they were both aware that despite countless peasant rebellions throughout Chinese history, the Asiatic social order had always been able to absorb its attackers and grow stronger. And, all agreed with Marx that the intrusion of Western imperialism in the nineteenth and early twentieth centuries had finally (although not completely) dislodged Asiatic social relations.

One of the major issues in developing an adequate theory of the Asiatic mode was how to account for the seeming anomaly of cities (the world's largest in the case of China), engaged in something resembling commerce, if the state and society were supposed to be locked into a static, immobile, agrarian structure. This was important both for Marx and for Max Weber, for both believed that commercial centers arose only as capitalism developed and were thus impossible in any meaningful sense in an Asiatic society. Marx skirted the problem of China by relying on sources that dealt primarily with India, although even their veracity remains dubious. The Asian city in his view had no autonomy whatsoever; it was either an administrative site, a garrison town, or a point at which foreign trade was transacted.

> In Asiatic societies, where the monarch appears as the exclusive proprietor of agricultural surplus, whole cities arise, which are at bottom nothing more than wandering encampments ... Asiatic history is a kind of indifferent unity of town and countryside (the really large cities must be regarded here merely as royal camps, as works of artifice erected over the economic construction proper).[29]

Max Weber stressed other factors, a constricting bureaucracy in particular, but his conclusions were the same: Oriental cities were not real cities in the Western mold.

Nakae was not restricted by ignorance when it came to the existence of Chinese cities. He had described them, the *i*, as centers for the ruling lineage in ancient times; and he had detailed his understanding of the structure of power in them, fully in accord with his ideas concerning Asiatic society. What he had not done was to draw his picture in any detail beyond the Eastern Chou. Ultimately, he ignored this problem. Early in his essay on Chinese feudalism, he states as a characteristic of China's Asiatic society that "aside from a few large cities, the entire country is broken up into village bodies which possess completely independent structures, [each] forming a small world" of its own. He reiterates this point at the end of this essay by associating it with Marx's view that the key to comprehending unchanging Asiatic societies lay in these "village bodies."[30]

Presumably Nakae meant by "village body" the equivalent of Marx's vague notion of the village commune, the Russian *mir* in his famous letter to Vera Zasulich (1849–1919). Marx did recognize the existence of a sense of community or *Gemeinschaft* in the Asiatic village system, a solidarity or proclivity to cooperate rather than compete as would have been the case in class societies under feudalism or capitalism. In his earlier writings he made no link between this cooperative spirit pervading societies that predated the development of individuality and the future "communist" inter-reliance of humanity; he insisted instead that Asiatic societies would have to be destroyed as a precondition to the creation of socialism. In later writings, as in his letter to Zasulich, the jump into socialism (without the otherwise necessary stages of development) came to seem more possible.[31]

Nakae held no such illusions about China. His picture of the Chinese population atomized into village bodies, all but incapable of lateral coordination, hopelessly trapped in an unchanging economic state of subservience, and all individually beholden to the emperor, the centerpiece of the Asiatic "great state form," is an exceedingly depressing one. Like the early Marx, Nakae looked to the intervention of capitalism and interdependence within the world economy as a beacon of progress away from stagnation. Whereas Marx's increasing disgust with European capitalism and imperialism led him to place more hope in the possibility of Asian societies' creating their own indigenous, non-capitalist paths to socialism, Nakae simply became more depressed.

Nakae's ideas about village body or village community exerted a strong though indirect influence on Japanese scholars after him, primarily through the intermediacy of Shimizu Morimitsu (b. 1904), who encountered Nakae's ideas when he was formulating theories that were to become part of a major debate after the war. Shimizu, who assisted in the editing and compiling of Nakae's writings for publication in 1950,[32] was one of the many researchers employed by the Research Department of the South Manchurian Railway Company whom Nakae knew in Peking when he was writing "On the Feudal System in China." Trained as a sociologist, although learned in the methods and sources of Sinology, Shimizu went to China to study the structures of its guilds, state, villages, and the family. The basic problem he posed for himself, in a series of essays published between 1936 and 1938, and revised for a book in 1939, was to explain the relationship between the organization of village society and the despotic power of the state. In this book, he acknowledged his agreement with Nakae that the imperial Chinese state from post-Chou times was the unitary "great state form"; but Shimizu devoted the bulk of his energies to the other side of the equation: the Chinese village.

Influenced, as Nakae had been, by the debate in Russia over the Asiatic mode of production, Shimizu argued that the cornerstone of Chinese despotism was the agrarian commune, or *kyōdōtai* as he called it, using a Japanese neologism in its first application to Chinese social organization in relation to despotism. (The term had been coined in the early twentieth century to translate the German word *Gemeinde*, or community, and was used by sociologists and anthropologists to stress the bonds that unite the constituent members of premodern social groupings; it was subsequently tied to the debates over the Asiatic mode of production.)

The rural *kyōdōtai* in China, Shimizu argued, were too isolated to unite or form horizontal links one with the other either for mutual benefit in matters like irrigation projects or for mutual resistance to the central imperial power. Instead, the need for water projects and the government's administrative capacity to carry them out reinforced the despotic control of the emperor.[33] This theory of *kyōdōtai* closely parallels Nakae's theory of *sonraku dantai* or village bodies. Shimizu quotes from Nakae's essay on feudalism to substantiate the claims that these self-regulating "village bodies" were always the basis of China's economic organization and that no intermediate, independent power existed between the village and the center. And, as if to underscore the importance of Nakae's ideas, Shimizu added: "These words have extremely profound implications." For example, if Chinese society could be characterized in the way Nakae had, then one might understand why a society millennia old had still not produced a feudal system; one could point, as Shimizu was doing in following Nakae's lead, directly to the structure of China's age-old social organization, the *kyōdōtai*.[34] Shimizu carried these thoughts into the debates on *kyōdōtai* and the Asiatic mode of production, which had an extended life eventually diverging from these origins. Yet, his conception of *kyōdōtai* as a primitive, isolated, microcosmic realm derives primarily from Nakae's earlier description of rural China.[35]

By a sad irony, Nakae's ideas through Shimizu's transmission had their greatest currency when their author was most obscure. Nakae came to be honored posthumously; but while his reputation grows on account of his moral example and his work is now widely available, the one essay he published during his lifetime is unlikely to be influential. In the late twentieth century, non-Marxist historians outside the socialist world no longer consider feudalism in China a topic of central importance, and strict adherence to schemes of developmental stages in history is no longer as popular as it once was. In fact, fifty years later, Nakae's essay on feudalism seems to have something pronouncedly wrongheaded about it. For one thing, the fundamentally counterfactual question of why feudalism did *not* develop is obviously no longer a burning issue to historians who do not expect it to develop everywhere (and are able to live with that fact). For another, scholarship has shown that there most assuredly were institutions of state and society between the center and the locality in pre–Opium-War China. Even the great stress on state control of irrigation has been shown to ignore many aspects of local initiative and control by the local gentry as well as other elements of local social organization. Nevertheless, Nakae's idea of *sonraku dantai* was seminal; and though the conclusions about *kyōdōtai* and the nature of Chinese social organization have changed, his and Shimizu's work were instrumental in directing scholarly inquiry to vital issues.

Part Three
Nakae's Mature Thought and Vision

Associates of Nakae Ushikichi. From left: Katō Koretaka, Suzue Gen'ichi, Sakatani Ki'ichi, Ts'ao Ju-lin, Itō Takeo, unidentified, at funeral service for Nakae, 1942.

SIX

Integrating the Past and the Present

Nakae put the finishing touches on his last major Sinological essay in January 1934, at which point he wrote an introduction. Pained by the fact that even his friends thought he was lost in some mysterious world of scholarly pedantry, Nakae took this opportunity to explain that, as far as he was concerned, the study of ancient history was anything but an escape from the real world. What follows is a translation of that introduction and an *explication du texte*, because its full implications have not hitherto been recognized.

A. Several years ago an old revolutionary, who died overseas, said to me in
2   amazement: "I can't imagine how you can really be interested in this ancient
3   stuff." Strangely enough, I can remember now, from about the same time,
4   the exact words a diplomatic official blurted out: "What is there possibly to
5   be gained from such things of three or four thousand years ago?"

B. All the more, now, with the "state of emergency in Japan," the kinds of
2   things I write about are not worth even so much as a drop of crude oil or a
3   scrap of aluminum. I can imagine, however, that back when classical studies
4   constituted "universal learning" in Chinese society, if a Chinese person had
5   made such a statement, he would have committed a crime of heresy and
6   probably paid for it with his head. The happiest thing for me is to be able
7   to write whatever I think, even if it is regarded as discarded scraps of wood
8   or bamboo.

C.   In the contemporary scholarly world, it is more than sufficient for one
2   researching the Chinese classics to possess but a small amount of land, bar-
3   ren with scarcely a ray of sunlight. If this barren land turns out to be bad, he
4   might choose to switch to something else; but by pushing a hoe, he can still
5   have hope that he may produce some, perhaps rather poor, crops. I would of
6   course never say that such a yield would provide food for the daily life of the
7   masses; but insofar as it is an inevitable product of the functioning of
8   human consciousness, I cannot imagine that it would be what Kant calls
9   "false to human nature." Yet, if you contemplate something qualitatively
10   different, something "non-human," replacing the life of humanity in which
11   we have persisted until now, then that would, needless to say, be something
12   else altogether. I would declare right here and now, however, that I myself,
13   unemployed and isolated, have neither the time nor the interest in idle spec-
14   ulation for its own sake.

D.   I was born the son of a poor man, and I guess my dabbling in the Chi-
2   nese classics has been reckless. In the last fifteen or so years, I've been able to
3   devote myself to it without the least worry because of the kindness of two
4   men, Ts'ao Ju-lin and Prince Saionji. When the plan for this essay was
5   roughly conceived, I wanted most to bring it to an end and depart; but I was
6   unable to fulfill this trivial desire, and it had to be printed in incomplete
7   form for which I feel a particularly deep sense of shame before these two
8   men. Foolish though I may be, I did exhaust my powers on this piece; and
9   I have the confidence that, should I read it at another time, I would not
10   embarrass myself. I offer this insignificant, little piece to these two gentle-
11   men, and I want both to express my great gratitude for their years of
12   decency as well as to present this as a farewell token in leaving this place to
13   which I have become so accustomed.

E.   I am profoundly grateful to the person who was my dearest friend when
2   I lived in Peking, Suzue Gen'ichi, for taking the time away from preparing
3   his own work to proofread this piece. Finally, as regards this short essay,
4   although I usually receive kindly instruction from senior scholars to whom
5   I have looked for corrections, this time I would like to add that, since I am
6   sending it off immediately and will soon be on my way all alone, although
7   rude, I must decline their guidance.[1]

These remarks, delivered on the eve of his departure for Japan and
the commencement of a life in which he would have been on his own,
were clearly intended both as parting words to his immediate friends
and benefactors and, more generally, as a succinct assertion of a long personal belief that the study of antiquity could yield meaning which

spoke directly to contemporary issues. All of his self-abnegation aside, Nakae has heady things to say in this introduction.

The "old revolutionary" (A1) was, according to Itō Takeo, Katayama Sen, the Japanese Communist whom Nakae housed for a time in June 1925. Katayama was on his way to the Soviet Union, but his passage through China coincidentally occurred just as the May Thirtieth Incident erupted in Shanghai. He traveled there several times from Peking, staying with Nakae when in the capital. Although Nakae offered him sanctuary, he and Katayama were not specially friendly. Nakae was never much impressed by the string of Japan Communist Party members who visited him in China, nor with intellectual Marxists generally. He refused to discuss "revolution" with them both to steer clear of trouble or suspicion for himself and to avoid this tireless subject with those most intent on its pursual and least prepared for it. Calling Katayama "old" was meant literally (not as the common East Asian term of affection), particularly in the context of the band of Japanese revolutionaries that had crossed his threshold. Katayama was 66 years of age when they met and had died in 1933, the year prior to the writing of this introduction. Nakae is citing Katayama (A2–3) here as typical of men of his kind, who were all but incapable of understanding that the study of the past, even the distant past, was not necessarily a fanciful exercise. But, Nakae is also using him as a straw man.

"The diplomatic official" (A4) was none other than his sister's relative by marriage, Yoshida Shigeru. Although Nakae actually met Yoshida only a few times at most, he uses Yoshida's words (A4–5) to juxtapose a revolutionary dedicated to overthrowing the Japanese state with a conservative official of the Japanese government and show that in his day, men of opposing political views share the myopic belief that only the contemporary can be relevant to life as lived. Hence, he "remembered" this concurrence of views "strangely" (A3), implying that one would expect his two informants to share no views whatsoever. For in the minds of both Katayama and Yoshida, as Nakae represents them, anything so old as the subjects he studied can be of no imaginable utility. But, Nakae is still setting up the point to be made in self-defense.

In fact, Nakae rhetorically agrees (B1–3): the more desperate things become, the more chaotic and terrifying the present seems, the more useless research and writing on ancient China is; pure irony, to be sure, which a closer examination of this sentence reveals. Nakae chose the simile "as a drop of crude oil or a scrap of aluminum" (B2-3) carefully, for crude oil and aluminum exemplify the very raw materials that Japan in its "state of emergency" (*hijō Nihon*, B1) required. The reference here, although somewhat obscure now, would not have been lost on any of his contemporary readers. From late 1931, following the Manchurian Incident, a sense of crisis in Japan was exacerbated by the unclear plans for expansion and domestic reform put forward by the extreme right wing and the military. There was a real fear that Japan might be isolated within the international arena. Taking their cue from a speech by the ultra-nationalist Minister of War, General Araki Sadao (1877-1966), the military in 1933 prepared a film under the title *Hijōji Nihon* (Japan in a state of emergency) which heightened this atmosphere of crisis.[2] In other words, Nakae is saying that indeed his writings cannot provide the Japanese with sustenance or natural resources, so essential to a nation poor in these materials and in a crisis; but what good are such things, he rhetorically implies, if the state no longer serves its people's interests? Thus, Nakae wants the reader to understand that no one can possibly claim that he in any way supports the repressive regime, doing "the kinds of things" (B2-3) he does.

Nakae then comes directly to one of his points. His next sentence (B3-6) refers to a point that is central to all his Sinological essays: In China before the contemporary era all learning was unified and nothing lay outside the ken of "classical studies" (*keigaku*, B3). It was "universal learning" (*banyūgaku*, B4) in the sense that it included all history, all literature, all science, every topic, every line of inquiry—in short, everything. In that context, to criticize *keigaku*, as Nakae himself had earlier done, or to insinuate that any statement concerning knowledge was worthless would, he argues, have been suicidal; for when *keigaku* was at its zenith, scholarship served the state.

So what has changed? What is the point of this juxtaposition of his work as useless in one context and seriously heretical in another? Contexts change, sometimes dramatically. Something that may have been regarded in one realm as treasonable (and presumably of the highest importance) is seen at a later date to be a complete and total waste of time. What is the point? Despite others' disapproval, Nakae is reasserting the importance of his research as the "happiest thing" (B6) for him; for this claim constitutes recognition of his ability to exercise what little freedom exists to him "to be able to write whatever I think" (B6–7). Indeed, contexts will change again, and what may now been taken "as discarded scraps of wood or bamboo" (B7–8), distinctly more appropriate similes in the traditional East Asian world, may be seen differently at another date. In other words, who is anyone else to decide the propriety of what one studies by investing one's own present needs and biases with excessive concern?

The renowned Sinologist Niida Noboru, writing in the immediate postwar period, took this phrase one step further, perhaps one step too far. He read in this phrase the intimation that Nakae's passion for the study of antiquity was left unsatisfied at the time, that he was, in fact, unable to enjoy the happiness which freedom to write as he pleased would bring. Niida also read countless critiques of the contemporary world into Nakae's Sinological discussions of ancient times—political oppression, inequality, and the like. Ultimately, in Niida's view, Nakae failed to generate a synthesis of his scholarly methodology as much for intellectual reasons as for his personal feelings of anguish.[3] There is much food for thought here, but one cannot help sensing that Niida has read something of his own agenda into Nakae's work. Without a doubt, Nakae drew sustenance from the knowledge that he was studying the lives of real human beings who had lived and suffered under harsh circumstances similar to those in which contemporary men and women found themselves. He did not however, study the past merely as an Aesopian medium for criticizing the present. Niida bent over backwards to appreciate Nakae's passion for antiquity, but he ultimately reinterpreted Nakae as someone who was concerned first and foremost with the contemporary and used the past to judge it. That is an oversimplification.

Paragraph C, the longest and most complex, turns the comparison of the first sentence of the previous paragraph, namely the value of scholarship as measured with respect to the worth or potential productivity of natural resources, into a metaphor. Nakae begins with a parting reference to "researching the Chinese classics . . . in the contemporary scholarly world" (C1–2). From that point until the last startling sentence of the paragraph, he develops this one metaphor into an extraordinarily extended conceit.

The contemporary world offers the scholar of ancient China a situation comparable to farming a "barren" strip of land with little "sunlight" (C2–3). You "push a hoe" over this "barren land" and, if it produces nothing, you can "switch to something else" (C4). The comparison of agricultural and scholarly work is not uncommon in East Asian writings. The farmer and the scholar have their respective pieces of terrain in which they labor and find personal fulfillment. Though the land may be barren or poor or in need of sunlight or rain (that is, though the scholar's area of research seems important only to him and is isolated from other research that could shed light on it), this is not a primary concern. He still works the land because it is his.

The word Nakae chose for "switch" was the heavily charged political term *tenkō*, which jumps out at the reader if only because it sharply conflicts with the agricultural metaphor. In the 1920s and early 1930s, numerous Japanese Marxists renounced their party affiliations and embraced the emperor-centered "national polity" (*kokutai*), the thin veneer covering Japanese jingoism. Several months before this piece was written, Sano Manabu and Nabeyama Sadachika, both of whom had visited Nakae in Peking and stayed with him, offered a joint statement of "conversion" or *tenkō*. Nakae does not belabor the issue. For those who persevere and do not "switch to something else" (C4) and sell their souls to the devil—that is, for those who continue to "push a hoe" (C4) in spite of the barrenness of the land, in spite of the opposition of acquaintances and social pressures—there is always the hope that they will be able to support themselves with some produce, even if the harvest proves to be "rather poor crops" (C5). That is to say, they may continue to entertain the hope that something positive will result from their efforts—not enough to save mankind, to which the next sentence alludes, but nothing to be ashamed of. After all, he implies, how much does one need to live if one is happy in one's little corner of the universe? If you decide that this is not enough, that you are going to save mankind through the work of your own hands, then surely "a yield" (namely, the concrete results of scholarly research) such as might be produced on a small plot of barren land would hardly have a major impact in the world or save mankind, or as Nakae put it, "provide food for the daily life of the masses" (C6–7). At this level of discourse, Nakae seems to be offering the scholar two choices: to continue to hoe or work in his field regardless of what others may say; or to switch to something else. The tenser the times for scholars and the more oppressive a regime, the more sharply do lines of choice tend to be drawn. The "state of emergency in Japan" (B1) was a tense time under an oppressive regime; and as a result Nakae does not offer the metaphorical farmer a wide range of options. The preferred option is to continue to hoe the tough row and not to switch. Nakae was fond in later years of citing Marx's quotation from Dante as it appears in the preface to *Das Kapital*: *"Segui il tuo corso, e lascia dir le genti* (Follow your own course, and let people talk)." (See p. 174 below.)

Nakae's point is not to absolve himself of any responsibility for the sufferings of his fellow man. It is precisely the converse. As we have seen in the earlier parts of this passage, he is saying that although the kind of work in which he has engaged, "researching the Chinese classics," may not solve all the problems of the world, it is not unrelated to those problems. And those who claimed to be the very mouthpiece of the masses were in the process of "switching" *en masse* into pawns of a repressive regime.

His next sentence is very important: "[I]nsofar as it is an inevitable product of the functioning of human consciousness, I cannot imagine that it would be what Kant calls 'false to human nature'" (C7–9). The "it" refers, of course, to his own work. "It" is a "product of . . . human consciousness" because its author, Nakae, is a reflecting human being; human beings think, read, and sometimes write. What they produce will, of necessity, forge links with other human beings who have done, are doing, and will do the same. In other words, in reading and writing and in being concerned with human beings of bygone times, Nakae lays claim to a place in the ongoing life of humanity; he does not seek escape from it. He offers no panacea for mankind's ills or a way to "provide food" for the hungry masses; he offers instead, much more modestly, a historical expression of mankind's search for humanity.

In this extremely brief reference to Kant, one can see the kernel of

Nakae's entire relationship to the philosopher of Königsberg and his work, the subject (in part) of Chapter Eight. We know from Nakae's marginal notations that he was reading Kant's *Critique of Practical Reason* at the time he composed the text under analysis. For Kant, "human nature" was not a category that varied or changed as a result of external circumstances or individual tastes. It was fundamentally moral and guided man to act in a morally appropriate fashion. Toward the end of Part I and again at the beginning of Part II of this *Critique*, Kant poses several negative instances which best illustrate what Nakae had in mind here.

> If human nature were not so constituted . . . everything would be mere cant; the law would be hated . . . The letter of the law (legality) would be met with in our actions, but the spirit of the law (morality) would not be found in our intentions . . . We would inevitably appear in our own eyes as worthless and depraved . . .
>
> The law of duty, through the positive worth which obedience to it makes us feel, finds easier access through the respect for ourselves in the consciousness of freedom. If it is well established, so that a man fears nothing more than to find himself on self-examination to be worthless and contemptible in his own eyes, every good moral disposition can be grafted on to this self-respect, for the consciousness of freedom is the best, indeed the only, guard that can keep ignoble and corrupting influences from bursting in upon the mind.[4]

In his next sentence, juxtaposed to the expression attributed to Kant, Nakae is considerably less subtle: "[I]f you contemplate something qualitatively different, something 'non-human,' replacing the life of humanity in which we have persisted until now, then that would . . . be something else altogether" (C9–12). The reference points superficially to a world in which people no longer act in concert with the moral precepts or character befitting humanity; a world in which neither Kant's designation of humans living as ethical beings in a society of laws nor Hegel's *Sittlichkeit* retain any meaning. It is an oblique reference to the horrific prospect that Japan and the Axis powers might win the world war which Nakae had seen on the horizon since the Manchurian Incident of 1931.

In light of that frightening possibility, which lay heavily on his mind every day from the early 1930s, Nakae wants to make it as clear as can be that his work is not "idle speculation for its own sake" (C13–14). The future of humanity was at stake here, and, even if he was in no position to cure all the ills of the world, he was not interested in wasting his time on trivialities. He apparently devoted these few weighty sentences to elucidating his frame of mind because his contemporaries failed to understand his motives, interests, and basic concerns; he was still smarting from Itō Takeo's inadvertent comment about pedantry.

The fourth paragraph (D) is an extended dedicatory note to his two long-term benefactors, Ts'ao Ju-lin and Prince Saionji. It reflects Nakae's deep sense of friendship and his excessive modesty. He was offering the essay that followed as a "farewell token" (D12) to Ts'ao and the Prince in anticipation of his departure for Japan. Ts'ao was already unable to help Nakae further with monetary support, because the Bank of Communications had collapsed. Earlier Saionji had helped arrange a multiple-year consultancy with no strings attached from the Research Department of the SMR.[5] Now, Nakae decided to return to Tokyo and put lingering family matters in order. About two weeks after arriving, he discovered that he was unable to carry on his studies there; and by the end of February he had returned to Peking for good. For all the modesty and self-abnegation of this paragraph, it concludes with the intriguingly self-confident clause, "I have the confidence that, should I read it [i.e., the essay that follows this introduction] at another time, I would not embarrass myself" (D9–10). It is as if Nakae were claiming that, in writing an essay on the organization of chapters in the *Shang-shu*, he had practiced what he had just preached in the introduction. For what could seem less important in the real world of 1934? He was cutting potential critics off in advance.

The last paragraph (E) is a strange mixture of gratitude to his close friend Suzue Gen'ichi and a mystifying rebuff to certain unnamed and unknown "senior scholars" (E4). Perhaps this was merely Nakae's way of saying that, if he had had more time to refine this essay and draw on the work of others, he would have been happy to do so. But, he was on the verge of a momentous time in his life; he was about to have to make a living on his own.

This two-page introduction contains numerous insights into Nakae's frame of mind. We have already seen how he viewed the world of "classical studies" in China's past. Only with that elucidation would the second paragraph of this piece make complete sense. The chapters that follow will examine the other ideas suggested here in the process of his intellectual maturation: the rise of militarism in Japan and World War II; the scholar and society, one's responsibility in an adverse age; the importance of German idealist thought, including Marx; and one man's relationship to humanity.

SEVEN

The Expatriate Vision

Nakae Ushikichi was a scholar who recognized without qualification that the self which is devoted to a particular scholarly object and the self which lives life in contemporary society are absolutely one and the same.

KATŌ KORETAKA[1]

After an unsuccessful attempt to repatriate during the winter of 1934, Nakae's decision to return to China was to all intents final. He spent these last eight, troubled years of his life, until sickness and the prodding of friends compelled him to enter Kyūshū University Hospital prior to his death in 1942, assiduously examining developments in the world around him and engrossed in the study of German idealist thought. Although he occasionally returned to a work on the *Shang-shu*, left unfinished at the time of his death, Nakae wrote nothing else Sinological.

The primary focus of his attention shifted; but, as he sought strenuously to point out in the text translated in Chapter Six, both his scholarship and his concern for the future of mankind were expressions of a common exercise of human freedom. They were linked in a way far more important than any apparent difference, for the principal object of Nakae's abiding concern was always mankind. All men and women, as he understood it, were bound from the distant past through the present and into the future by their places in a shared humanity. His work on ancient China had shown, for example, how much ordinary people then had suffered. And once, lest that lesson somehow be lost on his readers, as we have noted, Nakae went out of his way to accentuate it by exclaiming over how wretched the lives of the powerless had been.[2] Then he had stressed that past suffering was not merely a datum for the historian to file away somewhere, but the cause for sadness and concern, and a reality just as important as any other set of historical facts. Now the time had come for Nakae himself to examine the present, a time when humanity was again on the verge of great suffering.

One must be wary of so emphasizing his compassionate concerns as to see contemporary criticism throughout Nakae's Sinological writings. Observations of this sort abound in the postwar revival of interest in Nakae and his work. Niida Noboru, writing in 1950, passionately supported Nakae's claim that studying the past represented no escape from the present, for it was "fundamentally wrong to make contemporary relevance a criterion of evaluation." Niida then jumped to virtually the opposite extreme. He claimed that Nakae expressed his anguish in the contemporary world by criticizing the traditional authority of Confucianism and the downtrodden state of the masses of the Chinese people as "objects of rule" throughout Chinese history. Similarly, in Niida's view, Nakae's study of feudalism in China was initially motivated by the question of why China had never produced a modern state despite having had earlier contact with capitalist societies than Japan had. According to Niida, Nakae used his admittedly depressing portrayal of thorough domination by the state as a hidden attack on the contemporary rise of fascism in Europe and Japan.[3]

To the extent that all scholarship reflects a measure of autobiography, at least insofar as choice of topics is concerned, Niida's points seem fair enough. Nakae was deeply sorrowful about conditions of life in contemporary China, and this mood surely influenced his research as well. As much as Nakae may have wanted to demonstrate that present-day China's problems were longstanding ones, though, I seriously doubt whether he used pre-modern China solely to comment on contemporary China. As one scholar noted about Nakae in a similar vein years later, "It is very rare in contemporary Japan to find someone who so clearly demonstrates for us the iron law of historical reseach that, in order to understand antiquity, one has to understand the present."[4]

Why was Nakae so "rare" or different from the mainstream? What was it about his particular set of concerns that enabled him better than other Japanese at the time to sense the genuine calamities unfolding in East Asia and elsewhere? Before we can attempt answers to these questions, we have to look at the uniqueness of Nakae's position as an expatriate in the 1920s and 1930s and the development of his views on China, Japan, and their relations.

NAKAE AS EXPATRIATE

Nakae drifted into expatriatism. Unlike most expatriates, who choose to leave their native country out of a conscious dissatisfaction with economic, political, or intellectual conditions, Nakae left Japan on a lark and stayed in China because it became comfortable for him. Absorption in his studies and personal routine satisfied him for years; and it was only after the visit home in 1934 that he became aware that he no longer fitted the country or, to put it more the way he would have thought of it, the country was no longer fit for him.

The Japan he originally left was in a period of great intellectual excitement, but it was an excitement for which he cared nothing or of which he was completely unaware. It was not that his intellectual needs could not be met in Japan; he simply had none to speak of in the mid-1910s. He took up residence in a country whose people were suffering the ravages of imperialism as well as inept and corrupt government, civil war, and tremendous poverty. It was a country whose language he could read but not speak. At first, he did what many expatriates do: He sought out fellow nationals and old friends, remaining blissfully ignorant of what the natives were doing. His life changed dramatically, as we have seen, in 1919; and on his own in Japan the new Nakae would never have been able to support the life that Ts'ao Ju-lin and Prince Saionji enabled him to lead in China. Then one day it was 1934, and he realized that twenty years had passed since his arrival. His attempt to return to Japan only accentuated the fact that for him expatriatism had become a permanent condition.

In Nakae's case, as perhaps in others, loneliness accompanied the growing realization of this permanence. Solitude was something he both desired and regretted, a distance that offered him considerably more freedom than he would have had in Japan but that rendered him impotent. At the same time, his loneliness, as he suggested in the text analyzed in Chapter Six, was tinged with both a hint of self-pity and a kind of moral resolve. Less than a year before his death, he described this ambivalence in a letter to Suzue Gen'ichi: "I've recently felt that the flickering 'blessings' of solitude and loneliness, insofar as I've sensed them, have nonetheless been deeply captivating."[5] And, the next month, after a long passage on the fallen leaves and lonely trees of late autumn, he wrote: "I feel as though I'm straddling the world of sensation and the world beyond the senses."[6]

Convinced from the mid-1930s on of his alienation from life in Japan, Nakae set his mind on using the opportunity afforded by the decision to remain in China to gain the kind of clarity concerning the fate of mankind unavailable to him in Japan. Domestic political developments in Japan as well as the apparent inability of Japan's intellectuals to sustain any opposition to them enhanced Nakae's feelings of estrangement from his native land. In a letter of early 1939 to a friend, he described in great detail how much he despised Japanese intellectuals of recent times, particularly "intellectual Marxists." In their "attitudes toward life," he claimed, they demonstrate "no passion, no devotion, no duty, no sympathy, no perseverance; on the contrary, they are skeptical, derisive, temporizing, slanderous, cold, cowardly, and timid—at worst, anti-social, and at least, unethical. I keep as far away as possible from such intellectuals."[7] He was referring here primarily to the numerous Japanese Marxists and Communists who had in the previous few years made peace with the regime in Japan through a process of intellectual sleight of hand, somehow finding a unity of mission in the current right-wing ultra-nationalism and their own Marxism. From his safe port in Peking, Nakae saw them all as pusillanimous, driven by a keen desire to save their own skins, too afraid or too ignorant to carry out the dictates of their earlier convictions.

Sometime in 1938 or perhaps 1939 he received a letter from Sano Manabu from prison. Although best known for his early Communist activities and subsequent renunciation of the Communist movement in 1933, Sano had also by now taken up Sinological research and his letter asked Nakae something about an old Chinese text. Nakae showed the letter to his friend Ōta Ryōichirō (1905–1968) and said under his breath: "It would be better if Sano died in prison."[8]

Expatriatism is an especially rare phenomenon in the case of the Japanese,[9] so long an isolated, island people convinced of the uniqueness of their culture and the incapacity of the outside world to satisfy their needs. For a Japanese to choose an expatriate's existence requires a greater personal conflict with his society than would probably be the case for an American or European. If Nakae still harbored any illusions about his own relationship to his native land, the 1934 trip cured him immediately.

WHITHER JAPAN?

In mid-1932, just after he completed and had his essay on the *Kung-yang* tradition printed, Nakae made his first trip to Tokyo in eighteen years, presumably to meet with Prince Saionji and perhaps others as well. He was stunned by the changes in the city in which he had been raised. "In a word," he wrote to friends in China, "Tokyo is indeed the capital of a Japan in a period of total collapse. There may be a mood of revival amidst this decline, but how sad, alas, that those who sense this also feel the mood of bitterness and deterioration . . . Only in the instincts of living things that despise decay can a sense of hatred arise, finding the capital of Japan in this era of collapse unbearable." No mincing of words here; his response to kabuki in Tokyo was similar: "Art utterly devoid of a future!!! A sight richly clad in lethargy and ignorance. That's my impression in total."[10]

Nakae's general disaffection toward his homeland and his countrymen grew more severe through the 1930s, as both enhanced his increasingly gloomy picture. The real blow, though, had already come somewhat earlier, at the time of the Manchurian Incident of 18 September 1931. This well-known event that led to the Japanese occupation of Manchuria caused grief among most conscientious East Asians, although most Japanese hailed the occasion as the beginning of a new age in the East. Nakae began to tell virtually every one that visited him that this event was a harbinger of a coming world war in which Japan would be consumed in the conflagration.[11]

Particularly saddening to Nakae was the fact that Captain Imada Shintarō (1896–1949) of the Japanese Army had been the commander on the scene, ordered to lead the assault on Liu-t'iao-kou, the event that we now know as the Manchurian or Mukden Incident.[12] From an old family connection, Imada had long looked up to Nakae. In 1929 Imada was sent by the Army General Staff on an investigative mission into Shansi province, later to be stationed in Mukden. From time to time he visited Nakae in Peking and came to admire him even more deeply. Nakae had earlier met a variety of Japanese military men, some—such as Itagaki Seishirō (1885–1948) and Tsuda Shizue (1883–1964)—through the legation in Peking, others from the Kwantung Army. Nakae reserved a special affection for Imada and struck up a correspondence with him just after the Marco Polo Bridge Incident in 1937, the commencement of the Sino-Japanese War. When Nakae returned to Japan briefly in 1934, Imada arranged a meeting between him and his father's old friend, Tōyama Mitsuru, in Tokyo. It was a failure, punctuated by silence, awkwardness, and lack of politeness.[13]

In 1932 the Kwantung Army in Manchuria created the Japanese puppet state of Manchukuo, which at the time only Japan recognized. Nakae joined the rest of the world in refusing to recognize it as a legitimate regime. In 1934 he visited his old acquaintance Ting Shih-yuan in Tokyo where Ting was serving as minister to Japan from Manchukuo, and told him in no uncertain terms that he was serving a doomed "bogus state" (*wei-kuo*, J. *gikoku*) and that as a Chinese he should select an appropriate moment to extricate himself from it. Later that year he warned his close friend Katō Koretaka not to take a regular position with the SMR, because it would not stand him in good stead to have worked for an "agency" of Japanese imperialism when a prewar balance-sheet was compiled in the postwar period.[14]

Without joining an underground and physically resisting Japanese imperialism, Nakae chose to live his life in a manner in tune with his own conception of personal integrity. In a private act of resistance, he refused, for example, to follow the Japanese Army's imposition on Peking of Japanese time and continued to set his clocks by local Chinese time. He insisted to everyone with whom he spoke that Japan's aggression in Asia be called just that and not softened by the empty or euphemistic terms used to describe it by the government: *incident, holy war (seisen), state of emergency, Greater East Asian Co-Prosperity Sphere,* and the like. "China will probably become the center of world history in the second half of the twentieth century," he noted to Katō, whereas the Japanese continued to act like the "hicks of the universe."[15]

In July 1936 Nakae vacationed for several weeks at a beach near Shimabara in Kyūshū. He enjoyed his relaxation so much that the following summer he returned there. On the second or third day of his 1937 vacation, he learned of the Marco Polo Bridge Incident and recognized its gravity. He immediately repacked and returned to his home in Peking. From there he went directly to Tientsin where his old friend and former benefactor, Ts'ao Ju-lin, resided. Known for his long-standing pro-Japanese sympathies, Ts'ao had been under considerable pressure to join the Japanese puppet regime in North China. As Ts'ao admitted several years later, he owed his steadfast refusal to participate in such a collaborationist regime to Nakae's strongly worded counsel against it.[16]

WAR AND DEGRADATION

Nakae was now confirmed in his belief that Japan was set on a path of destruction and self-destruction. He could see no conceivable way a country like Japan could ever rule China. He told the lawyer and scholar Moriya Fumio (b. 1907) in 1937 that the Sino-Japanese War was just a prologue to a much larger world war. It was a conflict in which Japan would necessarily confront England and the United States and be demolished, "like a badger running into a locomotive."[17] Moreover, Japan's defeat was something to be hoped for; it was humanity's only chance.

While Nakae was unrelenting in his criticism of Japan's pursuit of the war and of the Axis cause generally, he kept open his lines of communication with military men and those harboring opposing points of view. There was a limit to his patience, as evidenced by his having the *Asahi shinbun* critic Sugiyama Heisuke (1895–1946) thrown out of his home in August 1937 for espousing ultranationalist views. Although he never published his opinions on current events, Nakae was open about them and wrote countless letters condemning Japan's role in the war. His stance became sufficiently well known in Peking that the military police claimed he was "an unpatriotic malcontent who clings to the city walls [of Peking] and frowns at the Holy War."[18]

Several themes run through Nakae's efforts to come to terms with the war, its development, and its meaning. He overcame his initial rage, alternately replacing it with gloom and hope, only to let it pour forth on subsequent occasions. Perhaps his most recurrent attitude toward the war was what might be called enlightened defeatism. To him it was a foregone conclusion that Japan could never win the war with China, let alone with the Western powers. Nakae moved beyond this rather obvious formulation to hope for an actual Allied victory. We see this in his correspondence, his conversations, and the private diary he kept from early 1939 until his death in mid 1942, written in the margins of primarily three books: Kant's *Kritik der reinen vernunft*, Hegel's *Phänomenologie des Geistes*, and Marx's *Das Kapital*.[19]

Nakae reserved special venom for the Axis leaders. In 1939 and 1940, he saw Hitler as an infantile, comic, albeit murderous, fool, full of bombast but pitifully inept. This view fitted well a popular image of Hitler, particularly as portrayed by Charlie Chaplin in his 1940 film *The Great Dictator*. In Mussolini, on the other hand, Nakae saw a clear and present danger. His view of Hitler changed as the German threat proved to his horror to be quite real, while his hatred of Mussolini only grew more and more intense. Nakae offered this dualistic picture of the two scourges of the twentieth century in a letter to Suzue Gen'ichi of late April 1940:

> I too have complete faith in the victory of the superior might of the Allies against Germany. In spite of this clear feeling, there's a major contradiction here, for the French and English hatred of Adolph Hitler as the embodiment of evil, the very spirit of the God of the Plague, isn't complete; rather, I sense a certain intimacy between them. He's certainly a scoundrel, but there's a kind of affability about him. When he roars and screams, there's a childishness there that's humorous. As a person, Hitler lacks all the qualities of the victorious hero . . . When he uses the arrogant expression *Blitzkrieg*, shadows and gloom (which shouldn't be present at all) drift up to the surface and pitifully suggest a painful sense that there's nothing whatsoever behind his perverse behavior. The opposite of Hitler is Mussolini who from head to toe

deserves only abhorrence. One day soon Fascist Italy will be compelled to enter the war, and the true value of that rat Mussolini will be bared before history—I pray inwardly for the commencement of this event.[20]

This view is echoed in his diary notations. Until the beginning of the bombings of London, perhaps as late as the invasion of Russia, Nakae did not see the real threat of the German war machine. For instance he remarked to himself in October 1939: "Hitler's tricks are getting clumsier and worse, and I can only assume that his last days will come before long." Several months later: "It looks like Hitler's downfall isn't necessarily so far off." In August 1940, the month before the commencement of the aerial bombardment of Great Britain: "Although the attack on Britain had been given a certain amount of priority since the 8th [of August], I doubt whether they'll accomplish as much as Hitler has claimed." And, in early October of 1940, after a month of Luftwaffe attacks on London: "Hitler's aerial *Blitzkrieg* has been less and less successful."[21]

After this point, and especially after the invasion of Russia, his image of Hitler changed, although not radically. In a letter written late in July 1941, he noted that Hitler, poised for the conquest of the Soviet Union, seemed pathetic from his pictures, not brawny like Mussolini.[22] Nakae had actually been surprised by the German invasion, but from that point forward he saw the only appropriate comparison for Hitler in Napoleon.

Mussolini, a figure who has popularly been seen as a buffoon or inept boor, was in Nakae's estimation the consummate villain. This view comes through more clearly from Nakae's diary than from his letters. One of his earliest notes, from September 1939, reads in part: "Once again Italy seems to be playing the opportunist. That scoundrel Mussolini has a well-deserved punishment awaiting him." Then, in April 1940, only four days after he wrote the letter, cited above, to Suzue: "Italy under Mussolini, whom I detest most of all, is going to have to enter the war. His true colors are now apparent, and soon he'll expose his ugliness to the entire world." And, two months later: "That despicable Mussolini has finally roused himself. He declared war on the afternoon of 10 June."[23]

Why he disliked Mussolini so much more than Hitler remains a mys-

tery for which we can offer only a tentative suggestion. Some of the solution to this puzzle lies in the public postures of the two men: Hitler was
a short figure who thoroughly lacked the physical might he demanded
of his countrymen; his ridiculous gestures virtually begged for a Chap-
linesque parody. Could this be a man planning a world conquest? In contrast, Mussolini was a physically huge, inflated, and immensely
pompous figure, claiming he would recreate the Roman Empire. At
least Mussolini looked the part, whereas Hitler appeared to Nakae to be
little more than a very bad joke. The attacks on London began to alter
this impression of Hitler. "I can imagine the joy of the British," he
noted in passing in a letter to Suzue of 14 September 1940, "when
Hitler's great army will be swallowed up in the Strait of Dover and the
North Sea."[24] The next day he recorded his sadness in the most moving
entry in his diary:

> The Nazi attack on London which began on the night of the 7th [of Sep-
> tember] has become more severe with each passing day, and since the 12th has
> carried to extremity sorrow such as is unprecedented.
>
> If the British people can weather this ordeal, then the German's amphibi-
> ous assault will be crushed and the enemy will vanish like the mist, just as in
> the case of Napoleon's designs of over 130 years ago. The Commander of
> these unparalleled air attacks is reported to be that scoundrel Goering,
> Hitler's right-hand man. It's just now the time of the harvest moon. The
> sound of the planes in the heavens, the earth ablaze in flames, the rounds of
> bullets glistening in the sky, the roar of cannons demolishing the pillars of
> heaven and the axis of the earth, the echoes of explosion and destruction, bil-
> lowing black smoke, the air full of stifling gunpowder—above all of this, the
> moon is shining. Such a scene, even in just the contemplation of it, makes
> one's blood boil and body seethe. And yet, if you ponder this further, beneath
> the moonlight covering all things equally, Churchill and Hitler, and the hell-
> ish sight of the world's greatest city in utter chaos, this may be regarded as a
> mere overture to the history of what's to come. Think of what the world will
> look like at this time next year. 15 Sept., a day before the harvest moon,
> 1940.[25]

NAPOLEON AND HISTORY

By 1940 Nakae had begun actively to use Napoleon's experiences in his attempted conquest of Russia (and the world) as a measure of Hitler's progress and eventual (hoped for) ruin. Nakae was certainly not the only observer conscious of the striking parallels between the "Little Corporal" from Corsica, leading the armies of the French Empire to countless military victories before a major campaign into the Russian Empire, and the Austrian corporal leading the forces of the German Reich to unprecedented military successes before a like invasion of Soviet Russia. From the start Nakae predicted an abysmal defeat for Hitler, just as had been the case with Napoleon. However, given his earlier views on Hitler's potential for success, one wonders whether Nakae based his prediction on historical lessons or false confidence.

His first mention of Napoleon appears in a letter to Suzue a year prior to Hitler's invasion of Russia. "From the results of the war in Europe thus far," he noted, "Hitler has succeeded in exploits [not attained] since Napoleon, but his future road will be ever so much more difficult. Contrary to popular ideas, I firmly hold to this view of mine which is unrelated to whether this fellow with his steamroller will be successful or not."[26] By mid 1940 Hitler had subjugated all the nations he had attacked, and Britain was expecting an amphibious landing at any moment. No one seriously believed that the Ribbentrop-Molotov peace treaty would deter a Nazi-Soviet war, but it did allow both sides a breathing spell to prepare for the hostilities. This was what Nakae had in mind when he referred to Hitler's "future road," implying the great difficulties he would face in Russia. Although his prediction was not exactly bold, he posed it in opposition to common views of the time; and he clung to it until his death. He was convinced that Hitler's invasion was doomed for all the reasons Napoleon's had failed.[27]

When the Wehrmacht did invade Russia in 1941, Nakae expressed "a little surprise." He was surprised not at Germany's actions but at the timing: "When you take into account Hitler's present position, his future outlook, and his character—[all] similar to Napoleon's in 1811— there's nothing to be too shocked about . . . My outlook on the conclusion of this incident overall hasn't changed in the least." In other words, he still believed Hitler was doomed. He was, however, well aware that no matter how often and how forcefully he invoked his optimistic views, the war still raged and Nazi troops marched forward. Immediately after the invasion, Nakae's analysis began to make the Hitler-Napoleon comparison more exact and more detailed. This letter continued: "However, Napoleon led the Grande Armée, personally investigated points for river crossings, and forded the Niemen River on 24 June 1812. It took two days for his entire army to cross. He crossed the Dnieper on 19 August. Compared to that, given the natural limitations of modern warfare, one can only wonder at the incomparable speed of the German Army now. Yet, they still have not occupied Minsk, Smolensk, Kiev, or Vitebsk."[28]

Having seized on the Napoleon comparison, Nakae was relentless. In the early days of the German invasion, the Nazis won astounding victories with great speed. For some reason, which ultimately proved to be correct, Nakae was led to believe that Russian resistance would outstrip the German war machine: "I think," he wrote Katō Koretaka in July 1941, "they're getting worried at Hitler's headquarters now that [they have met] a resistance far more stubborn and persevering than the Russian troops under Kutuzov's leadership in the war against Napoleon."[29]

Even when the Red Army appeared to be at its lowest ebb, he retained his faith, but no longer with the trace of wishful thinking. The Russo-German war was of "truly epochal" proportions: huge numbers of troops, long supply and battle lines, and battles that lasted from three days to a week. With the exception of the battle of Leipzig, which lasted four days, Napoleon fought rarely for more than a day in the early nineteenth century. The renowned battle of Borodino lasted two days and Napoleon won it, entered Moscow, and even then, Nakae noted, the Russians were badly hurt but not defeated. "King Pyrrhus of Epirus defeated the Roman army at an ancient site, but he exhausted [his forces] in the process and was spent. Napoleon too won a battle at Dresden, but he paid an extremely high price for it and was ultimately defeated at the battle of Leipzig. Hitler, a great fan and admirer of Napoleon Bonaparte, in his military successes accomplished over a short period of time, has far surpassed his mentor."[30] Here Nakae was simply noting that victory and defeat are not always what they seem. King Pyrrhus, whose name has come to signify a great defeat despite an apparent victory, and Napoleon, who won a Pyrrhic victory at Dresden, are to be taken as historical antecedents for Hitler. The implication is clearly that, as great as Hitler's victories might seem, so will his ultimate defeat be crushing.

Nakae's longest and more sustained comparison of Hitler and Napoleon appeared in a letter, also of July 1941, to Ogura Sōichi (b. 1909), a young man then employed in the Japanese Consulate in Tsingtao. After expressing initial surprise at the invasion, he explained that it was expected, given the Napoleonic footsteps in which Hitler was walking. "Just like Napoleon in 1812, Hitler has embarked on a great adventure [in Russia] with all his forces, while neglecting England and the United States . . . Post-Napoleonic historians saw the 1812 campaign against Russia as Napoleon's fatal defeat; but Napoleon, who could only envision certain victory, surely never so much as dreamed that it would end with his Grande Armée of 600,000 men sustaining nearly sixty per cent casualties in battle." By treating Napoleon as an ordinary mortal whose actions might prove instructive for predicting the results of Hitler's similar actions, Nakae sought to de-mythologize both men and treat them neither as gods nor as devils but as comprehensible men so that the present situation could be understood.

His letter to Ogura continued:

> When heroes soar into the heavens by the advance of their glorious deeds, the world affirms and praises their unrivaled position as geniuses. If we investigate the effects [of their actions] industriously and to the minutest detail, the historical lessons will reveal nothing strange in their accomplishments. For example – until 1804 the great conflagration of the French Revolution lay in Napoleon's hands; he was the purveyor of nationalism, a steamroller destroying old institutions, and the creator of a new society. But, at the time of the Russian invasion, he was already an avaricious adventurer, "an obese conqueror," seeking with old-style territorial cravings to block the spread of the new spirit which he himself was once responsible for propagating . . . My perspective on this unprecedentedly massive war hasn't changed in the least from what I've said earlier. The outbreak of Russo-German hostilities doesn't disturb this. If, by some accident, Hitler should win, then like Napoleon he'll compel Russia to make peace as quickly as possible.[31]

Here, as elsewhere, Nakae noted that Stalin was in a different position from Tsar Alexander, and that he might surprise the world and seize an opportunity to establish a tentative peace with Hitler.

NAKAE AND IMADA SHINTARŌ

The views we have thus far seen Nakae express on intellectual decay in Japan, the Japanese invasion of China, the war, and Hitler's demise have come from sources in which he was either writing for himself or speaking to people with whom he knew he shared values. His correspondence with Imada Shintarō of the Kwantung Army reveals that he held to these views and values when arguing with someone with whom he shared neither opinions nor values and that the lack of common ground between the two men necessitated a clearer formulation of his ideas. As noted above, Nakae and Imada had known each other for a number of years, and Nakae was painfully aware of Imada's central role in the Manchurian Incident. As Alvin Coox had noted of the planning for the Manchurian Incident, Imada "pushed even harder than Ishiwara [Kanji] and Itagaki [Seishirō] for lightning action; if they hesitated, he intimated, he would go it alone." They rushed ahead with the planning, fearful that an imperial order might stop them prematurely. Imada and others, intent on blaming the explosion on the Chinese, even forged a "Chinese maneuver order" which ended up in the hands of the Lytton Commission.[32]

War has a way of increasing the speed of upward mobility in the military, as Imada's rapid rise illustrates. A graduate of the Army War College in late 1925, he became a captain in the summer of 1927; he was first sent to China in August 1929. He was promoted to major in August 1933, made battalion commander in March of the following year, and sent to the Manchukuo Military Advisory Group of the Kwantung Army headquarters in March of 1935. He was promoted to lieutenant colonel in August 1937, to colonel in July 1939, and to major general in August 1943, the year after Nakae's death. He was well known as a member of the "Manchurian faction" in the Kwantung Army (along with Itagaki Seishirō, Katakura Tadashi [b. 1898], and others).[33]

Several weeks after the Marco Polo Bridge Incident in 1937, Nakae began writing to Imada at army headquarters in Tokyo; subsequent letters went to Korea, and from early 1942 to Shansi. Inexplicably, Nakae composed his entire correspondence with Imada in *sōrōbun*, the old epistolary style of Japanese. Perhaps Nakae wanted to elevate the level of the dialogue, particularly inasmuch as he soon began offering firm advice to Imada and the Kwantung Army about the course of their invasion of China. His letters were addressed to "Imada taikei," "Imada jinkei," "Imada rōkei," as well as an assortment of other heightened terms of endearment for friends. Only once, in the middle of 1938, did he suddenly shift to "Lieutenant Colonel Imada," perhaps as recognition of Imada's promotion.

Nakae's first communication to Imada had a tentative tone. He noted the scare in Peking, following the Marco Polo Bridge Incident, and the call to which Nakae refused to respond for all Japanese to report to the Legation. He sarcastically pointed out that it was probably even safer now for Japanese in North China: "While I was walking into the center of town [Peking] on the 29th [of July 1937], I heard considerable gunfire. It's not that I'm unhappy, for I enjoy taking walks. I can appreciate the might of the Imperial Army and at the same time marvel at the extraordinary situation in which we residents of Peking find ourselves." Although expressions like *state of emergency* had been current in Japan since the Manchurian Incident, only now, Nakae added, following the invasion did they assume real meaning for the Japanese people. He also promised a subsequent letter in which he would offer his "humble opinions . . . as one Japanese on the present Incident and the state of affairs."[34]

One important letter from Nakae to Imada, which apparently fulfilled this promise in part, has been lost. Nakae made reference to it in 1938 and Imada reconfirmed it after the war. In it Nakae warned of the great dangers that expanding and extending the invasion of China would cause. It was in this letter, which Imada passed around to Ishiwara Kanji (1886–1959) and others at General Staff Headquarters, that he made the cryptic statement: "Do not make Chiang Kai-shek into Ming T'ai-tsu!"[35] This line has been cited several times in the postwar laudatory literature on Nakae, although no one has as yet bothered to explain it. Taken out of context, the line lends itself to several explanations.

Ming T'ai-tsu (r. 1368–1398), despotic founder of the Ming dynasty, rose to power as the leader of an immense peasant army that expelled the Mongols from China. Perhaps Nakae was suggesting that a continued Japanese invasion and occupation of China would enable Chiang to rise to the top of the resistance, expel the foreign invaders, and eventually rule China in a despotic fashion. He was more likely intimating the possibility that the Nationalist regime and the Japanese could come to terms, with the latter hoisting Chiang to be the titular head of a puppet government. This suggestion implied Chiang's probable willingness to go along with such a plan, and Nakae was urging Imada and the rest of the military to oppose such a move in particular and the extension of the war with China in general.

In the late spring of 1938 Nakae urged Imada and the Japanese army to be as understanding or as sympathetic as possible in China. He used the German words *mitgefühlend* and *mitleiden* to convey his thought, adding the equivalents in the Christian, Buddhist, and Confucian traditions to note the essential universality of what brings and keeps people together. To violate this basic principle would be, he argued, expressing his worry, for the Japanese people to sacrifice a life of freedom for a single, specific objective. "It is my firm belief that a great commander must never forget, even as he sleeps, the necessity of always demonstrating this [principle] to each and every one of his troops active in the field."[36]

Whatever happened at the front, he claimed, affected the lives of those still back in the homeland. Nakae's point here was not exclusively to counsel solace for the poor Japanese at home, but for Imada and his fellows to consider that their actions in Manchuria and North China had international ramifications and could easily elicit an attack by another foreign power on Japan in which the common people would, as always, suffer the most. "I hope you'll give this your thoughts once again . . . Although there's nothing particularly odd about this rather ordinary [perception], a look at the surrounding circumstances may reveal something worthy of unrestrainable anxiety."[37]

In May 1938 Suzue Gen'ichi was living in Shanghai, researching materials on the history of the Chinese revolution. His friendship with Hu E-kung became closer at this time; and when, in an effort to reach Sino-Japanese peace, Hu began a series of meetings with Vice Admiral

Tsuda Shizue, Suzue acted as interpreter. On two occasions that May, Suzue traveled to Tokyo to confer with Imada at the General Staff Head-quarters. Suzue was, on behalf of Nakae, trying to describe the realities of the Japanese invasion to Imada in an effort to end the conflict.[38] Nakae's failure only confirmed his unhappy diagnosis that Japan was headed for destruction. Yet, he continued his attempts through the mail to counsel Imada.

Imada's letters to Nakae were never published and seem to have been lost or destroyed, but we can infer something of their content from Nakae's responses. In July 1938 he wrote to Imada that he had just received three pieces from him and commented on how worried Imada seemed. Nakae's conclusion implied agreement with something Imada had said: "I firmly believe that we must always act to improve the lives of our glorious people and that this must be continual. For that reason, I enthusiastically look forward to the time soon when the war will come to an end and [our] nearly 100 million people will be relieved of lives full of distress."[39] It appears that Imada had repeated to Nakae the popular wartime view in Japan that the war in Asia was aimed at better-ing the lives of the Japanese people. Nakae was responding that, if one were concerned with the future of the Japanese, an immediate end to the war was absolutely needed.

In this and earlier letters to Imada, unlike in his correspondence with anyone else or any of his other writings, he expressed much of his worry about the future course of the war in terms of the toll it was tak-ing on the ordinary Japanese people who would have to fight it and would suffer under the deprivations it would cause. Nakae was, of course, concerned with their lives, but he was specifically couching his appeals to Imada in logic and language calculated to gain an ear. Nakae was not ignorant of the widespread, popular jingoism in Japan; it sad-dened him greatly to see war on the Asian mainland glorified, with young Japanese boys being sent off to their deaths. One of his last diary entries, written shortly after the attack on Pearl Harbor, reads: "The [Japanese] people are enthralled by the results of the Pacific War . . . [hav-ing] obliterated all else from their minds. 2 Jan. 1942."[40]

Referring to his earlier warnings about the dire consequences of a pro-tracted war in China, Nakae wrote to Imada in August 1938 again expressing grave concerns. "The fact that 400 million people [i.e., China] and nearly 100 million [i.e., Japan] live separated by a body of water is a fact which cannot be obliterated by any power. Although the present, temporary situation is discouraging, the overall scene isn't at all. I have the most ardent wish that one day soon all will revert to the true path of morality."[41] One cannot help but note that Nakae's tone had become a bit more direct, even though he softened these comments at the end. Several days later he again wrote Imada, apologizing profusely in more typical self-abnegating fashion for having volunteered his views so forthrightly.[42] The purpose of this follow-up letter may have been to take some of the sting out of the tone, though not the content, of the previous one. Clearly, though, this was also a way for him to remind Imada of that previous letter and its content.

Early the next year, 1939, Nakae received a visit from a close friend of Imada's, Ushijima Tatsukuma (b. 1904), who served under Ishiwara Kanji and was a renowned judo star. What Nakae had to say to him specifically remains unknown, but Ushijima himself later testified to being greatly moved by the meeting. In a letter to Imada in April, Nakae referred obliquely to his conversation with Ushijima: "My views about the present situation which you may have already heard from Mr. Ushijima haven't changed a bit. The more the outside world undergoes ever greater changes, the more immovable my firm beliefs become."[43] Undoubtedly, he simply told Ushijima everything he had been telling Imada all along: that the war in China was insane and that Japan was doomed to fail. Late in the year he wrote in the margin of the last volume of Marx's *Capital*: "The Japanese Army took Nanning; they're probably at the end of their tether. The sky is clear, the wind cool. It's 9:30 a.m., 27 Nov. 1939."[44]

As was the case with his predictions about Hitler's demise, Nakae was ultimately proven correct; but his timing seems to have been influenced by his gloomy mood. In 1939 he began citing certain passages from the Bible to visitors and friends. One of his favorite passages, according to those closest to him, spoke to present concerns: "The [Red] Sea covered them, and they sank as lead in the mighty waters."[45] The quotation, Exodus 15:11, is from a song of praise sung by the Israelites after their deliverance from the Egyptian Army to the God in whom they placed their faith. Aside from the obvious allusion to his belief that the Japanese army in China would share a fate with Pharoah's troops several millennia earlier, perhaps this was another instance of Nakae's repeated efforts to demonstrate to his friends and acquaintances that the proper perspective on the present situation, seen with historical acuity and invested with boldness of trust and vision, could lead the way to avoiding grotesque errors.

In his last letter that year to Imada, dated 3 December 1939, Nakae mentioned having "unexpectedly run into the gallant figure of Ushijima yesterday . . . In his naiveté he understands your present situation, his will is calm, and [his mind] is strong." He then followed with a citation from the *Shuo-yuan* on the importance of being true to oneself.[46]

As if by contrast, Nakae went on to mention in heavily sarcastic language that "I was impolite to General Tada, whom I have yet to see in person, and surely wasted his valuable time by boldly making the empty chatter of a scholar." Lieutenant General Tada Hayao, a colleague of Imada's and a man Nakae himself had in fact met two decades earlier, was then Commander of Japan's North China Army. Nakae did not indicate what prompted their exchange, but we know from other sources, certainly known to Imada at the time, that Tada had tried (as he would again in 1940) to retain Nakae's services as an advisor on how best to save the situation in North China. In July of 1940, Prince Konoe Fumimaro (1891–1945), who had been concerned about the army's becoming bogged down in China, became Prime Minister a second time; and he also requested Nakae's advice. Nakae turned them both down flat. Under no circumstances was he going to become involved in the official Japanese activities of occupation.[47]

Whatever letters Nakae may have written Imada throughout 1940 are no longer extant. When we pick the correspondence up again in March 1941, Nakae has adopted a new tack. He no longer solely addresses the issue of the war, but now attempts to place it in a much larger philosophical context more typical of his correspondence with others. After briefly wishing him good health, Nakae launches into his newly fashioned theme: "Although truth does not exist apart from the present reality, that reality does not constitute truth in its entirety . . . This is not only so for individuals but for nations. '*Geist* [Spirit] mourns the loss of itself.' This is the condition of our times." This rather opaque citation, completely out of context, is to Hegel's *Phänomenologie des Geistes*, and its meaning is difficult to ascertain. As will become clearer in the next chapter, Nakae's point is to contrast sharply the ideal of ethical life (or *Sittlichkeit*) and genuine freedom with their antithesis—"something qualitatively different, something 'non-human,' replacing the life of humanity," as he put in the introduction analyzed in Chapter Six—which he saw dominating the contemporary world. To quote Hegel directly:

> This simple certainty of spirit within itself has a double meaning; it is quiet stability and solid truth, as well as absolute unrest, and the disappearance of the ethical order. It turns round, however, into the latter; for the truth of the ethical spirit lies primarily just in this substantial objectivity and trust, in which the self does not know itself as free individual, and which, therefore, in this inner subjectivity, in the self becoming free, falls into ruins. Since then its trust is broken, and the substance of the nation cracked, spirit, which was the connecting medium of unstable extremes, has now come forward as an extreme—that of self-consciousness grasping itself as essential and ultimate. This is *spirit* certain within itself, which *mourns over the loss of its world*, and now out of the purity of self produces its own essential being, raised above actual reality.[48]

One wonders whether Imada understood the elusive subtleties of German idealism here. Nakae's point, as I understand it, is a devastating critique of contemporary Japanese politics and the Japanese military machine, for they and their Axis allies were largely to blame for Spirit's lamentations.

This much of an explanation is sustained by the next portion of Nakae's letter: "Over the past ten years, there have been assorted twists and turns, but the stream at its source has now become a raging torrent which flows into a sea of darkness. Although in darkness, the sounds of rustling sea winds and the roar of the waves cannot deceive the ears and heart of even a foolish man. Honesty shines even when it's dark outside; and ostentation collapses even in brilliant light. This is as true for the individual as it is for the people."[49] Nakae's choice of a ten-year span pointedly located the beginning of the trouble in the Manchurian Incident in which Imada had played the central role in the explosion at Liu-t'iao-kou. The remainder of the letter was a direct continuation of the first part and a less direct extension of what he had been counselling Imada all along. His and his colleagues' actions had larger consequences, and service to truth required an unswerving fidelity in the face of the "twists and turns" of phenomena in everyday life.

Several weeks after Nakae mailed this letter, he wrote to Suzue in Shanghai and noted in passing a sudden visit from Imada. Their conversations went on for hours before Imada mentioned that he and others associated with Ishiwara Kanji's anti-Tōjō group had lost their posts. Nakae told Suzue that he had heard the news but only responded to Imada: "Is that so?"[50] Imada had been the commanding officer at a post in Korea since at least late 1939, and the proximity had facilitated visits to Nakae in Peking. By late 1941, Imada had been transferred to a position with the army at Lu-an in Shansi province, and all of Nakae's subsequent letters went there.

Nakae's last letters to Imada are exceedingly cryptic, full of references to old Chinese texts, mysteriously worded, and requiring a fair amount of detective work to sort out their meaning. Early in November 1941, he wrote: "Contrary to your hopes and expectations, 'They're going South of the city and will forget the North,' as Tu [Fu] said." Only in light of Nakae's letter of March 1941 does this make sense. When Nakae had reminded Imada of his role in the Manchurian Incident, he also intended it as a reminder that Imada may have expected that the invasion of China would end in Manchuria, but "they" (the Japanese Army) were now heading South deep into China proper. This letter continued:

> When we gaze at what has been created as a new pathway of history, as one part of the great principle shared by all men, as the great principle of humanity past and future in an immovable form beyond various narrow personal views and petty personal victories, we agree from our innermost heart with the sages of antiquity when they said that the 'Kingly Way' was vast and peaceful . . . I have perceived more and more that this is the true reason that human beings act morally and humanity is great.[51]

The first part of this excerpt contains a profoundly sarcastic reference to the "Kingly Way" (*wang-tao*, J. *ōdō*). Although the term had ancient roots in the Chinese classical tradition, Nakae was undoubtedly masking here an attack on the slogan of the "Kingly Way" then being appropriated in Manchuria and Japan to depict the form of government in the puppet regime in Manchukuo. In other words, it was being used as a slogan for Japanese imperialism, and Nakae had nothing but scorn for this perversion of truth.

He next wrote Imada about six weeks later, shortly after the attack on Pearl Harbor and the commencement of war in the Pacific. The thrust of this letter concerned the military strategies advanced by Karl von Clauswitz (1780–1831) and Sun-tzu (sixth century B.C.E.) and suggested that these old writings might have significance in the present war. The last lines touched on Tada Hayao and Ushijima Tatsukuma. With Tada, he now revealed relentless anger. Apparently Imada had written or said something critical of Tada to Nakae; "I agree with all your criticisms," Nakae wrote back and went on to condemn Tada in a variety of ways.[52] Sakatani Yoshinao remembers Nakae making a similarly negative assessment of Tada that year.

Nakae's mention of Ushijima is in a more positive vein. Over the years 1939–1941, Nakae had come to gain a certain affection for Ushijima. When Imada visited Nakae in these years, he often brought Ushijima along. In 1940 Tada Hayao discovered much to his surprise that Ushijima had already met Nakae. In his high-ranking military capacity, he asked Ushijima at that time to convey a (second) message to Nakae, requesting his assistance in resolution of Japan's situation in China. Nakae reportedly declined saying sarcastically: "What use [can they have] for an urchin in threadbare clothes?" Perhaps unaware of the great impression he had been making on Ushijima, Nakae offered him mild praise in the letter to Imada, written just ten days after their last meeting: "Ushijima is a passionate fellow, though rather much like those one reads about in the biographies of courageous warriors. I hope he'll be very successful as a pilgrim in pursuit of judo."[53]

Despite this mildly patronizing appraisal, Nakae must have genuinely liked Ushijima or he would not have continued seeing and talking with him. Their last meeting occurred on 11 December 1941, several days after the Japanese air attack on Pearl Harbor, an event of such proportions, Nakae told him, that few comparable could be cited throughout Japan's long history. At that time Nakae forcefully reiterated his belief that Japan was going to lose the war. Ushijima was deeply impressed by these meetings.

Late in the war, Ushijima and Major Tsunoda Tomoshige, who was also closely associated with Ishiwara Kanji, plotted the assassination of General Tōjō Hideki (1884–1948), in an attempt to bring the war to a rapid end. The attack was to take the form of a bomb thrown at Tōjō in the third week of July 1944, but their plans leaked out prematurely and were revealed to the authorities. They were arrested and sentenced to death, but their execution was stayed and they survived the war. Ushijima may have had many reasons for wanting to eliminate Tōjō, but, when he was caught and questioned, the statement he gave reads as follows: "Even now his words are unforgettable. It took place on 11 December 1941 in Peking; a great scholar by the name of Nakae Ushikichi resident there said: 'They've started a war with America, and so will be revealed a wretched fate for the Japanese as well as other peoples.' It's fair to say these words decided my subsequent actions."[54]

In November 1941 a mild influenza was going around Peking, and Nakae became afflicted. His marginal note of 16 December reads, "Was in bed from the 4th through the 14th—during this period, war broke out in the Pacific."[55] Chest discomfort continued through early 1942, and in mid March Nakae finally entered the Japanese-run Dōjin Hospital in Peking for x-rays. Twenty-three years before he had been treated at this hospital for injuries sustained in the demonstrations of 4 May 1919. His doctor discovered "serious pulmonary tuberculosis" and gave him "at most two years to live." At first the doctor was reluctant to inform Nakae of the seriousness of his illness, sure to cause him a great shock, although Katō ultimately did. The x-rays were forwarded to Kyūshū University Hospital where medical director Nakajima, a classmate of Nakae's from elementary school in nearby Kagoshima, reported that "there was hope." Suzue Gen'ichi, who had been cured of the same disease at Kyūshū University Hospital several years before, and Nakae's many other friends and acquaintances urged him to enter Dr. Nakajima's hospital. He wanted to remain at home in Peking; but ultimately they persuaded him to return to Japan, where his condition deteriorated rapidly, and he died on 3 August 1942.[56]

Through this period he maintained his contact with Imada. In early

April 1942, he wrote Imada's mother, a friend of his own mother, in Tokyo to report on his doctor's diagnosis but in an upbeat manner. Several days later he wrote to Imada himself. Noting that Imada had probably already heard the news of his illness, Nakae minimized the symptoms. Apparently Imada had offered through an intermediary, General Okamura Yasuji, Commander of the North China region and a man Nakae had known since his days with Banzai Rihachirō, to pay Nakae's medical expenses. Nakae turned him down, though not, it seems, for the reason that money from such a military figure was tainted; stubbornness and an unwillingness first to enter the hospital and later to embroil others in his illness compelled his refusal.

In this letter to Imada, Nakae was also responding to a question Imada had posed: Was the *Kung-yang Commentary* better than the *Tso-chuan*? Nakae had written extensively a decade earlier on the subject of these two commentaries, representing respectively the New Text and Old Text interpretations of the ancient classic *Ch'un-ch'iu* (Spring and autumn annals). He responded that the two texts in question each had distinctive strengths, but that the debate among specialists over their relative merit, which had raged since the Former Han dynasty, was of little use. Because they were qualitatively different, it was far too narrowly subjective, he counseled Imada, to assign one a higher place of importance. Then, suddenly, he shifted themes and wrote: "Circumstances in Europe are rapidly approaching a climax. Within a year things will reach a general conclusion. This should be more than evident to everyone."[57] It was Nakae's last piece of political commentary to Imada.

In early May, Katō wrote Imada a full report on Nakae's condition in response to a telegram of the previous day. Imada had apparently broached the topic of medical expenses because Katō brought it up himself. Katō reported that he had independently paid a visit to Ts'ao Ju-lin to talk over Nakae's condition. Ts'ao allegedly offered to pay for everything "out of a more than brotherly bond with Nakae for the past thirty years."[58]

Nakae dispatched his last extant letter to Imada only four days before departing Peking on 21 May 1942 for Kyūshū University Hospital. After discussing his plans and expectations, Nakae turned to his reading matter: "On my sick bed, I've begun reading Tolstoy's *War and Peace* for the first time . . . I've been extremely impressed, especially with his portrayal of the history of the war with Napoleon. I encourage you by all means to read it."[59] Few authors have expressed greater enmity for Napoleon ("who never even in exile displayed one trait of human dignity"[60]), or painted a more negative picture of him, than Tolstoy. One of the central themes of *War and Peace* concerns the historical inevitability of Napoleon's defeat. Such had been Nakae's metaphoric theme, with respect to Hitler, for some time.

Nakae made a point of assuming the post neither of a guru nor a pacifist to his many friends. He strictly forbade his younger acquaintances to call him *sensei*, a common term for one's teacher or simply one's senior. To say that war is hell and destructive should have been no revelation to anyone who heard him; to say it at a time when the war had been sanctified in Japan as "holy," became a more radical gesture, but it still was not an act of genius. Nakae's real prescience manifested itself when he predicted the wider war that would result from the Manchurian Incident and the war that was to come between Japan and the United States as a result of the Marco Polo Bridge Incident. He did not come to these assessments after a session with a crystal ball. By the same token, he greatly underestimated Hitler's capacities as a leader of a war machine, until the bombing of London and the invasion of Russia commenced.

What distinguished Nakae from his contemporaries was his unflinching attachment to personal principles that forbade, with the force of religious interdiction, any participation in the Japanese war effort. He had no desire to be a hero or a martyr, but he did choose to live his life with his dignity intact. That required his rejection of Tada Hayao's appeal for him to serve as an advisor, his advice to Ting Shih-yuan to remove himself from any contact with the Manchukuo government, his counsel to Ts'ao Ju-lin not to give in to pressure and join a puppet regime in North China, and his suggestion to Katō Koretaka not to accept an appointment from the SMR.

Nakae may not have been correct in every one of his predictions, but he had a keen sense of the tragic and devastating route the Japanese government and military were traveling, rare for a Japanese at that time. It is hard to describe, for example, what might have been Ushijima Tatsukuma's initial shock when he heard Nakae claim that the war Japan was pursuing in Asia was doomed to utter defeat and even more when he realized that Nakae hoped for that defeat. The nature of his relationship with Imada Shintarō, to whom Nakae repeatedly advocated an end to the war, and especially the nature of Imada's response to Nakae's haranguing are also impossible to fathom now.

Nakae's hope and personal belief that the Axis powers would lose the war have been presented here as a series of impressions and assessments, enhanced by his position away from Japan, where his voice would have been much more easily controlled. As someone who had rejected Japan and all the unfulfilled promises of Taishō democracy and who found that, even when he attempted to return home, it had become personally impossible, Nakae developed a unique perspective on developments in Japan. There were other Japanese expatriates living in China, but none attained the kind of diverse following nor expressed the kinds of views that Nakae did. In fact, it was far more common in the 1930s for previous left-wingers and scholars to "switch" tracks, jump on the ultranationalist bandwagon, and support Japanese expansionism as necessary and crucial for the future development of Japan.

Nakae's unique perspective and his views on the war were not purely a function of the distance that expatriatism allowed him. He possessed a kind of secular faith in a future for humanity, in which democracy and the genuine worth of every individual were to be fundamental. This deep faith demanded belief in a defeat for Germany, Italy, and Japan, as well as a victory for the Allies. There was more than wishful thinking at work here, far more. For Nakae, these ideals were grounded in a philosophical system he developed with the help of German idealism, in particular Kant, Hegel, and Marx, the three authors he was reading and rereading in the last years of his life. Nakae's relationship to German idealism and his own philosophical ideas are the subjects of the next chapter.

EIGHT

The Importance of German Idealism

"Perhaps there are still some children who have not eaten men? Save the children."
Lu Hsun[1]

Nakae's approach to the works of Kant, Hegel, and Marx—the trio on whom he concentrated in the mid 1930s—was not to consume all of their writings but to read their major works over and over again. He found in them the touch of philosophical brilliance linked with history that helped him sort out his own intellectual proclivities. The distant past, the horrific present, and the anticipation of a better future were now centrally linked through the one category that can be traced through his entire life and work: humanity. In the same way, the attraction to German idealism was part of his continuing effort to make philosophical sense of a world gradually going mad before his eyes. Where was truth to be found in all this tumult? Could it somehow be gleaned amid the much more obvious chaos? Was there any meaning to all this insanity? Was the world (and world history) moving forward or was it just moving toward annihilation?

As had been the case in his research on ancient China, Nakae was motivated in the first instance by methodological concerns. In his work on the Chinese classics, he had been interested in how the contemporary scholar enters the mind of a subject from the past, how one penetrates the world of antiquity, peeling away the layers of falsity that had massed themselves around the truth in the intervening centuries. In the

nische Bürgerkrieg des 19. Jahrhunderts für die europäische Arbeiterklasse. In England ist der Umwälzungsprocess mit Händen greifbar. Auf einem gewissen Höhenpunkt muss er auf den Kontinent rückschlagen. Dort wird er sich in brutaleren oder humaneren Formen bewegen, je nach dem Entwicklungsgrad der Arbeiterklasse selbst. Von höheren Motiven abgesehn, gebietet also den jetzt herrschenden Klassen ihr eigenstes Interesse die Wegräumung aller gesetzlich kontrolirbaren Hindernisse, welche die Entwicklung der Arbeiterklasse hemmen. Ich habe desswegen u. a. der Geschichte, dem Inhalt und den Resultaten der englischen Fabrikgesetzgebung einen so ausführlichen Platz in diesem Bande eingeräumt. Eine Nation soll und kann von der andern lernen. Auch wenn eine Gesellschaft dem Naturgesetz ihrer Bewegung auf die Spur gekommen ist, — und es ist der letzte Endzweck dieses Werks, das ökonomische Bewegungsgesetz der modernen Gesellschaft zu enthüllen — kann sie naturgemäße Entwicklungsphasen weder überspringen, noch wegdekretiren. Aber sie kann die Geburtswehen abkürzen und mildern.

Zur Vermeidung möglicher Missverständnisse ein Wort. Die Gestalten von Kapitalist und Grundeigenthümer zeichne ich keineswegs in rosigem Licht. Aber es handelt sich hier um die Personen nur, soweit sie die Personifikation ökonomischer Kategorien sind, Träger von bestimmten Klassenverhältnissen und Interessen. Weniger als jeder andere kann mein Standpunkt, der die Entwicklung der ökonomischen Gesellschaftsformation als einen naturgeschichtlichen Process auffasst, den Einzelnen verantwortlich machen für Verhältnisse, deren Geschöpf er social bleibt, so sehr er sich auch subjektiv über sie erheben mag.

Auf dem Gebiete der politischen Oekonomie begegnet die freie wissenschaftliche Forschung nicht nur demselben Feinde, wie auf allen anderen Gebieten. Die eigenthümliche Natur des Stoffes, den sie behandelt, ruft wider sie die heftigsten, kleinlichsten und gehässigsten Leidenschaften der menschlichen Brust, die Furien des Privatinteresses, auf den Kampfplatz. Die englische Hochkirche z. B. verzeiht eher den Angriff auf 38 von ihren 89 Glaubensartikeln als auf $1/39$

ihres Geldeinkommens. Heutzutage ist der Atheismus selbst eine culpa levis, verglichen mit der Kritik überlieferter Eigenthumsverhältnisse. Jedoch ist hier ein Fortschritt unverkennbar. Ich verweise z. B. auf das in den letzten Wochen veröffentlichte Blaubuch: „Correspondence with Her Majesty's Missions Abroad, regarding Industrial Questions and Trade's Unions." Die auswärtigen Vertreter der englischen Krone sprechen es hier mit dürren Worten aus, dass in Deutschland, Frankreich, kurz allen Kulturstaaten des europäischen Kontinents, eine Umwandlung der bestehenden Verhältnisse von Kapital und Arbeit ebenso fühlbar und ebenso unvermeidlich ist als in England. Gleichzeitig erklärte jenseits des atlantischen Oceans Herr Wade, Vicepräsident der Vereinigten Staaten von Nordamerika, in öffentlichen Meetings: Nach Beseitigung der Sklaverei trete die Umwandlung der Kapital- und Grundeigenthumsverhältnisse auf die Tagesordnung! Es sind dies Zeichen der Zeit, die sich nicht verstecken lassen durch Purpurmäntel oder schwarze Kutten. Sie bedeuten nicht, dass morgen Wunder geschehen werden. Sie zeigen, wie selbst in den herrschenden Klassen die Ahnung aufdämmert, dass die jetzige Gesellschaft kein fester Krystall, sondern ein umwandlungsfähiger und beständig im Process der Umwandlung begriffener Organismus ist.

Der zweite Band dieser Schrift wird den Cirkulationsprocess des Kapitals (Buch II) und die Gestaltungen des Gesammtprocesses (Buch III), der abschliessende dritte (Buch IV) die Geschichte der Theorie behandeln.

Jedes Urtheil wissenschaftlicher Kritik ist mir willkommnen. Gegenüber den Vorurtheilen der s. g. öffentlichen Meinung, der ich nie Koncessionen gemacht habe, gilt mir nach wie vor der Wahlspruch des grossen Florentiners:

Segui il tuo corso, e lascia dir le genti!

London, 25. Juli 1867.   **Karl Marx.**

A page with marginal notes, from Nakae Ushikichi's copy of Das Kapital.

last eight years of his life, however, he reoriented this concern and focused squarely on the contemporary world to look for a way to penetrate the confusion of the immediate present and sort out the true and meaningful from the false and transitory. The search took him back to Western philosophy and German idealism in particular. This reorientation was neither a volte-face nor sudden switch; nor does it reflect a discontent with or rejection of Sinological study. He had read Kant and Marx earlier, just as he continued to read old Chinese texts thereafter. In fact, it had been the work of the neo-Kantian, Georg Jellinek, that had helped prod him into a life of research and study years before.

In the late 1930s, Sakatani Yoshinao, then a high school student, began spending his summer vacations by visiting his family in Peking where his father Sakatani Ki'ichi, an old friend of Nakae's and heir to a peerage, served as head advisor to the North China Central Bank. Nakae took a special interest in Yoshinao, met with him frequently in Peking, and communicated with him regularly in long letters, laced with German expressions and classical Chinese quotations, clearly beyond the immediate understanding of a teenager but aimed at piquing his interests. "Is there a way to see through an age like our own?" he rhetorically asked the youngster in a letter of May 1940. The question was posed in part to encourage the young Sakatani not to believe everything he was being told in wartime Japanese schools and to continue studying on his own. In answer to himself, Nakae could not demonstrate that there was, indeed, a method to comprehend the present; he could only affirm how much depended on the need for it. "In an era in which the most advanced stage of history is about to unfold yet further, whatever decline or disorder there may be, if humanity had no confidence or foresight, why should human beings as part of the continuous, unbroken [chain of] humanity continue in the lives they have until now preserved for the 10,000 years since the dawn of history and seek to grow further."[2]

German idealism, particularly the works of Kant, Hegel, and Marx, provided something on the order of a prescriptive oracle for Nakae, or so it seems in his letters to young Sakatani. When writing to adults, Nakae adopted less the manner of a teacher, but he did not relinquish his highly optimistic philosophic vision. In 1940 he wrote his best friend Suzue Gen'ichi: "German idealism with the masterful achievements of Kant and Hegel might seem a little absurd, but I feel its rendering subjectivity complete, its making the individual's dignity supreme, and its caring for the functioning of our consciousness more than anything make it the most glorious product in the development of mankind to date. I rather doubt that idealism will be preserved in Hitler's Germany." German idealism, as the late Itō Takeo noted, became so important to Nakae because in it he found the greatest affirmation of humanity as the starting point, the subject of all consideration, philosophical or otherwise.[3]

Many books and articles in many languages have been written about Kant, Hegel, and Marx. What is needed here, therefore, is not so much an outline of their thought as an examination of those ideas that Nakae took from them. Looking at which of their ideas resonated with his concerns and were useful to him in developing his own philosophical convictions, and which ones he found lacking, will enable us to learn something about the thought and values of Nakae Ushikichi.

KANT

From Nakae's marginal notes in his copies of Kant's first two critiques, *Critique of Pure Reason* and *Critique of Practical Reason*,* we know that before 1934 he read the former twice (in 1924 and 1931) and the latter twice (in 1932 and 1933). From September 1936 through March 1937, he studied the *Critique of Pure Reason* with his young friend Katō Koretaka (who was then sixteen or seventeen years old) in the original German. Katō later recalled how Nakae labored with him over each passage again and again, without secondary writings or translations, but with long discussions, until it began to make some sense. When Katō one day brought along an essay by Heidegger on Kant, Nakae became angry: "You want to study *this* without having finished reading the classics? With that attitude let's quit right now!"[4] Nakae brooked no nonsense, although his style was usually softer.

In a letter of April 1941, he encouraged the young Sakatani Yoshinao

---

*Although Nakae read these works in German, here and throughout the chapter, quotations will be given in English translation, as will book titles.

to pursue his studies rigorously, regardless of what grades he received and even at the expense of loneliness. Shifting his tone, Nakae went on to note the inutility of the notion that life is all appearance or phenomena. Yet "the more the phenomenal world comes to dominate our minds . . . the more keenly we feel the mysteriousness of the mind, as Kant says at the end of his *Critique of Practical Reason*. Although truth does not lie outside the phenomenal world, the phenomenal world is not immediately truth [itself]. For, those who are conscious of and reflect on 'what is truth' and 'what is falsehood' are none other than ourselves [living in the phenomenal world], no matter how minute or powerless we may be."[5]

Indeed, Nakae was arguing, the more the world of immediate perceptions (that is, the realm of apparent reality) controls our daily lives, the more difficult we find sorting through the phenomena before us; the marvels of conscious existence can be overwhelming. And, yet, it is we little people who can and must see through this mysterious realm to the True and the False. Nakae claimed that he gained this insight from Kant. The conclusion of Kant's famous *Critique of Practical Reason*, to which he referred in his letter to Sakatani, reads as follows:

> Two things fill the mind with ever new and increasing admiration and awe, the oftener and more steadily they are reflected on: the starry heavens above me and the moral law within me. I do not merely conjecture them and seek them as though obscured in darkness or in the transcendent region beyond my horizon: I see them before me, and I associate them directly with the consciousness of my own existence. The former begins with the place I occupy in the external world of sense, and it broadens the connection in which I stand into an unbounded magnitude of worlds beyond worlds and systems of systems and into the limitless times of their periodic motion, their beginning and continuance. The latter begins from my invisible self, my personality, and exhibits me in a world which had true infinity but which is comprehensible only to the understanding—a world with which I recognize myself as existing in a universal and necessary (and not only, as in the first case, contingent) connection, and thereby also in connection with all those visible worlds. The former view of a countless multitude of worlds annihilates, as it were, my importance as an animal creature, which must give back to the planet (a mere speck in a universe) the matter from which it came, the matter which is for a little time provided with vital force, we know not how. The latter, on the contrary, infinitely raises my worth as that of an intelligence by my personality,

in which the moral law reveals a life independent of all animality and even of the whole world of sense—at least so far as it may be inferred from the purposive destination assigned to my existence by this law, a destination which is not restricted to the conditions and limits of this life but reaches into the future.[6]

Kant stressed in this vision of the overpowering capacity of the universe to make men sense the smallness of his own creation and at the same time feel the grandeur of creation itself that only humanity possesses the wherewithal to respond to moral law and to "a world . . . which is comprehensible only to the understanding."

Unlike the other animate creatures of the universe, in Kant's view, human beings possess the capacity to distinguish appearance from reality. They do this with Reason, and Reason operates with Ideas. For Kant, these Ideas serve to define the object of philosophical analysis, to set the standards for distinguishing true and false, and, ultimately, to enable the observer to separate appearance from reality.[7]

Central to Kant's philosophical system and to his impact on Nakae was this complex notion of morality. In a well known passage in the *Critique of Pure Reason*, Kant wrote: "Nothing is more reprehensible than to derive the laws prescribing what *ought to be done* from what *is done*, or to impose upon them the limits by which the latter is circumscribed."[8] Morality for Kant was a priori and at its core lay obligation or duty. Human beings, as ends in themselves fulfilled through happiness, are thus obligated by moral laws that arise from their practical reason. Happiness, though, cannot be confused with the satisfaction of immediate needs, for in Kant the former includes both needs (of all kinds) and the significant corrective of virtue.[9] Thus, for Kant and Nakae's understanding of him, two points need to be emphasized: Reason and morality, elemental to a human being's mental architecture, are prior to action; and all things in nature operate according to laws. But while non-rational beings act instinctively according to the demands of external "physical necessity," human beings may rationally observe the natural realm *and* can fashion their own actions because they are truly free. As such, human beings reside in both the sensible and the intelligible worlds, because they are able to live under moral obligation; they do not merely exist at the level of nature.[10]

What is the moral law to which the human will is attached? In his *Foundations of a Metaphysics of Morals*, Kant phrases it in the first person: "I should never act in such a way that I could not also will that my maxim should be a universal law." As A. R. C. Duncan has paraphrased this idea: "A rightful or dutiful [i.e., moral] action is then interpreted to be an action of such a kind that it should be possible without inconsistency to will the universal application of the maxim on which it is based."[11]

We have here the basis for the most famous of Kantian concepts, the categorical imperative. "Imperative" is best understood as an "ought" proposition. Two kinds of "ought" imply two kinds of imperative.

> An imperative is called hypothetical when it indicates which means must be willed or employed in order that something further . . . may be realized. [E.g., "He *ought* to go if he wants to see her"]. It is called categorical when it manifests itself as an unconditional [i.e., moral] demand that has no need to borrow its validity from some further end, but instead possesses its own validity in that it presents an ultimate, self-evident value. [E.g., "He *ought* to go"].[12]

There can be many hypothetical imperatives, but there is only one categorical imperative: "Act only according to that maxim by which you can at the same time will that it should become a universal law."[13]

A necessary precondition, according to Kant, for any practical reason, any moral action, is freedom. What merely *seems* impossible is no hindrance to freedom, for in Kant's understanding, freedom has the capacity to open the mind beyond the simply observable dimensions of reality. As Ernst Cassirer noted: "The causality of obligation is not confined to the actual, but is oriented toward what is not actual, indeed to what is empirically impossible."[14] Freedom of the individual will is the measure of human autonomy; for, in Kant's formulation of the categorical imperative, the free will is by definition a moral will.

What then is Kant's view of man? Men are rational entities, thinking members of a community. The more men exercise their freedom, the more their actions aim toward moral universalism; and this, in Kant's view, it is man's nature to do.[15] Various scholars have noted the great influence exercised by Rousseau over Kant in this area. Having previously overestimated the importance of pure thought, and by the same token denigrated the average man for being unable to do so, Kant noted, in an autobiographical fragment, that "Rousseau corrected me in this . . . I learned to honor man, and I 'find' that this attitude of mine [as an investigator] can give worth to all others in establishing the rights of mankind." [16]

Human beings do not live in isolation. As rational creatures, the full development of our reason requires a "process that can only be fully realized in the history of the human race," not as individuals. History for Kant embodied the evolution of mankind toward freedom, for "unless men are free to use their reason in public the progress of human enlightenment [namely, history] cannot continue."[17]

Kant formulated the categorical imperative slightly differently in his *Foundations of a Metaphysics of Morals*, in a way that addressed this issue of "humanity," the family of man, directly: "Act so that you treat humanity, whether in your own person or in that of another, always as an end and never as a means only."[18] "Humanity" for Kant, then, implied all rational beings among whom there had to be mutual respect simply because all are parts of a larger whole – humanity.

Even the most ardent defender of Kant would not deny that Kant's conception of the obligations imposed on the moral human agent is onerous. Kant's *Moralität* seems to demand an almost religious intention to do good, and Kant apparently hoped that others would be no less rigorous than he in this regard. He was well aware of the fact, though, that men continually fell short of perfection, and here he broke with Rousseau on the natural goodness of mankind. For Kant, only the moral will is naturally good; it is a goal for men to work toward recapturing.[19]

If anyone, however, aimed at such a high moral self-conception and wished it on others in a time of chaos, it was Nakae Ushikichi. Like Kant, Nakae lived most of his life single and with few friends; and, like Kant, Nakae kept a daily regimen so regular that one could set one's watch by it. Nakae's penchant for quotidian order possessed the additional element that by adhering to such a rigorous personal schedule, he preserved his integrity amid the prevalent decay of values all around. For Nakae this was the importance of philosophy: It was a guide to how one led one's life, not empty theorizing or complicated wordplay. With Kant, Nakae discovered the transcendence of an unconditional, unqualified morality, and a Reason that preceded the world of appearance in such a way as to assist in the essential task of separating falsity from truth in a world of decay.

Kant's notion that experience can never exhaust all that is real, the idea that there is more to reality than what is merely perceived, serves as background to establishing the a priori nature of moral reason. Nakae makes this point in his letter to Sakatani Yoshinao, with the added and equally important indication that such an approach provides the basis for a critique of contemporary society. The letter goes on to talk of the Mongol conquests, the Moslem invasion of Spain, all the havoc wrought, the death and destruction, with a clear indication that he means to compare these horrors with Japan's invasion of China. "Although you are but a middle school student today, historical con-sciousness" of these events "is very important," because they tell of a like time when all apparent reason was destroyed and people suffered greatly. He concludes with a suggestion he offered on other occasions and to others as well, to read Pierre Loti's *Les derniers jours de Pékin*, a melodramatic contemporary account of the devastation following the crushing of the Boxer Uprising by the Powers.[20]

Thus, several elements of Kant's larger philosophical system play important roles for Nakae. Kant's distinctive and rigorous notion of morality, his anti-empiricist conception of reality, his ultimate belief in the fellowship of humanity based on the categorical imperative, and his aspirations for freedom as the necessary precondition for the activity of the moral will all fit well with Nakae's own thought. Kant's successor in German idealist thought, Georg Wilhelm Friedrich Hegel, may have been even more influential.

HEGEL

One early August day in 1941, while Nakae was taking a walk through the streets of Peking with young Sakatani Yoshinao, he explained in a nutshell what appealed to him in German idealism from Kant to Hegel: "In a word, the fundamental spirit of German idealism lies in the prob-lem of how to live as a person. Thus, this fundamental spirit exists in the life (*Leben*) not so much of the 'philosopher' as unconsciously in the life of the direct and simple farmer who doesn't even know the first thing about philosophy" (literally, the *te* of *tetsugaku* or "philosophy").[21]

The one volume by Hegel that we know Nakae read several times, and the one which, by all accounts, exerted the most influence on him, was the *Phenomenology of Spirit*. In addition to layers of marginal notes in his copy, Nakae left thirty-three pages of continuous reading notes devoted to it. In Nakae's estimation, the book's greatness as a work of philosophy derived from the fact that it spoke directly to the concerns he expressed to Sakatani.

Nakae did not begin to tackle the *Phenomenology* until April 1940, two years before he died. He finished seventeen months later in September 1941 and immediately began to reread it. The second reading concluded in early 1942, and Nakae immediately began it for a third time. During the summer of 1941, Sakatani Yoshinao planned to go to Nakae's house every day to study the "Preface" to the *Phenomenology* with him in German, but soon stopped because of Nakae's severity. By this point, Nakae, like other intellectuals of his day, surely understood the importance of the "Preface" within the scheme of the larger text ("The Preface to the *Phenomenology*," wrote Herbert Marcuse in the same year, 1941, "is one of the greatest philosophical undertakings of all times."[22] "The most important of all Hegel texts . . . " wrote Hermann Glockner in 1940, "whoever has understood the preface to the *Phenomenology* has understood Hegel.")[23] Nakae knew that this was the place to begin a study of Hegel. Reading the *Phenomenology* during a major upheaval of the world order, he also knew he was studying a work written during the exciting and astonishing time when Napoleon's 1806 victories were changing not only the rule of Europe but its political imagination. Writing with enthusiasm for what seemed the dawning of a new and freer period, Hegel wrote of a spirit (*Geist*) moving in events and shaping them, a spirit that embraced all humanity and progressed through history, sometimes with tumult, enabling all mankind to move toward self-realization. It was this humanist strain in Hegel that appealed to Nakae, as it has to other twentieth-century political philosophers, especially certain Marxists and existentialists. It offered a promise of hope for the future as well as a means of making sense of the terrible present.

Several days before Napoleon's troops marched on Jena, where Hegel was teaching in 1806, Hegel wrote his friend and publisher, F. I. Niethammer (1766–1848), that he was sending the first half of his manuscript of the *Phenomenology* with the second half to follow. "If any part of this got lost, of course, I should hardly know what to do; I should hardly be able to reconstruct it." On the day (13 October 1806) Napoleon took Jena, Hegel sent perhaps his most famous letter, again to Niethammer: "The Emperor—this world soul—I saw riding through the city to a review of his troops; it is indeed a wonderful feeling to see such an individual who, here concentrated in a single point, sitting on a horse, reaches out over the world and dominates it." Although less than a decade later Hegel would marvel at the "tremendous spectacle of "an enormous genius destroy[ing] himself,"[24] in early October of 1806 the *anciens régimes* throughout Western Europe were finally crumbling, largely because of Napoleon's victories, and the future (even the present) was uncertain to say the least. As Robert Solomon points out:

> In 1806 . . . Hegel was dealing with an international situation unprecedented in the history of the modern world, which certainly seemed at the time, apocalyptic. He was the citizen of a non-nation whose sense of impotence makes our own sense of powerlessness seem self-induced by contrast. And most of all, in 1806, with the world at war, Hegel was reminding himself and everyone of the grand importance of *ideas*, of the way philosophy gives life a perspective and can be a source of inspiration and meaningfulness . . .
>
> In a world that has come to see ideas and collective enthusiasm with horror, Hegel becomes a gateway to a new world, where ideas are the key to consciousness, where the philosopher becomes the spokesman for the times and the prophet of a united humanity. It is a world in which archaic terms like "harmony" and "humanity" still make sense—indeed, still give us something to hope for.[25]

This enthusiasm with what the future held can be seen in the "Preface," which was written after he had completed the body of the *Phenomenology*: "It is surely not difficult to see that our time is a time of birth and transition to a new period. The spirit had broken with what was hitherto the world of its existence and imagination and is about to submerge all this in the past . . . To be sure, the spirit is never at rest but always engaged in ever progressing motion . . . [T]he spirit that educates itself matures slowly and quietly toward the new form, dissolving one particle of the edifice of its previous world after the other."²⁶

What then was the *Phenomenology* all about? Written as war engulfed and destroyed his world, what was the point? There are many points, but there is a grander perspective involving the book's overall intended impact. To quote Robert Soloman once again:

> The *Phenomenology* is a grand treatise in cosmic humanism; humanity is every-thing, in the guise of *Geist*, or "Spirit," and the purpose of Hegel's philosophy is to get us to appreciate ourselves as a unity, as all embracing humanity, and bring about the "self-realization of Spirit" . . . Hegel's "Spirit" is human spirit, and if it includes much more than just humanity (namely, everything), it is, nonetheless, a belligerently humanist demonstration that this is a human world in which all is but a stage for our own self-realization.²⁷

This reading of the *Phenomenology*, the humanist Hegel, has been the interpretation of philosophically oriented Marxists (such as Herbert Marcuse, Jürgen Habermas, and others of the Frankfurt School) as well as such existentialist thinkers as Alexandre Kojève and Jean Hyppolite. It also coincides with the interpretations of such sympathetic Hegel scholars as Shlomo Avineri and Walter Kaufmann.²⁸ More to the point, it approximates Nakae Ushikichi's reading of the *Phenomenology* and his understanding of Hegel's importance both in the history of philos-ophy and as an approach to the present.²⁹

Interestingly, nowhere in Nakae's letters, his reading and marginal notes, his scholarly writings, or the memoir literature about him do we find even passing mention of the thematic content of the *Phenomenol-ogy*. He does mention the great difficulty he had in reading it, as in sev-eral letters to Katō Koretaka: "Becoming at home with Hegel is difficult beyond belief. I only come to understand it after a week or two of real struggling." Or: "When I was reading Hegel [referred to in an avuncular Sino-Japanese style as "Hei-chan"] today . . . my head felt all glued to-gether, all motion ceased. I could only feel that these expressions like 'sich selbst' [oneself], 'wesentlich' [real], or 'Selbstbewusstsein' [self-consciousness] were dancing around on the paper as if written in Per-sian or something."³⁰ On occasion he analyzes the categories and terms that Hegel employed and complains at the inadequacy of Japanese equi-valents, preferring, for example, *chi* (as in *chishiki* or knowledge) over *gaku* to translate *Wissenschaft*.[31] It was not, however, the content of this book as such that so strongly influenced Nakae.

In the *Phenomenology*, Hegel sought to encompass the entire history of philosophy, arguing that all earlier philosophical views have been one-sided. The book unfolds as a critique of successive world views, beginning with that of the Greeks, told from within each system of thought, and taking each one as seriously as possible. By any estimation a major undertaking, as Walter Kaufmann notes: "The idea of arranging *all* significant points of view in such a single sequence, on a ladder that reaches from the crudest to the most mature, is as dazzling to contemplate as it is mad to try seriously to implement it."[32]

The word *phenomenology* meant for Hegel the study of the structures of experience. For Hegel there was no thing-in-itself, no realm of the noumenon into which the human mind could not enter. Phenomenology encompassed everything. By *Geist* or "Spirit," Hegel meant the *human* spirit, the spirit of *humanity*. Thus, the *Phenomenology of Spirit* implies the study of the structures of experience of humanity, from the Greeks through the present.[33]

By fashioning his massive undertaking as he did, Hegel sought to demonstrate "the rationality of the universe, the purpose and meaning of human life as a whole . . . [T]he grand purpose in the existence of Spirit *is* its recognition of its own reasons for being and, finally, the realization of its total activity." In addition, the *Phenomenology* constitutes a wholesale attack on the excesses of subjectivist individualism. Hegel shared with many Enlightenment thinkers the view that human beings had no meaning outside their society, their community, their culture. Commenting on the *Phenomenology*, Judith Sklar notes of Hegel's intent in this regard: "The greatest single obstacle to the quest for certain knowledge is the view of men as discrete entities, each one of whom must find his ends somewhere out there, when in reality they are together the creators of their selves and their common world."[34] Nakae put it more succinctly in a letter to Imada Shintarō: "The individual is confirmed through the people."[35]

In the realm of morality Hegel also sought to overstep Kant, and again he greatly influenced Nakae. Kant's conception of *Moralität* was an individual, subjective morality based ultimately on the categorical imperative. Hegel distinguished this kind of morality from a broader societal ethos, *Sittlichkeit* ("the Ethical World" or "ethical order," as it is used in the *Phenomenology*), an ethical community in which people interrelated not as individuals but as constituent members of the totality. From his early theological writings, Hegel's ideal for *Sittlichkeit* had been the ancient Greek *polis*, particularly Periclean Athens, in which religion had served as the community's cohesive glue. As he put it in the *Phenomenology*:

> In a free nation, therefore, reason is in truth realized. It is a present living spirit, where the individual not only finds his destiny, i.e. his universal and particular nature, expressed and given to him in the fashion of a thing, but himself is this essential being, and has also attainted his destiny. The wisest men of antiquity for that reason declared that wisdom and virtue consist in living in accordance with the customs of one's own nation.[36]

The notion of *Sittlichkeit* became central to the *Phenomenology*, in which Hegel also used the expression "spirit" to convey this sense of social unity or solidity. In the *Phenomenology*, it implies a "complex of customs, rituals, and practices that make up a society and make each one of us part of society . . . It is that set of behaviors through which we define ourselves, through which we learn what 'morality' is and what is right and wrong . . . a 'natural' synthesis of our moral sense and our social sense."[37] *Moralität* retains its place in Hegel's system and even sometimes takes precedence over *Sittlichkeit*; but, generally, morality for Hegel is truly completed only in a unified community, through *Sittlichkeit*.[38]

Sittlichkeit is closely related to Hegel's conception of freedom. When the subjective aims of the individual are thoroughly integrated into the communal life of society, he attains a state of freedom. The laws of the polity reflect and are reflected in the individual minds of each of the citizens of that polity. Again, this was Hegel's vision of Periclean Athens, a vision somehow oblivious to (troublingly so) the slave stratum upon which this idyllic world operated. "The happiness of the Athenians was due entirely to their being a free people."[39] The social component of freedom was important to Hegel; for he had witnessed how the drive to what he called "absolute freedom" had led to terror, not just as in revolutionary France but in general. When one man or a group imposed their notion of perfect freedom on a society, anything that stood in its way became the enemy of freedom and hence eminently detestable. Soon, a "social ethos" had given way to individual or subjective will posing as the general will and speaking in the name of "the people."[40]

In his first essay on ancient Chinese political thought, Nakae claimed to disagree sharply with "Hegel's view that places China at the lowest stage in his discussion of the spirit of freedom in world history." Later in his long essay, though, he cited Hegel's *Lectures on the Philosophy of World History* (in which the assessment was made) and said that the orthodox Chinese view of the state essentially embodied Hegel's notion of patriarchy. He also quoted from this book in his essay on the *Kung-yang* tradition to agree with Hegel that Chinese emperors never experienced the strife, well known in the West, between earthly or territorial power and religious authority. Later in this essay, Nakae again cited the same volume by Hegel, and argued that its idealist concept of history as something that transcends mere historical facts fitted well with the *Kung-yang Commentary* and the traditions it gave rise to. The latter text "was the vassal of the Idea, not its lord; historical facts are used as a medium for the Idea."[41]

In fact, a close reading of Nakae's work makes all too clear that, his disclaimer aside, he basically did agree with Hegel's placement of Chinese history at the lowest level of historical development. This point is further supported by Nakae's elucidation of the nature of Chinese society in his essay on "feudalism" in Chinese history.

After he began to read the *Phenomenology*, Nakae's understanding of Hegel expanded greatly. Despite the difficulties of the text, Nakae found it a deeply satisfying work. Shortly after he began, when it appears he was still struggling with the difficult "Preface," he wrote Katō Koretaka: "Hegel says that pure negativity is the movement of self-consciousness. I completely concur."[42] One can easily imagine Katō scratching his head, wondering just what it was that Nakae was agreeing with. *Negativity* here means for Hegel a confrontation with the factual (the way the world is), as opposed to the real (the potential for human fulfillment). As one works toward the self-consciousness Hegel has in mind (*self-confidence* may be a better term in English), one moves toward truth;

one eliminates the falsity that pervades the factual world of perceptions, as one continually distinguishes one's true self from the other. Everything contains negativity, opposition in motion, but "pure negativity" is the process of the self coming to know itself, or self-knowledge.[43]

Nakae was well aware that the text of the *Phenomenology* was completed rapidly at a confused time when Hegel's homeland was besieged by a foreign army, and he surely saw the similarities with his own predicament. Like Hegel he supported the victory of the "enemy" in the name of the furtherance of humanity. It was Hegel's particular gift, as far as Nakae was concerned, that he understood philosophy's proper calling to be its correct assessment of the present. If that necessitated a long historical perspective, it was not motivated by a desire to escape responsibility in dealing with the contemporary world. It was precisely to learn how to tell the truth from its perversion that required the long view, especially in turbulent times when the whole world was on the verge of cataclysm. Mankind in the ongoing process of coming to know itself, the achievement of "self-consciousness . . . the native land of truth," as Hegel stated in the *Phenomenology*,[44] provided the basis for Nakae's own philosophy of history.

MARX

The role of Marx's work in Nakae's thinking is considerably more difficult to sort out than that of Kant or Hegel. Much less difficult to read, Marx's writings exercised a powerful influence on Nakae's scholarship as well as on his own philosophical thought, although Nakae made explicit on any number of occasions that he was *not* a Marxist. The reasons for his aversion to the Marxist label are complex. In the opening paragraphs to his essay on feudalism in Chinese history, he had praised Mad'iar's position depicting the Asiatic basis of Chinese society. Whereas Mad'iar understandably held as closely as possible to Marxist theory, however, "since I am not a Marxist," Nakae averred, "I need not assume such an attitude."[45]

Nakae was not questioning the veracity of Marx's observations. He was rejecting the label "Marxist" because it seemed to necessitate accepting Marx's ideas as flawless science and the reaching of one's own conclusions before the completion of one's research; more importantly, it tied one to a group with whom Nakae wanted no part. He may have offered shelter to several of the major figures of the Japan Communist Party (JCP) in their time of need, but he had almost no respect for them as intellectuals, or *in maru* (short for "*in*tellectual *Mar*xists") as he disdainfully referred to them. He watched and listened to these "leaders," who claimed precisely the opposite of the role he had consciously chosen for himself as one of the masses, and all he heard was braggadocio about their experiences in prison and an incomplete understanding of Marx's writings.[46] Nakae chose his friends closely, and he counted no member of the JCP among them. He had equal, but less explicit, distaste for Chinese intellectual Marxists, which (as we have seen) he usually expressed in his scholarly work.

Thus, his rejection of the label "Marxist" for himself was to a large extent a rejection of organized Marxist politics and Communist parties who claimed to speak for "the people" but more likely typified the selfish individualism described in Hegel's concept of "absolute freedom." Katō Koretaka once noted in a letter to Suzuki Tadashi that "one might call Nakae a Marxist in the same sense that one might call Lu Hsun a Marxist."[47] His friend Ōta Ryōichirō noted a few years after Nakae's death that Nakae never doubted the veracity of Marx's theories "as the highest product of human knowledge," but he never once called himself a Marxist, much less a Communist.[48] What then did Marx and Marxism mean to Nakae?

From the mid 1920's on, Nakae read many of the writings of Marx and Engels, including *The Communist Manifesto, The Critique of the Gotha Program, The Civil War in France, The Poverty of Philosophy, A Contribution to the Critique of Political Economy,* and three editions of *Capital.*[49] It was *Capital,* though, that he read and reread in the last years of his life. He first began it late in December 1926, completing it and others works by Marx and about Marxism in the years 1926–1928. He returned to *Capital* in 1930; but it was not until February 1938 that he began his third and most diligent reading of this work, a project that consumed two full years. He finished the first volume in early March 1939, the second at the end of June, and the third in February 1940. By this time Nakae was devoting most of his reading to German idealism, and he followed his third reading of *Capital* with the plunge into Hegel's *Phenomenology* two months later.[50]

As in the case of his reading of Hegel, Nakae's many references to *Capital* almost always ignored the descriptive content of the work—the critique of capitalism and bourgeois political economy. He did agree in his written scholarly work with the views Marx expressed in *Capital* on the place of capitalism in world history, its emergence from feudal society, the relationship of economy to polity, the characteristics of Asiatic society, and the role of religion.[51] When he returned to *Capital* in the late 1930s, after his productive years as a Sinologist, Nakae was looking for something else in the text, something more along the lines of a philosophical guide to help make sense of chaos, as he found in the works of Kant and Hegel.

What is interesting, particularly from our perspective, is that he found Karl Marx, the philosopher and kindred spirit of Kant and Hegel, in *Capital*, the work of Karl Marx the economist. For the modern scholar who has, in addition to *Capital*, the *Grundrisse* and Marx's earlier philosophical and economic manuscripts, this is not difficult; but Nakae was reading before such materials were available and at a time when Marxists generally were less interested in the intellectual background to Marx's thought than in guided action. Nakae's understanding can only be termed remarkable. Shlomo Avineri has termed the similar discovery by the late Hungarian Marxist Georg Lukács (1890–1971) "an outstanding intellectual feat." Although Nakae did not develop the issues in Marxian thought so clearly or so creatively as Lukács had, his keying in on the theme of alienation was no less brilliant, particular when one realizes that he did it all alone. The guides he had to Marx and Marx's thought, books such as Franz Mehring's biography, depict the influence of Hegel and idealist thought on Marx in an absurd, Marxist caricature (a system of thought, with a neat tripartite dialectic, out of touch with the real world, waiting to be turned right side up), a view not unfamiliar even today.[52]

Nakae was fond of saying that the "reason Marxism is the greatest [system of] thought is that it is the most humanistic." He was particularly drawn to Marx's view of the historical subject pursuing a recovery from alienation, a notion undoubtedly developed from Hegel's conception of "self-consciousness." It was in this sense of "self-consciousness" that Nakae understood the term *humanity* (which he usually wrote with the Chinese characters *ningen* and glossed in Japanese syllabaries as *hyūmanitii*). It did not mean "human nature," but was drawn from the Hegelian-Marxian conception of world history. Nakae found in Marx the "principle of humanity" (*ningenshugi*, "humanism") transcending the alienation of the individual, at which point mankind would be able to realize real human nature.[53]

Marx used the idea of "critique" in the subtitle of *Capital: A Critical Analysis of Capitalist Production* as a specific kind of analysis similar to Kant's pioneering works. It implied an inquiry that sifted truth and falsity in an effort to pare away the layers of ideological obfuscation covering truth and to get directly to the problem: in this case, discovering the essence of capitalism.[54] Marx demonstrated this process brilliantly in his critique of the "fetishism of commodities," early in volume one. This penetrating search for a method and the critique it provided in separating truth from its perversion was precisely what impressed Nakae most about German idealist thought in general.

Much has now been written on the theme of alienation as central to Marx's entire intellectual project.[55] Although Marx dealt with it much more explicitly in his early manuscripts, a reader like Nakae who was well trained in German idealism could see the concept at work in *Capital* as well. As Louis Dupré had pointed out: "Though the term *alienation* virtually disappears from [Marx's] later writings, the idea of an objective separation between man and his self-realizing activity inspires his critique to the end."[56] Often in *Capital* Marx mentioned the historical necessity within the capitalist system of its own demise and the end as well of the "self-alienation" of mankind; for only in socialist society, Marx argued, would humanity for the first time take full control over its life. As one scholar has noted:

> Human history is therefore seen in terms of its most basic final outcome; as a necessary process of the elaboration and development of the human personality and its freedom. However, from Marx's point of view the issue was not so much to demonstrate the necessity of this process (this was already recognized by classical German philosophy), but rather to liberate this discovery from ideological illusions and place it on the firm foundation of real history, i.e., the development of the social relations of production.[57]

In *Capital* the concept of alienation takes on another dimension embedded in the modern definition of the term by referring not only to man's loss of his basic humanity but also to a loss of property, a loss of the power to control the product of his own labor in the capitalist system. This point is clearer in the *Grundrisse*, and it "remains the unspoken theme that guides the entire argument" of *Capital*.[58] Money is the symbol of this alienated state, or as Marx explained in the *Grundrisse*:

> Money thereby directly and simultaneously becomes the *real community* [*Gemeinwesen*], since it is the general substance of survival for all, and at the same time the social product of all. But . . . in money the community is at the same time a mere abstraction, a mere external, accidental thing for the individual, and . . . merely a means for his satisfaction as an isolated individual.[59]

Because the capitalist economy is oriented toward the commodity, its division of labor, according to Marx, turns man against the product of his own labor. Thus, capitalism's fetish for commodities represents in clearest form the alienation of mankind from his true nature. This particular point was recognized earliest from a reading of *Capital* by Lukács, whose understanding resembled Nakae's own.[60]

Like Kant and Hegel, Marx regarded history as a crucial dimension in philosophy, and he shared their unshakable belief in the rationality of history. Despite his ultimate wish to see the bourgeois order overthrown, Marx understood that proper understanding had to precede action. In other words, history, philosophy, scholarship, and politics were thoroughly interwoven; and at the center of it all lay a concern first and foremost with mankind. Nothing more neatly satisfied Nakae's own inclinations.

Nakae drew personal strength from the line from Dante quoted by Marx: *Sequi il tuo corso, e lascia dir le genti.* He used it to encourage others to independence of mind, especially the boys (his "young friends" or *wakai tomodachi*) who read texts with him in these last years. In the margin of his copy of *Das Kapital*, Nakae made a note, dated 20 April 1941: "Seventy-four years after these *iron words*," meaning seventy-four years after the publication in 1867 of volume one of the work (see p. 174). For Nakae, the epigram pointed to the strength needed to speak in a solitary voice under adverse conditions, to offer a perspective that not only went against prevailing opinion but assailed it.[61]

Nakae found himself doing just that; and having the strength to stem the tide, to stand by one's own, reasoned point of view in the face of the vast majority was immensely difficult. As those who were reading texts with him later noted, Nakae never sought to turn out young Kantians, Hegelians, or Marxists. He aimed at training them to think critically, and, in his estimation, German idealism was the best guide. Kant, Hegel, and Marx all shared a rejection of the world as it appeared in favor of a better world. This point was clearest in Marx's *Capital*, but Nakae did not intend to prepare these youngsters for lives at the barricades. He did want them to be able to distinguish the true from the false, especially when their own government and educational system was directly and daily assaulting them with lies. Kant's *Critique of Pure Reason*, Hegel's *Phenomenology of the Spirit*, and Marx's *Capital* were not, as he explained in a letter concerned with the last of these three to Suzue Gen'ichi, the sort of books "that high school and college students understand in the least."[62] They required great concentration and endless patience, but in Nakae's view the payoff was well worth it.

NAKAE USHIKICHI'S PHILOSOPHY OF LIFE

Although Nakae wrote no philosophical essays or treatises, his "philosophy" can be drawn from letters, conversations, marginal notes, and other scraps of information. What emerges is a sophisticated understanding of history, philosophically based in German idealism and Marx, primarily concerned with moral philosophy and combined with a stinging criticism of contemporary trends. At the center of his "system" is that elusive category of humanity.

In a letter from late 1938, Nakae noted to Suzue Gen'ichi: "I'm trying all alone to establish a *Lebensideologie* [philosophy of life], in conjunction with an environment of continual change, to derive from it as much as possible my individual activities in life, to unify it and make it consistent on that basis. This is extremely simple to talk about; quite a problem in fact."[63] Nakae was intensely aware of being "all alone" (when his dog Huang died in 1940, he was beside himself with grief);

but he also tried to draw strength and intellectual courage from this solitude, as someone who is not caught up in the whirlwind can stand back and scientifically observe it. Blinding change, a recurrent theme in his letters from the late 1930s onward, made accurate assessment of the direction toward which events were heading exceedingly difficult. However, with a powerful guide, a figurative road map of sorts, Nakae saw that a person could chart his own stance amid the chaos. "Kaleidoscopic changes, although increasingly bursting beyond their limits, have not shaken my beliefs one iota."[64] Kant, Hegel, and Marx helped Nakae answer the question he was always posing for himself and others: "How can we tell true from false?"

For much the same reason that he had refused to publish most of his Sinological work and rejected the label "Marxist," Nakae consciously selected an inconspicuous role for himself. He chose not to be a professional of any sort (academic, political, journalistic, or pedagogical). When addressed as "sensei," he usually responded rather harshly that he was nobody's teacher and nobody need address him with any superficially polite titles.[65] Nakae saw himself simply as one of the masses of humanity, a *seikatsusha* or living person, no more and certainly no less. Nakae's shyness buttressed this disinclination to leadership roles, but his intellectual stance had its own integrity.

The late Katō Koretaka planned but never wrote a biography of Nakae, which he had tentatively entitled "The Way for the Self-Conscious Masses." "Self-conscious" must be understood in the Hegelian-Marxian sense as fully aware or confident of self. The implied point was what Sakatani Yoshinao has referred to as "the fervent faith in the human race" at the core of Nakae's chosen way of life.[66] Despite his consistent plaint of loneliness and the omnipresent sadness one senses throughout his late years, Nakae retained a surprisingly optimistic view of the future.

He firmly believed that history moved according to laws of development drawn from Hegel and Marx. Following their idea of alienation, Nakae conceived of history as the ongoing process of the masses seeking to recover their lost humanity. This process could ultimately only be progressive; hence, history had to be moving forward, even if at present it might have seemed retrogressive. "World history," he told

Sakatani Yoshinao during their last chat in the summer of 1941, "advances in the direction of 'humanity.' In other words, what bears the burden of 'humanity' is alone the true *Träger* [bearer, conveyer] of world history. This is the law of the development of world history. However boastful of magnificence, that which does not move in the direction of a continually advancing 'humanity' must be crushed in the end." And no one could stand in for the masses: no party, no leader, just the masses themselves with whom Nakae sought to merge.[67]

He believed that assessing the world's present circumstances from the perspective of his inevitable advancement of humanity gave a new way of understanding what was happening—indeed, that any other view was a waste of time. "When I think about the [past] progress in human society," he wrote Suzue Gen'ichi, just after finishing *Capital* for the third time and at the point of beginning Hegel's *Phenomenology*, "I'm thankful from the bottom of my heart that when the extraordinary complexity of the present reality advances a step, there will be an age beyond any of the past in which life will happily be worth living." In a less sanguine moment the next year (1941), he wrote: "I have often thought that if the movement of history and the future of humanity are not *vernünftig* [intelligible] in the final analysis, then like our own trifling, minuscule lives, they're not worth a cent." [68]

> I fear errors or misreadings, but to . . . hesitate in the natural expression of one's capacity to seek truth is to abandon the development of humanity . . . Although truth has to be humble and selfless, these virtues absolutely will not be born from the cowardice . . . that panics in the face of error and loses heart in the face of misjudgment. With the power of our own conscience, we must [use] our capacity to seek truth, our courage, and our fortitude all to decide what is true and what is false.[69]

What in the present situation made such demands on the truth-discerning mind? The world of the late 1930s and early 1940s was moving with alacrity toward destruction with the rise of Nazism in Germany, Fascism in Italy, and militarism in Japan. Behind Nakae's predictions for collapse of the Axis Powers and the defeat of the Japanese military in China lay this abiding faith in the meaning of history and the ability of the well-trained mind to understand the pathway.

That was why Kant's distinction between the world of phenomenal experience and the true world of reality was so important to him.

Nakae repeated this lesson in a variety of garbs through his letters and conversations with the young Sakatani Yoshinao, who was being exposed in Japan to the official educational system and its version of the truth. In a letter of late April 1941, Nakae commended his young friend for not believing the "delirious utterances" of his high school teacher and for remaining faithful to a sense of truth. In a foreshadowing of latter-day computer wisdom, Nakae wrote Sakatani: "Nonsense gives birth only to nonsense."[70]

Nakae dealt further on this theme in a long letter the next month. Learning to differentiate truth from falsehood was not a matter, he argued, of copying a teacher or blindly following a leader; it was a matter of knowledge. It was a matter, moreover, of the will that breathes life into knowledge, for the ability to make any significant or discerning choice was a "manifestation of character. Courage, boldness, responsibility, self-confidence, discretion, and all such virtues originate in" personal character. He continued in this vein:

> "Is there any sort of future in an age like the one we're now in?"—nothing brings up a more ghastly and frigid feeling in me than when I hear such words nowadays. In an era in which the most advanced stage of history is about to develop even further, whatever collapse or disorder there may be, if one harbors no confidence or foresight, to what end will human beings, under the name of a continuous, unbroken humanity, continue in the lives they have until now preserved for the 10,000 years since the dawn of history? If scholarship suppressed mankind's aspirations in this direction, it would become if not poisoned learning, then dead learning.[71]

When Sakatani came to Peking that summer, Nakae told him that Japan and Germany were headed for an inevitable defeat. At this point, the young visitor balked, finding this prediction too much to accept. Nakae explained that, from the time of the occupation of the Sudetenland, the Nazis were building their external relations on the basis of conquerors and the conquered, a tremendous perversion of the proper, liberating direction for humanity in history. "Falseness cannot defeat truth. Germany must lose," he claimed.

> If the Axis Powers win and Nazi Germany and Japan cover the world with their systems of rule, do you think that there will be a reason for human life to go on? Do you think that humanity will want to continue living under them? . . . Something which rational human thought cannot bear cannot [ultimately] be victorious [in history]. If it could, history would have no meaning at all.[72]

Outside the context of a background in German idealism, this all sounds like so much wishful thinking; and to be sure, wishful thinking was not altogether absent. There was a further message specifically for Sakatani:

> And Japan is the same. You don't think that I'm simply a defeatist? If Japan were to proceed along its present lines and win victory, it would turn into [a nation of] military arrogance, bureaucratic self-righteousness, and skyrocketing prices, which the growth of a healthy and happy people can hope *never* to witness. So, rather than preserve the roots of the disease and spread the unhealthiness, it's better to lose the war and fundamentally whip the character of our people back into shape.[73]

Thus, Nakae's conception of world history incorporated the idea that history moved forward as humanity searched for itself and overcame alienation. Nakae's belief in the victory of progress in history meant that humanity would win out, and the forces devoted to its further enslavement (the Axis Powers) ultimately had to lose. "When you look at the present international conflict," he told Sakatani in their last chat, "clearly it's the democratic countries, not the Axis Powers, that are bearing the burden of 'humanity.' Final victory in the world war has to belong to the democratic nations. Nazi Germany must fall . . . This fact may not be so clear in the eyes of ordinary people, but with trained eyes it's perfectly clear."[74]

When doctrines were announced in Japan, like the New Order in East Asia, the Greater East Asian Co-Prosperity Sphere, the Holy War, and other cosmetic covers for outright Japanese imperialism, Nakae made a point of telling everyone who cared to listen what he thought of such ideas. Nonsense remained nonsense, and these nifty phrases were in fact transparent code words for aggression. Just as he had refused to act as a broker in Sino-Japanese relations on behalf of Prime Minister Konoe and Captain Tada, he flatly turned down an offer to be head of

the National Foundation University in the Japanese puppet state of Manchukuo. Katō Koretaka recalled being present when Nakae received a written invitation from Ōkawa Shūmei (1886–1957), a right-wing activist in
Manchukuo, to give lectures on East Asian politics so as to help calm down
the domestic scene in Japan; he tore the request into small pieces and deposited them in the garbage.[75] Nonsense belonged in its place of origin.

Nakae's wartime diaries, of course, show that he was just as eager to
see Germany and Italy defeated as he was to see Japan rescued from the
evil consequences of militarism, and his diagnosis of the historical
forces at work made him as confident in private as he was publicly of a
victory by the democratic countries over the Axis powers. In his diaries,
however, he expressed more pain at the great loss of life that would be
incurred in the process. In mid June 1940, he noted: "When I imagine
the imminent danger facing the French Army desperately holding back
the onslaught of the Germans who come pouring forth like a rushing
stream, such a tragic sight is simply appalling."[76]

In the last years of his life, he became more specifically concerned
with the road Japan was taking. Not an activist by inclination or philosophical bent, Nakae nonetheless tried through his letters to Imada Shintarō, his letters and talks with Sakatani Yoshinao and many others, and
the personal example of his consistent refusal to be involved with the
Konoe or Tōjō governments to counsel fellow Japanese on the disastrous course he saw the nation traveling. One detects a note of genuine anger and exasperation in diary entries such as in mid July 1940:
"The weak Yonai Cabinet has collapsed like a decayed log because of the
Army's extortion. Though it is presumed that the ever ambitious
Konoe, in spite of a lack of strength and capability, may rise out of the
trapdoor, the monkey show would remain a monkey show after all."
The man for whom Nakae reserved his special invective was neither
Konoe nor Tōjō, but Foreign Minister Matsuoka Yōsuke (1880–1946),
an ill-timed bad joke in human guise. He once told his friend Suzuki
Tadashi that "compared to Churchill—Konoe, Matsuoka, and Tōjō
were merely a laughingstock of poor actors."[77] He had, in fact, planned
to write and publish an essay entitled "Nihon kokumin ni tsugu" (Address to the Japanese people)—probably modeled on the "Address to the
German People" (1807–1808) of Johann Gottlieb Fichte (1762–1814)—in

which he would have addressed many of these issues, but his last illness prevented this work from being completed.⁷⁸

Given the depraved state of politics in Japan and the educational system's inculcation of an array of perversions and outright lies, Nakae decided that his small mission would be to try to recover a segment of Japan's youth. It is readily apparently that even an educated high school student would not be able to read Nakae's letters without considerable thought or assistance. (How many people quote regularly in their letters from Hegel's *Phenomenology*?) But, like the sessions in which Kant or Hegel was read in German, these letters and conversations were aimed at creating the basis for the youngsters to think critically for themselves. Japan had no immediate need, in Nakae's estimation, for a group of sectarian Kantians or Hegelians. Japan desperately needed a generation of people who could think critically, especially after the defeat Nakae so completely (and accurately) expected. Although the Japanese "people are enthralled by the results of the Pacific War [and have] obliterated all else from their minds,"⁷⁹ as he wrote in his diary shortly after the attack on Pearl Harbor, if Japan was to have a future, it was clearly not in war.

The future held no place for life-negating forces; it belonged, as a law of history, to humanity; and only democracy served the cause of humanity. Despite this firm belief, Nakae was not so naive as to think that things would just happen because the "laws of history" demanded it. Human beings with foresight, critical minds, and knowledge shared a great responsibility never to relinquish the struggle to search for truth and to let it be known. In the case of Japan, there were so few well trained souls that Nakae's fears were justified. His last letter to Sakatani Yoshinao made this point in a broader context, citing Hegel's *Phenomenology*, referring obliquely to Kant, and then continuing:

> Our lives are merely imaginary abstractions outside of [concrete] reality, but this present reality is not at all immovable and fixed. It is rather a ring of uninterrupted motion. It is surely not something we either can or must objectify in our reflection and contemplation. However great or overwhelming it may be, it is that much more instructive to us.

And, paraphrasing both Hegel and Marx:

History is the history of mankind. Its creation and transformation are always the creation and transformation of the history of humanity. Mankind lives in every corner of the globe, and living conditions in one region are integrated with the living relations throughout the total region. When the present war is over, we shall have to think in terms of some sort of cooperative postwar situation, unprecedented in history, and move toward recovery. I don't think that such an era is far off or imaginary.[80]

NINE

The Many Faces of Nakae Ushikichi

Nakae's death in August 1942 brought an end to the Nakae family line, for his marriage had ended in divorce with no children. It was a lonely end, with many of his friends still in war-torn China and his library still in Peking. His married sister, with whom he had quarreled long ago, did come to see him at Kyūshū University Hospital about a month before his death. By now they had made their peace, but how much comfort she could bring him is a matter of speculation. Just before her visit, he wrote in his diary, "30 June 1942. Sis is coming. We'll repress our passions somewhat." An entry of several weeks later reads, "28 July 1942. The threat of death presses closer. I'm fully resigned to it."[1]

Inasmuch as he had published but one article in his lifetime, Nakae might be remembered at best as a footnote to history had it not been for the determined efforts of a small group of friends and admirers. From the outset they were determined to see his work in print; but with a war going on, the first order of business after his death was to ensure that his library passed into responsible hands. During his many years in Peking Nakae had come to know several of the finest Japanese Sinologists of his generation. Among them, Ojima Sukema, who published the first short essay on Nakae as an afterword to a longer piece on Nakae Chōmin, had taught at Kyoto University and retained his contacts there. Katō Koretaka had learned from Nakae that he wished his books to be sent to the library of Kyoto University's Research Institute on Humanistic Sciences. Ojima was the natural person to complete the transfer.

In 1943, however, war still raged between China and Japan. In addition, a fair number of the books in Nakae's collection were proscribed by the authorities in Japan, such as certain Marxist works. Ojima's friend and colleague, Uchida Tomoo, who had worked for a time for the Research Department of the SMR, handled the details of packing the books and mailing them to Japan, with the help of a Chinese book dealer in Peking. The boxes in which the books had been packed were marked "public use" (*kung-yung* and no Japanese railway police at any of the checkpoints—Peking, Fengtien, Seoul, Pusan, and Shimonoseki—opened them. Uchida accompanied the books all the way to Kyoto and witnessed their safe arrival in the hands of the Research Institute.[2]

The group of friends and disciples who survived Nakae wanted his collection of books to remain in the same configuration as he had kept it. In other words, rather than having the books dispersed through the various categories of the larger university collection, they wanted it housed as it was, retaining the mixture of Chinese and Western books and reflecting Nakae's own mixed use of Western philosophy, social science, and classical Chinese materials.[3] They succeeded; and to this day, the entire collection has been maintained separately as the Nakae bunko (Nakae archive) in Kyoto University.

Their aim in keeping his library intact was to reflect the complexity and breadth of the man. If the collection were broken into its constituent parts, it would lose its distinctiveness, much as Nakae the man has little meaning unless all his component parts are considered together. In his fifty-three years Nakae seems to have lived three or four lives, although no single fully developed career. We have Nakae the spoiled brat as a student and pampered son; then there is Nakae the transformed scholar of ancient Chinese thought and society; there is Nakae the expatriate and critic of Japanese imperialism; and, finally, we have Nakae the student of German idealist philosophy and a budding thinker in his own right. Memoirists (there have, to this point, been no biographers) have gone to considerable pains to try to tie these different threads together. What was the central core of the man from which these varied "persons" arose?

The standard resolution of this problem has been to fall back on Nakae's own emphasis on the centrality of "humanity" to all human action and thought. In Nakae's usage "humanity" carried several connotations. While it implied the abstraction of human beings — mankind — it also involved his understanding of the categorical imperative as prescriptive. Many commentators have used Nakae's profound concern for the human race to link him with his altogether different father by citing Chōmin's deathbed statement that he would have felt compelled to try to rescue Louis XVI. While useful as far as it goes, such an approach is insufficient to account for all of Nakae's behavior or to describe his character fully, much less explain it.

As much as we tried to downplay the radical nature of Nakae's break with his own "profligate" youth in 1919, the serious man that emerged after reading Georg Jellinek and confronting the students in May was thoroughly different from the boy who preceded him. Just as war can change the lives of those personally involved in it, so Nakae's confrontation with the life-threatening incident in front of Ts'ao Ju-lin's home, his brush with death, at least catalyzed a process of maturation. It did not insure or prescribe, any more than his exposure to Jellinek's work did, that Nakae would subsequently become a devoted scholar, let alone a scholar of Chinese antiquities. His choice of that particular direction is difficult to explain other than to cite the obvious: He was living in China, he read Kanbun extremely well, and he worked from the start to devise a new approach to the classics.

This new approach involved bringing major Western works and traditions of philosophy, sociology, psychology, comparative religion, and anthropology to bear on an understanding of ancient China. It also relied heavily on Chinese textual traditions. As a result, Nakae asked a whole series of questions in his analysis of the past not previously addressed by scholars of ancient China, many still not addressed to this day. This search into the past began with the difficult question, usually ignored by historians as a methodological given, of how the contemplating mind of the researcher enters the minds of those living in times distantly removed in the past. Needless to say, this concern is not superfluous, although it may be insurmountable. That Nakae faced it, even if his resolution of it is not altogether satisfactory, remains important.

We noted in analyzing Nakae's long essay on ancient Chinese political thought how he broke into his own discussion with an occasional digression about the hardships experienced by men and women in the past.[4] He was apparently just as saddened by human suffering in the past as in the present. And, if he had had plans to publish this essay, in order to find a publisher he would surely have had to delete these sentences in the interests of the standards of "disinterested objectivity" of the scholarly community he so disliked.

His emphasis on and explanation of mankind's hardships and lack of freedom in the past emerged most strikingly in his essay on the question of feudalism in Chinese history. This topic gave him the opportunity to examine the nature of Chinese society from the Shang through the Ch'ing, the entire run. His conclusion, that it had changed little because of the Asiatic nature of despotic control especially from the Ch'in unification forward, sounds extraordinarily simple-minded now. Here Nakae's sadness at the state of Chinese suffering in the past and present seemed to have outweighed his reasoning as a historian. The recurrent problem of excessive power in the hands of an autocrat, a problem that no change of government for the previous two millennia had successfully attacked—in fact, each new regime had always taken advantage of the configuration of forces to seize despotic power for itself—could only mean, in the manner Nakae reduced it, that China possessed an Asiatic society and economy.

Humanity had suffered in the past, and that fact was perhaps even more important than all other historical facts. History, as Nakae began to conceive it more philosophically in the 1930s, was the process by which men overcame the alienation and hardship visited on them from time immemorial. In Nakae's view, we are all connected in the same historical, teleological struggle to recover the human decency (or, "humanity," in one of the senses used by Nakae) taken from us by those who have held control over our lives. For this reason and because Nakae was extremely shy, he had no interest in standing out from the mass. He not only sympathized with the hard life of the "masses" past and present; he saw himself as part of them.

The term *humanity* has several related nuances. It can imply all human beings—the masses—as in the title of the daily organ of the French Communist Party, *L'Humanité*. It can also imply an ethical conception of the interrelatedness of the human race, as when one acts out of a sense of humanity. Nakae used *humanity* with both of these meanings. These two senses of "humanity" are linked through Kant's categorical imperative, which is itself essentially a complex philosophical statement of the Golden Rule.

To act as you would have others act toward you (Confucius offered the same advice) is seen as the essence of being human. It is also the essence of friendship among human beings. For Kant, the ideal of "humanity" was a bond of mutual respect grounded in the moral will.[5] Because friendship in the sense of acting as a moral human being toward others was exceedingly important to Nakae, he cultivated friends his own age, his "young friends," and friends from every walk of life, even military and political leaders whose views he found thoroughly unacceptable.

Even expatriates—perhaps especially expatriates—crave the friendship of their fellow nationals. Like other foreigners in China and elsewhere, the Japanese had extensive services, clubs, restaurants, inns, and the like, sufficient to insulate desirous Japanese from any meaningful contact with the natives. Nakae effectively drifted into expatriatism, and he later developed a deeply felt estrangement from Japan; this turned to antipathy and only grew stronger with the passage of time, particularly after he tried to return home and found it psychologically impossible. As a result, he refused all but limited contact with anything Japanese.

From his position away from Japan, but not too far away, Nakae was able to see much more clearly than his contemporaries in Japan that the course the power-holders of the 1930s were taking would be disastrous. True to his sense of history and his faith in a better future for mankind, he knew that he had to oppose Japanese imperialism and militarism. Not an activist or a leader by inclination, not a member of any radical political party—we have seen how he despised Japanese Marxists, and many of them had apostatized to become supporters of Japanese imperialism—he had to be content communicating these views privately to everyone who would listen.

This is the origin of the confused mixture in the late Nakae of pessimist and optimist. He was serious, glum, conscious of his isolation (though, in a way, proud of it), and sad at the present state of the world.

In no extant picture of him is he ever smiling. By the same token, he retained an almost religious faith in the better future of humanity, following the demise he predicted for the Nazis, Fascists, and militarists.

Through scholarship he had been able to address issues in the development of humanity. In fact, historical research that failed to concern itself with human beings first and foremost, he had written, was "poisonous" or "dead." From the mid 1930s on, however, even he could no longer concern himself solely with the past. Suffering in the past surely was as important as that in the present; but one could do nothing about the past, except to understand it correctly. Although affecting the present was difficult, one could do something about the future. By gaining a proper perspective on the present, by being able to sift through all the rubble and ruin and come up with a method for discerning truth from falsity in a topsy-turvy world, one could pass on a critical vision to the next generation. Therefore, Nakae devoted the last years of his life to reading and rereading the great works of German idealism and trying to teach its main critical methods to younger men, such as Sakatani Yoshinao, and his other "young friends." In essence, this effort to separate the spurious from the true had been guiding him in his work both on the *Shang-shu* and on the *Kung-yang* schools, the effort to distinguish historical truth from *keigaku* truth.

Nakae's life did not end on a happy or thoroughly resolved note. The war was at one of its worst points when he became deathly ill. Japanese imperialism had reached its zenith. His contact in the Kwantung Army, Imada Shintarō, whom Nakae repeatedly counseled to restrain the war in China, was either incapable of doing so or chose not to. Nakae had not wanted to return to Japan, but it was there that he lay helplessly dying, rather than in China where he would have preferred to remain. "I'm becoming more and more aware of death as a real thing," he wrote several weeks before his death. "It's a little foolish to go and die in Fukuoka where I've come with the intention of living, but I've got no choice. Although my many thoughts have all mixed together, ultimately they're nothing at all. From anonymity I am absorbed back into anonymity."[6]

If Nakae had been known solely through his one published essay on feudalism in Chinese history, he might still have warranted a bit more than a stray footnote. "Community" or *kyōdōtai*, the concept he explored in the late 1920s, became a major issue among Chinese historians and sociologists in Japan in the late 1940s and 1950s. It remains so today, just as it is beginning to be recognized as an analytic tool in the West.

A group of ten of Nakae's friends and followers agreed shortly after his death to edit his unpublished writings for publication as a single volume. Just before Suzue Gen'ichi left for Peking to begin editorial work on the manuscripts, he was arrested in Manchuria by the military police of the Kwantung Army. Itō Takeo, Shimizu Morimitsu, Ojima Sukema, Kimura Eiichi, and others participated in editing and checking the essays. After considerable efforts by some of the most renowned Sinologists of the time, these essays appeared in book form in 1950.[7] The volume was soon greeted by glowing reviews, even from scholars like Niida Noboru and Kaizuka Shigeki who disagreed with several of the theses propounded in it.

Takeuchi Yoshimi was impressed by the strict organizational spirit and concern for method that runs through *Chūgoku kodai seiji shisō* and the overwhelming "human passion" of the author's search for truth. The legal scholar Kainō Michitaka found the book of great scholarly value, but went on to assess its lasting import: "When such a fine book as this one emerges from the narrow scope of being a scholars' favorite to becoming the kind of book enjoyed by the general public, then I think Japan will truly have become a civilized nation."

We cited at the outset the more recent, and rather lavish, praise of Hashikawa Bunzō, probably based on a reading of Nakae's letters which were published in 1964: "The keystone of his [Nakae's] greatness was an unbounded faith in and love of humanity combined with an historical vision so broad that he almost seemed to be the world spirit incarnate."[8] This evaluation obviously plays on the importance of Hegel's work to Nakae's philosophic concerns. More than the particular brilliance concerning this or that point, what appealed to all of these critics (and others as well) was Nakae's steadfast stance in opposition to Japanese imperialism, his outspoken criticism of it, and the clarity of his vision.

As early as 1950, when Nakae's book of essays was first published and reviewed, Niida Noboru understood immediately the connection for Nakae between the study of antiquities and contemporary concerns. In the dedication of his piece on the "P'an Keng" chapter of the *Shang-shu* to Prince Saionji, Nakae had written: "My humble essay may be trivial, but in my case I believe it to be an expression, however poor, of my consciousness of life."[9] Niida knew that this was not empty chatter. It was the whole point. Research and scholarship was dead if it was aimed solely at other researchers and scholars, and Nakae rejected this little world. It had to have a larger objective, in Nakae's case the largest possible: life itself, humanity. Niida was also aware that Nakae's claim, in the introduction (translated and analyzed in Chapter Six above) to the essay on the *Shang-shu*, to be "happy" because he could write as he wished was not an open admission of elation. Rather, it was equally a statement by Nakae that, as much as he may have wanted it, he could not enjoy that happiness at present.[10]

Nakae Ushikichi leaves a complex legacy. His scholarship has yet to receive any attention at all in the West, though it deserves considerable scrutiny. This is true particularly of his distinctive approach to the process of the formation of chapters in the *Shang-shu* and to his analysis of the development of *Kung-yang* schools, both of which involve severe critiques of the traditions of textual authority. Yet, on the one hand, Nakae would never have been happy to learn that only scholars were reading his essays (least of all scholars writing solely for other scholars), while on the other hand his writings are sufficiently difficult to make it all but impossible for anyone but scholars to comprehend them. Nakae simply did not like the academic world, even if his work retains value for it.

His intrinsically comparative approach to research presaged postwar developments in scholarship. Although many of the social scientists he used in his work are no longer fashionable, the borrowing of methodologies from parallel disciplines has become an article of faith, particularly since the war. His approach to German thought, especially German idealist philosophy, anticipated or was contemporaneous with trends in the European rediscovery of Hegel and the Hegelian core of Marx.

The strongest legacy Nakae leaves, especially for contemporary Japanese scholars, concerns his early, consistent, and unimpeachable stand against developments in Japan. Many in the left wing chose to "convert" to emperor worship rather than face the potentially deadly consequences of opposing the regime. Nakae chose what seemed to him the only humanly possible choice: The Japanese government (like their Nazi and Fascist allies in Europe) was the very incarnation of inhumanity, and one had to oppose it. If one did not stand up for human life, then could life have much value at all?

Appendix
Notes
Bibliography
Glossary
Index

Appendix
The War Diary (1939–1942) of Nakae Ushikichi

After World War II, autobiographical notations were found in the margins of three of Nakae's books. They were transcribed, arranged chronologically, and published as his diary. This appendix is a translation of that published diary.[1]

At the end of each diary entry below, the volume in which the original notation was found is given in brackets, using the following abbreviations:

H   Hegel, *Phänomenologie des Geistes*
K   Kant, *Kritik der reinen Vernunft*
M1   Marx, *Das Kapital*, volume 1
M2   Marx, *Das Kapital*, volume 2
M3.1   Marx, *Das Kapital*, volume 3, part 1
M3.2   Marx, *Das Kapital*, volume 3, part 2

1939

1.   Today, 2 January 1939, we've had beautiful weather. I heard the whistling sound of the pigeons[2] in the wind. 1:25 P.M. [*M1*]

2.   It's 1:55 and since morning it has seemed like a cold spring rain would fall. A constant drizzle has kept up. The last pieces of coal, which are about to burn up, occasionally make a sound in the stove. The important part of this morning's newspaper is the article about Chamberlain's long-winded protest to the Labour Party's vote of no confidence in defiance of his recognition of the Franco government in Spain. Until just a while ago, Little Boy [nickname for his dog Huang[3]] had been scratching his paws excitedly on the glass of the front door, but he has given that up and moseyed over to the western side of this house. 2 March 1939. [*M1*]

3. Today is the anniversary of my mother's death. The conflagrations of war about to flare up in Europe. 10:30 P.M., 17 April 1939, the weather is clear. [*M2*]

4. Today I heard the first cicadas. The sky was dense with clouds. 21 June 1939 (the time when they used to celebrate Boy's Festival, 1:30 A.M., 79°). (The issue of sealing off the British concession in Tientsin is all in turmoil.) [*M2*]

5. Cloudy, looks like rain. A cool, refreshing breeze like mountain air fills the house. 9:30 A.M., 24 June (Saturday) 1939, 77° indoors. (The blockade issue of the Tientsin Concession area is becoming increasingly complicated.) [*M2*]

6. 10:30 A.M., 19 July. For the first time in half a month, white light illuminates the azure sky. The hot weather is broiling. 83° indoors. [*M3.1*]

7. It's my fiftieth birthday. I have no money so I won't ask anyone over. Huang is sleeping pleasantly on his side in the next room. The cicadas are chirping furiously. 9:30 A.M., 14 August 1939, 77°. [*M3.1*]

8. Once again Italy seems to be playing the opportunist. That scoundrel Mussolini has a well deserved punishment awaiting him. 1:30 P.M., 6 September, it's about to rain but hasn't yet, a gloomy day, 69°. [*M3.1*]

9. It's the last two days of the annual mid-autumn festival. Leaves of the *huai* tree[4] seen through my window tremble golden in the setting sun. 4:00 P.M., 29 September 1939. Germany hasn't yet attacked the Balkans. Ribbentrop is in the Red Capital [Moscow] with the Turkish foreign minister. [*M3.1*]

10. Hitler's tricks are getting clumsier and worse, and I can only assume that his last days will come before long. The day before yesterday we had an autumn rain. Although the air is chilly, I still haven't lit the stove. I make do with my cotton clothing.

    [My old housekeeper] T'ung entered the German Hospital yesterday. The sky is gloomy, and a bleak atmosphere hovers over the garden. Noon, 17 October 1939, 59°. [*M3.1*]

11. The New Order in East Asia[5] is rapidly approaching a deadlock. Problems of industrial production, of *Warenbeschlagen* [a goods embargo] on foreign trade, and of distribution owing to the insufficiency of *Lebensmittel* [food] have become intertwined with diplomatic issues and the problem of commodity scarcities on Chinese markets. As a result, this situation is providing the *Triebhaus* [greenhouse] to foment popular lamentation and its heart-

breaking appeal that the first action for the settlement of the China Incident [i.e., Japan's occupation of China] will have to be an end to the war. My diagnosis of this "holy war" is that it has clearly entered the early stages of the third period [i.e., the end]. The wind is still; the light of the sun shines silently. 11:00 A.M., 2 November 1939. [*M3.2*]

12. The branches of my elm tree have been cut down. The Japanese Army took Nan-ning; they're probably at the end of their tether. The sky is clear, the wind cool. It's 9:30 A.M., 27 November 1939. [*M3.2*]

13. Received a letter from "Big Sis" [Okamoto Kikuko] saying that she'd gotten a phone call for Katō with the message that "Squire" [Tsujino Sakutarō] just passed away. For the last few days my phone has been disconnected because of apartment construction. The weather is fine; although a little cool, it feels just like Peking. 11:30 A.M., 5 December 1939 [*M3.2*]

14. Every day for the past week mellow weather has reigned supreme. Although at the brink of death, T'ung hasn't died. It has been five days already since I left him at his sickbed on a beautiful misty evening when there was a full moon in the sky. 5:00 A.M., 31 December 1939. 75°. [*M3.2*]

1940

15. Night has not yet turned to light; the atmosphere of dawn is vast and vague. 6:30 A.M., 1 January 1940. [*M3.2*]

16. T'ung died this morning, a little after 5:30. He was 43. I went over to Itō the dentist's place. The sky is clear and there's no wind, but the frigid atmosphere is unrelenting. 11:00 A.M., 4 January 1940. [*M3.2*]

17. T'ung's funeral procession went by the front gate of my house. The sound of the gong grieving over the dead burst into the sky like snowfall. 10:30 A.M., 8 January 1940. [*M3.2*]

18. The Abe Cabinet has fallen, and Yonai has formed a new cabinet. The [Japanese] occupation [of China] has entered stage two of the third period. Although the sky is clear, the air is chilly.

    In recent days, hearsay that the German Army was concentrating along the Belgian and Dutch borders has been circulating. It looks like Hitler's downfall isn't necessarily so far off. 11:00 A.M., 17 January 1940, 66°. Every morning since 4 January, I've been braving the cold wind to go visit Itō the dentist. [*M3.2*]

19. I've at last finished reading *Capital*. Although the sky is clear and the signs of spring still remain concealed, we nonetheless sense spring in the air through various sources like the glittering jasper. It is Chinese New Year's Eve, 7 February 1940. 12:00 noon, 60° indoors. My dog, "Little Boy," is already out in the garden, wanting the milk I usually give him there. A flock of sparrows chirp away merrily waiting for me and blissfully unaware of the sudden rise in grain prices. [*M3.2*]

20. The red-brick apartment looks like it's already finished being built; its white-painted windows scowl down on my garden. Still no one has come to rent it. 10:30 A.M., 7 March 1940, clear. [*M3.2*]

21. Today the Wang Ching-wei government was formed. The noisy sound of an airplane roared through the sky on this hazy spring day. I finally understand the meaning of this complicated section [*Capital,* vol. 2, ch. 20, part II.2, second to last paragraph]. 10:00 A.M., 30 March 1940. [*M2*]

22. Although the clove blossoms are half gone, my garden is full of fresh verdure, which seems to be trickling over the edge. Italy under Mussolini, whom I detest most of all, is going to have to enter the war. His true colors are now apparent, and soon he'll expose his ugliness to the entire world. The problem over Indonesia is increasingly defining a sharp difference between the opposing Japanese and American camps. 10:00 A.M., Sunday, 21 April 1940, with the warm wind and brilliant sun of late spring. [*M2*]

23. Huang has been sick for the past two days. [Since he was unable] to cough up phlegm, I removed it for him. Seeing him lying down by my chair in the guest room, I cannot help assuming that he is resigned to his imminent death. Fallen acacia blossoms are scattered all over my garden, leaving no space uncovered.

    4:00 P.M., 10 May 1940. Although the situation has grown tense in the Balkans, neither Germany nor Italy and, of course, neither England nor France has yet set off the fires of war.

    "Behold the feet of them who have buried thy husband are at the door and shall carry thee out." The Acts of the Apostles [*Acts* 5:9]. [*M2*]

24. Hitler has finally invaded the Netherlands and Belgium; Chamberlain has resigned and Churchill has replaced him. Churchill concluded his broadcast to the British people by urging an all-out effort "to overthrow, to exterminate these wild beasts who spring forth from their caves." 2:00 P.M., 12 May 1940. [*H*]

25. While I am fervently hoping for the victory of the British and the French, I heard with apprehension a report that the German Army was pursuing a ferocious course of attack and that Liège was already occupied. I'm afraid that the result of the fighting may turn out to be disadvantageous to England and France. Morning, 14 May 1940.

     The roles with their various forms of Hitler's latest movements. Yet it does not necessarily mean that the result of this battle will, fundamentally, alter the course of history. In any event, the result of this battle will merely be the expression of the latter [i.e., the course of history]. [*H*]

26. Last night Huang wandered about in great pain through the moonlit garden, furiously panting for almost the entire night. He fell asleep in the hallway for a moment, but he has just walked off now. There was a report of the fall of Brussels and Antwerp to the German Army. 10:00 A.M., 19 May 1940. [*H*]

27. Huang finally died this morning at 7:10. I heard the sound of their covering the hole—8:00 A.M., 24 May 1940—the sun shining, peaceful and quiet. (I suddenly remembered that I had severely scolded Huang yesterday—2:30 P.M.). [*H*]

28. Leopold [King of Belgium] has fallen. A proof that the modern state, itself created by war, finds it impossible to carry out a rapid war. Pathos for Huang has gradually changed to remembrance. 12:00 noon, 29 May, fierce wind. [*H*]

29. 31 May—in the midst of a life-and-death struggle, the Allied armies are trying to escape being surrounded by the German Army at Dunkirk and Calais. It is the eighth day since Huang's death, 11:00 A.M., raining since last night. [*H*]

30. That despicable Mussolini has finally roused himself. He declared war on the afternoon of 10 June. When I imagine the imminent danger facing the French Army desperately holding back the onslaught of the Germans, who come pouring forth like a rushing stream, such a tragic sight is simply appalling.

     "*La France subit de dures epreuves, mais la France ne peut mourir.*" [France has suffered difficult trials, but France cannot die]. Reynaud's words strongly resemble the cuckoo spitting up blood. Overcast, 10:00 A.M., 12 June. The flowers on the mulberry trees are blossoming. The remarkable earthen color of Huang's grave has faded. [*H*]

31. Paris has finally capitulated as an "unarmed city" (daybreak of the 14th) (only twenty days since they began a five-day attack).

    The Maginot Line has been broken through as if it were made of straw, and exhausted and weary French troops are running around in confusion before the German planes and tanks. It is as if the sole purpose of their feet were to save their necks. According to the reports of an English reporter who interviewed Hitler in his headquarters in Northern France, Hitler counted on superiority in military organization and in his command for ultimate victory, and has proclaimed that the so-called Fifth Column is a blanket term covering the disunity among the Allied forces. 10:30 P.M., 17 June. [*H*]

32. Pétain, like McMahon in past years, is still talking about *paix honorable;* I can't bear to listen to such disastrous [chatter]. 10:00 A.M., 19 June.

    A pair of fig trees were presented at Huang's memorial service. They have long trunks like the drawings of Western design. [*H*]

33. Hitler has yet to begin an attack on England. Despite the fact that President Roosevelt will without a doubt be elected for a third term, not a word about this has been mentioned. It's just as though he were holding a lute but concealing his face without playing it.

    The story of an Anglo-Japanese compromise over the issue of Burma has been talked about, and the American press is accusing it of being a new appeasement in the Far East.

    The weak Yonai Cabinet has collapsed like a decayed log because of the Army's extortion. Though it is presumed that the ever ambitious Konoe, in spite of a lack of strength and capability, may rise out of the trapdoor, the monkey show would remain a monkey show after all.

    Huang's old face has become increasingly vivid to me with the passing of time. 9:00 A.M., 16 July, clear. 78°. [*H*]

34. It is my fifty-first birthday, and I've invited Mrs. Tsujino, her son, and Katō for dinner.

    Although the attack on Britain has been given a certain amount of priority since the 8th, I doubt whether they'll accomplish as much as Hitler has claimed. British troops have completely evacuated China and the German press is discussing this with great enthusiasm, but it's wiser to see this move as an acceleration of the deepening rift in Anglo-Japanese antipathy. The color of the earth at Huang's grave has gradually turned—it's virtually all the same color now. 9:30 A.M., clear. 14 August 1940. 75°. [*K*]

35. I put on cotton clothing today, things from when Huang was still alive. I have never worn them in August. Long rainy spell, overcast. Clouds overwhelm the earth. It's 67° inside, 10:00 A.M., 23 August 1940. [*K*]

36. London is being subjected to fierce air raids. Although there was a raid over Berlin 23 days ago, the extent of the damage was incomparable. The Chinese dates haven't yet ripened; and though the wild chrysanthemums haven't blossomed, my garden is inundated with the autumn air. 11:30 A.M., 3 September. [*K*]

37. England and America have concluded an agreement over the leasing of land. It's like a tumultuous sensation that something may be afloat. A short rain fell; it was somber indoors, and I put on the electric lights. Morning, 5 September. [*K*]

38. The Nazi attack on London which began on the night of the 7th has become more severe with each passing day, and since the 12th has carried to extremity sorrow such as is unprecedented.

    If the British people can weather this ordeal, then the German's amphibious assault will be crushed and the enemy will vanish like the mist, just as in the case of Napoleon's designs of over 130 years ago. The Commander of these unparalleled air attacks is reported to be that scoundrel Goering, Hitler's right-hand man. It's just now the time of the harvest moon. The sound of the planes in the heavens, the earth ablaze in flames, the rounds of bullets glistening in the sky, the roar of cannons demolishing the pillars of heaven and the axis of the earth, the echoes of explosion and destruction, billowing black smoke, the air full of stifling gunpowder—above all of this, the moon is shining. Such a scene, even in just the contemplation of it, makes one's blood boil and body seethe. And yet, if you ponder this further, beneath the moonlight covering all things equally, Churchill and Hitler, and the hellish sight of the world's greatest city [London] in utter chaos, this may be regarded as a mere overture to the history of what is to come. Think of what the world will look like at this time next year. 15 September, a day before the harvest moon, 1940. [*K*]

39. The so-called *Blitzkrieg* over London which began on 8 August has increased in ferocity with each passing day, but they haven't forced the British to surrender so much as an inch. Rather, their land war, like Napoleon's plans of yesteryear, finds itself about to become a piece of empty bombast.

    On the 26th in Berlin, the Japanese-German-Italian military alliance was concluded, and it formalized the opposition of the Axis Powers to America. The principal focus of Sino-Japanese attention at present concerns how forceful a blow the [Japanese] attack on Yunnan from French Indo-China will deliver to the Chungking government.

It has rained steadily for the past few days. The cool and desolate air of late autumn has taken possession of the garden. 11:00 A.M., 29 September 1940. [*M3.1*]

40. The Japanese-German-Italian military alliance was signed on 27 September. Hitler's aerial *Blitzkrieg* has been less and less successful.

Together with the opening of the Burma Road, the World War will surely spread to the Far East. The air is clear and the leaves have been falling sporadically. 3:00 P.M., 7 Oct. 1940. [*M3.1*]

41. It was broadcast that as a result of Hitler's meetings with Pétain, Hitler's dream of Franco-German cooperation is about to be realized.

Neither Japan nor England nor America has yet begun any new activities with the opening of the Burma Road to traffic. The Japanese press reported that a new [Japanese] ambassador had arrived in Moscow and was in the midst of new negotiations concerning Russo-Japanese cooperation.

Only American diplomacy has become increasingly active. The stove has been lit for the past three days. There's no wind and the atmosphere has been clear. 10:00 A.M., 28 October. [*H*]

42. A light rain falling, and the leaves scattering here and there.

War between Italy and Greece has flared up, but the storm over the Balkans hasn't yet taken any sudden turns.

Talks have begun in Moscow between Japan and Russia, but it's difficult to guess what will come of them.

The world's attention is focused on the outcome of the presidential election in the United States the day after tomorrow. The hardening of American policy toward Japan has not waned in the least with each passing day. The New Order [of the Konoe government] is already facing criticism, and the government is having its ability questioned.

Hitler's coalition with Laval has effected a dream that the two men have long shared. 10:00, 3 November 1940. [*H*]

43. Roosevelt overwhelmingly clobbered Wilkie to become master of the White House for the third time.

Hitler attended the commemorative for the Munich uprising and roared that he would never compromise with Britain.

It is reported that Japan is rejoicing and dancing about at the celebration of her 2600th year. The cold wave has passed, the sun is shining brightly, the wind has died down. Sunday, 10 November 1940.

The "salaried men" living in the apartment next door were screaming "BANZAI" over and over again. 11:00, 11 November, no wind, beautiful rain. [*H*]

44. [Soviet Foreign Minister] Molotov arrived in Berlin on the 12th. The new consultations between these armed robbers and highwaymen have begun. They are also deliberating on how best to divide up their booties. 9:55 A.M., 13 November, the sun was out, but the wind was fierce. [*H*]

1941

45. Baldia fell on the 5th, and the bubble has popped for Italy's ambitions and dissolved like a spring snow. Morning, 7 January, 1941. Sky's warm. [*H*]

46. The bombing of London hasn't eased up at all on the British people. Only the success of a "landing operation" will prove to be the decisive key to the fate of the Three-Island Empire [Britain]. Because Italy is frustrated, the atmosphere in the Balkans over the past few days has been vibrating abnormally. It was reported that the Nazis are about to extend their tentacles over to Roumania and then to Bulgaria. Nazi pressure on the Vichy government has intensified recently. It looks like the major worry of the aging Pétain is whether to buckle under completely and offer Hitler his remnant navy or to flee to North Africa with his navy.

The lend-lease measure for military hardware has passed the House, and will undoubtedly get through the Senate. In view of the situation in Europe, which is getting more and more tense, after this measure has been passed, how will it affect the Far East? It seems that the world situation will develop toward a phase deserving our great interest. 11:00 A.M., 13 February 1941, cloudy. The lingering winter chills me to the bone. [*H*]

47. Although the prospects for war have become denser in the Balkans and the Pacific, nothing has exploded there yet. [Foreign Minister] Matsuoka's message, an application for mediation, was officially proclaimed in Moscow—it provoked a burst of laughter throughout the world. The British made an intentional statement that this was the result of a prearranged plan with Germany and Italy. The Nazis, who seemed to have been bowled over by this eccentric and ludicrous farce of Matsuoka's, claimed it was only Japan's wish, while Matsuoka himself was frightened at this reflection caused by his own farce and claimed that it was only his personal opinion. A recent source of laughter.

The ashen clouds hang low as the lingering cold is penetrating. (1:30 P.M., 22 February 1941). [*H*]

48. Chances for Japan to erupt against Great Britain and the United States: (1) the issue of the territorial transfer of Siam to French Indo-China; (2) negotiations with the Dutch East Indies; (3) innumerable other problems to worry about but can't be predicted—"chance occurrences."

    Lend-lease bill should quickly pass the Senate in a few days.

    At the Nazi Party commemoration Hitler said nothing about an invasion. He just boasted of the increasingly unlimited activities of his U-boats. England and America as well as the Axis Powers are sharpening their swords for before spring. The weather's recovered and I heard the flutes from the pigeons. 10:00, 28 February. [*H*]

49. [This note appears on the same page of *H* as the entry of 19 May 1940 (entry 26 above), which remarks on Huang's loitering about sick]. Reading again today. It has been nearly 9 months since Huang died. A dog [nicknamed Kozō] whom I found wandering about on Shui-mo Lane last winter, 20 December, and took back to my house, is now sitting where Huang used to be. 3:00 P.M., cloudy skies (5 March 1941). [*H*]

50. Hitler boasted that he would send troops into Yugoslavia and Greece, force the English troops out of the peninsula, and give Churchill the taste of a second Dunkirk. [Anthony] Eden and Chief of Staff Dale were in Athens and counterattacked in full. 1:00 P.M., 8 April 1941. Kakuichi [eldest son of Watase Shigeyoshi, named by Nakae] came over with his mother. [*H*]

51. The 13th, Russo-Japanese treaty signed. The [coming] commencement of hostilities with England and America has been accelerated. The start of the war is clearly going to accord with German advances into the Near East.

    The stormy weather of the last few days has run its course, and there is a bright sun out. The acacia buds have sprouted to the size of my thumb. 3:00 P.M., 15 April 1941, clear skies. [*K*]

52. It was broadcast that Yugoslavia and Greece have fallen, and that British troops are making a concerted withdrawal. The wind was powerful, and the sun bright and gloomy. 9:30 A.M. of the 28th anniversary of my mother's death, 17 April 1941. [*H*]

53. Seventy-four years after these iron words,[6] the joint British-Greek forces stubbornly defended against the German onslaught, like a raging billows, at Sicily.

    Berlin was bombed for the first time on Thursday for quite a few hours. Britain boasted that this was no reprisal, just the execution of their prearranged plan to the letter. English Minister Morrison said: "Make Hitler howl! Just as he bombed London at will, so we'll do the same to Berlin."

The German Army's invasion of Egypt is bogged down. 2:00 P.M., Sunday, 20 April 1941, no wind, sky cloudy. [*M1*]

54. With only a small number of troops, the British and Greek forces are now checking the Germans who are coming on in swarms, from within. I earnestly hope that the mountain pass at Olympus will turn into a second Thermopylae. 8:00 A.M., 21 April. [*H*]

55. The Balkan war that began on 6 April came to an end. It was announced that of the 60,000 British troops, 45,000 were returning alive. 9:00 A.M., 2 May 1941. The first fresh green after a rain in quite some time was a joy to behold. [*H*]

56. Read up to a point where someone was foolish enough to attach the pronunciation in Japanese syllabaries to the German words.[7] The situation in the war has gradually come to affect Asia, Australia, and the South Seas area, sites of natural resources for England and America. After sun-bathing, I felt my body and mind completely refreshed as though they'd been wiped clean. The sense that I'm not yet old swells up in me from the tips of my feet to the top of my head.

The sky is clear for the first time in a while, and the early summer brings rebirth to the sun, which shines sparklingly. Noon, 12 May 1941. [*H*]

57. Rudolph Hess, Vice-Premier of the Nazi Party, unexpectedly flew off alone in a Messerschmidt fighter plane and landed near Glasgow. He's caused a stir throughout the entire world—everyone wants to know his intentions. Will the Russo-German alliance come first or will the Anglo-American alliance be quicker? I've decided to read Hegel [*Phänomenologie des Geistes*] once again from the beginning.

The whistling birds are projecting their beautiful voices. 10:15 on a refreshing early summer morning (14 May 1941). [*H*]

58. It is four days since the anniversary of Huang's death. Kozō lies on his side where Huang used to.

The island of Crete fought a violent battle to the death. The [German battleship] *Bismarck*, which sank the [English battleship] *Hood*, has met with the same fate in the North Sea.

The sky is clear, the wind strong. 10:25 A.M., 28 May 1941. [*H*]

59. German troops are about to occupy Crete. The start of war between the United States and Germany is approaching, but they have not opened fire yet.

The scoundrel Darlan [Vichy admiral] has publicly announced cooperation with the Germans. Japan's negotiations with the Dutch East Indies
tend more toward rupturing.

No rain has fallen for the past few days; the wheat harvest was
announced to be 60% of an average year's. It looks like rain, concealed in the
cloudy sky, is about to fall. 9:00 A.M., 2 June 1941. [*H*]

60. Because of the Robin Moore incident and the freezing of German funds in
the United States, American-German relations have become increasingly
strained.

Although Damascus and Beirut are still in the hands of French troops,
it's only a matter of time. Perhaps the Russo-German pact will prolong [the
time] further. Dutch-Japanese negotiations have completely stagnated. Various conjectures are being advanced: (1) Will a tripartite alliance come about
in toto with the commencement of hostilities between Germany and America? (2) Will the American-Japanese problem provide a direct motive for
this? (3) Will Japanese-American relations remain neutral even if war erupts
between American and Germany?

It rained, cleared up, and the sun shone, but it's the end of the rainy sea-
son. 11:30 A.M., 17 June 1941. 71° [*H*]

61. Reports have it that Russo-German relations are at a critical juncture. In
order to be able to withstand Anglo-American opposition, have the Germans decided to subjugate the Soviet Union, running the risk of a pro-
tracted war? Or is this a mere gesture by the Germans? The real situation
has not yet become clear. 1:30, 21 June. [*H*]

62. War broke out between Germany and Russia on the 21st. It hasn't even been
two years since the signing of the Nazi-Soviet Pact of 23 August 1939. Flim-
siness in perfidious diplomatic relations seems as [effortless] as turning over
one's palm. 10:00 A.M., 23 June 1941, fine weather. [*H*]

63. [Prospective] results of the Russo-German war: (1) a complete German victory would extend [the war] with England and America, and would affect
the Sino-Japanese War: (2) a Russian victory, and Japan's position wouldn't
be too hard to imagine; (3) if it goes on for a long time, Anglo-American self-
confidence will increase and again Japan's position won't be too hard to
imagine. Morning, 23 June. [*H*]

64. Starting the war with Russia was without a doubt Hitler's greatest gamble. If
he can obtain and protect supply lines for a protracted war, perhaps he'll pro-

pose a *"blitz-*peace,"[8] and begin attacks on India and the Middle East. 24 June. [H]

65. I have heard reports that Riga, Vilna, Minsk, and Odessa have been occupied, but no confirmation as yet. No detailed reports have been announced by Berlin. Saturday, 28 June, a heavy rain fell last night and cleared up, and the green leaves are dripping with water. 9:00. [H]

66. Smolensk is exposed to the threats of the German forces advancing from the line of the Dvina River and also from the line between the Berezina and Dniester Rivers. The offensive and defensive battles at Smolensk may turn out to be [another] Sekigahara.[9] 9 July, eighteenth day since the start of the attack. [H]

67. The German invasion still has not slackened. The targeting of Leningrad from the northernmost tip as well as the south of Finland, the targeting of Leningrad from the Baltic coastline, and the occupation of Minsk and capture of Moscow from occupied Poland have all been raised as war objectives. 9:00 A.M., 20 July, 80° indoors. [H]

68. Konoe re-formed the cabinet on the 17th. Limitations have now been placed on ordinary travellers to Korea and Manchuria.

Although the Germans' three-pronged attack continues, Soviet resistance has not been frustrated and it fights on fiercely. The result is a gruesome scene of a mountain of corpses and a river of blood. Even if the Germans could possibly capture Leningrad and Kiev, it would clearly end in a Pyrrhic victory for them. 24 July, last night's rain has cleared up; the sunlight's reflection off the green leaves is exceptionally beautiful. 5:30 A.M., 76° indoors. [H]

69. The United States and England have promulgated orders freezing Japanese assets. July 27th: The price of Tōkabu [a leading stock]—on the Tokyo market—was at 94 yen. 10:00 A.M.

29th: It was announced that the Japanese Army and Navy have stationed troops in French Indo-China. 30 July.

As the Japanese occupation continues, no further orders (aside from the freeze) have been issued by the English or the Americans. Last Sunday a fierce wind and a pounding rain began around 8:00 in the evening. It's been clear today for the first time in a while. 2 August, 11:30 A.M. [H]

70. As a result of Roosevelt's meetings with Churchill in the Atlantic, an eight-point war objective was announced. The criticism of this in the various

national presses, to my surprise, has completely and totally missed the point. The two men wrote a joint letter to Stalin, requesting discussion of military cooperation. With the Soviet Union's ready consent, the configuration of conflict in the World War is on the verge of complete realization.

Germany has intensified its attack into the southern USSR. Odessa and Nikolaev are in serious danger. 11:30 A.M., 17 August, cloudy, 79°. [*H*]

71. Nikolaev has fallen, but Odessa is maintaining its thread of life, as is Kiev.
England and Russia are cooperating in trying to control Iran, and Germany has reacted by restraining Turkey.

Although Thailand has barely maintained its existence by keeping a balance over the two oppositional forces of Japan versus England and America, nothing whatsoever has changed the increasingly critical state of affairs in the Pacific. The heat has passed, and the autumn sunshine is penetrating. Cloudy morning, 25 August, 75°. [*H*]

72. I've been informed that Suzue Gen'ichi will be arriving today from Shanghai. 1:00 P.M., 28 August, clear, 75°. [*H*]

73. 11:20 A.M., 29 August 1941, clear skies, warm air. But I didn't get enough sleep last night; my head feels as heavy as lead. 77°
War has yet to break out in the Pacific. Nonetheless, Nazi Germany's fate is already becoming sealed. When I think back to this day one year ago, it seems as though life was much easier back then. [*H*]

74. On the basis of Konoe's letter to Roosevelt of the 28th, it looks like the negotiations are continuing. When I contemplate the fact that 90 million people are absorbed in anxiety over these negotiations, I am loath to speak of it as appalling.

Tsujino Toshio left Peking tonight to go back to Japan. The fall wind has been refreshing. 11:00 A.M., 3 September, clear. [*H*]

75. Although talks between the Americans and the Japanese haven't broken down, it looks like the eruption of war is a foregone conclusion. Leningrad, Odessa, and Kiev have all fallen. (Was it a false report which stated that Leningrad had been invaded by a division camped along its outskirts and that part of Odessa had been occupied?) The Russo-German war is about to enter its third month.

The wild camomile are blooming like crazy and the fall insects are buzzing away. 10:00 A.M., 20 September, 69° indoors. [*H*]

76. Reports from the German Army have it that as a result of this battle which began on 2 October, Timochenko's main force has been surrounded by the Germans who advanced from the direction of Vyazma and Bryansk; the seventy strongest and best trained divisions in the Soviet Army are now on the verge of total annihilation. In the same report it was boasted that the Bolshevik military might would be totally crushed within three months of the commencement of the war, and that the English dream of a war on two fronts had completely dissipated into the mist.

    9:00 A.M., 10 October 1941. It's the Double Ten holiday,[10] but the sky is gloomy. [*H*]

77. The new offensive begun by Germany on 2 October has, as Hitler declared, captured the attention of the entire world to an event that will decide the fate of the Russo-German war. Although reports from the German Army boast that the Russians are surrounded and that their obstinate resistance has become merely the fighting of a cornered beast, the truth is not at all clear. There's no doubt that Hitler is staking his entire strength on this invasion. What has taken place in the Japanese-American negotiations has, as usual, not been reported to the outside world. All the same, there is no doubt that the tension between Japan and America had approached increasingly dangerous proportions. 11:00 A.M., 12 October. Clear skies, cool air. 57°. [*H*]

78. Reports have it that Borodino, Kaluga, and Tula have been occupied. The Soviet Army's position is pathetic and gloomy. 2:00 P.M., 13 October. [*H*]

79. Turned on the stove in the eastern room.

    The Germans attacked Moscow, and it seems that their sharp advances have been somewhat blunted. We haven't yet been relieved of worry, though. 15 October. [*H*]

80. The Konoe Cabinet collapsed last night. The German invasion has still not been checked. 17 October, the sun is shining but there's a wind. [*H*]

81. The critical situation facing Moscow has gotten worse and worse. The ambassadors stationed there have moved to Kazan. Odessa finally fell, and the Crimean peninsula is isolated.

    Konoe's successor is Tōjō, and for the first time since the Manchurian Incident, a military cabinet (which had been expected to form but didn't) finally emerged.

    A stove will be on from today forward in the study too. 9:00 A.M., 18 October, the sun is shining brightly. [*H*]

82. It seems that German advances have been somewhat checked at Kalinin and Orel, but Moscow's position hardly warrants optimism as yet. The German Army will doubtless make their final surge before the winter freeze sets in.

    Tōjō's new cabinet is reportedly continuing the negotiations with the United States, but there's no doubt about their outcome.

    The ruling bureaucracy is revived, and their opposition to financial and industrial capitalists is complete. 10:00 A.M., 20 October, sunny and windy. [H]

83. Apparently the Germans have moved into the final stage of their assault on Moscow. For the past week this has been the most important point in the present war. 10:30 A.M., 3 November, no wind and clear skies. [H]

84. Mr. Kurusu was unexpectedly sent to America on the 5th on the pretext of assisting [Ambassador] Nomura. Thus, Japanese-American negotiations are again reportedly bound by a single hope. Yet it seems the real intent of the Japanese government will be to claim how endlessly patient and prudent they have been in exerting all possible effort without a reward. In this way they can whip up popular sentiment for a coming rupture [with the United States]. If they believe that by doing this the Japanese-American negotiations will somehow take a sudden turn, they're crazy. 9:00 A.M., 6 November, clear. [H]

85. With Kurusu's dispatch to America, the argumentative tone in the Japanese press has become more and more aggressive, nothing short of a "war of nerves." The attitude of the authorities has become more clumsy and thoughtless—it's really deplorable. 10:30, 7 November, clear. [H]

86. The conquest of Moscow and Leningrad would seem impossible within as early as this year. The Germans find consolation in their victories in the Ukraine, the Donetz Basin, and their complete subjugation of the Crimea.

    The Japanese-American talks, unrelated to Kurusu's arrival in the United States, are pressing ever closer to the decisive rupture. 2:00 P.M., Saturday, 8 November 1941. No wind, the sun high in the sky. [H]

87. Despite Kurusu's arrival in America, the American side's attitude remains one of extremely indifferent nonchalance. Even though there are political functions served by this, much of the future of Japanese-American relations can be predicted.

    Special meetings began on the 15th for an emergency military budget of 3.8 billion yen.

The mist had remained since yesterday, and the late fall air has been very cold. 11:30 A.M., Sunday, 16 November. [*H*]

88. The Nazis have desperately attacked Moscow. This is serving notice on the great outcome of this attack to government circles back in Berlin. The situation over the past few days has been focused on the final squaring of accounts between Germany and Russia within this year.

   Although England's invasion of North Africa has had some military success, it looks like it won't proceed as planned.

   The Japanese-American negotiations seem to have entered the stage just prior to rupture. It's about to rain now and we've had plenty of wind. The sky is cloudy, and they forecast snow to be falling early in the year. 11:30 A.M., 26 November 1941. [*H*]

89. Was in bed from the 4th through the 14th—during this period, war broke out in the Pacific.[11] 10:30 A.M., 16 December 1941. The snow in the garden hasn't yet melted. The sun shining. [*H*]

90. Hong Kong surrendered yesterday. The sun is bright, but the wind has been fierce since the snowfall. The temperature is still 7° below zero. 10:30 A.M., 26 December 1941. [*H*]

91. Hour by hour the decisive battle at Manila presses on. This will determine the fate of the Philippines.

   The British Army in Libya captured Benghazi. The sun is shining after the snowfall, but the wind is cold. 11:00 A.M., 27 December. [*H*]

1942

92. The [Japanese] people are enthralled by the results of the Pacific War. They've obliterated all else from their minds and press on with the war. The sun is shining. 2 January 1942. [*H*]

93. Reading this [Hegel's *Phänomenologie des Geistes*] for the third time. 11:00 A.M., 3 January 1942. The sun shines silently. [*H*]

94. With the fall of Manila, the Pacific War completed period one. It is a matter of interest for us to watch the direction the Japanese military authorities will pursue—to attack the Dutch East Indies immediately or to concentrate on maintaining control over the seas between the occupied areas and the home country.

   The Soviet Union has slowly but steadily advanced in recovering lost territory this winter. The German Army, assuming a thoroughly defensive posture, is only holding its own.

Although the moon is out, it's as if it isn't—the clouds are of an ashen white color. 9:30 A.M., 9 January 1942. [*H*]

95. I had the limbs of my *huai* tree hewn for two reasons: to purify the limb from which a poverty-stricken Chinese had hanged himself and to obtain some firewood. I hired three workers, one just a child, and gave them nine *yuan*.

The occupation of the island of Celebes is almost complete.

The cold wave passed several days ago, and the sun is now shining. 10:30, 15 January 1942. [*H*]

96. 9:30 A.M. of the 28th day since my sickness began. Singapore fell last night. 16 February 1942. [*H*]

The diary ends with this note. Shortly thereafter, on 13 March, Nakae was informed that he was suffering from terminal pulmonary tuberculosis. He died on 3 August 1942.

Abbreviations
Used in the Notes and Bibliography

CKSS Nakae Ushikichi. *Chūgoku kodai seiji shisō* (Ancient Chinese Political Thought). Tokyo, Iwanami shoten, 1975.

CTM *Chōmin o tsugu mono* (The Man Who Followed [Nakae] Chōmin). Ed. Sakatani Yoshinao. Tokyo, privately published by Sakatani Yoshinao, 1960.

NB Nakae bunko. Archive of Nakae Ushikichi's library, Research Institute of Humanistic Sciences, Kyoto University.

NGZ *Nakae Ushikichi no ningenzō* (Nakae Ushikichi's View of Humanity). Ed. Sakatani Yoshinao and Suzuki Tadashi. Nagoya, Fūbaisha, 1980.

NUH *Nakae Ushikichi to iu hito, sono seikatsu to shisō to gakumon* (A Man Called Nakae Ushikichi, His Life, Thought, and Learning). Ed. Sakatani Yoshinao. Tokyo, Daiwa shobō, 1979.

NUS *Nakae Ushikichi shokanshū* (The Letters of Nakae Ushikichi). Ed. Suzue Gen'ichi, Itō Takeo, and Katō Koretaka. Tokyo, Misuzu shobō, 1964.

Notes

PREFACE

1. See Marius Jansen, "Japan and the Chinese Revolution of 1911," in John K. Fairbank and Kwang-ching liu, eds., *The Cambridge History of China*, vol. 11, *Late Ch'ing, 1800–1911, Part 2* (Cambridge, 1980), p. 339.
2. Marius Jansen, *The Japanese and Sun Yat-sen* (Cambridge, Mass., 1954). See, more recently, his textbook, *Japan and China: from War to Peace, 1894–1972* (Chicago, 1975).
3. See, for example, Akira Iriye, *After Imperialism: The Search for a New Order in the Far East, 1921–1931* (Cambridge, Mass., 1965); Noriko Kamachi, *Reform in China: Huang Tsun-hsien and the Japanese Model* (Cambridge, Mass., 1981); and several of the essays in Akira Iriye, ed., *The Chinese and the Japanese: Essays in Political and Cultural Interactions* (Princeton, 1980).

INTRODUCTION

1. Hashikawa Bunsō [Bunzō], "Anti-war Values—the Resistance in Japan," tr. Robert Vargo, *Japan Interpreter* 9.1:91. For similarly positive views, see Ienaga Saburō, *The Pacific War: World War II and the Japanese*, tr. Frank Baldwin (New York, 1978), pp. 87–88.
2. Hasegawa Nyozekan, "Tsuiokudan," speech delivered 3 August 1946, in *Nakae Ushikichi go kaiki kinenkai, kiroku*, in *NUH*, p. 253.
3. Takeuchi Yoshimi, "*Chūgoku kodai seiji shisō*, shinri tsuikyū no ningen teki jōnetsu," *Tosho* (November 1950), in *NGZ*, p. 318.
4. Kinoshita Junji, "Doko ni dorama wa naritatsu ka," *Gunsō* (April–May 1967), in *NUH*, p. 27.
5. Kōtoku Shūsui, *Chōmin sensei* (Tokyo, 1960), p. 38. See also Matsunaga Shōzō's interesting commentary on this statement by Chōmin, in his "Itsutsu no mondōtai: Chōmin no hōhō," in Kinoshita Junji and Etō Fumio, eds. *Nakae Chōmin no sekai* (Tokyo, 1977), p. 137.

1. BACKGROUND: *NAKAE USHIKICHI'S YEARS IN JAPAN*

1. Kuwabara Takeo, "Ningen no Chōmin," in Kuwabara Takeo, ed., *Nakae Chōmin no kenkyū* (Tokyo, 1966), p. 22; Robert Jay Lifton, Shūichi Katō, and Michael Reich, *Six Lives, Six Deaths: Portraits from Modern Japan* (New Haven, 1979), p. 123.

2. The most famous writer of the Tokugawa era who adopted the style of Ssu-ma Ch'ien was Rai San'yō (1780–1832). His works were used through the early Meiji period as examples of elegant Kanbun. See W. G. Beasley and Carmen Blacker, "Japanese Historical Writing in the Tokugawa Period (1603–1868)," in W. G. Beasley and E. G. Pulleyblank, eds., *Historians of China and Japan* (London, 1961), pp. 259–263; Herschel Webb, "What Is the *Dai Nihon Shi*?" *Journal of Asian Studies* 19.2:135–149. Chōmin shared, of course, none of San'yō's infatuation with the imperial house.

3. Kuwabara, pp. 23–25, 29; Lifton, pp. 125–6, 131; Margaret B. Dardess, *A Discourse on Government: Nakae Chōmin and his "Sansuijin keirin mondō,"* Occasional Papers No. 10, Western Washington State College (Bellington, Washington, 1977), p. 2. In his final work, *Ichinen yūhan*, dictated on his deathbed, Chōmin wrote: "The people's rights are the highest principle, and freedom and equality are the ultimate justice. They cannot be monopolized by the West." Cited in Lifton, p. 133. For an annotated edition of this last text, see Nakae Chōmin, *Ichinen yūhan*, in *Nakae Chōmin zenshū*, vol. 10, ed. Matsumoto Sannosuke (Tokyo, 1983), pp. 129–218.

4. Lifton, pp. 133–134.

5. Dardess, pp. 4–5. For the text of Chōmin's translation with a modern Japanese translation and extensive notes by Shimada Kenji, see *"Minyaku yakkai* genbun, yomikudashi bun, narabi ni chūkai," in Kuwabara Takeo, ed., *Nakae Chōmin no kenkyū*, pp. 177–246; reprinted in *Nakae Chōmin zenshū*, vol. 1, ed. Ida Nobuya (Tokyo, 1983), pp. 65–200. See also Shimada Kenji, "Chōmin no aiyōgo ni tsuite," in Kinoshita Junji and Etō Fumio, ed., *Nakae Chōmin no sekai* (Tokyo, 1977), pp. 226–232; Matsumoto Sannosuke, "Minken no tetsugaku: Nakae Chōmin," in his *Meiji seishin no kōzō* (Tokyo, 1981), pp. 77–100.

6. The view that Nakae Chōmin hoped for distribution in China and Korea is potentially substantiated by Professor Shimada Kenji's discovery in a Shanghai library several years ago of a Chinese edition of the first half of the translation; it had been published circa 1898, the year of the Hundred Days Reform. See Shimada Kenji, "Nakae Chōmin *Minyaku yakkai* no Chūgoku han," *Dōhō* 40:1. The Chinese edition of the text carried the title *Min-yueh t'ung-i.*

7. Lifton, p. 139. See the various essays by Kinoshita Junji and Matsunaga Shōzō, in Kinoshita Junji and Etō Fumio, eds., *Nakae Chōmin no sekai* (Tokyo, 1977). The translations are Dardess, *Discourse on Government;* and Nakae Chōmin, *A Discourse by Three Drunkards on Government,* tr. Nobuko Tsukui (Tokyo, 1984).

8. Matsumoto Ken'ichi, "Nakae Chōmin to Tōyama Mitsuru," in Takeuchi Yoshimi and Hashikawa Bunzō, eds., *Kindai Nihon to Chūgoku*, vol. 1 (Tokyo, 1974), pp. 87–98.

9. Sugita Tei'ichi, "Yū-Shin yokan," in Saika Hakuai, *Sugita Kakuzan ō* (Tokyo, 1928), pp. 582–585; Joshua A. Fogel, *Politics and Sinology: The Case of Naitō Konan (1866–1934)*, (Cambridge, Mass., 1984), p. 14; Hashikawa Bunsō [Bunzō], "Japanese Perspectives on Asia: From Dissociation to Coprosperity," in Akira Iriye, ed., *The Chinese and the Japanese*, pp. 331–333.

10. Matsumoto Ken'ichi, p. 100; Dardess, pp. 6, 19–20, 25–26.

11. For discussions of the divergences between Nakae and Tōyama as they became even clearer in their disciples, see Matsumoto Ken'ichi, pp. 95–96, 99; Yamaguchi Kōsaku, *Itan no genryū: Nakae Chōmin no shisō to kōdō* (Tokyo, 1961), pp. 59–61.

12. Takeuchi Chibi, "Chichi Chōmin no omoide," *Tosho* 189:16.

13. Kuwabara, p. 30; Shūichi Katō, comments in Lifton, pp. 145–147.

14. Ueyama Shumpei, "Chōmin no tetsugaku," in Kuwabara Takeo, ed., *Nakae Chōmin no kenkyū* (Tokyo, 1966), pp. 38–39; Lifton, p. 142.

15. "Nakae Ushikichi nenpu," compiled by Katō Koretaka and Sakatani Yoshinao, in *NUH*, p. 293.

16. Takeuchi Chibi, p. 17; Katō Koretaka, "Chōmin no ko," *Dōsetsu* (*n.s.*) 1:102–106, in *NGZ*.

17. Takeuchi Chibi, p. 19; Katō Koretaka, "Chōmin no ko," pp. 107–110.

18. "Nakae Ushikichi nenpu," p. 293; Katō Koretaka, "Chōmin no ko," pp. 110–113.

19. "Nakae Ushikichi nenpu," pp. 293–294; Katō Koretaka, "Chōmin no ko," p. 113; Kuwabara, p. 33.

20. Ojima Sukema, *Nakae Chōmin* (Tokyo, 1949), p. 62; Suzuki Tadashi, "Ikyō no koten teki yuibutsuronsha: Nakae Ushikichi ron," *Shisō no kagaku* (December 1961), reprinted in his *Kindai Nihon no risei* (Tokyo, 1972), p. 141.

21. *NUS*, pp. 297–299. For corroboration concerning Chōmin's great love of wild peaches, see his brief reminiscence of them in Nakae Chōmin, *Ichinen yūhan*, p. 174.

22. Letter to Suzue Gen'ichi, dated 14 August 1940, in *NUS*, p. 192.

23. As quoted in Lifton, pp. 114–115.

24. Takeuchi Chibi, p. 20; Katō Koretaka, "Chōmin no musume," in *NUH*, pp. 139–141.

25. Letter to Katō Koretaka, dated 1 August 1941, in *NUS*, pp. 329–330.

26. Suzuki Tadashi, "Ikyō no koten teki yuibutsuronsha," p. 141.

27. Ts'ao Ju-lin, *I-sheng chih hui-i* (Taipei, 1970), pp. 20–25; "Nakae Ushikichi nenpu," p. 294. See also Madeleine Chi, "Ts'ao Ju-lin (1876–1966): His Japanese Connections," in Akira Iriye, ed., *The Chinese and the Japanese*, pp. 140–160.

28. "Nakae Ushikichi nenpu," pp. 294–295; Katō Koretaka, "Chōmin no musume," in *NUH*, p. 140. On Takeuchi Tsuna, who was a leader of the Jiyūtō and later an

overseas developer and entrepreneur, see J. H. Dower, *Empire and Aftermath: Yoshida Shigeru and the Japanese Experience, 1878–1954* (Cambridge, Mass., 1979), pp. 14–17.

29. "Nakae Ushikichi nenpu," p. 295; Emma Goldman, *Living My Life*, ed. Richard and Anna Maria Drinnon (New York, 1977), pp. 473–474, 476–477. On Kōtoku's relationship to Nakae Chōmin, see F. G. Notehelfer, *Kōtoku Shūsui: Portrait of a Japanese Radical* (Cambridge, 1971), pp. 20–26, 32–33.

30. "Nakae Ushikichi nenpu," p. 295; Takada Taijun, "*Nakae Ushikichi shokanshū*, kakumei ki no Chūgoku to Nihonjin," *Asahi jānaru* (7 February 1965), in *NUH*, p. 227; Nakamura Shintarō, "Nakae Ushikichi to Katayama Sen," in his *Son Bun kara Ozaki Hotsumi e* (Tokyo, 1975), p. 140. Concerning the Morito Incident, see *Nihon rekishi daijiten* (Tokyo, 1968–1970), vol. 9, p. 289; Richard H. Mitchell, *Thought Control in Prewar Japan* (Ithaca, 1976), pp. 39–44. The editor of the journal that published Morito's piece, Ōuchi Hyōe (1888–1980), also received a fine and short prison term; he has written several essays on Nakae Ushikichi.

31. "Nakae Ushikichi nenpu," p. 296; Katō Koretaka, "Chōmin no ko," pp. 122–123.

2. A LIFE TRANSFORMED: THE 1910s

1. Georg Jellinek, *System der subjektiven öffentlichen Rechte* (Darmstadt, Wissenschaftlische Buchgesselschaft, 1892), p. 81, as cited and translated in Rupert Emerson, *State and Sovereignty in Modern Germany* (New Haven, 1928), p. 84.

2. "Nakae Ushikichi nenpu," p. 296; Kaji Ryūichi, "Sūkiden, Nakae Ushikichi kun," *Asahi hyōron* (August 1947), in *CTM*, p. 58; Itō Takeo, *Mantetsu ni ikite* (Tokyo, 1964), p. 80; Ono Katsutoshi, "Nakae san o omou," *Tōyōshi kenkyū* (January–February 1943), reprinted as "'Wakai tomodachi' ni yoru tsuioku: Nakae san o omou," in *CTM*, p. 66.

3. Ernest P. Young, *The Presidency of Yuan Shih-k'ai: Liberalism and Dictatorship in Early Republican China* (Ann Arbor, 1977), pp. 170–172, quotation from p. 172. I have found Chinese translations of four books by Ariga on modern diplomacy and contemporary politics: See Huang Fu-ch'ing, *Chinese Students in Japan in the Late Ch'ing Period*, tr. Katherine P. K. Whitaker (Tokyo, 1982), pp. 262, 265; Sanetō Keishū, *Chūgokujin Nihon ryūgaku shi* (Tokyo, 1960), pp. 272–273.

4. Young, pp. 171, 296; "Ts'ao Ju-lin," in *Biographical Dictionary of Republican China*, ed. Howard L. Boorman and Richard C. Howard, vol. 3 (New York, 1968), pp. 299–300.

5. *Biographical Dictionary of Republican China*, vol. 3, pp. 299–302; Young, p. 219; Ts'ao Ju-lin, *passim*; Madeleine Chi, "Bureaucratic Capital in Operation: Ts'ao Ju-lin and His New Communications Clique, 1916–1919," *Journal of Asian Studies* 34.2:675–688, esp. pp. 681, 686; Madeleine Chi, "Ts'ao Ju-lin," p. 146.

6. See Yamamoto Shirō, "Terauchi naikaku jidai no Nit-Chū kankei no ichimen: Nishihara Kamezō to Banzai Rihachirō," *Shirin* 64.1:1–36. Banzai's predecessor in

China as representative of the Japanese Army was Lieutenant-General Aoki Norizumi (1859–1924), who stayed on after Banzai's arrival. Nakae came to know
both men, and through them he met other high-ranking members of the Japanese military. See Satō Kōseki, *Aoki Norizumi* (Tokyo, 1943).

7. "Nakae Ushikichi nenpu," pp. 296–297.

8. All three men became generals by the mid 1930s, and all were deeply involved
in Japanese military activities in China. Among the voluminous materials in
this field, see for example: Madeleine Chi, "Ts'ao Ju-lin," pp. 146, 153–154;
Lloyd Eastman, "Facets of an Ambivalent Relationship: Smuggling, Puppets,
and Atrocities during the War, 1937–1945," in Akira Iriye, ed., *The Chinese and
the Japanese*, p. 291; B. Winston Kahn, "Doihara Kenji and the North China
Autonomy Movement, 1935–1936," in Alvin D. Coox and Hilary Conroy, eds.,
China and Japan: A Search for Balance Since World War II (Santa Barbara, 1978),
pp. 177–207; Yoji Akashi, "A Botched Peace Effort: The Miao Pin *Kōsaku*,
1944–1945," in Coox and Conroy, pp. 267–274; "Nakae Ushikichi nenpu," p.
297. On Ting Shih-yuan, see the rather confusing biography of him in *Who's
Who in China* (Shanghai, 1925), pp. 720–721. He was apparently associated
with Japanese interests as early as the early 1920s, and this characterized his subsequent biography.

9. Letter to Imada Shintarō, dated 11 June 1938, in *NUS*, p. 345.

10. "Nakae ushikichi nenpu," pp. 297–298.

11. Takeuchi Minoru, "Nihonjin ni totte no Chūgoku zō," in his *Nihonjin ni totte
no Chūgoku zō* (Tokyo, 1966), p. 388.

12. Ōta Ryōichirō, "Kaisō no Nakae Ushikichi," *Jiron* (November 1946), in *NGZ*, p.
23; Itō Takeo, *Mantetsu ni ikite*, p. 80; and Etō Shinkichi and Hsu Shu-chen,
Suzue Gen'ichi den (Tokyo, 1984), p. 40.

13. See, for example, Mitsuda Ikuo, "Nakae Ushikichi ni tsuite," *Nihon bungaku*
(April 1972), in *NUH*, p. 56; "Nakae Ushikichi nenpu," p. 298.

14. Frank O. Miller, *Minobe Tatsukichi: Interpreter of Constitutionalism in Japan* (Berkeley, 1965), p. 12. See also Rōyama Masamichi, in Rōyama Masamichi, et al.,
"Nihon ni okeru seijigaku no kako to shōrai: tōron," *Seijigaku* 1:45 (1950).

15. Miller, pp. 13, 14, 16; Rōyama Masamichi, *Nihon ni okeru kindai seijigaku no hattatsu* (Tokyo, 1949), p. 82; and Matsumoto Sannosuke, "Nihon kenpōgaku ni
okeru kokkaron no tenkai, sono keiseiki ni okeru hō to kenryoku no mondai o
chūshin ni," in Fukuda Kan'ichi, ed., *Seiji shisō ni okeru Seiō to Nihon*, vol. 2 (Tokyo, 1961), pp. 172–173.

16. Emerson, pp. 35, 38; Miller, p. 8; and Matsumoto Sannosuke, "Nihon kenpōgaku," pp. 215–216, 219.

17. Emerson, pp. 60–61, 71–73, quotation from p. 73. The fullest treatment of
Jellinek's juristic theories can be found in two books: Fernando de los Rios y
Urruti, *Estudios Jurídicos* (Buenos Aires, 1959), especially the chapter entitled
"La Doctrina de Jellinek," pp. 113–174; and Reinhard Holubek, *Allgemeine*

Staatslehre als empirische Wissenschaft: eine Untersuchung am Beispiel von Georg Jellinek (Bonn, 1961). Rios y Urruti, incidentially, translated *Allgemeine Staatslehre* into Spanish. Arnold Brecht has also credited Jellinek with developing the idea of "Scientific Value Relativism," ordinarily attributed to Max Weber; see Arnold Brecht, *Political Theory: The Foundations of Twentieth-Century Thought* (Princeton, 1967), pp. 220–221.

18. Cited in Emerson, p. 84.
19. *Allgemeine Staatslehre* (Berlin, 1900); 2nd edition, 1905; 3rd edition, edited by his son Walter Jellinek (1885–1955), 1914. See Hollerbach, p. 253.
20. Miller, pp. 26, 28, 30–31, 43–44, 63; and Matsumoto Sannosuke, "Nihon kenpōgaku," pp. 169, 207–208.
21. Miller, pp. 40, 45, 71–72, 192, quotation from p. 45; and Ienaga Saburō, *Minobe Tatsukichi no shisō teki kenkyū* (Tokyo, 1964), pp. 129, 137, 150, 171.
22. The following account is based on: Chow Tse-tsung, *The May Fourth Movement: Intellectual Revolution in Modern China* (Cambridge, Mass., 1960), pp. 84–116; Wang Yun-sheng, *Liu-shih-nien lai Chung-kuo yü Jih-pen*, vol. 7 (Tientsin, 1932–1934), pp. 334–335; Chia I-chün, *Wu-ssu yun-tung chien-shih* (Peking, 1951), pp. 32–33; and Ch'en Tuan-chih, *Wu-ssu yun-tung chih shih te p'ing-chia* (Shanghai, 1935), p. 235.
23. Cited in Chow, p. 108.
24. *The North-China Herald*, vol. 131, no. 2700, 10 May 1919, pp. 347, 348.
25. Itō Takeo, *Mantetsu ni ikite*, pp. 78–79; Itō Takeo, "Hashigaki," in Suzue Gen'ichi, *Chūgoku kaihō tōsō shi* (Tokyo, 1953), p. 2. Suzuki Tadashi tends to support this explanation of the May Fourth Incident; see his "Ikyō no koten teki yuibutsuronsha," pp. 144–145. On Lin Ch'ang-min and his "role" in the May Fourth Incident, see *Biographical Dictionary of Republican China*, vol. 2, pp. 368–372; and Chi, "Ts'ao Ju-lin," pp. 149–150. Andrew Nathan (pp. 158–160) convincingly argues that the Peking cliques were surprised by the events of May 4 and immediately sought to use them for their own interests. The Research Clique was so called because it originated in a group of men commissioned by the Yuan government to do the research necessary for drafting a constitution.
26. Fujiwara Kamae, *Pekin nijūnen: Chūgoku no taidō to Nihon no jogen* (Tokyo, 1959), pp. 360–363, from a eulogy first published shortly after Lin's death.
27. Ts'ao Ju-lin, pp. 151–159; *Biographical Dictionary of Republican China*, vol. 1, pp. 127–129; Chow, pp. 112–113; Mitsuda Ikuo, pp. 57–59.
28. Po Ch'i-ch'ang, *Wu-ssu yun-tung wen-chi*, comp. Hua-chung kung-hsueh-yuan Ma-k'o-ssu Lieh-ning chu-i ts'e-liao-shih (Wuhan, 1957), p. 173; Ts'ao Ju-lin, pp. 151–159.
29. "Another Chinese account" comes from Ch'en Tuan-chih, p. 235. *The North-China Herald*, 10 May 1919, p. 345; its editors were merciless to Ts'ao, running the headline for this story (p. 348): "DOWNFALL OF TS'AO THE MIGHTY. MINISTER LITERALLY BITES THE DUST." Memoirist K'uang Hu-sheng

corroborates Ch'en's account, in *Wu-ssu ai-kuo yun-tung*, vol. 1 (Peking, 1979), p. 496. See most recently a long and fairly evenly balanced account in P'eng Ming, *Wu-ssu yun-tung shih* (Peking, 1984), pp. 286–288. Nakae is misidentified as a newspaperman by Hsu Te-heng, "Ch'u chien pu-hsi ssu, lai pa Chung-kuo chiu," *Hung-ch'i* 5:52 (1979).

30. Matsukata Saburō, "Rō Pekin no kankai," *Sekai* (October 1948), in *NGZ*, p. 76; Ōnishi Itsuki, "Tsuiokudan," *Nakae Ushikichi go kaiki kinenkai, kiroku*, speech delivered 3 August 1946, in *NGZ*, p. 248; Nakamura Shintarō, p. 142.

31. "Nakae Ushikichi nenpu," p. 299; Suzuki Tadashi, "Ko no naka no fuhensha," *Sekai* (October 1967), in *NGZ*, p. 352.

32. Hanzawa Hiroshi, "Nakae Ushikichi to Tachibana Shiraki," in Takeuchi Yoshimi and Hashikawa Bunzō, eds., *Kindai Nihon to Chūgoku*, vol. 2 (Tokyo, 1974), pp. 85–101; Katō Koretaka, "Aru nichijō seikatsu," *Dōsetsu* n.s. 5 (May 1965), in *NGZ*, pp. 127–140; "Nakae Ushikichi nenpu," p. 299; Katō Koretaka, "Nakae Ushikichi to shinbun," *Kumamoto nichinichi shinbun*, 14 October 1971, in *NUH*, pp. 137–138; Ōuchi Hyōe, "Engerusu no 'shō mihon': *Nakae Ushikichi shokanshū* wa omoshiroi," *Misuzu* 74 (July 1965), in *NGZ*, p. 327; Yamamoto Hideo, *Tachibana Shiraki* (Tokyo, 1977), p. 34.

33. Nakae Ushikichi, "*Byōchū nikki* shō: shi no toko no kiroku," in *NGZ*, pp. 418–430; and Katō Koretaka, "Chishiki to seikatsu," *Nōgyō gijutsu* (November 1948), in *NGZ*, p. 99.

34. "Nakae Ushikichi nenpu," pp. 299, 305.

35. Etō Shinkichi, "Suzue Gen'ichi, aru megumarezaru seishun," *Sekai* 216 (December 1963), pp. 192, 193, 196–198; Etō Shinkichi, "Nihonjin no Chūgoku kan: Suzue Gen'ichi o megutte," *Shisō* 445:5. These essays and one other have been revised and included in Etō Shinkichi, *Nihon no shinro* (Tokyo, 1969). Most thoroughly handled in Etō and Hsu, *Suzue Gen'ichi den*, pp. 1–13.

36. Etō, "Nihonjin no Chūgoku kan," pp. 6–7; Etō, "Suzue Gen'ichi," pp. 198–200; Itō Takeo, "Suzue Gen'ichi to sono jidai," *Sekai* (May 1950), in *NGZ*, p. 62; Itō Takeo, "Ajia no kenkyūsha: Suzue Gen'ichi," *Ajia no mondai* 2.3, in *CTM*, pp. 226–227; Etō and Hsu, *Suzue Gen'ichi den*, pp. 16–18, 23–24. For an analysis of *all* of Suzue's essays for these publications, see Etō and Hsu, pp. 18–20, 26–29.

37. Etō Shinkichi, "Suzue Gen'ichi," p. 201.

38. Etō Shinkichi, "Suzue Gen'ichi," p. 202; Chow, p. 152, 164n; Etō and Hsu, pp. 36–37. In these first years of his immersion in China, Suzue became particularly close to Shih Yang (also known as Chao Shih-yen, d. 1923), a CCP member, a lawyer, for a time the chairman of the Shanghai General Labor Union, and a leader in the famous Peking-Hankow Railway Strike of 1923. He used his expertise in the law to serve as a legal advisor to the Hankow rickshaw pullers in their fight with the rickshaw companies, and he helped them to form a union in 1921. He also served from 1921 to 1922 as the Hupeh head of the Labor Secretariat within the CCP. He was executed by warlord Wu P'ei-fu (1874–1939). See Jean

Chesneaux, *The Chinese Labor Movement: 1919–1927,* tr. H. M. Wright (Stanford, 1968), pp. 179, 196, 403.

Among Suzue's other early Chinese friends were Hsieh Lien-ch'ing, a leader in the Peking student movement, who later withdrew from left-wing politics altogether; and Ch'eng Heng, who went to study in Japan under Suzue's influence and died of illness when he was still young.

Another Chinese friend from these early years was Huang Jih-k'uei. Huang had been a leader of the student movement at Peking University and, after 20 May 1919, in Nanking and Shanghai as well. He later became chairman of the Student Union of China and an active participant in the Society for the Study of Marxist Theory (1920–1921). In 1924 he accepted an assistant professorship at Peking University; and as the head of the Chinese Socialist Youth Corps, he remained an active leader of the left-wing movement in China. Huang provided Suzue with great quantities of original documents concerning the radical movement.

39. Itō Takeo, *Mantetsu ni ikite,* pp. 64–65; Itō Takeo, "Suzue Gen'ichi to sono jidai," pp. 61–62; Itō Takeo, "Hashigaki," pp. 1–5. It was through Itō, that the SMR in 1929 published Suzue's first major work, *Chūgoku musan kaikyū undō shi* (A history of the Chinese proletarian movement), as the book was titled when it was reissued after the war.

    Also in 1922 Suzue made the acquaintance of Hu E-kung, a leader of the 1911 Revolution, political figure at China's first National Assembly, and, at the time of their meeting, a teacher. Hu provided assistance, monetary and other, to Suzue for his entire life. Through him, Suzue was introduced to the famous painter Ch'i Pai-shih (1863–1957) with whom he became close personal friends over the years. When Suzue died in 1945, he was buried in the Japanese cemetery in Peking; and at his request Ch'i Pai-shih agreed to inscribe the epitaph on his tombstone. Sakatani Yoshinao, "Kaisetsu," in Suzue Gen'ichi, *Chūgoku kakumei no kaikyū tairitsu,* ed. Sakatani Yoshinao, vol. 2 (Tokyo, 1972), p. 210; Etō and Hsu, pp. 37–39.

40. Etō and Hsu, pp. 49, 70–72, 87–90, 104–115.

41. Katō Koretaka, "Kenja to chinpin: Suzue Gen'ichi no omoide," *Ajia kenkyū* 8.4 (December 1961), in *NGZ,* p. 180. Etō and Hsu (p. 101) suggest this first meeting occurred "around 1924." Suzue later married Takeuchi Namiko, the eldest daughter of Nakae's sister.

PART II: PENETRATING THE WORLD OF ANCIENT CHINA

3. POLITICS AND THOUGHT

1. Poem from *Shih-ching* in Arthur Waley, tr., *The Book of Songs* (Boston, 1937), p. 320.
2. Ojima Sukema, "Atogaki," in his *Chūgoku shisō shi*, rev. ed. (Tokyo, 1968), pp. 419–421; Ojima Sukema, *Chūgoku no shakai shisō* (Tokyo, 1967), pp. 445–452; "Nakae Ushikichi nenpu," p. 299; Ojima Sukema, "Nakae Chōmin," in Hayashi Shigeru, ed., *Nakae Chōmin shū* (Tokyo, 1967), pp. 436–438; Fogel, pp. 113–121.
3. Takeuchi Yoshimi, pp. 318–319; "Nakae Ushikichi nenpu," p. 301.
4. Nakae Ushikichi, "Chūgoku kodai seiji shisō shi," in *CKSS*, pp. 3–4, 7, 8.
5. Nakae Ushikichi, "Chūgoku kodai seiji shisō shi," pp. 18–19. Nakae's copy of Lewis Morgan's *Ancient Society* (New York, 1877) is dated 12 November 1921 on the frontispiece in Nakae's hand. He also cites the following three works in this context: on 9 January 1922, Karl Vorländer, *Geschichte der Philosophie*, vol. 1 (Leipzig, 1921); on 28 August 1922, Hermann Rehm, *Geschichte der Staatsrechtswissenschaft* (Freiburg and Leipzig, 1896); and with no date for the citation, Eduard Zeller, *Die Philosophie der Griechen in ihrer geschichtlichen Entwicklung* (Leipzig, 1920–1923); all in NB.
6. Nakae Ushikichi, "Chūgoku kodai seiji shisō shi," pp. 20–22; and Nakae's edition (dated 13 February 1922) of Gustav Le Bon, *Psychologie der Massen*, tr. Rudolph Eisler (Leipzig, 1919), in NB.
7. Nakae Ushikichi, "Chūgoku kodai seiji shisō shi," p. 22; Nakae's edition of Ernest Renan, *The Life of Jesus* (London, 1924), in NB. From the section of Renan's work that Nakae underlined in red, we can see that he was interested not so much in Jesus himself as he was in how one reconstructs a past era or a person from whom we have no extant writings. This again elicits from Nakae a comparison with Socrates. Nakae also looked closely at Renan's concern to wash away the layers of accumulated sediment imposed on antiquity in the intervening 2000 years.
8. See K. C. Chang, *Early Chinese Civilization: Anthropological Perspectives* (Cambridge, Mass., 1976), pp. 61–64.
9. Nakae Ushikichi, "Chūgoku kodai seiji shisō shi," pp. 24–28. Itō Takeo remembers that in the early 1920s in Peking, Nakae organized a scholarly discussion group of men from various professions and dubbed it the Mumeikai (Anonymous Society). At their first session Nakae presented a piece entitled "Yū no igi ni tsuite" (On the meaning of *i*) where he first developed these ideas on the conception of the "state" in ancient China. See Itō Takeo, "Pekin no kagakusha Nakae Ushikichi," *Tōkyō shinbun* (28 April 1950), in *NGZ*, pp. 39–40. See also Nakae's edition (dated 29 December 1923) of Wilhelm Wundt, *Völkerpsychologie: Eine Untersuchung der Entwicklungsgesetze von Sprache, Mythus, und Sitte*, vol. 8 (Leipzig, 1914–1920), in NB. Nakae read through several of Wundt's works

a few times, and left his complete set of this work well marked up. From his reading and marginal notes we know that Nakae was reading Wundt's *Einleitung in die Philosophie* (Leipzig, 1921) throughout 1922. Nakae has marked the preface of his copy with the date 4 December 1922, and p. 1 with 14 January 1922. His notes concern only comparisons with ancient Chinese texts. He also began reading Wundt's *System de Philosophie* (Leipzig, 1919) early that year; p. 1 of his copy is dated 8 January 1922.

10. Nakae Ushikichi, "Chūgoku kodai seiji shisō shi," pp. 29–32. Major works cited here, in addition to many Chinese texts, include Julius Lippert, *Kulturgeschichte der Menschheit in ihrem organischen Aufbau*, vol. 2 (Stuttgart, 1886–1887) to show that ancient Greece and Rome shared certain political, economic, and religious aspects of the ancient state with China; Theodor Mommsen, *Römische Geschichte* (Berlin, 1919–1921) to demonstrate similarities in defense preparations; Karl Bücher, *Die Entstehung der Volkswirtschaft*, vol. 1 (Tübingen, 1920), to characterize the economic nature of the ancient state as *geschlosse Hauswirtschaft* or private household economy; and Numa Denis Fustel de Coulanges, *The Ancient City: A study of the religion, laws, and institutions of Greece and Rome*, tr. Willard Small (Boston, 1901) on religion in the ancient state. Nakae wrote the date 6 July 1923 in his copy of Lippert, no date in Mommsen, 29 October 1921 in Bücher, and 21 May 1924 in Fustel de Coulanges, all of which remain in NB. In his own introduction, Fustel de Coulanges (1839–1889) remarked that one had to examine the religious ideas of a people as the oldest and most basic element of ancient life. Nakae inserted a marginal note at this point in his copy of the book (p. 12) to the effect that this statement was important in the study of ancient China. See also Nakae Ushikichi, "Chūgoku kodai seiji shisō shi," pp. 126–131.

11. Kaizuka Shigeki, "Atogaki," in *Kaizuka Shigeki chosakushū*, vol. 1 (Tokyo, 1976), pp. 386, 388.

12. Nakae Ushikichi, "Chūgoku kodai seiji shisō shi," pp. 32–41. Nakae relied heavily on traditional Chinese (particularly Ch'ing) scholarship to construct elements of his argument here. He strongly disagreed, for instance, with Cheng Hsuan (127–200) and Sun I-jang (1848–1908) on specific points, the latter having argued that the well-field system was an idealized method of tax collection. He agreed with Liang Li-sheng's (1748–1793) view that, contrary to traditional scholarship, Shang Yang (d. 338 B.C.E.) was not solely to blame for the destruction of the well-field system; what Shang was doing merely legalized the changes in the ways of life of his day.

13. Nakae Ushikichi, "Chūgoku kodai seiji shisō shi," pp. 42–44. On a similar point concerning comparisons of myth and taboo, Nakae cites Wundt, *Völkerpsychologie*, vol. 4 (in which his first notation is dated 20 May 1923). Throughout his copy of this book, Nakae jotted in numerous places the marginal notes, "compare with China."

14. Nakae Ushikichi, "Chūgoku kodai seiji shisō shi," pp. 44–45. On the need for a unified vision to avoid reaching arbitrary conclusions, Nakae cites the work of Rudolph Stammler, *Wirtschaft und Recht nach der materialistischen Geschichtsauffassung: Eine sozialphilosophische Untersuchung* (Leipzig, 1914). His copy is dated 16 June 1921.

15. Ienaga Saburō, *Minobe Tatsukichi no shisō teki kenkyū*, pp. 129, 137, 150; Matsumoto Sannosuke, p. 193; Ishida Takeshi, *Kindai Nihon seiji kōzō no kenkyū* (Tokyo, 1956), p. 299; Rōyama Masamichi, *Nihon ni okeru kindai seijigaku no hattatsu*, p. 90.

16. William Kluback, *Wilhelm Dilthey's Philosophy of History* (New York, 1956), pp. 40, 59–61, 65, 69; H. P. Rickman, *Wilhelm Dilthey: Pioneer of the Human Studies* (Berkeley, 1979), pp. 6–7, 10, 52–53, 65, 123–142, 148–149, 153–155; H. P. Rickman, "General Introduction," to Wilhelm Dilthey, *Pattern and Meaning in History: Thoughts on History and Society,* tr. and ed. Rickman (London, 1971), pp. 17–18, 22, 30, 32–36, 40–41, 51; Rudolph A. Makkreel, *Dilthey: Philosopher of the Human Studies,* (Princeton, 1975), pp. 242–246, 306–313; Theodore Plantinga, *Historical Understanding in the Thought of Wilhelm Dilthey* (Toronto, 1980), pp. 98–121; Otto Friedrich Bollnow, *Dirutai sono tetsugaku e no annai,* tr. Asō Ken (Tokyo, 1977), pp. 185–197, 311–325.

17. Kluback, p. 69.

18. Nakae Ushikichi, "Chūgoku kodai seiji shisō shi," pp. 48–50, 52–63. Among the many comparisons offered here, Nakae discusses how the name of one particular ethnic group often became the generic name for other groups of the same race; and he cites William Stubbs, *The Constitutional History of England, in its Origin and Development,* vol. 1 (Oxford, 1891); Karl Julius Beloch, *Griechische Geschichte,* vol. 1 (Strassburg and Berlin, 1913–1924). Stubbs is dated 13 December 1924 and Beloch is dated 9 December 1924 in Nakae's copies in NB.

19. Nakae Ushikichi, "Chūgoku kodai seiji shisō shi," pp. 52–63. In attacking List's classification scheme for societal development, used by Liang Ch'i-ch'ao, Nakae relies on the work of Karl Bücher and Eugen von Philippovitch, *Grundriss der politischen Oekonomie,* vol. 1 (Tübingen, 1920), his copy of which is dated 4 August 1921. Both are in NB.

20. Nakae Ushikichi, "Chūgoku kodai seiji shisō shi," pp. 69–70. On the economy and its influence in history, Nakae cites Edwin R. A. Seligman, *The Economic Interpretation of History* (New York, 1917). His copy (in NB) is first dated 6 July 1921; he apparently completed reading it on 21 July 1921.

21. This discussion of the *i* and its economy in ancient China comes from Nakae Ushikichi, "Chūgoku kodai seiji shisō shi," pp. 70–83.

22. Nakae Ushikichi, "Chūgoku kodai seiji shisō shi," pp. 106–112.

23. Nakae Ushikichi, "Chūgoku kodai seiji shisō shi," p. 86. To make this comparison, he cites the work of Franz Oppenheimer, *Der Staat* (Frankfurt, 1919), his copy of which is dated 8 March 1922 (in NB).

24. Nakae Ushikichi, "Chūgoku kodai seiji shisō shi," pp. 112–116. See also Ludwig Gumplowicz, *Allgemeines Staatsrecht* (Innsbruck, 1907) and Oppenheimer. Nakae's copies of both are in NB; the first page of this Gumplowicz is dated 23 September 1924, the last page 6 March 1925.

25. Nakae Ushikichi, "Chūgoku kodai seiji shisō shi," pp. 105–112, 116, 121–123, quotation from p. 123. Henry Sumner Maine, *Ancient Law: Its connection with the early history of society and its relation to modern ideas* (London, 1894); in NB, undated. Scholars of Shang China still agree with Nakae's assessment of the deprivations endured by the powerless in ancient China. As K. C. Chang puts it, "The aristocracy's hold on the lower classes was obviously total, sanctioned by fiction and enforced by might . . . [T]he Shang period witnessed the beginning in this part of the world of organized large-sale exploitation of one group of people by another within the same society, and the beginning of an oppressive governmental system to make such exploitation possible." K. C. Chang, pp. 55, 57.

26. Nakae Ushikichi, "Chūgoku kodai seiji shisō shi," pp. 92–97, 102–105.

27. Nakae Ushikichi, "Chūgoku kodai seiji shisō shi," pp. 133–136.

28. Nakae Ushikichi, "Chūgoku kodai seiji shisō shi," pp. 148–153, citing numerous examples, in particular the pioneering work of Juan Yuan (1764–1849). The contemporary Chinese scholar Ting Shan is usually credited with interpreting the oracle bone character *tsu* to mean a "military unit," but Nakae clearly anticipated him. See Ting Shan, *Chia-ku wen so-chien shih-tsu chi ch'i chih-tu* (Peking, 1956), p. 33; K. C. Chang, *Shang Civilization* (New Haven, 1980), pp. 163–165, 196–196.

29. Nakae Ushikichi, "Chūgoku kodai seiji shisō shi," pp 153–156, 160–161, 162–163, 165, 173–174, 193–195. Wundt, *Völkerpsychologie* and Jellinek, *Allgemeine Staatslehre,* in NB. Nakae relies especially on the formulation by Huang Tsung-hsi (1610–1985) of how Ch'in Shih Huang-ti remolded the power and function of the ruler, citing the first chapter ("On the ruler") of Huang's famous *Ming-i tai-fang lu* (A plan for the prince).

30. Nakae Ushikichi, "Chūgoku kodai seiji shisō shi," pp. 176–190, 201–204.

31. On Renan, see Lewis Freeman Mott, *Ernest Renan* (New York, 1921); and "Ernest Renan," in *Encyclopedia of the Social Sciences,* vol. 13 (New York, 1948), pp. 285–287.

32. On Gumplowicz, see Lester F. Ward, "Ludwig Gumplowicz," *American Journal of Sociology* 15:410–413 (1909); Harry Elmer Barnes, "Ludwig Gumplowicz," in *International Encyclopedia of the Social Sciences,* vol. 6 (New York, 1968), pp. 293–295. On Bücher, see Bert F. Hoselitz, "Theories of Stages of Economic Growth," in Bert F. Hoselitz, et al., eds., *Theories of Economic Growth* (New York, 1960), pp. 193–238; and Edouard Will, "Trois quarts de siècle de recherches sur l'économies grecque antique," *Annales* 9:7–19 (1954). On Oppenheimer, see Paul Honigsheim, "The Sociological Doctrines of Franz Oppenheimer: An Agrarian Philosophy of History and Social Reform," in Harry E. Barnes, ed., *An*

Introduction to the History of Sociology (Chicago, 1948), pp. 332–352.

33. On Morgan, see Carl Resek, *Henry Lewis Morgan: American Scholar* (Chicago, 1960); Leslie A. White, "Henry Lewis Morgan," in *International Encyclopedia of the Social Sciences,* vol. 10 (New York, 1968), pp. 196–198. On Lippert, see "Julius Lippert: An Autobiographical Sketch," tr. A. W. Small, *American Journal of Sociology* 19:145–165 (1913); George Peter Murdock, "Introduction," in Julius Lippert, *The Evolution of Culture,* tr. G. P. Murdock (New York, 1931), pp. v–xxxii. On Wundt, see Edwin G. Boring, *A History of Experimental Psychology* (New York, 1929), pp. 316–347; and Edwin Boring, "Wilhelm Wundt," in *International Encyclopedia of the Social Sciences,* vol. 16 (New York, 1968), pp. 581–586.

34. On Mommsen, see William Warde Fowler, "Theodor Mommsen: His Life and Work," in *Roman Essays and Interpretations* (Oxford, 1920), pp. 250–268; Wilhelm Weber, "Theodor Mommsen," in *Encyclopedia of the Social Sciences,* vol. 10 (New York, 1948), pp. 576–577. On Beloch, see William Scott Ferguson, "Karl Julius Beloch," in *Encyclopedia of the Social Sciences,* vol. 2 (New York, 1948), pp. 507–508.

35. On Stammler, see Vladimir S. Simkhovitch, "Rudolph Stammler," *Educational Review* 27:236–251 (March 1904). On Fustel de Coulanges, see Jean M. Tourneur, *Fustel de Coulanges* (Paris, 1931).

36. Albert Hermann Post, *Die Geschlechtsgenossenschaft der Urzeit und die Entstehung der Ehe* (Oldenburg, 1875), citations from pp. 51, 119, 120; Wilhelm Windelband, *Die Geschichte der neueren Philosophie, in ihrem Zusammenhange mit der allgemeinen Kultur und den besonderen Wissenschaften* (Leipzig, 1919), citation from vol. 2, p. 2, both in NB.

37. Nakae ikō shuppan iinkai, "Batsu," in *CKSS,* p. 666.

38. Kimura Eiichi, "Shōin," to Nakae Ushikichi, "Shōsho gairon," *Shinagaku* 12.1–2:1–2 (September 1946); Nakae's essay appears on pp. 5–68, and it is reprinted in *CKSS,* pp. 579–634.

39. Nakae Ushikichi, "Shōsho gairon," pp. 581–586, 591.

40. Nakae Ushikichi, "Shōsho gairon," pp. 586–607.

41. Nakae Ushikichi, "Shōsho gairon," pp. 619–629.

42. Cited by Nakae Ushikichi, "Hashigaki" (Introduction), to "Sho nijūkyū hen ni kansuru shikan ni tsuite (1)," in *CKSS,* p. 448. This introduction is translated in full with commentary in Chapter Six below.

4. A CRITIQUE OF CLASSICISM

1. "Nakae Ushikichi nenpu," p. 302.

2. Nakae's copies of the following books, with his notations of dates, are all in NB: Karl Marx, *Das Kapital: Kritik der politischen Oekonomie,* ed. Friedrich Engels, 3 vols. (Hamburg, 1922); Karl Marx, *Zur Kritik der politischen Oekonomie,* ed.

Karl Kautsky (Berlin, 1924), dated 15 July 1928 by Nakae; N. Lenin, *Imperialism: The Last Stage of Capitalism* (London, n.d.), dated 13 January 1927 on p. 1, 16 January 1927 on the last page; Rosa Luxemburg, *Einführung in die Nationalökonomie*, ed. Paul Levi (Berlin, 1925), dated 5 January 1927 on p. 1, 15 February 1927 on the last page; N. Bucharin, *Theorie des historischen Materialismus: Gemeinverständliches Lehrbuch der Marxistischen Soziologie*, tr. Frida Rubiner (Berlin, 1922), dated 9 May 1926; Immanuel Kant, *Kritik der reinen Vernunft*, ed. Theodor Valentiner (Leipzig, 1919); Woldemer Oskar Döring, *Das Lebenswerk Immanuel Kants* (Lübeck, 1916), dated 20 August 1921; Max Weber, *Wirtschaftsgeschichte: Abriss der universalen Sozial- und Wirtschaftsgeschichte*, ed. S. Hellman and M. Palyi (Munich and Leipzig, 1924), dated 26 October 1926; Émile Durkheim, *The Elementary Forms of Religious Life: A Study in Religious Sociology*, tr. Joseph Ward Swain (London, 1926), dated 29 July 1925.

3. Shirakawa Shizuka, *Kōkotsubun no sekai, kodai In ōchō no kōzō* (Tokyo, 1972), p. 253; Herrlee Glessner Creel, *Studies in Early Chinese Culture: First Series* (Baltimore, 1937), pp. 1–9; Kaizuka Shigeki, ed., *Kodai In teikoku* (Tokyo, 1967), pp. i–xiii.

4. See, for example, the essays by Hayashi Taisuke collected in his *Shina jōdai no kenkyū* (Okazaki, 1944). Among Tazaki Masayoshi's work on ancient China, see his *Ukō ron* (Tokyo, 1920); and *Ōdō tenka no kenkyū* (Kyoto, 1926). On Hayashi's life and work, see Kaizuka Shigeki, "Hayashi Taisuke," in *Ajia rekishi jiten*, vol. 7 (Tokyo, 1961), p. 411.

5. Seventeenth: James Legge and Clae Waltham, tr., *Shu ching: Book of History* (Chicago, 1971), p. 85. Eighteenth: David N. Keightley, *Sources of Shang History: The Oracle-Bone Inscriptions of Bronze Age China* (Berkeley, 1978), pp. 185, 203. Nineteenth: K. C. Chang, *Shang Civilization*, p. 7. See also the helpful table of Shang kings, based on the *Shih-chi*, drawn up by Joey Bonner, *Wang Kuo-wei: An Intellectual Biography* (Cambridge, Mass., 1986), pp. 188–189, which places P'an Keng nineteenth.

6. K. C. Chang, *Shang Civilization*, p. 11.

7. On this kettle of fish, see Ku Chieh-kang, *Ku-shih pien*, vol. 1 (Peking, 1926), p. 201, where he argues that "P'an Keng" is the only genuine Shang material in the *Shang-shu*, although he later changed his mind and thought it a Chou forgery; Creel, pp. 64–69, who argues that the entire chapter was a forgery of later vintage; Paul Wheatley, *The Pivot of Four Quarters: A Preliminary Enquiry into the Origins and Character of the Ancient Chinese City* (Chicago, 1971), pp. 13–14, 420, who argues that "P'an Keng" was clearly not a pre-Chou text because it reflects Chou conceptions of urbanism and probably was written in the late Western Chou, revised in the Eastern Chou; Ho Ping-ti, *The Cradle of the East: An Inquiry into the Indigenous Origins of Techniques and Ideas of Neolithic and Early Historic China, 5000–1000 B.C.* (Hong Kong, 1975), p. 308, who argues that "P'an Keng" has now been authenticated archeologically, although no other scholar

seems to be aware of his source here; Ch'en Meng-chia, *Yin-hsü pu-tz'u tsung-shu* (Peking, 1956), pp. 580–581, who argues that "P'an Keng" is a forgery from the middle of the Western Chou; Matsumoto Masaaki, *Shunjū Sengoku ni okeru Shōsho no tenkai* (Tokyo, 1966), pp. 425–432, who disagrees with many of the theories naming "P'an Keng" as a forgery because of their lack of scholarly rigor, but who ultimately argues that it was a forgery (from the middle of the Warring States period) on the basis of numerous points; Chang Hsi-t'ang, *Shang-shu yin-lun* (Sian, 1958), pp. 198–199, who argues that style and word usage would place composition in the early Chou, not the Shang and not the late Spring and Autumn period as some have proposed.

8. Chu Hsi, *Chu-tzu yü-lei*, ed. Li Ching-te (Taipei reprint, 1970), ch. 78 (vol. 5, p. 3147).

9. Nakae Ushikichi, "Shōsho Hankō hen ni tsuite," in *CKSS*, pp. 289–299.

10. Nakae Ushikichi, "Shōsho Hankō hen ni tsuite," pp. 307–313, 317, 319–325. Nakae points out (p. 310) that Liu Feng-lu (1776–1829) and Chuang Shu-tsu (1750–1816) before him noted that the "people" were not meant to be excluded in the first section of the "P'an Keng" chapter. Creel (pp. 64–69) complains that this entire chapter is "long and . . . rather tedious," and ultimately condemns the whole thing as a fraud. He, like countless scholars before and after him, apparently never considered separating the parts of "P'an Keng" to place them in relation to each other. Nakae seems to have transcended both the classicist's overly reverential approach to the "sanctified" text and the iconoclastic irreverence of many of the May Fourth generation and their disciples, who were too quick to declare passages and entire texts spurious.

11. Nakae Ushikichi, "Shōsho Hankō hen ni tsuite," pp. 313–314.

12. Ho Ping-ti, p. 308. K. C. Chang (*Shang Civilization*, p. 226) cites a number of Chinese scholars with views similar to Professor Ho's. Chang (pp. 226–227) offers a much more sober assessment of *chung*, generally consistent with Nakae's position; and he quotes from a 1973 summary by Chang Cheng-lung that closely approximates Nakae's interpretation:

> "Chung-jen" were farmers, and were the fighting men in wars. They . . . usually occupied a very lowly position, opposite the . . . nobility. They had no title to land . . . and they were securely tied up with agricultural collectives, controlled by the . . . rulers, were conscriptd to become soldiers, paid tributes, and performed labor services. When they were soldiers they would become slaves when captured, and if they refused to become soldiers they and their families would instantly become slaves also. Their lives and their possessions were controlled by the king and the nobles, being in essence their tools and possessions. [Chang Cheng-lang, "P'u-tz'u p'ou t'ien chi ch'i hsiang-kuan chu wen-t'i," *K'ao-ku hsueh-pao* 1:117 (1973)]

13. Nakae Ushikichi, "Shōsho Hankō hen ni tsuite," p. 314.
14. Nakae Ushikichi, "Shōsho Hankō hen ni tsuite," pp. 315–317, 325–326. One Chinese scholar, Yang Yun-ju, has suggested that a serious problem exists between what the parts of the "P'an Keng" chapter allege to describe and their actual order of composition, but he has not developed the analysis beyond noting these issues for further study. See his *Shang-shu ho-ku* (Sian, 1959), pp. 94–118.
15. Kaizuka Shigeki, *Chūgoku no kodai kokka*, in *Kaizuka Shigeki chosakushū*, vol. 1 (Tokyo, 1976), pp. 153–154, 155–156.
16. Nakae Ushikichi, "Sho nijūkyū hen ni kansuru shiken ni tsuite (1): Kōkō keitō Shohen o ronzu," in *CKSS*, p. 492.
17. Nakae Ushikichi, "Sho nijūkyū hen (1)," pp. 450–453, 458–459. Ikeda Suetoshi, a contemporary scholar of the *Shang-shu*, once noted that Nakae's distinction between *keigaku* historical facts and general historical facts was particularly important. See Ikeda Suetoshi, "Shōsho tsūkai kō (1)," *Hiroshima daigaku bungakubu kiyō* 30.2:8–9 (March 1971).
18. See Creel, p. 59; and Kaizuka Shigeki, *Chūgoku no kodai kokka*, pp. 86–88.
19. Nakae Ushikichi, "Sho nijūkyū hen (1)," pp. 454, 455, 460–487.
20. James Legge and Clae Waltham, pp. 146–152; Nakae Ushikichi, "Sho nijūkyū hen (1)," pp. 502, 503–511.
21. Nakae Ushikichi, "Sho nijūkyū hen (1)," pp. 513–521.
22. According to Clae Waltham, "Legge found this document ['Tzu ts'ai'] lacking in unity and said of it that it was the translator's greatest comfort that it was short." Legge and Waltham, p. 128.
23. Nakae Ushikichi, "Sho nijūkyū hen (1)," pp. 521–536.
24. Legge and Waltham, p. 229; Nakae Ushikichi, "Sho nijūkyū hen (1)," pp. 555–561, 566–568, 574–576.
25. Nakae Ushikichi, "Sho nijūkyū hen ni kansuru shiken ni tsuite (2): Rakkō keitō Shohen o ronzu," in *CKSS*, pp. 637–639, 641–643.
26. Nakae Ushikichi, "Sho nijūkyū hen (2)," pp. 645–647, 655–657, quotation on p. 657.
27. Nakae Ushikichi, "Sho nijūkyū hen (2)," p. 659.
28. Naitō Konan, "Shōsho keigi," *Shinagaku* 1.7 (March 1921), in *Naitō Konan zenshū*, ed. Naitō Kenkichi and Kanda Kiichirō, vol. 7 (Tokyo, 1970), pp. 9–23, quotation on p. 22. For comments on the brilliance of this essay, see, for example, Matsumoto Masaaki, p. 341; Kimura Eiichi, "Nakae Ushikichi shi icho *Chūgoku kodai seiji shisō* ni tsuite," *Tōhō gakuhō* 19 (December 1950), in *CTM*, pp. 193–195; Ojima Sukema, "*Chūgoku kodai seiji shisō* ni tsuite," *Tosho* (August 1950), in *NGZ*, p. 324. The reason I suggest that Nakae may have seen Naitō's essay is that *Shinagaku* was among the few Japanese journals he read, as evidenced by a number of citations to it. Also, his friend Ojima Sukema published several articles in the early 1920s in *Shinagaku*, and Nakae cited them on occasion.

29. Nakae Ushikichi, "Kuyōden oyobi Kuyōgaku ni tsuite," in *CKSS*, pp. 329, 333–338.
30. Nakae Ushikichi, "Kuyōden," pp. 345–346.
31. Nakae Ushikichi, "Kuyōden," pp. 348, 351–352, 354–357, 359–363.
32. Nakae Ushikichi, "Kuyōden," pp. 363–369.
33. Nakae Ushikichi, "Kuyōden," pp. 370–372, 385–386, 387–390, 393–395.
34. George Kennedy, "Interpretation of the *Ch'un-ch'iu*," *Journal of the Oriental Society* 62:40–48 (1942). Nakae's textual analysis of the *Ch'un-ch'iu* ("Kuyōden," pp. 401–409) closely parallels Kennedy's.
35. Nakae Ushikichi, "Kuyōden," pp. 410–422, 432–435.
36. *Harvard-Yenching Institute Sinological Index Series. Supplement No. 11: Combined Concordances to Ch'un-ch'iu, Kung-yang, Ku-liang and Tso-chuan*, vol. 1 (Taipei, 1965), pp. 4, 25, 487; James Legge, tr., *The Chinese Classics*, vol. 5: *The Ch'un ts'ew with the Tso chuen* (Hong Kong, 1861–1872), pp. 1, 3, 37, 39, 833.
37. Nakae Ushikichi, "Kuyōden," pp. 396, 440–444, quotation on p. 441.
38. Niida Noboru, "Yūmon no sho: Nakae shi ni okeru Tōyō shakai no mikata," *Chūgoku kenkyū* 13 (September 1950), in *CTM*, p. 183; Kimura Eiichi, "Nakae Ushikichi shi icho *Chūgoku kodai seiji shisō* ni tsuite," pp. 196–199.
39. Matsumoto Masaaki, *Shunjū Sengoku ni okeru Shōsho no tenkai;* Hihara Toshikuni, *Shunjū Kuyōden no kenkyū* (Tokyo, 1976); Ueno Kenchi, *Nihon Saden kenkyū chojutsu nenpyō* (Tokyo, 1975). The fullest treatment I have been able to find of the *Kung-yang* school is Ch'en Chu, *Kung-yang-chia che-hsueh* (Shanghai, 1929).
40. Nakae's edition of Hegel's *Vorlesungen über die Philosophie der Weltgeschichte* (Leipzig, Felix Meiner, 1920) is now lost: See *Nakae bunko mokuroku*, no. 11 in series *Shinchaku tosho geppō* (Kyoto, 1964), p. 18. On Nakae's reading and rereading Kant, see "Nakae Ushikichi nenpu," pp. 301, 304, 305, 306, 308. See Nakae's copies of Wilhelm Windelband, *Einleitung in die Philosophie* (Tübingen, 1923), which he dated 16 June 1925; Windelband, *Die Geschichte der neueren Philosophie*, dated 14 October 1921; Wilhelm Dilthey, *Einleitung in die Geisteswissenschaften: Versuch einer Grundlegung für das Studium der Gesellschaft und der Geschichte* (Leipzig, 1923), undated; Heinrich Rickert, *Die Probleme der Geschichtsphilosophie* (Heidelberg, 1924), undated; Georg Simmel, *Die Probleme der Geschichtsphilosophie: Eine erkenntnistheoretische Studie* (Munich and Leipzig, 1922), dated 15 July 1922; all in NB. In addition, Nakae also made use of several other major turn-of-the-century works, all in NB, by historians of philosophy, such as Ernst Bernheim, *Lehrbuch der historischen Methode* (Leipzig, 1894), in which Nakae's notes cover only the sections on "Geschichtsphilosophie" and give no date; Friedrich Ueberweg, *Grundriss der Geschichte der Philosophie*, 4 volumes (Berlin, 1915–1926); Eduard Zeller, *Grundriss der Geschichte der Griechischen Philosophie* (Leipzig, 1920), undated; Eduard Meyer, *Geschichte des Altertums* (Stuttgart and Berlin, 1925), dated both 5 November 1925 and 6 October 1926.

41. On Windelband, see R. G. Collingwood, *The Idea of History* (New York, 1956), pp. 166–168; H. Stuart Hughes, *Consciousness and Society: The Reorientation of European Social Thought 1890–1930* (New York, 1961), pp. 189–190, 194–195; Hayden V. White, "Wilhelm Windelband," in *The Encyclopedia of Philosophy*, vol. 8 (New York, 1967), pp. 320–322.

42. On Rickert, see R. G. Collingwood, A. E. Taylor, and F. C. S. Schiller, "Are History and Science Different Kinds of Knowledge?" *Mind* 31:425–466 (1922); Maurice Mandelbaum, *The Problem of Historical Knowledge: An Answer to Relativism* (New York, 1938), pp. 119–147; Robert Anchor, "Heinrich Rickert," in *The Encyclopedia of Philosophy*, vol. 7 (New York, 1967), pp. 192–195. On Simmel's views on the philosophy of history, see Mandelbaum, pp. 101–119; Collingwood, *The Idea of History*, pp. 170–171; Rudolph H. Weingartner, *Experience and Culture: The Philosophy of Georg Simmel* (Middletown, 1962).

43. Wilhelm Bauer, *Einführung in das Studium der Geschichte* (Tubingen, 1921), as cited in R. G. Collingwood, *The Idea of History*, p. 175.

44. See, for example, Nakae's marginal notes in his copy of Richert's *Die Problem der Geschichtsphilosophie*, p. 61: "I couldn't disagree more." Or, p. 114: "Why isn't this a little more impressive?" Or, p. 115: "What a horrible attitude to take." Or, p. 125: "So, in the final analysis, is philosophy of history a field of learning that cannot be established?" See also Nakae's subtle thrust at Rickert in "Kuyōden," p. 345.

5. THE NATURE OF THE CHINESE POLITY

1. George Wilhelm Friedrich Hegel, *The Philosophy of History*, tr. Carl J. Friedrich and Paul W. Friedrich, in Carl J. Friedrich, ed., *The Philosophy of Hegel* (New York, 1965), p. 46.

2. Suzuki Tadashi, "Ikyō no koten teki yuibutsuronsha: Nakae Ushikichi ron," p. 146; and W. Lenin, *Sämliche Werke* (Vienna, 1927–1931).

3. Nakae Ushikichi, "Ei Ō no Shōyū to Chō Gi no Shōo to ni tsuite," in *CKSS*, p. 211. Most sources give the figure of thirty as the size of the run Nakae ordered for this essay's printing; see, for example, Nakae shi ikō shuppan iinkai, "Batsu," in *CKSS*, p. 666. One source gives the figure fifty: "Nakae Ushikichi nenpu," p. 304.

4. Nakae Ushikichi, "Ei Ō no Shōyū," pp. 212–231.

5. Itō Takeo, "Nakae Ushikichi no shoken," in *NGZ*, p. 40.

6. Arif Dirlik, *Revolution and History: The Origins of Marxist Historiography in China, 1919–1937* (Berkeley, 1978), pp. 96–97. Dirlik notes that the leaders in the debate, Kuo Mo-jo (1892–1978) and T'ao Hsi-sheng (b. 1893), became interested in earlier periods of Chinese history only as a result of this debate. Nakae's article

was published as "Shina no hōken seido ni tsuite," *Mantetsu Shina gesshi* 8.1 (January 1931).

7. Nakae Ushikichi, "Chūgoku no hōken seido ni tsuite," in *CKSS*, p. 249. In the *CKSS* edition of this essay, the editors have substituted "Chūgoku" for the original "Shina," reflecting postwar usage.

8. Nakae Ushikichi, "Chūgoku no hōken seido ni tsuite," p. 236.

9. Nakae Ushikichi, "Chūgoku no hōken seido ni tsuite," p. 270.

10. Nakae Ushikichi, "Chūgoku no hōken seido ni tsuite," pp. 233–234.

11. Nakae Ushikichi, "Chūgoku no hōken seido ni tsuite," p. 237; and letter from Katō Koretaka to Sakatani Yoshinao, dated 15 February 1947, in Katō Koretaka, *Pekin no Nakae Ushikichi, aru kosei no kiroku* (Tokyo, 1984), p. 165.

12. Nakae Ushikichi, "Chūgoku kodai seiji shisō shi," pp. 29–30, 126–130.

13. Nakae Ushikichi, "Chūgoku no hōken seido ni tsuite," pp. 242, 244, 246–248.

14. Nakae Ushikichi, "Chūgoku no hōken seido ni tsuite," pp. 249–257.

15. For a good treatment of this whole issue in scholarship from around the world, as well as the elaboration of one particular view, see Tanigawa Michio, *Medieval Chinese Society and the Local "Community,"* tr. Joshua A. Fogel (Berkeley, 1985).

16. Nakae Ushikichi, "Chūgoku no hōken seido ni tsuite," pp. 258–265.

17. Nakae Ushikichi, "Chūgoku no hōken seido ni tsuite," p. 266.

18. Nakae Ushikichi, "Chūgoku no hōken seido ni tsuite," pp. 266–270.

19. Nakae Ushikichi, "Chūgoku no hōken seido ni tsuite," pp. 264–65, 271–279; Frederick Engels, *Anti-Dühring* (Moscow, 1959), p. 253; and Nakae's undated copy of Engels, *Herrn Eugen Dühring's Umwälzung der Wissenschaft* (Stuttgart, 1921).

20. Nakae Ushikichi, "Chūgoku no hōken seido ni tsuite," pp. 236–237.

21. Nakae Ushikichi, "Chūgoku no hōken seido ni tsuite," pp. 280–281, quotations on p. 281.

22. Nakae Ushikichi, "Kuyōden oyobi Kuyōgaku ni tsuite," pp. 330–334, 336–367, 372, 411–412; and Nakae Ushikichi, "Chūgoku no hōken seido ni tsuite," p. 282.

23. The foregoing is drawn primarily from the excellent work by Marian Sawer, *Marxism and the Question of the Asiatic Mode of Production* (The Hague, 1977), pp. 5–6, 12–13, 16–19, 22, 24–31, 33, 37–38. See also, Basil Guy, *The French Image of China Before and After Voltaire*, vol. 21 of *Studies on Voltaire and the Eighteenth Century* (Geneva, 1963); E. Rose, "China as a Symbol of Reaction in Germany, 1830–1880," *Comparative Literature* 3:57–76 (1951); Lawrence Krader, *The Asiatic Mode of Production: Sources, Development and Critique in the Writings of Karl Marx* (Assen, The Netherlands, 1975), pp. 19–79; G. W. F. Hegel, *The Philosophy of History*, p. 44; and Shlomo Avineri, *Hegel's Theory of the Modern State* (Cambridge, 1972), pp. 122–125. Sawer (p. 26) notes: "The idea that Eastern nations lacked within themselves the conditions for further organic development was to become the dominant theme of nineteenth-century writing on Oriental despotism."

24. Karl Marx, *Grundrisse: Foundations of the Critique of Political Economy,* tr. Martin Nicolaus (Harmondsworth, 1973), pp. 472–473, 474, 484, 493; and Sawer, pp. 44–51, 53–54, 56.

25. For a detailed treatment of the concept of the Asiatic mode of production and the debates over it, see my "The Debates over the Asiatic Mode of Production in Soviet Russia, China, and Japan," *American Historical Review* 93.1:57–79 (February 1988).

26. "Lajos Magyar [Liudvig Ignat'ievich Mad'iar]," in *Great Soviet Encyclopedia,* vol. 15, p. 321; Liudvig Mad'iar, *Ekonomika sel'skogo khoziaistva v Kitae* (Moscow, 1928); partial Chinese translation by Tsung Hua, *Chung-kuo nung-ts'un ching-chi chih t'e-hsing* (Shanghai, 1930); complete translation (with additional materials) by Ch'en Tai-ch'ing and P'eng Kuei-ch'iu, *Chung-kuo nung-ts'un ching-chi yen-chiu* (Shanghai, 1930); and chapter twelve translated by Li Min-ch'ang, *Chung-kuo ching-chi yen-chiu,* stenographic copy, Moscow, 1929, held in the collection of the Hoover Institution, Stanford University. See also Sawer, pp. 86–88. Dirlik (p. 191) misreads a work by Ho Kan-chih to say that this work appeared first in 1930; the Chinese translation was published in 1930, two years after the book appeared in Russian. In fact, it was translated two times and a beginning was made on a third. Mad'iar's second book, *Ocherki po ekonomike Kitaia* (Moscow, 1930), was translated into Chinese (in full) by Hsu Kung-ta, *Chung-kuo ching-chi ta-kang* (Shanghai, 1933). The actual initiator of the debate in the Soviet Union was another Hungarian exile by the name of Evgenii Varga (1879–1964). On Varga, see "Evgenii Samuilovich Varga," in *Great Soviet Encyclopedia,* vol. 4, p. 509; "Yevgeni Samoilovich Varga," in *Encyclopaedia Judaica,* vol. 16, col. 69–70; Anne M. Bailey and Josep R. Llobera, eds., *The Asiatic Mode of Production: Science and Politics* (London, 1981), pp. 51–52; Peter Knirsch, *Eugen Varga* (Berlin, 1961); obituary notice in *New York Times,* 9 October 1964, p. 39; Sawer, pp. 52, 76, 81–85.

27. Liudvig Mad'iar, "The Legitimacy of the AMP," tr. Robert Croskey, in *The Asiatic Mode of Production,* ed. Bailey and Llobera, pp. 83–84, from Mad'iar's introduction to M. D. Kokin and G. Papaian, *"Tszin'-Tian": Agrarnyi stroi drevnogo Kitaia* (Leningrad, 1930). For a discussion of this book and Mad'iar's introduction, see V. N. Nikiforov, *Sovetskiie istoriki o problemakh Kitaia* (Moscow, 1970), pp. 231–233. Kokin and Papaian argued in the body of their book that the *ching-t'ien* or well-field system of distant antiquity represented the Chinese manifestation of the rural commune. Since the state in theory owned all the land, rent and tax became one, another important element of the Asiatic mode of production. Mad'iar, Kokin, and Papaian all agreed, as did the other Aziatchiki, that private property was not unknown in ancient (Asiatic) China, but the principle that provided the society's undergirding lacked a full-fledged conception of private property. It was also understood that the heyday of the Asiatic mode was over, but the Aziatchiki claimed in addition that feudalism still did not characterize contemporary Chinese social relations. As concerned the prospects for the coming

Chinese revolution, to which all eyes were glued, they argued that China's bourgeoisie was still weak, inexperienced, and unprepared to assume the leadership of the revolution. Thus, China was ready for a social revolution. That view put them dangerously, in many cases fatally, close to Trotsky's position that the Chinese revolution need be socialist (because the Chinese economy could be characterized as capitalist), although they disagreed completely with Trotsky's assessment of the fundamental social forces at work in China.

28. Letter from Katō Koretaka to Sakatani Yoshinao, dated 15 February 1947, in Katō Koretaka, *Pekin no Nakae Ushikichi*, pp. 165–166; and Niida Noboru, p. 183.

29. Karl Marx, *Grundrisse*, pp. 467, 479.

30. Nakae Ushikichi, "Chūgoku no hōken seido ni tsuite," pp. 237, 281.

31. Letter to Verz Zasulich, dated 8 March 1881, in *The Letters of Karl Marx and Frederick Engels*, tr. Saul Pavoder (Englewood Cliffs, 1979), pp. 335–336; also appended to Marx, *Pre-Capitalist Economic Formations*, tr. Jack Cohen (New York, 1971), pp. 144–145; George Lichtheim, "Oriental Despotism," in his *The Concept of Ideology* (New York, 1967), p. 75; Shlomo Avineri, *The Social and Political Thought of Karl Marx* (Cambridge, 1968), pp. 152–153; and Sawer, pp. 63–64.

32. Nakae shi ikō shuppan iinkai, "Batsu," in *CKSS*, pp. 664–665; Takagi Motoyasu, "Ippan keika hōkoku," in *NUH*, p. 243; and Hirota Hiroo, "Tsuiokudan," in *NUH*, pp. 257–258.

33. Shimizu Morimitsu, *Shina shakai no kenkyū* (Tokyo, 1939), pp. 1–2, 83–84, 120, 127–128. Shimizu claimed that he agreed with the views of Yokogawa Jirō (another SMR researcher who continued to live in China for many years after Japan's defeat in WWII) that the scattered, isolated nature of rural Chinese villages, each within its own universe, provided the basis for a low level of productivity and required the intrusion of a higher authority to provide the mechanism for irrigation works. Yokogawa regarded the village *kyōdōtai* as synonymous not with primitive communalism, but with an immediately subsequent transitional era from common or public to private notions of property. And, he believed, this village *kyōdōtai* was an essential element of the Asiatic mode of production in China. Yokogawa Jirō, "Shina ni okeru nōson kyōdōtai to sono isei ni tsuite, hitotsu no gimon no teishutsu to shite," *Keizai hyōron* 2.5:2–3, 6, 8, 13, 15, 21, 24, 32, 36–37 (July 1935); and Hatada Takashi, "Chūgoku ni okeru senseishugi to 'sonraku kyōdōtai' riron," *Chūgoku kenkyū* 13 (October 1950), as reprinted in his *Chūgoku sonraku to kyōdōtai riron* (Tokyo, 1973), p. 56.

34. Shimizu Morimitsu, pp. 129–130, 141–142, 162, 305, quotation on p. 129. As a sociologist, though, Shimizu ultimately was not so attracted to the theories of Marx, Mad'iar, or Wittfogel, as he was to Emile Durkheim's notion of *société segmentaire* as descriptive of the dispersed nature of rural China. Nor was Shimizu so completely convinced as Nakae by the Marxist notion that the key to the demise of an unchanging China, previously mired in a stagnant social structure of villages and despotism, was the invasion of Western capital.

35. *Kyōdōtai* theory has become a virtual industry in postwar Japan and applied to countless societies around the globe. By the late 1920s and early 1930s, Japanese scholars had come to use it in two related ways: as synonymous with Marx's "primitive communalism" and hence a pre-class society; and as a sense of linkage (authentic or imposed) between members of the same social network to enable the smooth handling of all sorts of problems that might arise.

It was in this connection during the debates over the Asiatic mode of production in Japan that *kyōdōtai* and the Asiatic mode became associated. Some used the two concepts interchangeably and meant by them a primitive social organization predating the emergenece of class antagonisms. In addition, the characteristics of societies described by the concepts of *kyōdōtai* and the Asiatic mode of production often elicited in the minds of scholars the older idea of stagnation or lack of social change as something distinctive to the Orient, and with it came the overpowering image of Oriental despotism. However simplistically put, this was essentially the picture as portrayed by Nakae Ushikichi and Shimizu Morimitsu.

Drawing on his training as a sociologist, Shimizu was the first scholar to apply the term and theory of *kyōdōtai* to Chinese social organization in an attempt to describe its relationship to despotism. In fact, of course, Nakae had already done work along similar lines without using the terminology of *kyōdōtai;* and through their personal acquaintanceship, Shimizu had access to Nakae's printed but unpublished essays. His citations to Nakae's esays on "feudalism" in China and the history of ancient Chinese thought show that he was familiar with Nakae's research.

Nonetheless, Shimizu's work marked a giant step ahead in the study of Chinese society. Subsequent scholarly appraisals, such as those of Hirano Yoshitarō, Kainō Michitaka, and Matsumoto Yoshimi, have all dealt directly with the problem of *kyōdōtai* as initially put forth by Shimizu, although nothing even remotely resembling agreement exists. In fact, the general tendency of postwar scholarship in Japan has moved away from the picture of *kyōdōtai* as elaborated by Shimizu, largely in response to the fact, as perceived after the war, that stagnation could not possibly characterize a China engulfed in a Communist revolution.

In the mid 1930s, however, in China as well as Japan, the concept of a rural *kyōdōtai* (Chinese, *kung-t'ung-t'i*) could be found in the pages of journals of social and economic history. One scholar by the name of Liu Hsing-t'ang, who clearly was able to read Japanese, alternatively translated the Marxist idea of the village commune as *nung-ts'un kung-she* and *nung-ts'un kung-t'ung-t'i*. He claimed that many scholars saw it as one important reason why Asiatic society had stagnated. Despite changes in China's basic mode of production and the major jolt caused by the intrusion of Western capital at the time of the Opium War, he argued, remnants of *kyōdōtai* still seriously impeded China's social development. See Liu Hsing-t'ang, "T'ang-tai chih kao-li-tai shih-yeh," *Shih-huo* 1.10:8, 15 (April 1935);

Liu Hsing-t'ang, "Chung-kuo she-hui fa-chan hsing-shih chih t'an-hsien," *Hsin sheng-ming* 2.9:7, 24, 26–27 (October 1935); and Liu Hsing-t'ang, "Chung-kuo ching-chi fa-chan te pen-chih," *Wen-hua p'i-p'an* 2.2–3:188–207 (1935).

Under the influence of both Max Weber and Karl Marx, more creative Japanese social scientists in the postwar period have developed a whole science of *kyōdōtai*. Two extremely important events fueled this development: the end of the war, which brought an end to domestic Japanese repression of left-wing intellectuals; and the discovery (in 1939) and translation into Japanese (in 1947) of Marx's manuscript, *Pre-Capitalist Economic Formations*. The text was found in the Marx-Engels Archives in the Soviet Union, and Japanese was the first foreign language into which it was translated, with the possible exception of Russian.

Ōtsuka Hisao (b. 1907), Japan's leading theoretician of *kyōdōtai*, has generated over the years an elaborate system in which *kyōdōtai* is no longer simply the organization of a primitive, classless society or a transitional stage following it. In the mid 1930s he began reading the works of Marx and Weber with an eye to their views on the fate of the village structure as societies developed marketing systems. Before the war, but particularly after it and the land reform carried out by the occupation in Japan, Ōtsuka had been intrigued by the remnants of the village *kyōdōtai* and the process of its dissolution before the intrusion of capital. Yet, he knew well that capital had long preceded capitalism.

With the publication of Marx's *Pre-Capitalist Economic Formations*, Ōtsuka began to build his sociological system based on *kyōdōtai*. His first major work was *Kyōdōtai no kiso riron* (Tokyo, 1955), based on lectures given at Tokyo University in the early 1950s. In his view, a distinctive *kyōdōtai* emerges corresponding to each of the various ascending stages of societal development. Thus, all pre-capitalist forms of social and economic organization—Asiatic, ancient, feudal, or whatever—generated an appropriate *kyōdōtai*. The mode of production, the kind of *kyōdōtai*, and the form of exploitation unite in a triumvirate specific to each historical stage. Eventually, Ōtsuka argued, *kyōdōtai* dissipates with the rise of bourgeois capitalism. See Ōtsuka Hisao, *Kyōdōtai no kiso riron*, in *Ōtsuka Hisao chosakushū*, vol. 7 (Tokyo, 1971), pp. 6–8; Ōtsuka Hisao, "Kyōdōtai kaitai no kiso teki shojōken, sono riron teki kōsatsu," in *Ōtsuka Hisao chosakushū*, vol. 7, pp. 107–33; Fukutomi Masami, *Kyōdōtai to shoyū no genri: Shihonron taikei to kōgi no keizaigaku no hōhō* (Tokyo, 1970), pp. 365–366, 368; Ōta Hidemichi, "Ōtsuka Hisao," in *Nihon no rekishika*, ed. Nagahara Keiji and Kano Masanao (Tokyo, 1976), pp. 345–356; and Mimori Sadao, "Nihon ni okeru kyōdōtai no kenkyū," in *Kyōdōtai no kenkyū*, vol. 2 (Tokyo, 1958), pp. 63–65.

In Marx's conception, individuals have historically not been able to live completely in isolation; instead, they form mutual bonds. And in pre-capitalist society, Ōtsuka argues, the communal nature of *kyōdōtai* makes social integration possible. As Marx notes in *Pre-Capitalist Economic Formations*, the development of exchange leads to a process of individuation and atomization that ultimately renders group life useless. Exchange, no longer the communal solidarity of *kyōdōtai*, becomes the arbiter of social cohesion with the advent of capitalism. Thus, in pre-capitalist society, the level of productive capacity gives rise to a distinctive form of social cohesion represented by a distinctive *kyōdōtai*, and this in turn generates a distinctive mode of production. See Karl Marx, *Pre-Capitalist Economic Formations*, p. 96; and Shiozawa Kimio, *Ajia teki seisan yōshiki ron* (Tokyo, 1970), pp. 193–198. Also, in postwar *kyōdōtai* theory, "Asiatic" no longer usually applies solely to Asian societies, but has become a generic term for a mode of production preceding the ancient stage but following the primitive, classless commune.

6. INTEGRATING THE PAST AND THE PRESENT

1. Nakae Ushikichi, "Hashigaki" (Introduction), to "Sho nijūkyū hen ni kansuru shiken ni tsuite (ichi): Kōkō keitō Shohen o ronzu," in *CKSS*, pp. 448–449.
2. *Nihon kin-gendai shi jiten* (Tokyo, 1978), p. 573.
3. Niida Noboru, pp. 178–181.
4. Immanuel Kant, *Critique of Practical Reason, and Other Writings in Moral Philosophy*, tr. and ed. Lewis White Beck (Chicago, 1949), pp. 249–250, 258.
5. Itō Takeo reported Nakae to have said upon initial receipt of this money, "The money I receive is for research expenses. If there are any demands for counter-service on my part as 'consultant,' then I refuse it. When my research is complete, however, I will send you a copy of it." Itō Takeo, *Mantetsu ni ikite*, p. 82. See also Suzuki Tadashi, "Ikyō no koten teki yuibutsuronsha: Nakae Ushikichi ron," p. 148; and Itō Takeo, "Nakae Ushikichi no shokan," in *NGZ*, p. 41.

7. THE EXPATRIATE VISION

1. Katō Koretaka, "Chishiki to seikatsu," p. 91.
2. Nakae Ushikichi, "Chūgoku kodai seiji shisō shi," p. 123.
3. Niida Noboru, pp. 178–181, quotation on p. 178.
4. Kuno Osamu, "*Nakae Ushikichi no ningenzō*, rekishi kenkyū no tessoku no migoto na jitsubutsu kyōji," *Tōkyō shinbun* (27 July 1970), in *NUH*, p. 234.
5. Letter to Suzue Gen'ichi, dated 4 October 1941, in *NUS*, p. 240.
6. Letter to Suzue Gen'ichi, dated 12 November 1941, in *NUS*, p. 242.
7. Letter to Suzue Gen'ichi, dated 7 March 1939, in *NUS*, p. 113.
8. Ōta Ryōichirō, p. 30. "Nakae Ushikichi nenpu" (p. 312) claims that this letter arrived "around" October 1940.
9. Tsurumi Yoshiyuki's attempted typology of Japanese who left their native land for long periods of time is suggestive but unsuccessful: Tsurumi Yoshiyuki,

"Nihonjin banare no ikikata ni tsuite, teichaku to idō no hōhō," *Shisō no kagaku* (June 1972), in *NUH,* pp. 63–91.

10. Letter to Hama Masao and Kimura Eiichi, dated 16 June 1932, in *NUS,* pp. 273–274. See also Takeda Taijun, p. 229.

11. Kimura Eiichi, "Nakae Ushikichi shi icho *Chūgoku kodai seiji shisō* ni tsuite," p. 200; "Nakae ushikichi nenpu," p. 304; and Katō Koretaka, "Kakuretaru minshu-shugisha, senji no Nakae Ushikichi shi," *Hyōron* (October 1948), in *NGZ,* pp. 79–80.

12. Imai Seiichi, *Taiheiyō sensō shi 1: Manshū jihen* (Tokyo, 1971), pp. 265–266; and Umemoto Sutezō, *Zenshi Kantōgun* (Tokyo, 1978), pp. 107, 109.

13. "Nakae Ushikichi nenpu," pp. 300, 303, 307; and *NUS,* p. 342, fn. 1.

14. Katō Koretaka, "Kakuretaru minshushigisha," p. 80. Katō says that Nakae offered his advice to Ting in 1933; but it has to have been 1934, as confirmed by "Nakae Ushikichi nenpu," p. 307.

15. Letter to Imada Shintarō, dated 24 July 1938, in *NUS,* p. 81; letter to Suzue Gen'ichi, dated 12 March 1940, in *NUS,* p. 173; letter to Imada Shintarō, dated 19 August 1938, in *NUS,* p. 341; and Katō Koretaka, "Nakae Ushikichi to shinbun," p. 136.

16. "Nakae Ushikichi nenpu," pp. 308, 309; and Katō Koretaka, "Kakuretaru min-shushugisha," p. 80.

17. Tsubokawa Ken'ichi, "Pekin no natsu," *Nihonkai sakka* n.s. 13 (March 1965), in *NGZ,* p. 205; Moriya Fumio, "Nakae Ushikichi shi no koto," in *NUH,* p. 212 (from his *Shakai kagaku e no shisaku,* Tokyo, Aoki shoten, 1975); and Katō Kore-taka, "Kakuretaru minshushugisha," p. 83.

18. "Nakae Ushikichi nenpu," pp. 309, 313.

19. Although he never mentioned this diary to anyone, there is a cryptic remark in a letter of 21 October 1941 to Sakatani Yoshinao (in *NUS,* pp. 381–382) that sug-gested its existence: "Every year, just at the time when the leaves on the trees are greenest and most luxuriant, some birds—I don't know their name—fly over-head, making a beautiful, high-pitched sound; and into my ragged study each year they bring the truly joyous noise of birdsong. Somewhere on a page of a book by Marx or Kant are written words to the effect of 'the birds have come with their characteristic whistling sound' and the date." Several months earlier, on 14 May 1941, on a page of his copy of Hegel's *Phänomenologie,* Nakae had written almost precisely these words (See Appendix, no. 57).

20. Letter to Suzue Gen'ichi, dated 25 April 1940, in *NUS,* p. 176.

21. See Appendix, nos. 10, 18, 34, 40.

22. Letter to Suzue Gen'ichi, dated 31 July 1941, in *NUS,* p. 231. His diary entry for 12 October 1941 (Appendix, no. 77) suggests a change toward a more balanced view: "The new offensive which Germany began on 2 October has, as Hitler declared, captured the attention of the entire world to an event which will decide the fate of the Russo-German war. Although reports from the German Army

boast that the Russians are surrounded and that their obstinate resistance has become merely the fighting of a cornered beast, the truth is not at all clear. There's no doubt that Hitler is staking his entire strength on this invasion."

23. See Appendix, nos. 8, 22, 30.

24. Letter to Suzue Gen'ichi, dated 14 September 1940, in *NUS*, p. 192.

25. See Appendix, no. 38.

26. Letter to Suzue Gen'ichi, dated 14 July 1940, in *NUS*, p. 186.

27. See Appendix, no. 44.

28. Letter to Suzue Gen'ichi, dated 7 July 1941, in *NUS*, pp. 227–228. See also the letter written two days earlier, 5 July 1941, to Katō Koretaka, in *NUS*, p. 318.

29. Letter to Katō Koretaka, dated 11 July 1941, in *NUS*, p. 323.

30. Letter to Suzue Gen'ichi, dated 31 July 1941, in *NUS*, pp. 230–231.

31. Letter to Ogura Sōichi, dated 10 July 1941, in *NUS*, p. 363, 365.

32. Alvin Coox, *Nomonhan: Japan Against Russia, 1939* (Stanford, 1985), pp. 29, 31, 32. Coox (p. 599, n. 6) adds the following: "According to a colorful account by consul Morishima Morito, Imada went out personally on a handcar with a railway man and forced him to set off the charge."

33. Hata Ikuhiko, *Gun fashizumu undō shi* (Tokyo, 1972), pp. 182–183, 414; Mark R. Peattie, *Ishiwara Kanji and Japan's Confrontation with the West* (Princeton, 1975), pp. 245–246; and Yokoyama Shinpei, *Hiroku Ishiwara Kanji* (Tokyo, 1971), p. 152. Knowledge of Imada's personal history comes from a personal communication from Alvin Coox.

34. Letter to Imada Shintarō, dated 19 August 1937, in *NUS*, pp. 341–342.

35. Nakae's reference appears in his letter to Imada Shintarō, dated August 1938, in *NUS*, p. 348; and fn. 1 on same page for citation to Imada.

36. Letter to Imada Shintarō, dated 19 May 1938, in *NUS*, pp. 343–344.

37. Letter to Imada Shintarō, dated 19 May 1938, in *NUS*, p. 344.

38. "Nakae Ushikichi nenpu," p. 310.

39. Letter to Imada Shintarō, dated 13 July 1938, in *NUS*, p. 347.

40. See Appendix, no. 92.

41. Letter to Imada Shintarō, dated 11 August 1938, in *NUS*, p. 348.

42. Letter to Imada Shintarō, dated 16 August 1938, in *NUS*, p. 249.

43. Letter to Imada Shintarō, dated 11 April 1939, in *NUS*, p. 350; and "Nakae Ushikichi nenpu," p. 311.

44. See Appendix, no. 12.

45. "Nakae Ushikichi nenpu," p. 312.

46. Letter to Imada Shintarō, dated 3 December 1939, in *NUS*, pp. 350–351.

47. "Nakae Ushikichi nenpu," p. 312; letter to Imada Shintarō, dated 3 December 1939, in *NUS*, p. 351; and *NUS*, p. 351, fn. 1.

48. Letter to Imada Shintarō, dated 3 March 1941, in *NUS*, p. 352. The citation from Hegel's *Phenomenology* follows the translation by J. B. Baillie, *The Phenomenology of Mind* (New York, 1967), p. 711, emphasis added. This section of the text

by Hegel is much abbreviated in the edition translated by A. V. Miller, *Phenomenology of Spirit* (Oxford, 1977), p. 580. Nakae's intellectual relationship to Hegel will be handled in considerably more detail in Chapter Eight.

49. Letter to Imada Shintarō, dated 3 March 1941, in *NUS*, p. 352.

50. Letter to Suzue Gen'ichi, dated 18 March 1941, in *NUS*, p. 216.

51. Letter to Imada Shintarō, dated 4 November 1941, in *NGZ*, pp. 434–435; and Sakatani Yoshinao's commentary on it, in *NGZ*, pp. 439–440.

52. Letter to Imada Shintarō, dated 20 December 1941, in *NGZ*, p. 436; and Sakatani Yoshinao, in *NGZ*, pp. 441–442.

53. *Shishi Ushijima Tatsukuma den*, ed. Ushijima Tatsukuma sensei koki kinenkai, 1974, as cited in Saktani Yoshinao, "*Shokan* hoi," in *NGZ*, pp. 442–443; and letter to Imada Shintarō, dated 20 December 1941, in *NGZ*, p. 436.

54. As cited in Sakatani Yoshinao, "*Shokan* hoi," in *NGZ*, p. 443. On Ushijima and Tsunoda's plot to assassinate Tōjō, see Hosaka Masayasu, *Tōjō Hideki to tennō no jidai*, vol. 2 (Tokyo, 1980), pp. 112, 127; and John Toland, *The Rising Sun: The Decline and Fall of the Japanese Empire, 1936–1945* (New York, 1970), pp. 524–525.

55. See Appendix, no. 89.

56. "Nakae Ushikichi nenpu," pp. 313–315; letter to Imada Shintarō's mother, dated 3 April 1942, in *NUS*, pp. 354–355; and letter from Katō Koretaka to Sakatani Yoshinao, dated 27 March 1942, in Katō, *Pekin no Nakae Ushikichi*, pp. 152–153.

57. Letter to Imada Shintarō's mother, dated 3 April 1942, in *NUS*, p. 354–355; and letter to Imada Shintarō, dated 14 April 1942, in *NUS*, p. 356.

58. Letter from Katō Koretaka to Imada Shintarō, dated 2 May 1942, in Katō, *Pekin no Nakae Ushikichi*, pp. 155–160, quotation on p. 155.

59. Letter to Imada Shintarō, dated 17 May 1942, in *NUS*, p. 357.

60. Leo Tolstoy, *War and Peace*, tr. Constance Garnett (New York, 1931), p. 1011.

8. The Importance of German Idealism

1. Lu Hsun, "A Madman's Diary" (April 1918), in *Selected Works of Lu Hsun*, vol. 1 (Peking, 1956), p. 21.

2. Letter to Sakatani Yoshinao, dated 31 May 1941, in *NUS*, p. 379.

3. Letter to Suzue Gen'ichi, dated 14 September 1940, in *NUS*, pp. 193–194; and Itō Takeo, "Nakae Ushikichi no shokan," pp. 50–52. The rise of Hitler and a widespread misunderstanding of Hegel and German idealism motivated Herbert Marcuse at precisely this time to write *Reason and Revolution* and attempt to destroy any possible imputation of a link between Nazism and Hegelian thought. His last paragraph reads in part: "The social and political theory responsible for the development of Fascist Germany was, then, related to Hegelianism in a completely negative way. It was anti-Hegelian in all its aims and principles. No better witness to this fact exists than the one serious theorist of Nationalism Socialism,

Carl Schmitt, [who] ... summarizes the entire process [of the development of Hegelian thought] in the striking statement that on the day of Hitler's ascent to power 'Hegel, so to speak, died.'" Marcuse, *Reason and Revolution: Hegel and the Rise of Social Theory* (1941; reprint Boston, 1969), pp. 418–419.

4. Katō Koretaka, "Keiko no omoide," *Kyōiku kenkyū* (May 1956), in *NGZ*, p. 165; and "Nakae Ushikichi nenpu," in *NUH*, p. 304.

5. Letter to Sakatani Yoshinao, dated 11 April 1941, in *NUS*, pp. 368–370.

6. Immanuel Kant, *Critique of Practical Reason, and Other Writings in Moral Philosophy*, tr. and ed. Lewis White Beck (Chicago, 1949), pp. 258–259.

7. See Norman Kemp Smith, *A Commentary to Kant's 'Critique of Pure Reason'* (New York, 1962), pp. 308–321.

8. Immanuel Kant, *Critique of Pure Reason*, tr. Norman Kemp Smith (New York, 1965), p. 313 (B375).

9. On this last point, see Lewis White Beck, "Introduction," in Immanuel Kant, *Critique of Practical Reason*, pp. 20, 23, 40–41; and John R. Silber, "Kant's Conception of the Highest Good as Immanent and Transcendent," *Philosophical Review* 68.5:480, 490 (October 1959).

10. A. R. C. Duncan, *Practical Reason and Morality: A Study of Immanuel Kant's Foundations for a Metaphysics of Morals* (London, 1957), pp. 102, 104, 134, 136–138, 141–142.

11. Immanuel Kant, *Foundations of the Metaphysics of Morals*, tr. Lewis White Beck (Indianapolis, 1959), p. 18; A. R. C. Duncan, p. 67. Duncan (p. 121) notes further:

> The conception of moral law also involves the imposition of restrictions on the agent's freedom of action. We have already pointed out that when we speak of any situation in which we are called upon to act as a moral situation, we mean that that situation makes certain demands upon us which are independent of what we may happen to want to do in that situation. The moral demands of a situation may coincide with what we should like to do, but frequently they do not. Our personal inclinations are part of the total situation and may have to be taken into account in determining what the moral demands of the situation are. Once we know what the situation demands of us morally, however, we cannot alter the demands of the situation by urging that we would rather do something else. It is because a moral situation makes demands upon us in this way that the conception of a moral law has grown up alongside the primary concept of legal rules which gives the word 'law' its basic meaning.

See also Herman-J. de Vleeschauwer, *The Development of Kantian Thought: The History of a Doctrine*, tr. A. R. C. Duncan (Toronto, 1962), pp. 118–119, 124.

12. Ernst Cassirer, *Kant's Life and Thought*, tr. James Haden (New Haven, 1981), p. 245; and bracketed examples suggested by A. R. C. Duncan, pp. 106–110.

13. Kant, *Foundations of the Metaphysics of Morals*, p. 38.

14. Cassirer, p. 254.

15. Lucien Goldman, *Immanuel Kant,* tr. Robert Black (London, 1971), p. 223.

16. As cited in Lewis White Beck, "Introduction," p. 7. Cassirer (p. 414) gets a little carried away in this regard:

> Kant's attitude toward mankind was defined by the pure and abstract medium of the moral law; but even in this law itself he recognized and at the same time honored the highest force of human personality. Therefore the idea of humanity and of freedom was not for him a politico-social ideal, but it became the lever by which he displaced the entire intellectual and spiritual world, and lifted it from its hinges. The idea of the 'primacy of practical reason' implied a transformation of the basic conception of theoretical reason itself: the new feeling and the new consciousness of humanity led to a universal 'intellectual revolution,' only in which did it find its final and decisive footing.

17. H. S. Riess, "Kant and the Right of Rebellion," *Journal of the History of Ideas* 17.2:187 (1956). See also Lewis White Beck, "Kant and the Right of Revolution," *Journal of the History of Ideas* 32:411–422 (1971).

18. Kant, *Foundations of a Metaphysics of Morals,* p. 47.

19. Smith, *A Commentary to Kant's 'Critique of Pure Reason',* pp. lvii–lix.

20. Letter to Sakatani Yoshinao, dated 11 April 1941, in *NUS,* pp. 370–371, quotation on p. 370; and Sakatani Yoshinao, "Hachigatsu jūgonichi to Nakae san no omoide," *Hana no wa* (September 1950), reprinted as "Sekai shi shinten no hōsoku," in *NUH,* p. 215.

21. Sakatani Yoshinao, "Ningen, kono kōki naru mono," *Seiryū* (February 1955), in *NGZ,* p. 234.

22. Herbert Marcuse, p. 97.

23. Hermann Glockner, *Hegel,* vol. 2 (1940), as cited in Walter Kaufmann, *Hegel: Reinterpretation, Texts, and Commentary* (Garden City, New York, 1965), p. 363.

24. Three letters to Niethammer, dated 8 October 1806, 13 October 1906, and 29 April 1814, as cited in Kaufmann, *Hegel: Reinterpretation, Texts, and Commentary,* pp. 315–315, 336.

25. Robert C. Solomon, *In the Spirit of Hegel: A Study of G. W. F. Hegel's Phenomenology of Spirit* (New York, 1983), pp. 29.

26. Translated in Kaufmann, *Hegel: Texts and Commentary,* p. 20. Other translations of this important portion of the text demonstrate both the possibilities and the difficulties Hegel bequeathed his translators. J. B. Baillie's translation:

> For the rest it is not difficult to see that our epoch is a birth-time, and a period of transition. The spirit of man has broken with the old order of things hitherto prevailing, and with the old ways of thinking, and is in the mind to let them all sink into the depths of the past . . . [T]he spirit of the time, growing slowly and quietly ripe for the new form it is to assume, disintegrates one fragment after another of the structure of its previous world. [*The Phenomenology of Mind,* p. 75.]

A. V. Miller's translation:

Besides, it is not difficult to see that ours is a birth-time and a period of transition to a new era. Spirit has broken with the world it has hitherto inhabited and imagined, and is of a mind to submerge it in the past ... [T]he Spirit in its formation matures slowly and quietly into its new shape, dissolving bit by bit the structure of its previous world. [*Phenomenology of Spirit*, p. 6.]

27. Solomon, p. 7.

28. Marcuse, esp. pp. 91–120; Jürgen Habermas, *Knowledge and Human Interests*, tr. Jeremy Shapiro (Boston, 1972), pp. 43–44ff; Alexandre Kojève, *Introduction to the Phenomenology of Spirit*, ed. Allan Bloom, tr. James H. Nichols, Jr. (New York, 1969); Jean Hyppolite, *Genesis and Structure of Hegel's Phenomenology of Spirit*, tr. Samuel Cherniak and John Heckman (Evanston, 1974); Shlomo Avineri, *Hegel's Theory of the Modern State*, esp. pp. 64–6; Georg Lukács, *The Young Hegel: Studies in the Relations between Dialectics and Economics*, tr. Rodney Livingstone (Cambridge, Mass., 1976), esp. pp. 442–536; J. Loewenberg, *Hegel's Phenomenology: Dialogues on the Life of the Mind* (La Salle, Ill., 1965), which speaks (p. x) of "the spirit of humanism pervading the *Phenomenology*." This is also central to Walter Kaufmann's interpretation in his *Hegel: Reinterpretation, Texts, and Commentary*.

29. For Nakae's view, see his letter to Suzue Gen'ichi, dated 14 May 1940, in *NUS*, pp. 177–178, where he speaks of the *Phenomenology* as a brilliant examination of the direction of human life.

30. Letter to Katō Koretaka, dated 1 May 1940 and 5 July 1941, in *NUS*, pp. 311, 315–316.

31. Letter to Suzue Gen'ichi, dated 17 November 1940, in *NUS*, p. 203.

32. Kaufmann, *Hegel: Texts and Commentary*, p. 149. Kaufmann continues: "To sum up: the greatness of the *Phenomenology* lies both in its conception, which is in part brilliant and fruitful, and in a lot of its detail: but some aspects of the conception are absurd, and some of the details bizarre." Judith Sklar notes: "The *Phenomenology of Spirit* as a whole is an immense funeral oration at the graveside of speculative philosophy. Inevitably the Greeks dominated Hegel's remembrances, for they had begun, set the ends and determined the form of the search for certain knowledge which had now been completed ... A new age had been born, but it was impossible to know what form it would take. Hegel was no crystal-gazer. Instead, he devoted himself to recapturing and reliving the past, to knowing what it was possible to know perfectly"; Judith Sklar, "Hegel's 'Phenomenology': An Elegy for Hellas," in *Hegel's Political Philosophy: Problems and Perspectives*, ed. Z. A. Pelczynski (Cambridge, 1971), p. 73.

33. Solomon, pp. 10, 33–35, 158–159, 196–197, quotation from p. 197, which continues: "Spirit is the consciousness that knows itself, and so every twist and turn

in the history of philosophy regarding knowledge and truth is at the same time a twist and turn in our conception of ourselves. Thus the history of philosophy is also a kind of auto-biography, a *Bildung* in which humanity as a whole comes to understand itself. The *Phenomenology* is essentially our collective memoirs, clarifying finally what we now find that we are. So viewed, the *Phenomenology* is a treatise on *self-identity*, what each of us, and all of us, ought to think of ourselves." Avineri, *Hegel's Theory of the Modern State*, pp. 64–65; Avineri (p. 65) notes that "the title *Phenomenology of Spirit*, which implies the ultimate reality, *Geist*, is manifest in its phenomenological appearances and intelligible through them." See also Kaufmann, *Hegel: Reinterpretation, Texts, and Commentary*, pp. 163–165; and Charles Taylor, *Hegel* (Cambridge, 1975), pp. 80–94, 127–139.

34. Robert Solomon, pp. 181–182; Sklar, "Hegel's 'Phenomenology,'" p. 74. Sklar notes (p. 85) Hegel's long and profound admiration for the character of Antigone: "It was Antigone's great merit that although she did not understand the origins of the law which she so heroically defended, she never thought of herself as an individual expressing a personal morality." See also Kaufmann, *Hegel: Reinterpretation, Texts, and Commentary*, pp. 69, 273.

35. Letter to Imada Shintarō, dated 3 March 1941, in *NUS*, p. 352.

36. Baillie translation, pp. 375, 378, quotation on p. 378; Miller translation, pp. 212, 214, quotation on p. 214. Translations identical, save Miller's capitalizing of "Reason." Judith Sklar, *Freedom and Independence: A Study of the Political Ideas of Hegel's Phenomenology of Mind* (Cambridge, 1976), pp. 13, 74.

37. Solomon, pp. 152–153; and Avineri, *Hegel's Theory of the Modern State*, pp. 137–138. At one point in the *Phenomenology* (p. 214 in the Miller translation) Hegel defines *Sittlichkeit* as follows: "the customs and laws in their entirety are a *specific* ethical substance . . . Further, therefore, the single individual consciousness as its exists in the real ethical order, or in the nation, is a solid unshaken trust in which Spirit has not, for the individual, resolved itself into its *abstract* moments, and therefore he is not aware of himself as being a pure individuality on his own account." The Baillie translation (pp. 378–379) is similar.

38. Richard Norman, *Hegel's Phenomenology: A Philosophical Introduction* (New York, 1976), pp. 72–77; Solomon, p. 153; Taylor, p. 378. Taylor (pp. 385, 388) continues: "[I]n the Greek polis, men identified themselves with its public life; its common experiences were for them the paradigm ones. Their most basic, unchallengeable values were those embodied in this public life, and hence their major duty and virtue was to continue and sustain this life. In other words, they lived fully by their *Sittlichkeit*. But the public life of each of these poleis was narrow and parochial," as the case of Socrates proved, when individual morality transcended this *Sittlichkeit*. Only "the rational state will restore *Sittlichkeit*, the embodiment of the norms in an ongoing public life . . . This integration of individuality and *Sittlichkeit* is a requirement we can deduce from the Idea. But this

is also Hegel's way of formulating and answering the yearning of his age to unite somehow the radical moral autonomy of Kant and the expressive unity of the Greek polis."

39. Sklar, *Freedom and Independence,* pp. xiv, 74, quotation on p. 74; and Norman, *Hegel's Phenomenology,* p. 54.

40. Baillie translation, pp. 599–610; Miller translation, pp. 355–363. As Charles Taylor suggests, the Cultural Revolution under Mao Tse-tung's guidance provides a latter-day example, as in the Terror following 1789, of this "absolute freedom." See Taylor, pp. 416–418.

41. Nakae Ushikichi, *CKSS,* pp. 42–43, 104, 333, 356, 360–361, quotations from pp. 42–43, 361. Nakae's copy of this Hegel text is now lost: *Nakae bunko mokuroku,* p. 20.

42. Letter to Katō Koretaka, dated 1 May 1940, in *NUS,* p. 312. This sentence is an excellent example of the mixture of languages Nakae often used in his letters to close friends. It reads: "Heigeru iwaku reine Negativität wa Selbstbewusstein no Bewegung nari to, mattaku dōkan mōshisōrō."

43. Baillie translation, p. 80; Kaufmann translation in *Hegel: Texts and Commentary,* p. 28; and Miller translation, p. 10. See Marcuse, pp. 110–115; Taylor, pp. 110–11; and Solomon, pp. 256–247, 282. In his essay on the *Kung-yang Commentary* (*CKSS,* pp. 437–438), Nakae noted that the conception of change and movement in the *Spring and Autumn Annals* was not of a "self-negating" or dialectical sort. Hence, Hegel's "absolüte Negativität" did not apply here.

44. Baillie translation, p. 219; Miller translation, pp. 104–105.

45. Nakae Ushikichi, *CKSS,* p. 237.

46. Reference to *in maru* in letter to Suzue Gen'ichi, dated 11 October 1935, in *NUS,* p. 27. Etō Shinkichi, "*Nakae Ushikichi shokanshū,* shinri e no shinkō kokuhaku," *Ajia kenkyū* 12.1 (April 1965), in *NGZ,* pp. 336, 338; Kaji Ryūichi, "Sūkiden, Nakae Ushikichi kun," in *CTM,* p. 59; and Sakatani Yoshinao, "Ningen, kono kōki naru mono," p. 233.

47. Letter of Katō Koretaka to Suzuki Tadashi, dated 15 December 1969, in Sakatani Yoshinao, "Nakae Ushikich zō no saigen no tame ni" (August 1978), in *NUH,* p. 151.

48. Ōta Ryōichirō, p. 31.

49. These volumes, all in German of course and replete with Nakae's marginalia, can now be found in NB.

50. "Nakae Ushikichi nenpu," pp. 302, 303, 310–312. In the NB, see, for example: Karl Marx, *Das Kapital: Kritik der politischen Oekonomie,* ed. Friedrich Engels, packed with notes; Karl Marx, *Zur Kritik der poliltischen Oekonomie,* ed. Karl Kautsky (Berlin, 1924), dated by Nakae 15 July 1928; Rosa Luxemburg, *Einführing in die Nationalökonomie,* dated 5 January 1927 on p. v, and 15 February 1927 on final p. 293; Friedrich Engels, *Der Ursprung der Familie, des Privateigentums und des Staats* (Stuttgart, 1921), dated 1 August 1926 on final p. 188; Lenin,

Imperialism: The Last Stage of Capitalism, dated 13 January 1927 on p. 7, and 16 January 1927 on final p. 152; N. Bucharin, *Theorie des historischen Materialismus*, dated 9 May 1926 on p. 1, and both 16 October 1926 and 19 November 1926 on final p. 366; and Heinrich Cunow, *Die Marxsche Geschichts-, Gesellschafts- und Staatstheorie: Grundzüge der Marxschen Soziologie* (Berlin, 1923), dated 8 April 1927 on p. 17. Aikō Katsuya claims that in his sole meeting with Nakae in Peking (in February 1939) Nakae told him not to read translations of Marx: "Get as close to Marx himself as possible. Do as I'm doing. Right now I'm in my tenth reading of volume one" of *Capital;* Aikō Katsuya, "Pekin to Tōkyō o musubu su-jiito," in *NUH,* p. 209. There is no evidence to support Nakae's having read *Capital* ten times, and there is no corroborative evidence for this conversation.

51. See, for example, Nakae Ushikichi, *CKSS*, pp. 281–281, 314, 331, 412.

52. Avineri, *The Social and Political Thought of Karl Marx*, p. 96, referring to the essays by Georg Lukács collected in his *History and Class Consciousness: Studies in Marxist Dialectics*, tr. Rodney Livingstone (London, 1971). For the caricatured view of Hegelian and German idealist thought among the books that Nakae had read, see, for instance, Franz Mehring, *Karl Marx: The Story of His Life*, tr. Edward Fitzgerald (Ann Arbor, 1969), e.g., pp. 127–128 (where Hegel is referred to as "amongst the best brains of all time"); and Nikolai Bukharin, *Historical Materialism: A System of Sociology* (New York, 1934), e.g., pp. 62, 65, 74–75 (where Hegel's dialectic is described as the famous triad "thesis-antithesis-synthesis"). On the total absence of this triad from Hegel's writings, see Kaufmann, *Hegel: Reinterpretation, Texts, and Commentary*, p. 168.

53. Sakatani Yoshinao, "Ningen, kono kōki naru mono," p. 233; Karl Marx, "Critique of the Hegelian Dialectic and Philosophy as a Whole," in *The Economic and Philosophic Manuscripts of 1844*, tr. Martin Milligan (New York, 1971), pp. 170–193, esp. pp. 173–180, 184; C. Boey, *L'Aliénation dans "La Phénoménologie de l'Esprit" de G. W. G. Hegel* (Paris, 1970); Louis Dupré, "Hegel's Concept of Alienation and Marx's Reinterpretation of It," *Hegel-Studien* 7:217–236 (1972), esp. pp. 217, 222–233; and Katō Koretaka, "Chishiki to seikatsu," p. 100.

54. Derek Sayer, *Marx's Method: Ideology, Science and Critique in Capital* (Atlantic Highlands, 1979), p. 105; and Kant, *Critique of Pure Reason*, p. 3.

55. See, for example, István Mészáros, *Marx's Theory of Alienation* (London, 1970); and Bertell Ollman, *Alienation: Marx's Conception of Man in Capitalist Society* (Cambridge, 1980), esp. pp. 73–127 on "Marx's Conception of Human Nature."

56. Louis Dupré, *Marx's Social Critique of Culture* (New Haven, 1983), p. 5, also p. 18; and Alan Swingewood, *Marx and Modern Social Theory* (New York, 1975), pp. 89, 91.

57. Roman Rosdolsky, *The Making of Marx's 'Capital,'* tr. Pete Burgess (London, 1977), pp. 414–415.

58. Louis Dupré, *Marx's Social Critique of Culture*, p. 43.

59. Karl Marx, *Grundrisse*, pp. 225–226.

60. Georg Lukács, "Reification and the Consciousness of the Proletariat," in *History and Class Consciousness,* pp. 84–87. See also Louis Dupré, *Marx's Social Critique of Culture,* pp. 37–38, 44, 46, 48, 49.
61. Karl Marx, *Capital: A Critical Analysis of Capitalist Production,* tr. Samuel Moore and Edward Aveling, ed. Frederick Engels (New York, 1947), p. xx; and Appendix, no. 53.
62. Letter to Suzue Gen'ichi, dated 23 March 1939, in *NUS,* p. 115.
63. Letter to Suzue Gen'ichi, dated 31 October 1938, in *NUS,* pp. 94–95.
64. Letter to Suzue Gen'ichi, dated 19 April 1941, in *NUS,* p. 219.
65. See, for example, Matsukata Saburō, p. 75; and letter to Sakatani Yoshinao, dated 31 May 1941, in *NUS,* p. 375.
66. Letter of Katō Koretaka to Sakatani Yoshinao, dated 6 December 1969, in Sakatani, "Nakae Ushikichi zō no saigen no tame ni," in *NUH,* pp. 149–150; and Sakatani Yoshinao, "Ningen, kono kōki naru mono," p. 232.
67. Sakatani Yoshinao, "Sekai shi shinten no hōsoku," in *NUH,* p. 219.
68. Letters to Suzue Gen'ichi, dated 14 May 1940 and 18 March 1941, in *NUS,* pp. 177–178, 217.
69. Letter to Suzue Gen'ichi, dated 22 May 1941, in *NUS,* p. 223. Similarly, in a letter to Ogura Sōichi, dated 17 February 1941 (in *NUS,* p. 361): "I firmly believe and am secure in the fact that the course which human history has hitherto traversed will not be for it to retrogress; and I believe that the course of the world (*Weltlauf*) learned herein will provide us with the best gauge" for the future.
70. This is another example of Nakae's multilingual sentences: "*Nonsensu*" *no naka kara umarete kuru mono wa yahari issō ni nonsensu no nanimono igai ni meiyō nari.* Letter to Sakatani Yoshinao, dated 30 April 1940, in *NUS,* p. 373.
71. Letter to Sakatani Yoshinao, dated 31 May 1941, in *NUS,* pp. 378, 379.
72. Sakatani Yoshinao, "Sekai shi shinten no hōsoku," pp. 215–216.
73. Sakatani Yoshinao, "Sekai shi shinten no hōsoku," p. 216.
74. Sakatani Yoshinao, "Sekai shi shinten no hōsoku," p. 219.
75. Katō Koretaka, "Kakuretaru minshushugisha," p. 87; Katō Koretaka, "Chishiki to seikatsu," pp. 95–96; and Hanzawa Hiroshi, p. 91.
76. Appendix, no. 30.
77. For Nakae's view of Konoe, see Appendix, no. 33; and Ogura Sōichi, "Nakae Ushikichi no hito to shisō," *Saiken* (April 1964), reprinted as "Aru tetsujin no omoide: Nakae Ushikichi no hito to shisō," in *NGZ,* p. 297. On Matsuoka, see Appendix, no. 57; and Sakatani Yoshinao, "Tsuioku henpen: Nakae Ushikichi no taiwa kara," *Misuzu* 82–83 (March–April 1966), in *NGZ,* p. 258. On Nakae's view of Tōjō as Japan's nearest thing to Stalin, see Sakatani Yoshinao, "Tsuioku henpen," p. 256. On all three Japanese leaders, see Suzuki Tadashi, "Ikyō no koten teki yuibutsuronsha: Nakae Ushikichi ron," p. 150.
78. Ogura Sōichi, "Minshushugi no tetsujin Nakae Ushikichi no shōgai," *Nōrin shunjū* (March 1953), reprinted as "Wasureenu hito no shōgai," in *NGZ,* p. 313.

79. Appendix, no. 92.
80. Letter to Sakatani Yoshinao, dated 15 January 1942, in *NUS*, pp. 383–384.

9. *THE MANY FACES OF NAKAE USHIKICHI*

1. Nakae Ushikichi, *"Byōchū nikki* shō, shi no toko no kiroku," notes dated 30 June 1942 and 28 July 1942, pp. 428, 432.
2. Uchida Tomoo, "'Nakae bunko' hannyū no kotodomo," *Dōshisha hōgaku* 91 (March 1965), in *NUH*, pp. 265–266, 268–269, 271–273, 277, 279, 284–286.
3. Uchida Tomoo, in *NUH*, p. 274.
4. Nakae Ushikichi, "Chūgoku kodai seiji shisō shi," in *CKSS*, p. 123.
5. H. J. Paton, "Kant on Friendship," *Proceedings of the British Academy* (1956), pp. 48, 65–65.
6. Nakae Ushikichi, *"Byōchū nikki* shō," note dated 8 June 1942, p. 425.
7. Nakae shi ikō shuppan iinkai, "Batsu," in *CKSS*, pp. 663–672.
8. Takeuchi Yoshimi, p. 317; Kainō Michitaka, *"Chūgoku kodai seiji shisō*, kōki ni michita sho," *Yomiuri shinbun*, 21 June 1950, in *NUH*, p. 223; and Hashikawa Bunsō, "Antiwar Values," p. 91.
9. Nakae Ushikichi, "Shōsho Hankō hen ni tsuite," in *CKSS*, p. 284.
10. Niida Noboru, p. 180.

APPENDIX

1. This translation of Nakae's diary is made from "Senji no danshō," in *NGZ*, pp. 377–396. In addition Nakae left scattered notes of a similar type in the margins of several of his other books, now in NB. These include the following:

   a. Really hot, four days before leaving for Dairen. 11 July 1934.

   b. Aug. 6, 1934, third day since returning from Dairen. [In Immanuel Kant, *Kritik der praktischen Vernunft*.]

   c. The sparrows fell with the grasshoppers. They died. Three sparrows lay fallen before me under the persimmon tree. (5 March 1937, there's a fair amount of snow on the ground this morning.)
   The snow is all gone.

   d. 26 March 1937. Today I bathed my entire body in the sun. It's 11:20 A.M. The blue sky, the sounds of the flutes in the pigeons [see note 2, below], and the snow falling off the roof. All is in harmony and leisure as the snow melts. [In Arthur Schopenauer, *Die Welt als Wille und Vorstellung*.]

   e. I wrote another letter today. 13 August 1934, 1:30 P.M. [In Karl Marx, *Das Kapital*, 1933 edition, note in introduction by Lenin to this edition.]

   f. I did a major cleaning today. 9 July 1935, 9:30 A.M. [In Wilhelm Wundt, *Völkerpsychologie*, vol. 4.]

g. Planned [to read this far] by 10 April 1938. (Reached only p. 413 by that date). Finished on 4 May. (The day that [Suzue] Gen'ichi left for Shanghai).

Gorgeous weather, the endless sound of airplanes. [In Wundt, vol. 5.]

Nakae also left four marginal notes beside his reading notes to Hegel's *Phenomenology*. They cover a short period of time and all deal with the same topic.

a. Huang [see note 3, below] is dying. It's a day of great melancholy. 2:30 P.M., 23 May 1940.

b. Afternoon of the day Huang died. 1:30 P.M., 24 May 1940, early summer day. I feel very lonely.

c. Morning of the day after Huang's death. Morning's light shines as usual. 8:30 A.M., Saturday, 25 May [1940].

d. At 11:00 today a telegram arrived from [Tsujino] Toshio. Sunday morning, two days after Huang's death. Last night got a return letter from Suzue Gen'ichi. There has been no decline at all in my sorrow. I see two footprints on the ground in the garden, and my feelings are much the same as they were on the day of Huang's death.

2. Some well-to-do families in Peking used to sew tiny flutes into the wings of pigeons, which would cause a whistling sound over the city when they flew by.

3. *Huang* literally means "yellow"; but Huang is also a common Chinese surname, which gave the dog a certain integrity.

4. *Sophora japonica*, a tree which grows in North China; its flowers are used for a yellow dye.

5. Original in Chinese and English as "New Order in East Asia."

6. Reference to the date of *Capital*'s preface (1867), seventy-four years prior to this entry. The "iron words" refer to Marx's quotation from Dante at the end of the preface: "Segui il tuo corso, e lascia dir le genti" (Follow your own course, and let people talk). For a photocopy of this page, see p. 174 above.

7. Nakae's copy of the *Phenomenology* was a second-hand book in which the previous owner had made Japanese notes next to the German original from time to time.

8. Nakae puns here on the expression *dengeki sakusen* (*Blitzkrieg*) by using *heiwa* (peace) instead of *sakusen* (war).

9. The final battle in which the forces of Tokugawa Ieyasu completed their conquest of Japan in 1600.

10. Anniversary of the 1911 Chinese Revolution, celebrated every 10 October.

11. Nakae always referred to the "Pacific War" (*Taiheiyō sensō*), never the "Great East Asian War" (*dai Tō-A sensō*) as it was called in Japan.

Bibliography of Works Consulted

Aikō Katsuya 愛甲勝矢 . "Pekin to Tōkyō o musubu sujiito" 北京と 東京を結ぶすじ糸 (The thread linking Peking and Tokyo), in *NUH*.

Akashi, Yoji. "A Botched Peace Effort: The Miao Pin *Kōsaku*, 1944–1945," in Alvin D. Coox and Hilary Conroy, eds., *China and Japan: A Search for Balance Since World War II.* Santa Barbara, ABC-Clio, 1978.

Akisawa Shūji 秋澤修二 . *Shina shakai kōsei* 支那社會構成 (The structure of Chinese society). Tokyo, Hakubaisha, 1939.

Anchor, Robert. "Heinrich Rickert," in *The Encyclopedia of Philosophy*, Vol. 7. New York, The Macmillan Company & The Free Press, 1967.

Avineri, Shlomo. *Hegel's Theory of the Modern State.* Cambridge, Cambridge University Press, 1972.

——— . *The Social and Political Thought of Karl Marx.* Cambridge, Cambridge University Press, 1968.

Bailey, Anne M. and Josep R. Llobera, eds. *The Asiatic Mode of Production: Science and Politics.* London, Routledge & Kegan Paul, 1981.

Barnes, Harry Elmer. "Ludwig Gumplowicz," in *International Encyclopedia of the Social Sciences,* Vol. 6. New York, The Macmillan Company, 1968.

Beasley, W. G., and Carmen Blacker. "Japanese Historical Writing in the Tokugawa Period (1603–1868)," in W. G. Beasley and E. G. Pulleyblank, eds., *Historians of China and Japan.* London, Oxford Univesity Press, 1961.

Beck, Lewis White. "Kant and the Right of Revolution," *Journal of the History of Ideas* 32:411–422 (1971).

Beloch, Karl Julius. *Griechische Geschichte,* Vol. 1. Strassburg and Berlin, K. J. Trübner, Walter de Gruyter, u. Vereinigung Wissenschaftlicher Verleger, 1913. [NB]

Bernheim, Ernst. *Lehrbuch der historischen Methode.* Leipzig, Verlag von Duncker & Humblot, 1894. [NB]

Biographical Dictionary of Republican China. Ed. Howard L. Boorman and Richard C. Howard. 4 vols. New York, Columbia University Press, 1968.

Boey, C. *L'Aliénation dans "La Phénomenologie de l'Esprit" de G. W. F. Hegel.* Paris, Desclée de Brouwer, 1970.

Bollnow, Otto Friedrich. *Dirutai sono tetsugaku e no annai* ディルタイその哲学への案内 (Dilthey, guide to his philosophy), tr. Asō Ken 麻生建. Tokyo, Miraisha, 1977.

Bonner, Joey, *Wang Kuo-wei: An Intellectual Biography.* Cambridge, Harvard University Press, 1986.

Boring, Edwin G. *A History of Experimental Psychology.* New York, Appleton, 1929.

———. "Wilhelm Wundt," in *International Encyclopedia of the Social Sciences,* Vol. 16. New York, The Macmillan Company, 1968.

Brecht, Arnold. *Political Theory: The Foundations of Twentieth-Century Thought.* Princeton, Princeton University Press, 1967.

Bucharin, N. *Theorie des historischen Materialismus: Gemeinverständliches Lehrbuch der Marxistischen Soziologie,* tr. Frida Rubiner. Berlin, Verlag der Kommunistischen Internationale, 1922. [NB]

Bücher, Karl. *Die Entstehung der Volkswirtschaft,* Vol. 1. Tübingen, Verlag der H. Lauppschen Buchhandlung, 1920. [NB]

Bukharin, Nikolai. *Historical Materialism: A System of Sociology.* New York, International Publishers, 1934.

Cassirer, Ernst. *Kant's Life and Thought,* tr. James Haden. New Haven, Yale University Press, 1981.

Chang Hsi-t'ang 張西堂. *Shang-shu yin-lun* 尚書引論 (Guide to the *Book of History*). Sian, Shan-hsi jen-min ch'u-pan-she, 1958.

Chang, K. C. *Early Chinese Civilization: Anthropological Perspectives.* Cambridge, Harvard University Press, 1976.

———. *Shang Civilization.* New Haven, Yale University Press, 1980.

Ch'en Chu 陳柱. *Kung-yang-chia che-hsueh* 公羊家哲學 (The philosophy of Kung-yang scholars). Shanghai, Chung-hua shu-chü, 1929.

Ch'en Meng-chia 陳夢家. *Yin-hsü pu-tz'u tsung-shu* 殷虛卜辭綜述 (Compendium of the divinational writings from Yin remains). Peking, K'o-hsueh ch'u-pan-she, 1956.

Ch'en Tuan-chih 陳端志. *Wu-ssu yun-tung chih shih te p'ing-chia* 五四運動之史的評價 (A historical assessment of the May Fourth Movement). Shanghai, Sheng-huo shu-tien, 1935.

Chesneaux, Jean. *The Chinese Labor Movement: 1919–1927,* tr. H. M. Wright. Stanford, Stanford University Press, 1968.

———. "Le mode de production asiatique: quelques perspectives de recherche," *La Pensée* 114:33–55 (January-February 1964).

———. "Où en est la discussion sur 'le mode de production asiatique'?" *La Pensée* 122: 40–59 (July-August 1965); 129:33–46 (September-October 1966); 138:47–55 (March-April 1968).

Chi, Madeleine. "Bureaucratic Capital in Operation: Ts'ao Ju-lin and His New Communications Clique, 1916–1919," *Journal of Asian Studies* 34.2:675–688 (May 1975).

———. "Ts'ao Ju-lin (1876–1966): His Japanese Connections," in Akira Iriye, ed., *The Chinese and the Japanese: Essays in Political and Cultural Interactions.* Princeton, Princeton University Press, 1980.

Chia I-chün 賈逸君 . *Wu-ssu yun-tung chien-shih* 五四運動簡史 (A short history of the May Fourth Movement). Peking, Hsin-ch'ao shu-tien, 1951.

Chow Tse-tsung. *The May Fourth Movement: Intellectual Revolution in Modern China.* Cambridge, Harvard University Press, 1960.

Chu Hsi 朱熹 . *Chu-tzu yü-lei* 朱子語類 (Recorded sayings of Master Chu). Vol. 5. Ed. Li Ching-te 黎靖德 . Taipei reprint, Cheng-chung shu-chü, 1970, *chüan* 78.

Collingwood, R. G. *The Idea of History.* New York, Oxford University Press, 1956.

———, A. E. Taylor, and F. C. S. Schiller. "Are History and Science Different Kinds of Knowledge?" *Mind* 31:426–466 (1922).

Coox, Alvin D. *Nomonhan: Japan Against Russia, 1939.* Stanford, Stanford University Press, 1985.

——— and Hilary Conroy, eds. *China and Japan: A Search for Balance Since World War II.* Santa Barbara, ABC-Clio, 1978.

Creel, Herrlee Glessner. *Studies in Early Chinese Culture: First Series.* Baltimore, Waverly Press, 1937.

Cunow, Heinrich. *Die Marxsche Geschichts-, Gesellschafts- und Staatstheorie: Grundzüge der Marxschen Soziologie.* Berlin, J. H. W. Dietz Nachf., 1923. [NB]

Dardess, Margaret B. *A Discourse on Government: Nakae Chōmin and his Sansuijin keirin mondō.* Occasional Papers No. 10, Western Washington State College. Bellington, Washington, 1977.

Dilthey, Wilhelm. *Einleitung in die Geisteswissenschaften: Versuch einer Grundlegung für das Studium der Gesellschaft und der Geschichte.* Leipzig, B. G. Teubner, 1923. [NB]

Dirlik Arif. *Revolution and History: The Origins of Marxist Historiography in China, 1919–1937.* Berkeley, University of California Press, 1978.

Diskussia ob aziatskom sposobe proizvodstva (Discussion on the Asiatic mode of production). Moscow and Leningrad, Gosudarstvennoie sotsial'no-ekonomicheskoie izdatel'stvo, 1931.

Döring, Woldemer Oskar. *Das Lebenswerk Immanuel Kants.* Lübeck, Verlag von Charles Coleman, 1916. [NB]

Dower, J. H. *Empire and Aftermath: Yoshida Shigeru and the Japanese Experience,*

1878–1954. Cambridge, Council on East Asian Studies, Harvard University, 1979.

Duncan, A. R. C. *Practical Reason and Morality: A Study of Immanuel Kant's Foundations for a Metaphysics of Morals.* London, Thomas Nelson and Sons, 1957.

Dupré, Louis, "Hegel's Concept of Alienation and Marx's Reinterpretation of It," *Hegel-Studien* 7:217–236 (1972).

——. *Marx's Social Critique of Culture.* New Haven, Yale University Press, 1983.

Durkheim, Émile. *The Elementary Forms of Religious Life: A Study in Religious Sociology,* tr. Joseph Ward Swain. London, George Allen & Unwin, 1926. [NB]

Eastman, Lloyd. "Facets of an Ambivalent Relationship: Smuggling, Puppets, and Atrocities during the War, 1937–1945," in Akira Iriye, ed., *The Chinese and the Japanese: Essays in Political and Cultural Interactions.* Princeton, Princeton University Press, 1980.

Emerson, Rupert. *State and Sovereignty in Modern Germany.* New Haven, Yale University Press, 1928.

Encyclopaedia Judaica: Das Judentum in Geschichte und Gegenwart, Vol. 8. Berlin, Verlag Eschkol A. G., 1931.

Encyclopedia Judaica. Jerusalem, Ktav, 1971.

Engels, Frederick [Friedrich]. *Anti-Dühring.* Moscow, Foreign Languages Publishing House, 1959.

Engels, Friedrich. *Herrn Eugen Dühring's Umwälzung der Wissenschaft.* Stuttgart, J. H. W. Dietz, 1921. [NB]

——. *Der Ursprung der Familie, des Privateigentums und des Staats.* Stuttgart, J. H. W. Dietz Nachf., 1921. [NB]

Etō Shinkichi 衛藤瀋吉 . "*Nakae Ushikichi shokanshū, shinri e no shinkō kokuhaku*" 中江丑吉書簡集真理への信仰告白   (The Letters of Nakae Ushikichi, a profession of faith in truth), *Ajia kenkyū* 12.1 (April 1965), as reprinted in *NGZ.*

——. "*Nihonjin no Chūgoku kan: Suzue Gen'ichi o megutte*" 日本人の中国観：鈴江言一をめぐって   (A Japanese view of China: On Suzue Gen'ichi), *Shisō* 445:1–15 (July 1961).

——. *Nihon no shinro* 日本の進路   (Japan's road forward). Tokyo, Tokyo University Press, 1969.

——. "*Suzue Gen'ichi, aru megumarezaru seishun*" 鈴江言一ある惠まれざる青春   (Suzue Gen'ichi, an unfortunate youth), *Sekai* 216:192–203 (December 1963).

——. "*Zoku Suzue Gen'ichi, gekijō to ōkai*" 続・鈴江言一，激情と韜晦 (More on Suzue Gen'ichi, passion and self-concealment), *Sekai* 225:160–168 (September 1964).

—— and Hsü Shu-chen 許淑真 . *Suzue Gen'ichi den* 鈴江言一伝 (A biography of Suzue Gen'ichi). Tokyo, Tokyo University Press, 1984.

Ferguson, William Scott. "Karl Julius Beloch," in *Encyclopedia of the Social Sciences*, Vol. 2. New York, The Macmillan Company, 1948.

Fogel, Joshua A. "The Debates Over the Asiatic Mode of Production in Soviet Russia, China, and Japan," *American Historical Review* 93.1:56–79 (February 1988).

——. *Politics and Sinology: The Case of Naitō Konan (1866–1934)*. Cambridge, Council on East Asian Studies, Harvard University, 1984.

Fowler, William Warde. "Theodor Mommsen: His Life and Work," in *Roman Essays and Interpretatic* Oxford, The Clarendon Press, 1920.

Fujiwara Kamae 藤原鎌兄. *Pekin nijūnen: Chūgoku no taidō to Nihon no jogen* 北京二十年：中国の胎動と日本の助言 (Twenty years in Peking, China stirring and Japanese advice). Tokyo, Heibonsha, 1959.

Fukutomi Masami 福富正美. *Kyōdōtai to shoyū no genri: Shihonron taikei to kōgi no keizaigaku no hōhō* 共同体と所有の原理：資本論体系と広義の経済学の方法 ("Community" and the basic principles of ownership, the organization of *Capital* and the methods of economics in the broader sense). Tokyo, Miraisha, 1970.

Fustel de Coulanges, Numa Denis. *The Ancient City: A study of the religion, laws, and institutions of Greece and Rome*, tr. Willard Small. Boston, Lothrop, Lee & Shepard Co., 1901. [NB]

Garushiants, Iuri M. "Ob aziatskom sposobe proizvodstva" (On the Asiatic mode of production), *Voprosy istorii* 2:83–100 (1966).

Godes, M. "Itogi diskussiia ob aziatskom sposobe proizvodstva" (Conclusions of the discussion on the Asiatic mode of production), in *Diskussiia ob aziatskom sposobe proizvodstva po dokladu M. Godesa* (Discussion on the Asiatic mode of production from the report of M. Godes). Moscow and Leningrad, Gosudarstvennoie sotsial'no-ekonomischeskoie izdatel'stvo, 1931.

Goldman, Emma. *Living My Life,* ed. Richard and Anna Maria Drinnon. New York, The New American Library, 1977.

Goldmann, Lucian. *Immanuel Kant,* tr. Robert Black. London, Humanities Press, 1971.

Gumplowicz, Ludwig. *Allgemeines Staatsrecht*. Innsbruck, Verlag der Wagner'schen Universitäts Buchhandlung, 1907. [NB]

Guy, Basil. *The French Image of China Before and After Voltaire*. Vol. 21 of *Studies on Voltaire and the Eighteenth Century*. Geneva, Institut et Musée Voltaire, 1963.

Habermas, Jürgen. *Knowledge and Human Interests*, tr. Jeremy Shapiro. Boston, Beacon Press, 1972.

Hanzawa Hiroshi 判沢弘. "Nakae Ushikichi to Tachibana Shiraki" 中江丑吉と橘樸 (Nakae Ushikichi and Tachibana Shiraki), in Takeuchi Yoshimi and Hashikawa Bunzō, eds., *Kindai Nihon to Chūgoku* 近代日本と中国 (Modern Japan and China), Vol. 2. Tokyo, Asahi shinbunsha, 1974.

Harvard-Yenching Institute Sinological Index Series. Supplment No. 11: Combined Concordances to Ch'un-ch'iu, Kung-yang, Ku-liang and Tso-chuan, Vol. 1. Taipei, Ch'eng-wen Publishing Company, 1965.

Hasegawa Nyozekan 長谷川如是閑 . "Tsuiokudan" 追憶談 (Remembrances), in *Nakae Ushikichi go kaiki kinenkai, kiroku* 中江丑吉五回忌記念会，記録 (Transcript of the commemorative meeting for the fifth anniversary of the death of Nakae Ushikichi), as reprinted in *NUH*.

Hashikawa Bunsō [Bunzō] 橋川文三 . "Anti-war Values—the Resistance in Japan," tr. Robert Vargo. *Japan Interpreter* 9.1:86–97 (Spring 1974).

——. "Japanese Perspectives on Asia: From Dissociation to Coprosperity," in Akira Iriye, ed., *The Chinese and the Japanese: Essays in Political and Cultural Interactions.* Princeton, Princeton University Press, 1980.

——. "Wakai hitobito e" 若い人びとへ (To young people), in *NUH*.

Hata Ikuhiko 秦郁彦 . *Gun fashizumu undō shi* 軍ファシズム運動史 (A history of the fascist movement in the military). Tokyo, Kawade shobō, 1972.

Hatada Takashi 旗田巍 . "Chūgoku ni okeru senseishugi to 'sonraku kyōdōtai' riron" 中国における専制主義と「村落共同体」理論 (Despotism in China and the theory of the "village community"), *Chūgoku kenkyū* 13 (October 1950), as reprinted in *Chūgoku sonraku to kyōdōtai riron* 中国村落と共同体理論 (Chinese villages and the theory of *kyōdōtai*). Tokyo, Iwanami shoten, 1973.

Hayashi Taisuke 林泰輔 . *Shina jōdai no kenkyū* 支那上代の研究 (Studies of Chinese antiquity). Okazaki, Shinkōsha, 1944.

Hegel, Georg Wilhelm Friedrich. *The Phenomenology of Mind,* tr. J. B. Baillie. New York, Harper Torchbooks, 1967.

——. *Phenomenology of Spirit,* tr. A. V. Miller, Oxford, The Clarendon Press, 1977.

——. *The Philosophy of History,* tr. Carl J. Friedrich and Paul W. Friedrich, in Carl J. Friedrich, ed., *The Philosophy of Hegel.* New York, Random House, 1965.

Heller, Herman. "George Jellinek," in *Encyclopaedia of the Social Sciences,* Vol. 8. New York, The Macmillan Company, 1932.

Hihara Toshikuni 日原利國 . *Shunjū Kuyōden no kenkyū* 春秋公羊伝の研究 (Studies of the *Spring and Autumn Annals* and the *Kung-yang Commentary*). Tokyo, Sōbunsha, 1976.

Hirata Shōroku 平田小六 . "Peking no Nakae Ushikichi" 北京の中江丑吉 (Nakae Ushikichi of Peking), *Tōkyō shinbun,* 28 April 1950, as reprinted in *NGZ*.

Hirota Hiroo 広田弘雄 . "Tsuiokudan" 追憶談 (Remembrances), in *Nakae Ushikichi go kaiki kinenkai, kiroku* 中江丑吉五回忌記念会，記録 (Transcript of the commemorative meeting for the fifth anniversary of the death of Nakae Ushikichi), as reprinted in *NUH*.

Ho Ping-ti. *The Cradle of the East: An Inquiry into the Indigenous Origins of Techniques and Ideas of Neolithic and Early Historic China, 5000–1000 B.C.* Hong Kong, The Chinese University of Hong Kong and The University of Chicago Press, 1975.

Hollerbach, Alexander. "Georg Jellinek," in *International Encyclopedia of the Social Sciences*, Vol. 8. New York, The Macmillan Company, 1968.

Holubek, Reinhard. *Allgemeine Staatslehre als empirische Wissenschaft: eine Untersuchung am Beispiel von Georg Jellinek.* Bonn, Bouvier u. Co. Verlag, 1961.

Honigsheim, Paul. "The Sociological Doctrines of Franz Oppenheimer: An Agrarian Philosophy of History and Social Reform," in Harry E. Barnes, ed., *An Introduction to the History of Sociology.* Chicago, University of Chicago Press, 1948.

Hosaka Masayasu 保阪正康. *Tōjō Hideki to tennō no jidai* 東條英機と天皇の時代 (The era of Tōjō Hideki and the emperor), Vol. 2. Tokyo, Gendai jānarizumu shuppankai, 1980.

Hoselitz, Bert F. "Theories of Stages of Economic Growth," in Bert F. Hoselitz et al., eds., *Theories of Economic Growth.* New York, Free Press, 1960.

Hsu Te-heng 許德珩. "Ch'u chien pu-hsi ssu, lai pa Chung-kuo chiu" 鋤奸不惜死,来把中国救 (Risk death to weed out the wicked and save China), *Hung-ch'i* 5:49–56 (1979).

Huang Fu-ch'ing. *Chinese Students in Japan in the Late Ch'ing Period,* tr. Katherine P. K. Whitaker. Tokyo, The Centre for East Asian Cultural Studies, 1982.

Hughes, H. Stuart. *Consciousness and Society: The Reorientation of European Social Thought, 1890–1930.* New York, Vintage Books, 1961.

Hyppolite, Jean. *Genesis and Structure of Hegel's Phenomenology of Spirit,* tr. Samuel Cherniak and John Heckman. Evanston, Northwestern University Press, 1974.

Ienaga Saburō 家永三郎. *Minobe Tatsukichi no shisō teki kenkyū* 美濃部達吉の思想的研究 (A study of the thought of Minobe Tatsukichi). Tokyo, Iwanami shoten, 1964.

——. *The Pacific War: World War II and the Japanese,* tr. Frank Baldwin. New York, Pantheon Books, 1978.

Ikeda Suetoshi 池田末利. "Shōsho Rakkō kai (jō)" 尚書洛誥解(上) (An explanation of the Lo-kao chapter of the *Shang-shu*, part 1), in *Uno Tetsuto sensei hakuju shukuga kinen Tōyōgaku ronsō* 宇野哲人先生白寿祝賀記念東洋学論叢 (Essays in East Asian studies presented to Dr. Uno Tetsuto in commemoration of his ninety-ninth birthday). Tokyo, Tōhō gakkai, 1974.

Ikeda Suetoshi 池田末利. "Shōsho tsūkai kō (1)" 尚書通解稿(1) (Draft annotation of the *Shang-shu*), *Hiroshima daigaku bungakubu kiyō* 30.2:1–118 (March 1971).

Imai Seiichi 今井清一. *Taiheiyō sensō shi 1: Manshū jiken* 太平洋戦争

史 1 ：満州事件 (The Pacific War 1: The Manchurian Incident). Tokyo, Aoki shoten, 1971.

Iriye, Akira. *After Imperialism: The Search for a New Order in the Far East, 1921–1931.* Cambridge, Harvard University Press, 1965.

——, ed. *The Chinese and the Japanese: Essays in Political and Cultural Interactions.* Princeton, Princeton University Press, 1980.

Ishida Takeshi 石田雄. *Kindai Nihon seiji kōzō no kenkyū* 近代日本政治構造の研究 (A study of the structure of modern Japanese politics). Tokyo, Miraisha, 1956.

Ishidō Kiyotomo 石堂清倫. "*Nakae Ushikichi shokanshū:* Nihon no kindai ga unda hirui no nai zunō" 中江丑吉書簡集：日本の近代"が"生んた比類のない頭脳 (The Letters of Nakae Ushikichi, an incomparable mind born of modern Japan), *Yomiuri shinbun,* 8 January 1965, as reprinted in *NUH.*

Itō Michiharu 伊藤道治. *Chūgoku kodai ōchō no keisei, shutsudo shiryō o chūshin to suru In-Shū shi no kenkyū* 中国古代王朝の形成出土資料を中心とする殷周史の研究 (The formation of kingship in ancient China: A study of Shang and Chou history based on archeological finds). Tokyo: Sōbunsha, 1976.

Itō Takeo 伊藤武雄 "Ajia no kenkyūsha: Suzue Gen'ichi" アジアの研究者：鈴江言一 (Scholar of Asia: Suzue Gen'ichi), *Ajia no mondai* 2.3 (March 1955), as reprinted in *CTM.*

——. "Hashigaki" はしがき (Foreword), in Suzue Gen'ichi, *Chūgoku kaihō tōsō shi* 中國解放闘争史 (A history of the struggle for the liberation of China). Tokyo, Ishizaki shoten, 1953.

——. "Fumetsu no yūjō: *Nakae Ushikichi shokanshū* no kankō o oete" 不滅の友情：中江丑吉書簡集の刊行を了えて (An indestructible friendship, completion of the publication of the letters of Nakae Ushikichi), *Misuzu* 69 (February 1965), as reprinted in *NUH.*

——. *Mantetsu ni ikite* 満鉄に生きて (Life along the South Manchurian Railway). Tokyo, Keisō shobō, 1964.

——. "Nakae Ushikichi no shokan" 中江丑吉の書簡 (The letters of Nakae Ushikichi), *Shisō* (January 1963), as reprinted in *NGZ.*

——. "Pekin no kagakusha Nakae Ushikichi" 北京の科学者中江丑吉 (Nakae Ushikichi, scientist of Peking), *Tōkyō shinbun,* 28 April 1950, as reprinted in *NGZ.*

——. "Suzue Gen'ichi to sono jidai" 鈴江言一とその時代 (Suzue Gen'ichi and his age), *Sekai* (May 1950), as reprinted under the title "Manadeshi Suzue Gen'ichi no koto" 愛弟子鈴江言一のこと (On Suzue Gen'ichi, beloved disciple), in *NGZ.*

——. "Takeuchi Yoshimi no shi ni kaishite ko Nakae Ushikichi o kaisō suru" 竹内好の死に会して故中江丑吉を回想する (Remembering the late Nakae Ushikichi at the death of Takeuchi Yoshimi), *Chūgoku kenkyū geppō* (March 1977), as reprinted in *NUH*.

——, Okazaki Kaheita 岡崎嘉平太 , and Matsumoto Shigeharu 松本重治 . *Warera no shōgai no naka no Chūgoku* わ れ ら の 生 涯 の な か の 中 国 (China in our careers). Ed. Sakatani Yoshinao 阪谷芳直 and Tai Kuo-hui 戴國煇. Tokyo, Misuzu shobō, 1983.

Jansen, Marius. *Japan and China: from War to Peace, 1894-1972.* Chicago, Rand McNally, 1975.

——. "Japan and the Chinese Revolution of 1911," in *The Cambridge History of China,* Vol. 11, *Late Ch'ing, 1800-1911, Part 2.* Ed. John K. Fairbank and Kwang-ching Liu. Cambridge, Cambridge University Press, 1980.

——. *The Japanese and Sun Yat-sen.* Cambridge, Harvard University Press, 1954.

Jellinek, Georg. *Allgemeine Staatslehre.* Berlin, O. Häring, 1900; 2nd ed., 1905. 3rd ed., Walter Jellinek, ed., Berlin, Verlag von Julius Springer, 1914.

——. *The Declaration of the Rights of Man and of Citizens: A Contribution to Modern Constitutional History,* tr. Max Farrand. New York, Henry Holt and Company, 1901.

"Julius Lippert: An Autobiographical Sketch," tr. A. W. Small, *American Journal of Sociology* 19:145-165 (1913).

Kahn, B. Winston. "Doihara Kenji and the North China Autonomy Movement, 1935-1936," in Alvin D. Coox and Hilary Conroy, eds., *China and Japan: A Search for Balance Since World War II.* Santa Barbara, ABC-Clio, 1978.

Kainō Michitaka 戒能通孝 . "*Chūgoku kodai seiji shisō,* kōki ni michita sho" 中国古代政治思想,香気に満ちた書 (Ancient Chinese Political Thought, a book full of fragrance), *Yomiuri shinbun,* 21 June 1950, as reprinted in *NUH*.

Kaizuka Shigeki 貝塚茂樹. "Atogaki" 後がき (Afterword), in *Kaizuka Shigeki chosakushū* 貝塚茂樹著作集 (The writings of Kaizuka Shigeki), Vol. 1. Tokyo, Chūō kōron sha, 1976.

——. *Chūgoku no kodai kokka* 中国の古代国家 (The ancient Chinese state), in *Kaizuka Shigeki chosakushū,* Vol. 1. Tokyo, Chūō kōron sha, 1976.

——. "Hayashi Taisuke" 林泰輔 , in *Ajia rekishi jiten* アジア歴史事典 (Encyclopedia of Asian history), Vol. 7. Tokyo, Heibonsha, 1961.

——. *Kodai In teikoku* 古代殷帝国 (The ancient Yin empire). Tokyo, Misuzu shobō, 1967.

Kaji Ryūichi 嘉治隆一 . "Sūkiden, Nakae Ushikichi kun" 数奇伝,中江丑吉君 (A checkered life, Nakae Ushikichi), *Asahi hyōron* (August 1947), as reprinted in *CTM*.

——. "Sūkiden, Suzue Gen'ichi kun" 数奇伝,鈴江言一君 (A checkered life, Suzue Gen'ichi), *Asahi hyōron* (August 1947), as reprinted in *CTM*.

Kamachi, Noriko. *Reform in China: Huang Tsun-hsien and the Japanese Model.* Cambridge, Council on East Asian Studies, Harvard University, 1981.

Kanesaki Satoshi 金崎賢 . "Iishirenu shitashisa, Nakae Ushikichi shi to watakushi" 云ひ知れぬ親しさ，中江丑吉氏と私 (An inexpressible closeness, Mr. Nakae Ushikichi and myself), *Tō-A shinpō*, 26 August 1942, as reprinted in *NUH*.

Kant, Immanuel. *Critique of Pure Reason,* tr. Norman Kemp Smith. New York, St. Martin's Press, 1965.

——. *Critique of Practical Reason, and Other Writings in Moral Philosophy,* tr. and ed. Lewis White Beck. Chicago, University of Chicago Press, 1949.

——. *Foundations of the Metaphysics of Morals,* tr. Lewis White Beck. Indianapolis, Bobbs-Merrill Company, 1959.

——. *Kritik der praktischen Vernunft.* Leipzig, Verlag von Felix Meiner, 1920. [NB]

——. *Kritik der reinen Vernunft,* ed. Theodor Valentiner. Leipzig, Felix Meiner, 1919. [NB]

Katō Koretaka 加藤惟孝 . "Aru nichijō seikatsu"或る日常生活(A certain daily life), *Dōsetsu* n.s. 5 (May 1965), as reprinted in *NGZ*.

——. "Chishiki to seikatsu"知識と生活 (Knowledge and life), *Nōgyō gijutsu* (November 1948), as reprinted in *NGZ*.

——. "Chōmin no ko"兆民の子 (Chōmin's child), *Dōsetsu* n.s. 1 (April 1964), as reprinted in *NGZ*.

——. "Chōmin no musume" 兆民の娘 (Chōmin's daughter), *Gifu nichinichi shinbun*, 4 November 1971, as reprinted in *NUH*.

——. "Kakuretaru minshushugisha, senji no Nakae Ushikichi shi" 隠れたる民主主義者，戦時の中江丑吉氏 (A hidden advocate of democracy, Mr. Nakae Ushikichi during the war), *Hyōron* (October 1948), as reprinted under the title "Senji no Nakae Ushikichi" 戦時の中江丑吉 (Nakae Ushikichi during the war), in *NGZ*.

——. "Keiko no omoide"稽古の思い出(Memories of instruction), *Kyōiku kenkyū* (May 1956), as reprinted in *NGZ*.

——. "Kenja to chinpin: Suzue Gen'ichi no omoide" 賢者と珍品：鈴江言一の憶い出 (Sage and rarity, memories of Suzue Gen'ichi), *Ajia kenkyū* 8.4 (December 1961), as reprinted in *NGZ*.

——. "Kōdan ni tsuite"講談について (On narrative), *Nōkyō no kyōsai* (December 1962), as reprinted in *NUH*.

——. "Nagayo san no koto"長与さんのこと (About Nagayo), *Dōsetsu* n.s. 4 (November 1964), as reprinted under the title "Nagayo Yoshirō to no hannichi" 長与善郎との半日 (Half a day with Nagayo Yoshirō), in *NGZ*.

——. *"Nakae Ushikichi shokanshū ni yosete"* 中江丑吉書簡集に寄せて (On the Letters of Nakae Ushikichi), *Chūgoku* 16 (March 1965), as reprinted in *NGZ*.

——. "Nakae Ushikichi to Shinbun" 中江丑吉と新聞 (Nakae Ushikichi and the press), *Kumamoto nichinichi shinbun,* 14 October 1971, as reprinted in *NUH.*

———. *Pekin no Nakae Ushikichi, aru kosei no kiroku* 北京の中江丑吉 ，ある個性の記録 (Nakae Ushikichi of Peking, record of an individual). Ed. Sakatani Yoshinao 阪谷芳直 . Tokyo, Keisō shobō, 1984.

———. "Pekin no tomodachi, Shōwa jūninen no Pekin ni te" 北京の友達，昭和十二年の北京にて (My Peking friend, in Peking in 1937), *Dōsetsu* 9 (March 1937), as reprinted in *NUH.*

———. "Shi no hibi" 死の日々 (Days of death), *Dōsetsu* n.s. 12 (November 1969), as reprinted in *NGZ.*

Kaufmann, Walter. *Hegel: Reinterpretation, Texts, and Commentary.* Garden City, New York, Doubleday & Company, 1965.

———. *Hegel: Texts and Commentary.* Garden City, Anchor Books, 1965.

Kawamura Gen 河村原 . "Sei-Shū jidai no yū to ri ni tsuite" 西周時代の邑と里について (The i and the li in the Western Chou period), *Shisō* 30:77–90 (January 1983).

Keightley, David N. *Sources of Shang History: The Oracle-Bone Inscriptions of Bronze Age China.* Berkeley, University of California Press, 1978.

Kennedy, George A. "Interpretation of the *Ch'un-ch'iu,*" *Journal of the American Oriental Society* 62:40–48 (1942).

Kimura Eiichi 木村英一 . "Nakae Ushikichi shi icho *Chūgoku kodai seiji shisō ni tsuite*" 中江丑吉氏遺著中国古代政治思想について (On Ancient Chinese Political Thought, by Mr. Nakae Ushikichi), *Tōhō gakuhō* 19 (December 1950), as reprinted in *CTM.*

———. "Shōin" 小引 (Brief introduction) [to Nakae Ushikichi, "Shōsho gairon"], *Shinagaku* 12.1–2:1–5 (September 1946).

Kinoshita Junji 木下順二 . "Doko ni dorama wa naritatsu ka" どこにドラマは成り立つか (What constitutes drama?), *Gunsō* (April–May 1967), as reprinted in *NUH.*

——— and Etō Fumio 江藤文夫 , eds. *Nakae Chōmin no sekai* 中江兆民の世界 (The world of Nakae Chōmin). Tokyo, Chikuma shobō, 1977.

Kitaura Sentarō 北浦千太郎 . "Tsuiokudan" 追憶談 (Remembrances), in *Nakae Ushikichi go kaiki kinenkai, kiroku* 中江丑吉五回忌記念会記録 (Transcript of the commemorative meeting for the fifth anniversary of the death of Nakae Ushikichi), as reprinted in *NUH.*

Kluback, William. *Wilhelm Dilthey's Philosophy of History.* New York, Columbia University Press, 1956.

Knirsch, Peter. *Eugen Varga.* Bibliographische Mitteilungen des Osteuropa-Instituts an der Freier Universität Berlin 5. Berlin, Osteuropa-Institut, 1961.

Kojève, Alexandre. *Introduction to the Phenomenology of Spirit,* ed. Allan Bloom, tr. James H. Nichols, Jr. New York, Basic Books, 1969.

Kokin, M. D. and G. Papaian. *"Tszin'-Tian": Agrarnyi stroi drevnogo Kitaia (Ching-*

t'ien, the agrarian structure of ancient China). Leningrad, Izdatel'stvo Lenin-gradskogo vostochnogo instituta im. A. S. Enukidze, 1930.

Kōtoku Shūsui 幸德秋水 . *Chōmin sensei* 兆民先生 (My teacher, [Nakae] Chōmin). Tokyo, Iwanami shoten, 1960.

Krader, Lawrence. *The Asiatic Mode of Production: Sources, Development and Critique in the Writings of Karl Marx*. Assen (The Netherlands), Van Gorcum & Comp. B. V., 1975.

Ku Chieh-kang 顧頡剛. *Ku-shih pien* 古史辨 (Controversies in ancient history), Vol. 1. Peking, P'u-she, 1926.

K'uang Hu-sheng 匡互生 . *Wu-ssu ai-kuo yun-tung* 五四爱国运动 (The patriotic May Fourth Movement), Vol. 1. Peking, Chung-kuo she-hui k'o-hsueh ch'u-pan-she, 1979.

Kuno Osamu 久野收. "*Nakae Ushikichi no ningenzō*, rekishi kenkyū no tessoku no migoto na jitsubutsu kyōji" 中江丑吉の人間像歷史研究 の鉄則のみごとな実物教示 (Nakae Ushikichi's View of Humanity, splendid substantive lessons of the iron laws of historical research), *Tōkyō shinbun*, 27 July 1970, as reprinted in *NUH*.

Kuwabara Takeo 桑原武夫 . "Ningen no Chōmin" 人間の兆民 (Chō-min, the person), in Kuwabara Takeo, ed., *Nakae Chōmin no kenkyū* 中江兆民の研究 (Studies of Nakae Chōmin). Tokyo, Iwanami shoten, 1966.

Le Bon, Gustav. *Psychologie der Massen*, tr. Rudolph Eisler. Leipzig, Alfred Kröner, 1919. [NB]

Legge, James, tr. *The Chinese Classics*, Vol. 5: *The Ch'un ts'ew with the Tso chuen*. Hong Kong, Lane, Crawford & Co., 1861–1872.

—— and Clae Waltham, tr. *Shu ching: Book of History*. Chicago, Henry Regnery Company, 1971.

Lenin, W. *Imperialism: The Last Stage of Capitalism*. London, Communist Party of Great Britain, n.d. [NB]

——. *Sämliche Werke*. Vienna and Berlin, Verlag für Literatur und Politik, 1927–1931. [NB]

Lichtheim, George. "Oriental Despotism," in his *The Concept of Ideology*. New York, Random House, 1967.

Lifton, Robert Jay, Shūichi Katō, and Michael Reich. *Six Lives, Six Deaths: Protraits from Modern Japan*. New Haven, Yale University Press, 1979.

Lippert, Julius. *Kulturgeschichte der Menschheit in ihrem organischen Aufbau*, Vol. 2. Stuttgart, Verlag von Ferdinand Enke, 1886–1887. [NB]

Liu Hsing-t'ang 劉興唐 . "Chung-kuo ching-chi fa-chan te pen-chih" 中國 經濟發展的本質 (The basic nature of the development of the Chinese economy), *Wen-hua p'i-p'an* 2.2–3:188–207 (1935).

——. "Chung-kuo she-hui fa-chan hsing-shih chih t'an-hsien" 中國社會發展

形式之探險 (An exploration of the forms of the development of Chinese society), *Hsin sheng-ming* 2.9:7–27 (October 1935).

——. "T'ang-tai chih kao-li-tai shih-yeh" 唐代之高利貸事業 (The profession of usury in the T'ang dynasty), *Shih-huo* 1.10:8–15 (April 1935).

Loewenberg, J. *Hegel's Phenomenology: Dialogues on the Life of the Mind.* La Salle, Ill., The Open Court Publishing Co., 1965.

Lu Hsun. "A Madman's Diary" (April 1918), in *Selected Works of Lu Hsun*, Vol. 1. Peking, Foreign Languages Press, 1956.

Lukács, Georg. *History and Class Consciousness: Studies in Marxist Dialectics,* tr. Rodney Livingstone. London, Merlin Press, 1971.

——. *The Young Hegel: Studies in the Relations between Dialectics and Economics,* tr. Rodney Livingstone. Cambridge, MIT Press, 1976.

Luxemburg, Rosa. *Einführung in die Nationalökonomie,* ed. Paul Levi. Berlin, E. Laub'sche Verlagsbuchhandlung, 1925. [NB]

Mad'iar, Liudvig. *Chung-kuo ching-chi ta-kang* 中國經濟大綱 (Outline of the Chinese economy), tr. Hsu Kung-ta 許共達. Shanghai, Hsin sheng-ming shu-chü, 1933.

——. *Chung-kuo ching-chi yen-chiu* 中國經濟研究 (A study of the Chinese economy), tr. Li Min-ch'ang 李民長. Stenographic copy. Moscow, 1929.

——. *Chung-kuo nung-ts'un ching-chi chih t'e-hsing* 中國農村經濟之特性 (The nature of the economy of the Chinese rural village), tr. Tsung Hua 宗華. Shanghai, Pei-hsin shu-chü, 1930.

——. *Chung-kuo nung-ts'un ching-chi yen-chiu* 中國農村經濟研究 (Studies in China's rural economy), tr. Ch'en Tai-ch'ing 陳代青 and P'eng Kuei-ch'iu 彭桂秋. Shanghai, Shen-chou kuo-kuang she, 1930.

——. *Ekonomika sel'skogo khoziaistva v Kitae* (The agrarian economy of China). Moscow, Gosudarstvennoie izdatel'stvo, 1928.

——. "The Legitimacy of the AMP," tr. Robert Crosky, in Anne M. Bailey and Josep Llobera, eds., *The Asiatic Mode of Production: Science and Politics.* London, Routledge and Kegan Paul, 1981.

——. *Ocherki po ekonomike Kitaia* (Works on the economy of China). Moscow, Izdatel'stvo kommunisticheskoi akademii, 1930.

"Magyar, Lajos [Liudvig Ignat'ievich Mad'iar]," in *Great Soviet Encyclopedia*, Vol. 15. Moscow, Sovietskaia Entsiklopediia Publishing House, 1974.

Maine, Henry Sumner. *Ancient Law: Its connection with the early history of society and its relation to modern ideas.* London, John Murray, 1894. [NB]

Makkreel, Rudolph A. *Dilthey: Philosopher of the Human Studies.* Princeton: Princeton University Press, 1975.

Mandelbaum, Maurice. *The Problem of Historical Knowledge: An Answer to Relativism.* New York, Liveright Publishing Corporation, 1938.

Marcuse, Herbert. *Reason and Revolution: Hegel and the Rise of Social Theory.* Boston, Beacon Press, 1969.

Marx, Karl. *Capital: A Critical Analysis of Capitalist Production,* tr. Samuel Moore and Edward Aveling, ed. Frederick Engels. New York, International Publishers, 1947.

——. *A Contribution to the Critique of Political Economy.* New York, International Publishers, 1970.

——. *The Economic and Philosophic Manuscripts of 1844,* tr. Martin Milligan. New York, International Publishers, 1971.

——. *Grundrisse: Foundations of the Critique of Political Economy,* tr. Martin Nicolaus. Harmondsworth, Penguin Books, 1973.

——. *Das Kapital: Kritik der politischen Oekonomie,* ed. Friedrich Engels. 3 vols. Hamburg, Otto Meissner Verlag, 1922. [NB]

——. *Das Kapital: Kritik der politischen Oekonomie,* ed. Karl Kautsky. 3 vols. Berlin, J. H. W. Dietz, Nachf., 1928. [NB]

——. *Das Kapital: Kritik der politischen Oekonomie,* ed. Marx-Engels-Lenin Institute. Vol. 1: Vienna and Berlin, Verlag f. Literatur u. Politik, 1932. Vols. 2 and 3: Moscow and Leningrad, Verlagsgenossenschaft Auslandischer Arbeiter in d. UdSSR, 1933. [NB]

——. *Zur Kritik der politischen Oekonomie,* ed. Karl Kautsky. Berlin, J. H. W. Dietz Nachf., 1924. [NB]

——. *Pre-Capitalist Economic Formations,* tr. Jack Cohen, ed. Eric J. Hobsbawm. New York, International Publishers, 1971.

—— and Frederick Engels. *The Letters of Karl Marx and Frederick Engels,* tr. Saul Pavoder. Englewood Cliffs, N.J., Prentice-Hall, 1979.

Matsukata Saburō 松方三郎. "Rō Pekin no kankai" 老北京の感懐 (My feeling about an old Peking hand), *Sekai* (October 1948), as reprinted in *NGZ*.

Matsumoto Ken'ichi 松本健一. "Nakae Chōmin to Tōyama Mitsuru" 中江兆民と頭山満 (Nakae Chōmin and Tōyama Mitsuru), in Takeuchi Yoshimi 竹内好 and Hashikawa Bunzō 橋川文三, eds., *Kindai Nihon to Chūgoku* 近代日本と中国 (Modern Japan and China), Vol. 1. Tokyo, Asahi shinbunsha, 1974.

Matsumoto Masaaki 松本雅明. *Shunjū Sengoku ni okeru shōsho no tenkai* 春秋戰國における尚書の展開 (The development of the *Book of History* in the Spring and Autumn and Warring States periods). Tokyo, Kazama shobō, 1966.

——. "Shōsho Rakkō hen no seiritsu" 尚書洛誥篇の成立 (The formation of the Lo-kao chapter of the *Shang-shu*), in *Uno Tetsuto sensei hakuju shukuga kinen Tōyōgaku ronsō* 宇野哲人先生白寿祝記念東洋学論叢 (Essays in East Asian studies presented to Dr. Uno Tetsuto in commemoration of his ninety-ninth birthday). Tokyo, Tōhō gakkai, 1974.

——. "Shōsho Kōkō hen no seiritsu" 尚書康誥篇の成立 (The formation of the K'ang-kao chapter of the *Shang-shu*), *Hōbun ronsō* 39:39–60 (March 1977).

——. "Shōsho Shukō hen no seiritsu, Rakuyū kensetsu e no dōtei" 尚書酒誥篇の成立、洛邑建設への道程 (The formation of the Chiu-kao chapter of the *Shang-shu*, the process leading to the establishment of the "city" of Lo), in *Mikami Tsugio hakushi shōju kinen Tōyō shi kōkogaku ronshū* 三上次男博士頌寿記念東洋史考古学論集 (Essays in East Asian history and archeology presented to Professor Mikami Tsugio in commemoration of his seventieth birthday). Kyoto, Hōyū shoten, 1979.

——. "Shōsho Tashi hen no seiritsu, rekishi ishiki no suii ni tsuite" 尚書多士篇の成立、歴史意識の推移について (The formation of the To-shih chapter of the *Shang-shu*, concerning transformations in historical consciousness), in *Egami Namio kyōju koki kinen ronshū—minzoku bunka hen* 江上波夫教授古稀記念論集民族文化篇 (Essays commemorating the seventieth birthday of Professor Egami Namio, ethnographic and cultural section). Tokyo: Yamakawa shuppansha, 1976–1977.

Matsumoto Sannosuke 松本三之助. "Minken no tetsugaku: Nakae Chōmin" 民権の哲学：中江丑吉 (The philosophy of human rights: Nakae Chōmin), in *Meiji seishin no kōzō* 明治精神の構造 (The structure of the Meiji spirit). Tokyo, Nihon hōsō shuppan kyōkai, 1981.

——. "Nihon kenpōgaku ni okeru kokkaron no tenkai, sono keiseiki ni okeru hō to kenryoku no mondai o chūshin ni" 日本憲法学における国家論の展開、その形成期における法と権力の問題を中心に (The development of conceptions of the state with a focus on the issues of law and authority in the formative period of Japanese constitutionalism), in Fukuda Kan'ichi 福田歓一, ed., *Seiji shisō ni okeru Seiō to Nihon* 政治思想における西欧と日本 (Western Europe and Japan in political thought), Vol. 2. Tokyo, Tokyo University Press, 1961.

Matsunaga Shōzō 松永昌三. "Itsutsu no mondōtai: Chōmin no hōhō" 五つの問答体：兆民の方法 (Five questions and answers, Chōmin's method), in Kinoshita Junji and Etō Fumio, eds., *Nakae Chōmin no sekai*. Tokyo, Chikuma shobō, 1977.

Mehring, Franz. *Karl Marx: The Story of His Life*, tr. Edward Fitzgerald. Ann Arbor, The University of Michigan Press, 1969.

Mészáros, István. *Marx's Theory of Alienation*. London, Merlin Press, 1970.

Meyer, Eduard. *Geschichte des Altertums*. Stuttgart and Berlin, J. G. Cotta, 1925. [NB]

Miller, Frank O. *Minobe Tatsukichi: Interpreter of Constitutionalism in Japan*. Berkeley, University of California Press, 1965.

Mimori Sadao 三森定男. "Nihon ni okeru kyōdōtai no kenkyū" 日本における共同体の研究 (Japanese studies of the "community"), in

Kyōdōtai no kenkyū 共同体の研究 (Studies of "community"), Vol. 1. Tokyo, Risōsha, 1958.

Mitchell, Richard H. *Thought Control in Prewar Japan.* Ithaca, Cornell University Press, 1976.

Mitsuda Ikuo 満田郁夫. "Nakae Ushikichi ni tsuite" 中江丑吉につい て (On Nakae Ushikichi), *Nihon bungaku* (April 1972), as reprinted in *NUH.*

Mommsen, Theodor. *Römische Geschichte.* Berlin, Weidmannsche Buchhandlung, 1919–1921. [NB]

Morgan, Lewis Henry. *Ancient Society.* New York, Henry Holt and Co., 1877. [NB]

Moritani Katsumi 森谷克己. *Ajia teki seisan yōshiki ron* アジア的生産 様式論 (On the Asiatic mode of production). Tokyo, Ikuseisha, 1937.

Moriya Fumio 守屋典郎. "Nakae Ushikichi shi no koto" 中江丑吉氏 のこと (About Mr. Nakae Ushikichi), in Moriya Fumio, *Shakai kagaku e no shisaku* 社会科学への思索 (Thoughts on social science). Tokyo, Aoki shoten, 1975, as reprinted in *NUH.*

Mott, Lewis Freeman. *Ernest Renan.* New York, D. Appleton and Company, 1921.

——. "Ernest Renan," in *Encyclopedia of the Social Sciences,* Vol. 13. New York, The Macmillan Company, 1948.

Murdock, George Peter. "Introduction," in Julius Lippert, *The Evolution of Culture,* tr. G. P. Murdock. New York, The Macmillan Company, 1931.

Nabeyama Sadachika 鍋山貞親. "Pekin senkō" 北京潜行 (Traveling incognito in Peking), in *NUH.*

——. *Watakushi wa Kyōsantō o suteta, jiyū to sokoku o motomete* 私は共産 党をすてた、自由と祖國を求めて (I abandoned the Communist Party, in search of freedom and the motherland). Tokyo, Daitō shuppansha, 1949.

Naitō Konan 内藤湖南. "Shōsho keigi" 尚書稽疑 (Doubts about the *Book of History*), *Shinagaku* 1.7 (March 1921), as reprinted in Naitō Kenkichi 内 藤乾吉 and Kanda Kiichirō 神田喜一郎, eds., *Naitō Konan zenshū* 内藤湖南全集 (Collected works of Naitō Konan), Vol. 7. Tokyo, Chikuma shobō, 1970.

Nakae bunko mokuroku 中江文庫目録 (Catalogue of the Nakae bunko). Number 11 in series, *Shinchaku tosho geppō* 新着図書月報 (New library arrivals monthly). Kyoto, Kyōto daigaku jinbun kagaku kenkyūjo toshoshitsu, 1964.

Nakae Chōmin 中江兆民. *A Discourse by Three Drunkards on Government,* tr. Nobuko Tsukui. Tokyo, Weatherhill, 1984. See also Dardess.

——. *Ichinen yūhan* 一年有半 (One year and a half), in Matsumoto Sannosuke 松本三之助, ed., *Nakae Chōmin zenshū* 中江兆民全 集 (Collected works of Nakae Chōmin), Vol. 10. Tokyo, Iwanami shoten, 1983.

Nakae shi ikō shuppan iinkai 中江氏遺稿出版委員會 (Committee for the posthumous publication of Nakae [Ushikichi's] manuscripts). "Batsu" 跋 (Postscript), in *CKSS.*

Nakae Ushikichi 中江丑吉 . "Byōchū nikki shō: shi no toko no kiroku"病中日記抄 : 死の床の記録 (Extracts from *Diary of an Illness,* a deathbed record), in *NGZ.*

——. *Chūgoku kodai seiji shisō* 中國古代政治思想 (Ancient Chinese political thought). Tokyo, Iwanami shoten, 1975.

1. "Chūgoku kodai seiji shisō shi" 中國古代政治思想史 (History of ancient Chinese political thought), pp. 1–210. [July 1925].

2. "Ei Ō no shōyū to Chō Gi no Shoo to ni tsuite" 衞鞅の商邑と張儀の商於とに就いて (On Shang-i of Shang Yang and Shang-yü of Chang I), pp. 211–231. [July 1930.]

3. "Chūgoku no hōken seido ni tsuite" 中國の封建制度に就いて (On the Chinese feudal system), pp. 233–282. [December 1930.] Published as "Shina no hōken seido ni tsuite" 支那の封建制度について (On the Chinese feudal system) in *Mantetsu Shina gesshi* 8.1 (January 1931).

4. "Shōsho Hankō hen ni tsuite" 尚書殷庚篇に就いて (On the P'an-keng chapter of the *Shang-shu*), pp. 283–326. [August 1931.]

5. "Kuyōden oyobi Kuyōgaku ni tsuite" 公羊傳及公羊學に就いて (On the *Kung-yang Commentary* and the Kung-yang school), pp. 327–445. [June 1932.]

6. "Sho nijūkyū hen ni kansuru shiken ni tsuite (ichi): Kōkō keitō Shohen o ronzu" 書廿九篇に關する私見に就いて (一):唐誥系統書篇を論す" (My views on the twenty-nine chapters of the *Book of History* [Part 1]: An analysis of the chapters of the *Book of History* in the system of the "K'ang kao" chapter), pp. 447–576. [January 1934.]

7. "Shōsho gairon" 尚書概論 (An outline of the *Book of History*), pp. 579–634. [1924.]

8. "Sho nijūkyū hen ni kansuru shiken ni tsuite (ni): "Rakkō keitō Shohen o ronzu" 書廿九篇に關する私見に就いて (二) : 洛誥系統書篇を論す" (My views on the twenty-nine chapters of the *Book of History* [Part 2]: An analysis of the chapters of the *Book of History* in the system of the "Lo kao" chapter), pp. 635–662. [1935.]

——. "Senji no danshō" 戰時の斷章 (Wartime diary), in *NGZ.*

——. Untitled, unpublished reading notes on G. W. F. Hegel, *Phänomenologie des Geistes.*

"Nakae Ushikichi nenpu" 中江丑吉年譜 (Chronological biography of Nakae Ushikichi). Compiled by Katō Koretaka and Sakatani Yoshinao, in *NUH.*

Nakae Ushikichi go kaiki kinenkai, kiroku 中江丑吉五回忌記念会.記

録(Transcript of the commemorative meeting for the fifth anniversary of the death of Nakae Ushikichi), as reprinted in *NUH*.

Nakae Ushikichi no ningenzō 中江丑吉の人間像 (Nakae Ushikichi's view of mankind), ed. Sakatani Yoshinao and Suzuki Tadashi. Nagoya, Fūbaisha, 1980.

Nakae Ushikichi shokanshū 中江丑吉書簡集 (The letters of Nakae Ushikichi), ed. Suzue Gen'ichi, Itō Takeo, and Katō Koretaka. Tokyo, Misuzu shobō, 1964.

Nakae Ushikichi to iu hito, sono seikatsu to shisō to gakumon 中江丑吉という人，その生活と思想と学問 (A man called Nakae Ushikichi, his life, thought, and learning), ed. Sakatani Yoshinao. Tokyo, Daiwa shobō, 1979.

Nakamura Shintarō 中村新太郎 . *Son Bun kara Ozaki Hotsumi e* 孫文から尾崎秀実へ (From Sun Yat-sen to Ozaki Hotsumi). Tokyo, Nit-Chū shuppan, 1975.

New York Times, 9 October 1964.

Nihon kin-gendai shi jiten 日本近現代史事典 (Historical dictionary of modern and contemporary Japan). Tokyo, Tōyō shinpōsha, 1978.

Nihon rekishi daijiten 日本歴史大事典 (The great encyclopedia of Japanese history). Tokyo, Kawade shobō, 1968–1970.

Niida Noboru 仁井田陞 . "Yūmon no sho: Nakae shi ni okeru Tōyō shakai no mikata" 憂問の書：中江氏における東洋社会の見方 (A work of anguish: Mr. Nakae's view of East Asian society), *Chūgoku kenkyū* 13 (September 1950), as reprinted in *CTM*.

Nikiforov, V. N. *Sovetskiie istoriki o problemakh Kitaia* (Soviet historians on Chinese problems). Moscow, Izdatel'stvo "Nauka," 1970.

Norman, Richard. *Hegel's Phenomenology: A Philosophical Introduction*. New York, St. Martin's Press, 1976.

The North-China Herald, Vol. 131, no. 2700, 10 May 1919.

Notehelfer, F. G. *Kōtoku Shūsui: Portrait of a Japanese Radical*. Cambridge, Cambridge University Press, 1971.

Ogura Sōichi 小倉倉一 . "Nakae Ushikichi no hito to shisō" 中江丑吉の人と思想 (Nakae Ushikichi, the man and his thought), *Saiken* (April 1964), as reprinted in *NGZ*.

——— . "Minshushugi no tetsujin Nakae Ushikichi no shōgai" 民主主義の哲人中江丑吉の生涯 (The career of Nakae Ushikichi, democratic philosopher), *Nōrin shunjū* (March 1953), as reprinted under the title "Wasureenu hito no shōgai" 忘れ得ぬ人の生涯 (The career of an unforgettable man), in *NGZ*.

——— . "Suzue Gen'ichi shi no omoide, wasureenu hito" 鈴江言一氏の思い出，忘れえぬ人 (Reminiscences of Mr. Suzue Gen'ichi, an unforgettable person), *Saiken* (September 1966), as reprinted under the title "Wasureenu hito: Nakae san to Suzue san no koto" 忘れえぬ人：中江さんと 鈴江さんのこと (Unforgettable people: Nakae and Suzue) in *NUH*.

Ojima Sukema 小島祐馬 . *Chūgoku shisō shi* 中国思想史 (A history of Chinese thought), rev. ed. Tokyo, Sōbunsha, 1968.

———. "*Chūgoku kodai seiji shisō* ni tsuite" 中国古代政治思想につ いて (On [Nakae Ushikichi's] *Ancient Chinese Political Thought*), *Tosho* (August 1950), as reprinted in *NGZ*.

———. *Chūgoku no shakai shisō* 中国の社会思想. (Chinese social thought). Tokyo, Chikuma shobō, 1967.

———. *Nakae Chōmin* 中江兆民. Tokyo, Kōbundō, 1949.

———. "Nakae Chōmin" 中江兆民 , in Hayashi Shigeru 林茂 , ed., *Nakae Chōmin shū* 中江兆民集 (Writings by Nakae Chōmin). Tokyo, Chikuma shobō, 1967.

Ōkita Saburō 大来佐武郎 . "Pekin funin" 北京赴任 (To my appointment in Peking), in *NUH*.

Ollman, Bertell. *Alienation: Marx's Conception of Man in Capitalist Society*, 2nd ed. Cambridge, Cambridge University Press, 1980.

Ōnishi Itsuki 大西斎 . "Tsuiokudan" 追憶談 (Remembrances), in *Nakae Ushikichi go kaiki kinenkai, kiroku* 中江丑吉五回忌記念会 ,記録 (Transcript of the commemorative meeting for the fifth anniversary of the death of Nakae Ushikichi), as reprinted in *NUH*.

Ono Katsutoshi 小野勝年 . "Nakae san o omou" 中江さんを憶う (Remembering Nakae), *Tōyōshi kenkyū* (January-February 1943), as reprinted under the title "'Wakai tomodachi' ni yoru tsuioku: Nakae san o omou" 若 い友だちによる追憶：中江さんを憶う (The reminiscences of "young friends": Remembering Nakae), in *CTM*.

Oppenheimer, Franz. *Der Staat*. Frankfurt, Literarische Anstalt Rütten & Loenig, 1919. [NB]

Ōshima Kan'ichi 大島寛一 . "Rō Pekin, Nakae Ushikichi san" 老北京，中 江丑吉さん (An old Peking hand, Nakae Ushikichi), in *NUH*.

Ōta Hidemichi 太田秀通 . "Ōtsuka Hisao" 大塚久雄 , in Nagahara Keiji 永原慶二 and Kano Masanao 鹿野政直 , eds., *Nihon no reki-shika* 日本の歴史家 (Historians of Japan). Tokyo, Nihon hyōronsha, 1976.

Ōta Ryōichirō 大田遼一郎 . "Kaisō no Nakae Ushikichi" 回想の中 江丑吉 (Nakae Ushikichi in my memory), *Jiron* (November 1946), as reprinted in *NGZ*.

Ōtsuka Hisao 大塚久雄 . "Kyōdōtai kaitai no kiso teki shojōken, sono riron teki kōsatsu" 共同体解体の基礎的諸条件 ,その理論 的考察 (The basic conditions for the breakdown of the "community," a theoretical examination of it), in *Ōtsuka Hisao chosakushū* 大塚久雄著作 集 (The writings of Ōtsuka Hisao), Vol. 7. Tokyo, Iwanami shoten, 1971.

———. *Kyōdōtai no kiso riron* 共同体の基礎理論 (The basic theory of

the "community"), in *Ōtsuka Hisao chosakushū* (The writings of Ōtsuka Hisao), Vol. 7. Tokyo, Iwanami shoten, 1971.

Ōuchi Hyōe 大内兵衛 . "*Chōmin o tsugu mono*, Pekin ni kakureta itten no ryōshin" 兆民を継じ゛その，北京にかくれた一点、の 良心 (The man who followed [Nakae] Chōmin, a conscience hidden in Peking), *Kōbe shinbun*, 27 August 1960, as reprinted in *NUH*.

———. "Engerusu no 'shō mihon': *Nakae Ushikichi shokanshū* wa omoshiroi" エンゲルスの゛小見本」：『中江丑吉書簡集』はおもし ろい (On the model of Engels: The letters of Nakae Ushikichi are interesting), *Misuzu* 74 (July 1965), as reprinted in *NGZ*.

Ozaki Shōtarō 尾崎庄太郎 . "Ajia teki seisan yōshiki ronsō" アジア的 生産様式論争 (The debate over the Asiatic mode of production), in *Ajia teki seisan yōshiki ron* アジア的生産様式論 (On the Asiatic mode of production). Tokyo, Hakubaisha, 1949.

Paton, H. J. *The Categorical Imperative: A Study in Kant's Moral Philosophy*. London, Hutchinson & Co., 1965.

———. "Kant on Friendship," *Proceedings of the British Academy* (1956), 45–66.

Peattie, Mark R. *Ishiwara Kanji and Japan's Confrontation with the West*. Princeton, Princeton University Press, 1975.

P'eng Ming 彭明 . *Wu-ssu yun-tung shih* 五四运动史 (A history of the May Fourth Movement). Peking, Jen-min ch'u-pan-she, 1984.

Philippovitch, Eugen von. *Grundriss der politischen Oekonomie*, Vol. 1. Tübingen, T. C. B. Mohr, 1920. [NB]

Plantinga, Theodore. *Historical Understanding in the Thought of Wilhelm Dilthey*. Toronto, University of Toronto Press, 1980.

Po Ch'i-ch'ang 白歧昌. *Wu-ssu yun-tung wen-chi* 五四运动文辑 (Writings of the May Fourth Movement), comp. Hua-Chung kung-hsueh-yuan Ma-k'o-ssu Lieh-ning chu-i ts'e-liao-shih 华中工学院馬克思列宁主义资料室 . Wuhan, Hu-pei jen-min ch'u-pan-she, 1957.

Post, Albert Hermann. *Die Geschlechtsgenossenschaft der Urzeit und die Entstehung der Ehe*. Oldenburg, Schulzesche Buchhandlung, 1875. [NB]

Rehm, Hermann. *Geschichte der Staatsrechtswissenschaft*. Freiburg and Leipzig, J. C. B. Mohr, 1896. [NB]

Reiss, R. S. "Kant and the Right of Rebellion," *Journal of the History of Ideas* 17.2: 179–192 (1956).

Renan, Ernest. *The Life of Jesus*. London, Watts & Co., 1924. [NB]

Resek, Carl. *Henry Lewis Morgan: American Scholar*. Chicago, University of Chicago Press, 1960.

Rickert, Heinrich. *Die Probleme der Geschichtsphilosophie*. Heidelberg, Carl Winters Universitätsbuchhandlung, 1924. [NB]

Rickman, H. P. "General Introduction," to Wilhelm Dilthey, *Pattern and Meaning in History: Thoughts on History and Society,* tr. and ed. H. P. Rickman. London, George Allen & Unwin, 1971.

———. *Wilhelm Dilthey: Pioneer of the Human Studies.* Berkeley, University of California Press, 1979.

Rios y Urruti, Fernando de los. *Estudios Jurídicos.* Buenos Aires, Ediciones Jurídicas Europa-America, 1959.

Rosdolsky, Roman. *The Making of Marx's 'Capital,'* tr. Pete Burgess. London, Pluto Press, 1977.

Rose, E. "China as a Symbol of Reaction in Germany, 1830–1880," *Comparative Literature* 3:57–76 (1951).

Rōyama Masamichi 蠟山政道. *Nihon ni okeru kindai seijigaku no hattatsu* 日本における近代政治學の發達 (The development of modern political science in Japan). Tokyo, Jitsugyō no Nihon sha, 1949.

———, Hori Toyohiko 堀豐彦, Oka Yoshitake 岡義武, Nakamura Akira 中村哲, Tsuji Kiyoaki 辻清明, and Maruyama Masao 丸山真男. "Nihon ni okeru seijigaku no kako to shōrai: tōron" 日本における政治學の過去と將來：討論 (Discussion of the past and future of political science in Japan), *Seijigaku* 1:35–82 (1950).

Sakatani Ki'ichi 阪谷希一. "Tōko kakusha ni ko Nakae Ushikichi kei o omou" 塘沽客舍に故中江丑吉兄を憶ふ (Remembering my friend, the late Nakae Ushikichi, at an inn in T'ang-ku), notes dated August 1946, in *NUH.*

Sakatani Yoshinao 阪谷芳直. "Entenkō" 炎天行 (Walks under the blazing sun), in *CTM.* Reprinted in *NGZ.*

———. "Hachigatsu jūgonichi to Nakae san no omoide" 八月十五日と中江さんの思い出 (August 15 and memories of Nakae), *Hana no wa* (September 1950), as reprinted under the title "Sekai shi shinten no hōsoku" 世界史進展の法則 (The laws of development in world history), in *NGZ.*

———. "Kaisetsu" 解説 (Explanation), in Suzue Gen'ichi, *Chūgoku kakumei no kaikyū tairitsu* 中国革命の階級対立 (Class struggle in the Chinese revolution), Vol. 2, ed. Sakatani Yoshinao. Tokyo, Heibonsha, 1972.

———. "Katō Koretaka shokan to Nakae zō" 加藤惟孝書簡と中江像 (Katō Koretaka's letters and the image of Nakae), in *NUH.*

———. "Nakae Ushikichi" 中江丑吉, in *Kōtō gakkō gendaibun no kenkyū* 高等学校現代文の研究 (Studies of contemporary prose for high school). Tokyo, Kadogawa shoten, 1983.

———. "Nakae Ushikichi no ikō ni tsuite" 中江丑吉の遺稿について (On Nakae Ushikichi's surviving manuscripts), in *NUH.*

———. "Nakae Ushikichi zō no saigen no tame ni" 中江丑吉像の再現

の ため に (Toward a rediscovery of the image of Nakae Ushikichi), in *NUH*.

——. "Ningen, kono kōki naru mono" 人間、この高貴なるもの (A human being, this noble entity), *Seiryū* (February 1955), as reprinted in *NGZ*.

——. "Tsuioku henpen: Nakae shi to no taiwa kara" 追憶片々：中江氏との対話から (Scattered memories, from conversations with Mr. Nakae), *Misuzu* 82–83 (March–April 1966), as reprinted under the title "Tsuioku henpen: Nakae Ushikichi to no taiwa kara" 追憶片々：中江丑吉との対話から (Scattered memories, from conversations with Nakae Ushikichi), in *NGZ*.

——, ed. *Chōmin o tsugu mono* 兆民をつぐもの (The man who followed [Nakae] Chōmin). Tokyo, privately published by Sakatani Yoshinao, 1960.

Sanetō Keishū さねとうけいしゅう. *Chūgokujin Nihon ryūgaku shi* 中国人日本留學史 (The history of Chinese students in Japan). Tokyo, Kuroshio shuppan, 1960.

Satō Kōseki 佐藤垢石. *Aoki Norizumi* 青本宣純. Tokyo, Bokusui shobō, 1943.

Sawer, Marian. *Marxism and the Question of the Asiatic Mode of Production*. The Hague, Martinus Nijhoff, 1977.

Sayer, Derek. *Marx's Method: Ideology, Science and Critique in "Capital."* Atlantic Highlands, Humanities Press, 1979.

Seligman, Edwin R. A. *The Economic Interpretation of History*. New York, Columbia University Press, 1917. [NB]

Schopenhauer, Arthur. *Die Welt als Wille und Vorstellung*. Leipzig, Philipp Reclam, n.d. [NB]

Shimada Kenji 島田慶次. "Chōmin no aiyōgo ni tsuite" 兆民の愛用語について (On Chōmin's favorite language usage), in Kinoshita Junji and Etō Fumio, eds., *Nakae Chōmin no sekai*. Tokyo, Chikuma shobō, 1977.

——. "*Minyaku yakkai* genbun, yomikudashi bun, narabi ni chūkai" "民約訳解"原文、よみくだ"し文、ならびに注解 (The original text of the translation of the *Social Contract*, with annotations), in Kuwabara Takeo 桑原武夫, ed., *Nakae Chōmin no kenkyū* 中江兆民の研究 (Studies of Nakae Chōmin). Tokyo, Iwanami shoten, 1966. Reprinted in Ida Nobuya 井田進也, ed., *Nakae Chōmin zenshū* 中江兆民全集 (Collected works of Nakae Chōmin), Vol. 1. Tokyo, Iwanami shoten, 1983.

——. "Nakae Chōmin *Minyaku yakkai* no Chūgoku han" 中江兆民"民約訳解"の中国版 (A Chinese edition of Nakae Chōmin's translation of the *Social Contract*), *Dōhō* 40:1 (October 1981).

Shimizu Morimitsu 清水盛光. *Shina shakai no kenkyū* 支那社會の研究 (A study of Chinese society). Tokyo, Iwanami shoten, 1939.

Shiozawa Kimio 塩澤君夫. *Ajia teki seisan yōshiki ron* アジア的生産様

式 論 (On the Asiatic mode of production). Tokyo, Ochanomizu shobō, 1970.

Shirakawa Shizuka 白川静. *Kōkotsubun no sekai, kodai In ōchō no kōzō* 甲骨文 の世界，古代殷王朝の構造 (The world of oracle bones, the structure of the ancient Yin dynasty). Tokyo, Heibonsha, 1972.

Silber, John R. "Kant's Conception of the Highest Good as Immanent and Transcendent," *Philosophical Review* 68.4:469–494 (October 1959).

Simkhovitch, Vladimir S. "Rudolph Stammler," *Educational Review* 27:236–251 (March 1904).

Simmel, Georg. *Die Probleme der Geschichtsphilosophie: Eine erkenntnistheoretische Studie.* Munich and Leipzig, Verlag von Duncker & Humblot, 1922. [NB]

Sklar, Judith. *Freedom and Independence: A Study of the Political Ideas of Hegel's Phenomenology of Mind.* Cambridge, Cambridge University Press, 1976.

——. "Hegel's 'Phenomenology': An Elegy for Hellas," in Z. A. Pelczynski, ed., *Hegel's Political Philosophy: Problems and Perspectives.* Cambridge, Cambridge University Press, 1971.

Smith, Norman Kemp. *A Commentary to Kant's 'Critique of Pure Reason.'* New York, Humanities Press, 1962.

Solomon, Robert C. *In the Spirit of Hegel: A Study of G. W. F. Hegel's Phenomenology of Spirit.* New York, Oxford University Press, 1983.

Stammler, Rudolph. *Wirtschaft und Recht nach der materialistischen Geschichtsauffassung: Eine sozialphilosophische Untersuchung.* Leipzig, Veit & Comp., 1914. [NB]

Stubbs, William. *The Constitutional History of England, in its Origin and Development,* Vol. 1. Oxford, The Clarendon Press, 1891. [NB]

Suda Teiichi 須田禎一. "*Nakae Ushikichi no ningenzō,* honmono no shisōka, rōkotaru gōri shisō o tsuranuku" 中江丑吉の人間像，ほんものの思想家，牢固たる合理思想を貫く (Nakae Ushikichi's view of humanity, a genuine thinker penetrated with steadfast rational thought), *Tosho shinbun,* 18 July 1970, as reprinted in *NUH.*

Sugita Tei'ichi 杉田定一. "Yū-Shin yokan" 遊清餘感 (Impressions of a visit to China), in Saika Hakuai 雜賀博愛, *Sugita Kakuzan ō* 杉田鶏山翁 (Venerable Sugita Kakuzan). Tokyo, Kakuzankai, 1928.

Suzuki Tadashi 鈴木正. "Ikyō no koten teki yuibutsuronsha: Nakae Ushikichi ron" 異郷の古典的唯物論者：中江丑吉論 (Classical materialist in a foreign land: On Nakae Ushikichi). *Shisō no kagaku* (December 1961). Reprinted in Suzuki Tadashi. *Kindai Nihon no risei* 近代日本の理性 (Reason in modern Japan). Tokyo, Keisō shobō, 1972.

——. "Jinsei no shi: Nakae Ushikichi" 人生の師：中江丑吉 (A teacher for life: Nakae Ushikichi), *Asahi shinbun,* 28 April 1971, as reprinted in *NUH.*

——. "Ko no naka no fuhensha, Nakae Ushikichi ron" 個のなかの普遍者：中江丑吉論 (A universalist within an individual: On Nakae Ushikichi), *Sekai* (October 1967), as reprinted in *NGZ.*

Swingewood, Alan. *Marx and Modern Social Theory.* New York, John Wiley & Sons, 1975.

Takagi Motoyasu 高木基安. "Ippan keika hōkoku" 一般経過報告 (General progress report), as reprinted in *NUH.*

Takahashi Kazumi 高橋和巳. "Mizukara senkusha taru koto o kinjitsuzuketa senkusha" 自ら先駆者たることを禁じっづけた先駆者 (A pioneer who continually forbid himself to be a pioneer), in *NUH.*

Takeda Taijun 武田泰淳. *"Nakae Ushikichi shokanshū,* kakumei ki no Chūgoku to Nihonjin" 中江丑吉書簡集，革命期の中国と日本人 (The Letters of Nakae Ushikichi, China in a revolutionary period and the Japanese), *Asahi jānaru* (7 February 1965), as reprinted in *NUH.*

Takeuchi Chibi 竹内千美. "Chichi Chōmin no omoide" 父兆民の思い出 (Memories of my father [Nakae] Chōmin), *Tosho* 189:16–21 (May 1965).

Takeuchi Minoru 竹内実. "Nihonjin ni totte no Chūgoku zō" 日本人にとっての中国像 (Japanese images of China), in his *Nihonjin ni totte no Chūgoku zō.* Tokyo, Shunjūsha, 1966.

Takeuchi Yoshimi 竹内好. *"Chūgoku kodai seiji shisō,* shinri tsuikyū no ningen teki jōnetsu" 中国古代政治思想，真理追求の人間的情熱 (*Ancient Chinese Political Thought,* human enthusiasm in pursuit of truth), *Tosho* (November 1950), as reprinted in *NGZ.*

Tanigawa Michio 谷川道雄. *Medieval Chinese Society and the Local "Community,"* tr. Joshua A. Fogel. Berkeley, University of California Press, 1985.

Taylor, Charles. *Hegel.* Cambridge, Cambridge University Press, 1975.

Tazaki Masayoshi 田崎仁義. *Ōdō tenka no kenkyū* 王道天下の研究 (Studies in the realm of the kingly way). Kyoto, Naigai shuppan, 1926.

——. *Ukō ron* 禹貢論 (On the "Yü-kung"). Tokyo, Kokumin keizai zasshi sha, 1920.

Tejima Masaki 手嶋正毅. "Pekin ryūgaku jidai" 北京留学時代 (My period of study in Peking), in *NUH.*

Ter-Akopian, N. B. "Razvitie vzgliadov K. Marksa i F. Engel'sa na aziatskii sposob proizvodstva i zemledel'cheskuiu obshchinu" (The development of the views of K. Marx and F. Engels on the Asiatic mode of production and rural society), *Narody Azii i Afriki* 2:74–88 (1965); 3:70–85 (1965).

Ting Shan 丁山. *Chia-ku-wen so-chien shih-tsu chi ch'i chih-tu* 甲骨文所見氏族及其制度 (The clan and its organization as seen in oracle bone inscriptions). Peking, K'o-hsueh ch'u-pan-she, 1956.

Tökei, Ferenc. *Sur le mode de production asiatique.* Budapest, Akadémiai Kiadó, 1966.

Toland, John. *The Rising Sun: The Decline and Fall of the Japanese Empire: 1936–1945.* New York, Random House, 1970.

Tolstoy, Leo. *War and Peace*, tr. Constance Garnett. New York, Modern Library, 1931.

Tourneur, Jean M. *Fustel de Coulanges*. Paris, Bouvin, 1931.

Ts'ao Ju-lin 曹汝霖 . *I-sheng chih hui-i* 一生之回憶 (Memoirs of a life). Taipei, Ch'uan-chi wen-hsueh ch'u-pan-she, 1970.

Tsubokawa Ken'ichi 坪川健一 . "Pekin no natsu" 北京の夏 (Summer in Peking), *Nihonkai sakka* n.s.13 (March 1965), as reprinted in *NGZ*.

Tsurumi Yoshiyuki 鶴見良行 . "Nihonjin banare no ikikata ni tsuite, teichaku to idō no hōhō" 日本人ばなれの生き方について，定着と移動の方法 (How to live away from Japanese, fixity and means of movement), *Shisō no kagaku* (June 1972), as reprinted in *NUH*.

Uchida Tomoo 内田智雄 . "'Nakae bunko' hannyū no kotodomo" 中江文庫」搬入のことども (Matters concerning the transfer of the Nakae bunko), *Dōshisha hōgaku* 91 (March 1965), as reprinted in *NUH*.

Ueberweg, Friedrich. *Grundriss der Geschichte der Philosophie*. 4 vols. Berlin, E. S. Mittler & Sohn, 1915–1926. [NB]

Ueno Kenchi 上野賢知 . *Nihon Saden kenkyū chojutsu nenpyō* 日本左伝研究著述年表 (Chronological record of Japanese writings on the *Tso-chuan*). Tokyo, Tōyō bunka kenkyūjo, 1975.

Ueyama Shunpei 上山春平 . "Chōmin no tetsugaku" 兆民の哲学 (Chōmin's philosophy), in Kuwabara Takeo, ed., *Nakae Chōmin no kenkyū* 中江兆民の研究 (Studies of Nakae Chōmin). Tokyo, Iwanami shoten, 1966.

Ulmen, G. L. *The Science of Society: Toward an Understanding of the Life and Work of Karl August Wittfogel*. The Hague, Mouton Publishers, 1978.

Umemoto Sutezō 楳本捨三 . *Zenshi Kantōgun* 全史関東軍 (The complete history of the Kwantung Army). Tokyo, Keizai ōraisha, 1978.

Varga, Eugen. *Ocherki po problemam politekonomii kapitalizma* (Works on the problems of the political economy of capitalism). Moscow, Izdatel'stvo politicheskoi literatury, 1965.

"Varga, Evgenii [Eugen] Samuilovich," in *Great Soviet Encyclopedia*, Vol. 4. Moscow, Sovetskaia Entsiklopediia Publishing House, 1974.

Vleeschauwer, Herman-J. de. *The Development of Kantian Thought: The History of a Doctrine*, tr. A. R. C. Duncan. Toronto, Thomas Nelson and Sons, 1962.

Vorländer, Karl. *Geschichte der Philosophie*, Vol. 1. Leipzig, Felix Meiner, 1921. [NB]

Waley, Arthur, *The Book of Songs*. Boston, Houghton Mifflin, 1937.

Wang Yun-sheng 王芸生 . *Liu-shih-nien lai Chung-kuo yü Jih-pen* 六十年來中國與日本 (China and Japan over the past sixty years), Vol. 7. Tientsin, Ta-kung-pao-she, 1932–1934.

Ward, Lester F. "Ludwig Gumplowicz," *American Journal of Sociology* 15:410–413 (1909).

Webb, Herschel. "What Is the *Dai Nihon Shi?*" *Journal of Asian Studies* 19.2:135–149 (February 1960).

Weber, Max. *Wirtschaftsgeschichte: Abriss der universalen Soziol- und Wirtschafts-geschichte,* ed. S. Hellman and M. Palyi. Munich and Leipzig, Duncker & Humblot, 1924. [NB]

Weber, Wilhelm. "Theodor Mommsen," in *Encyclopedia of the Social Sciences,* Vol. 10. New York, The Macmillan Company, 1948.

Weingartner, Rudolph H. *Experience and Culture: The Philosophy of Georg Simmel.* Middletown, Wesleyan University Press, 1962.

Wheatley, Paul. *The Pivot of Four Quarters: A Preliminary Enquiry into the Origins and Character of the Ancient Chinese City.* Chicago, Aldine Publishing Company, 1971.

White, Hayden V. "Wilhelm Windelband," in *The Encyclopedia of Philosophy,* Vol. 8. New York, The Macmillan Company and The Free Press, 1967.

White, Leslie A. "Henry Lewis Morgan," in *International Encyclopedia of the Social Sciences,* Vol. 10. New York, The Macmillan Company, 1968.

Who's Who in China. Shanghai, The China Weekly Review, 1925.

Will, Édouard. "Trois quarts de siècle de recherches sur l'économie grecque antique," *Annales* 9:7–19 (1954).

Windelband, Wilhelm. *Einleitung in die Philosophie.* Tübingen, Verlag von J. C. B. Mohr, 1923. [NB]

——. *Die Geschichte der neueren Philosophie, in ihrem Zusammenhange mit der allgemeinen Kultur und den besonderen Wissenschaften,* Vol. 2. Leipzig, Breitkopf & Hartel, 1919. [NB]

Wittfogel, Karl A. *Oriental Despotism: A Study in Total Power.* New Haven, Yale University Press, 1957.

Wundt, Wilhelm. *Einleitung in die Philosophie.* Leipzig, Verlag von S. Hirzel, 1921. [NB]

——. *Völkerpsychologie: Eine Untersuchung der Entwicklungsgesetze von Sprache, Mythus, und Sitte,* Vols. 4, 8. Leipzig, Alfred Kröner Verlag, 1914–1920. [NB]

——. *System der Philosophie.* Leipzig, Alfred Kröner, 1919. [NB]

Yamaguchi Kōsaku 山口光朔 . *Itan no genryū: Nakae Chōmin no shisō to kōdō* 異端の源流：中江兆民の思想と行動 (The roots of heresy: Nakae Chōmin's thought and actions). Tokyo, Hōritsu bunkasha, 1961.

Yamamoto Hideo 山本秀夫 . *Tachibana Shiraki* 橘樸. Tokyo, Chūō kōronsha, 1977.

Yamamoto Shirō 山本四郎 . "Terauchi naikaku jidai no Nit-Chū kankei no ichimen: Nishihara Kamezō to Banzai Rihachirō" 寺内内閣時代の日中関係の一面：西原亀三と坂西利八郎 (One side of Sino-Japanese relations during the period of the Terauchi Cabinet: Nishihara Kamezō and Banzai Rihachirō), *Shirin* 64.1:1–36. (January 1981).

Yang Yun-ju 楊筠如. *Shang-shu ho-ku* 尚書覈詁 (An examination of the *Book of History*). Sian, Shan-hsi jen-min ch'u-pan she, 1959.

Yokogawa Jirō 横川次郎. "Shina ni okeru nōson kyōdōtai to sono isei ni tsuite, hitotsu no gimon no teishutsu to shite" 支那における農村共同体とその遺制について，一つの疑問の提出として (On the rural "community" and what it bequeathed in China, a tentative proposal), *Keizai hyōron* 2.5:2–38 (July 1935).

Yokoyama Shinpei 横山臣平 . *Hiroku Ishiwara Kanji* 秘録石原莞爾 (The secret story of Ishiwara Kanji). Tokyo, Fuyō shobo, 1971.

Young, Ernest P. *The Presidency of Yuan Shih-k'ai: Liberalism and Dictatorship in Early Republican China*. Ann Arbor, University of Michigan Press, 1977.

Zeller, Eduard. *Grundriss der Geschichte der Griechischen Philosophie*. Leipzig, O. R. Reisland, 1920. [NB]

——. *Die Philosophie der Griechen in ihrer geschichtlichen Entwicklung*. Leipzig, O. R. Reisland, 1920–1923. [NB]

Glossary

Ajia teki seisan yōshiki アジア的生産樣式

Ajia teki shakai アジア的社會

Ajia teki shakai keizai アジア的社會經濟

Amano Motonosuke 天野元之助

An Lu-shan 安祿山

An-yang 安陽

anego 姐御

Anfu 安福

Aoki Masaru 青木正兒

Aoki Norizumi 青木宣純

Araki Sadao 荒木貞夫

Ariga Nagao 有賀長雄

Asahi shinbun 朝日新聞

Asakawa Norihiko 淺川範彦

banyūgaku 萬有學

Banzai Rihachirō 坂西利八郎

biri ビリ

Chang Ping-lin 章炳麟

Chang Tsung-hsiang 章宗祥

Chao-chia-lou 趙家樓

Chao Shih-yen 趙世炎

Ch'en-pao 辰報

Ch'eng Heng 程衡

Cheng Hsuan 鄭玄

chi 知

Ch'i Pai-shih 齊白石

chia-fa 家法

Chia K'uei 賈逵

Chidōkan 致道館

Ch'ien Ta-hsin 錢大昕

Ch'ih Yu 蚩尤

Chin-pu-tang 進步黨

"Ching-kao Jih-pen jen shu" 警告日本人書

ching-t'ien 井田

chishiki 知識

Chōshuntei 長春亭

Chou 周

Chou-li 周禮

chu-tzu 諸子

Ch'u 楚

chuan 傳

Chuang Shu-tsu 莊述祖

Chuang-tzu 莊子

Ch'un-ch'iu 春秋

chung 眾

Ch'ung-chen 崇貞

dai kokka tai 大國家體

dai Shinatsū 大支那通

dai Tō-A sensō 大東亞戰爭

Daigaku nankō 大學南校

Dai'ichi kōtō gakkō
第一高等学校

dengeki 電撃

Doihara Kenji 土肥原賢二

Dōjin 同仁

dokuritsu shitsuka keizai
獨立室家經濟

fang 方

Feng 封

feng-chien 封建

fu 婦

Fu Sheng 伏生

Fujiwara Kamae 藤原鎌兄

Fujiwara Masafumi 藤原正文

Furuno Inosuke 古野伊之助

gaku 學

gensei teki 現世的

Genyōsha 玄洋社

Ginza 銀座

Han Ching-ti 漢景帝

Han-fei-tzu 韓非子

Han Wu-ti 漢武帝

Hashikawa Bunzō 橋川文三

Hashikawa Tokio 橋川時雄

Hayakawa Jirō 早川次郎

Hei-chan 黑チャン

*Heigeru iwaku reine Negativität -
wa Selbstbewusstsein no Bewegung nari to, mattaku dōkan
mōshisōrō:* 黒根児曰く
reine Negativität Selbstbewusstsein の Bewegung 也と,
全同感申候

heiwa 平和

hijō Nihon 非常日本

Hijōji Nihon 非常時日本

Hirano Yoshitarō 平野義太郎

Hiraoka Kōtarō 平岡浩太郎

Ho Hsiu 何休

Hōchikoku 法治國

Hokumon shinpō 北門新報

hōtō burai 放蕩無頼

Hozumi Yatsuka 穗積八束

Hsieh Lien-ch'ing 謝廉清

hsin 心

hsing 姓

hsü 序

Hsün-tzu 荀子

hua 華

huai 槐

Huan 桓

Huang 黄

Huang Jih-k'uei 黄日葵

Huang-shou-i 黄獸醫

Huang Tsung-hsi 黄宗羲

Hu Ch'iu-yuan 胡秋原

Hu E-kung 胡鄂公

hyūmanitii ヒューマニティー

i ("settlement") 邑

i (2) ("alien") 夷

I-ching 易經

Ichikawa Shōichi 市川正一

Imada jinkei 今田仁兄

Imada rōkei 今田老兄

Imada Shintarō 今田新太郎

Imada taikei 今田大兄

Imazeki Tenpō 今關天彭

in maru インコル

Indo no karasu 印度の烏

Inukai Tsuyoshi 犬養毅

Ishimoto Kenji 石本憲治

Ishiwara Kanji 石原莞爾

Itagaki Seishirō 板垣征四郎

Itō Daihachi 伊藤大八

Iwakura 岩倉

Izumo 出雲

jiko seigen 自己制限

Jinbun kagaku kenkyūjo
人文科學研究所

Jiyūtō 自由黨

jung 戎

Juan Yuan 阮元

Kagoshima 鹿兒島

Kaneko Motozaburō 金子元三郎

Kangaku 漢學

"K'ang kao" 康誥

K'ang Shu 康叔

K'ang Yu-wei 康有為

Katakura Tadashi 片倉衷

Katayama Sen 片山潛

Katō Hiroyuki 加藤弘之

Katō Kōmei 加藤高明

keigaku 經學

Kei-Shin nichinichi shinbun
京津日日新聞

ko-ming 革命

Koishikawa-ku 小石川區

Kōjimachi 麴町

Kokumintō 國民黨

Kokuryūkai 黑龍會

kokutai 國體

Konoe Fumimaro 近衛文麿

Kosuge Isamu 小菅勇

Kozō 子僧

Ku-liang 穀梁

Kuan-yin-ssu 觀音寺

kung-t'ung-ti 共同體
Kung-tzu i-shih 公子益師
Kung-yang chuan 公羊傳
kung-yung 公用
K'ung An-kuo 孔安國
K'ung Yin-ta 孔穎達
Kunikida Doppo 國木田獨步
kuo 國
Kuo Mo-jo 郭沫若
Kuraishi Takeshirō
　　　倉石武四郎
Kurihara Ryōichi 栗原亮一
Kurusu 來栖
kyōdōtai 共同體

Liang Ch'i-ch'ao 梁啟超
Liang Li-sheng 梁履繩
"Li cheng" 立政
Li Chi 李季
Li-chi 禮記
Li Yuan-hung 黎元洪
"Li-yun" 禮運
lin 麟
Lin Ch'ang-min 林長民
Liu E 劉鶚
Liu Feng-lu 劉逢祿
Liu Hsin 劉歆
Liu Pang 劉邦
Liu-t'iao-kou 柳條溝
Lo Chen-yü 羅振玉
"Lo kao" 洛誥

Lu 魯
Lu Cheng-hsiang 陸徵祥
Lu Tsung-yü 陸宗輿
Lü Chen-yü 呂振羽
"Lü hsing" 呂刑
Lü Pu-wei 呂不韋
Lü-shih ch'un-ch'iu 呂氏春秋

man 蠻
Mantetsu Shina gesshi 滿鐵支那月誌
Matsui Satoko 松井里子
Matsumoto Yoshimi 松本善海
Matsuoka Yōsuke 松岡洋右
Matsuzaki Tsuruo 松崎鶴雄
Miao 苗
min 民
Min-yueh t'ung-i 民約通義
ming 命
Ming-i tai-fang lu 明夷待訪錄
Ming T'ai-tsu 明太祖
ming-te shen-fa 明德慎罰
Minobe Tatsukichi
　　　美濃部達吉
Morishima Morito 森島守人
Morito Tatsuo 森戶辰男
Motozono-chō 元園町
Mumeikai 無名會

Nagayo Yoshirō 長與善郎
Nakae bunko 中江文庫
Nakae Chibi 中江千美

Nakae Iyoko　中江弥子

Nakae Motosuke　中江元助

Nakajima　中島

Nanbara Shigeru　南原繁

Natsume Sōseki　夏目漱石

Neguro　ネグロ

Nihonbashi　日本橋

Nihon kenpō　日本憲法

"Nihon kokumin ni tsugu"
　日本國民に告ぐ

ningen　人間

ningenshugi　人間主義

Nippori　日暮

Nishihara Kamezō　西原亀三

Nishizato Tatsuo　西里竜夫

Nomura　野村

"Nonsensu" no naka kara umarete
　kuru mono wa yahari issō ni
　nonsensu no nanimono igai ni
　meiyō nari　「ノンセンス」の中
　から生れて來るものは矢張
　リ一層にノンセンスの何物
　以外に没有也．

Nosaka Sanzō　野板参三

nü　女

nung-ts'un kung-she　農村公社

nung-ts'un kung-t'ung-t'i
　農村共同體

ōdō　王道

Okamoto Kikuko　岡本菊子

Okamoto Torao　岡本寅男

Okamura Yasuji　岡村寧次

Ōkawa Shūmei　大川周明

Ōkubo Toshimichi
　大久保利通

Ōnishi Itsuki　大西齋

Onozuka Kiheiji
　小野塚喜平次

Otaru　小樽

Ou-yang Hsiu　歐陽修

Ozaki Yukio　尾崎行雄

"P'an Keng chih cheng"
　般庚之政

pang　邦

Pekin koi　北京戀

Pekin Mantetsu geppō　北京滿鐵月報

p'ien　篇

P'i Hsi-jui　皮錫瑞

Rai San'yō　頼山陽

Saionji Kinmochi　西園寺公望

Sakamoto Ryōma　坂本龍馬

sakusen　作戰

Sano Manabu　佐野學

san-shih　三時

*Sansuijin keirin mondō*三醉人經綸問答

Sasaki Tadashi 佐々木忠

seihin 清貧

seijigaku 政治學

seiji gakujutsu 政治學術

seiji gakusetsu 政治學説

seiji shisō 政治思想

Seiri sōdan 西理叢談

seisen 聖戰

seitai 政體

sensei 先生

shang 尚

Shang-i 商邑

Shang-shu 尚書

Shang Yang 商鞅

Shang-yü 商於

she-chi 社稷

shen 神

shih 市

Shih-chi 史記

Shih-ching 詩經

shih-fa 師法

Shih Huang-ti 始皇帝

Shih Ssu-ming 史思明

Shih Yang 施洋

Shimizu Yasuzō 清水安三

Shimoda Utako 下田歌子

Shimotoshima 下豊島

shinjin 新人

Shin Shina 新支那

shisō 思想

Shu-ching 書經

Shui-mo 水磨

Shun 舜

Shun-t'ien shih-pao 順天時報

Shuo-wen chieh-tzu 説文解字

Shuo-yuan 説苑

shuzoku teki kokka 種族的國家

Sonezaki 曽根崎

sonraku dantai 村落團體

sōrōbun 候文

ssu-kuo 四國

Ssu-ma Ch'ien 司馬遷

Su Chao-cheng 蘇兆徵

su-wang 素王

Sugiyama Heisuke 杉山平助

Sun I-jang 孫詒讓

Sun-tzu 孫子

Sung T'ai-tsu 宋太祖

Suzue Gen'ichi 鈴江言一

ta-i 大義

Ta-kung-pao 大公報

"Ta shih" 大誓

ta-tsai 大宰

Tachibana Shiraki 橘樸

Tada Hayao 多田駿

t'ai-p'ing 太平

Taiheiyō sensō 太平洋戰爭

taikei 體系

Taishō nichinichi shinbun 大正日日新聞

Takehaya 竹早

Takehaya-chō 竹早町

Takeshima-chō 武島町

Takeuchi Namiko 竹内浪子

Takeuchi Toraji 竹内虎治

Takeuchi Tsuna 竹内綱

"T'ang shih" 湯誓

T'ao Hsi-sheng 陶希聖

Tarui Tōkichi 樽井藤吉

Tasaka Sadao 田板貞雄

Tatsuridō 達理堂

tenkō 轉向

Teikoku kenpō 帝國憲法

Terauchi Masatake 寺内正毅

tetsugaku 哲學

ti 狄

ti-tao 狄道

t'ien-i 天意

t'ien-ming 天命

Ting Shan 丁山

Ting Shih-yuan 丁士源

"To fang" 多方

"To shih" 多士

Tōkabu 東株

Tokugawa Ieyasu 德川家康

Tōyama Mitsuru 頭山滿

Tōyō gakkan 東洋學館

Ts'ao Chih 曹植

Ts'ao P'i 曹丕

Ts'ao Ts'ao 曹操

Tso-chuan 左傳

tsu 族

Tsuda Shizue 津田靜枝

Tsujino Sakujirō 辻野朔次郎

Tsujino Toshio 辻野俊雄

Tsunoda Tomoshige 津野田知重

Tu Fu 杜甫

Tu Lin 杜林

Tuan Ch'i-jui 段祺瑞

Tuan Yü-ts'ai 段玉裁

Tung Chung-shu 董仲舒

Tung Tso-pin 董作賓

T'ung 佟

Tzu-chih t'ung-chien 資治通鑑

"Tzu ts'ai" 梓材

Uchida Ryōhei 内田良平

Uesugi Shinkichi 上杉慎吉

Ushijima Tatsukuma 牛島辰熊

wakai tomodachi 若い友だち

wang-che 王者

Wang Ching-wei 汪精衛

Wang Ch'ung 王充

Wang Kuo-wei 王國維

Wang Ming-sheng 王鳴盛

Wang Shu-chih 王樞之

Wang Su 王肅

wang-tao 王道

Wang Tzu-yen 王子言
Watase Kakuichi 渡瀬革一
Watase Shigeyoshi 渡瀬成美
wei-kuo (gikoku) 偽國
wei-shu 緯書
"Wei tzu" 微子
Wen 文
"Wen-hou chih ming" 文侯之命
"Wu i" 無逸
Wu P'ei-fu 吳佩孚
Wu Ta-ch'eng 吳大澂

Ya-hsi-ya sheng-ch'an fang-shih 亞細亞生產方式
Yamada 山田
Yao 堯

"Yao tien" 堯典
Yeh-lü Ch'u-tsai 耶律楚材
Yen Jo-chü 閻若璩
Yin 殷
Yonai 米内
Yoshida Shigeru 吉田茂
Yoshikawa Kōjirō 吉川幸次郎
"Yū no igi ni tsuite" 邑の意義について
Yūrakuchō 有樂町
Yü 禹
"Yü kung" 禹貢
Yuan Shih-k'ai 袁世凱

Zenrinkan 善隣館
zokuchi teki kokka 屬地的國家

Index

Harvard East Asian Monographs